THE OMNI DIET

THE
OMNI
DIET

The Revolutionary
Program to Lose Weight,
Reverse Disease, and
CHANGE YOUR LIFE FOREVER

Tana Amen, BSN, RN

RODALE.

Exclusive direct mail edition published by Rodale Inc. in May 2014
by arrangement with St. Martin's Press, New York, NY.

© 2013, 2014 by Tana Amen, B.S.N., R.N.
Foreword © 2013 by Daniel G. Amen, M.D.

Printed in the United States of America
Rodale Inc. makes every effort to use acid-free ♾, recycled paper ♾.

The brain scans on page 114 are courtesy of Amen Clinics, Inc.
Book Design by Richard Oriolo
Exercise Photographs by Tony Lattimore Photography

Library of Congress Cataloging-in-Publication Data is on file with the publisher.
ISBN 978–1–62336–381–9

2   4   6   8   10   9   7   5   3   1   Direct mail hardcover

We inspire and enable people to improve their lives and the world around them.
For more of our products, visit rodalestore.com or call 800-848-4735

To my amazing family for your support, love, and encouragement. To Daniel, my husband, for never doubting me. And to my daughter, Chloe, who always challenges me. This perfect blend of ingredients is a sure recipe for success.

[CONTENTS]

PART FIVE

OMNI RECIPES

[FOREWORD]

EVEN THOUGH YOUR BRAIN MAKES up only 2 percent of your body's weight—about 3 pounds—it uses 20–30 percent of the calories you consume. It is the most energy-hungry organ in your body. The nutrition you give your brain is either helping it to function properly and repair itself, or hurting and tearing down the most important organ in your body.

The overall health of your body plays a major role in the health of your brain and your mind. There are now twenty-two scientific studies reporting that as your weight goes up, the size and function of your brain go down. The first study outlining this relationship between weight and brain function was performed by my friend Dr. Cyrus Raji and his colleagues. Reading it made me lose 20 pounds. I was not going to do anything that would shrink my brain! When it comes to the brain, size matters. After I published two studies from the Amen Clinics replicating Dr. Raji's findings, I coined the term "Dinosaur Syndrome" to describe this phenomenon—big body, little brain, on your way to becoming extinct. Knowing the science made it clear to me that I had to reach people and teach them to get healthy now. You literally have no time to waste. And as I learned more and more about the connection between physical health and brain health, I understood that nutrition was the centerpiece of healing.

My wife, Tana, has been my partner in getting and staying truly healthy and in educating others about the amazing power of nutritious food. Her reputation as a wellness expert has spread. These days, nearly everywhere she goes people ask Tana—whom they fondly refer to as the Brain Doctor's wife—for health and nutrition advice. Friends, neighbors, the parents and teachers at our daughter's school, people we meet when we travel to Amen Clinics all over the United States—they all want to know how they can improve the health of their brain and body by changing what they eat.

When people do what Tana suggests, they often get immediate dramatic and positive health benefits. We have been astonished by the many phone calls and e-mails she receives from people who have lost weight, eliminated body pain, gotten off medications, improved their energy, gained strength, and normalized their bowels—simply by following her advice.

When I saw the impact Tana was having on the people she met and worked with, I asked her to write the cookbooks for my national public television specials. My audience loved her and raved about the benefits that they experienced when they followed her program. Then, when I was tapped by Pastor Rick Warren to help put together the Daniel Plan, a wide-ranging health plan created for Saddleback Church, I knew Tana would be the perfect coach. Together with our friends Mehmet Oz and Mark Hyman we helped 15,000 people to lose 250,000 pounds during the Daniel Plan's first twelve months. Whenever we speak together and people ask for advice about nutrition and supplements, I always defer to Tana: "Ask the Brain Doctor's wife! She's the nutrition expert!"

TANA HAS A PASSION FOR health. She trained as a nurse at Loma Linda University, in Loma Linda, California, a town whose residents are famous for their longevity. When we met, she was a neurosurgical intensive care nurse working with the sickest patients in the hospital. She saw firsthand the deadly effects of a lifetime of poor lifestyle and food choices, as people with obesity, diabetes, heart disease, and other chronic illnesses succumbed to early deaths. She also saw the dramatic transformations that took place when patients took charge of their health and changed their diets, reversing the destructive path of their illnesses, lowering their need for medication, and renewing their energy and health.

As Tana has discovered in her life and among the many people she has helped over the years, when it comes to good health, food can be your best medicine or your worst enemy. The typical Western diet of bad fat, salt, and sugar—think cheeseburgers, fries, and sodas—promotes inflammation and has been associated with depression, attention deficit disorder (ADD), dementia, heart disease, cancer, diabetes, and obesity. But, there is good news: If you start making better choices today you will quickly notice that you have more energy, better focus, a better memory, better moods, and a slimmer, sexier waistline. You can also lower your risk of developing a range of chronic diseases, such as heart disease, high blood pressure, type 2 diabetes, obesity, and cancer. Making healthier choices can even reverse the course of certain conditions, in some cases reducing or eliminating the need for medication. A number of new studies have reported that a healthy diet, just like the plan in *The Omni Diet,* is associated with dramatically lower risks of Alzheimer's disease and depression.

As you eat your way to good health, you will also enjoy yourself. Eating the Omni Diet way has completely changed my attitude toward food: It can be healthy and be amazingly tasty. The Omni Diet was the start of a wonderful relationship with food. Rather than being a slave to foods that were hurting me, I willingly enjoyed a range of wonderful foods that boosted my health and made me feel good about myself. I used to be like a yo-yo: I would crave bad food, overeat, feel lousy, hate myself in the process, crave bad food to feel better. . . . It was way too much drama. Since eating the way discussed in this book, I have never eaten better. It affects everything in my life in a positive way. I don't want fast food anymore, because it makes me tired and stupid. Instead, I want the right food that makes me smarter. And, contrary to what most people think, eating in a brain-healthy way is not more expensive—it will actually save you money. Your medical bills will be lower, your productivity will skyrocket, your outlook will be brighter, and your waistline will be trimmer. Feeling amazing is priceless.

The Omni Diet is the program we use at the Amen Clinics to help our patients get and stay healthy. The principles Tana and the Omni Diet use are good for your brain *and* for your body. The Omni Diet is smart, science based, and easy to follow. Tana guides you in a very practical, step-by-step way as you incorporate new ways of eating into your life. She has hundreds of tips and suggestions to get you started and to help you succeed. I can tell you from personal experience that she is the perfect teacher, cheerleader, and coach—exactly the person you want on your side to guide you toward a new way of eating, and a new way of living.

Take it from a physician, neuroscientist, and brain health expert: With Tana as your guide, you can feel healthier than ever before. Get ready, pay attention, and be inspired—*The Omni Diet* may very well extend and save your life. It will absolutely change it for the better.

Daniel G. Amen, M.D.

Introduction: The Omni Way

**The doctor of the future will no longer treat the human frame with
drugs, but rather will cure and prevent disease with nutrition.**

—THOMAS EDISON

I LOVE FOOD. I THINK it matters. I've experienced the effects of food
(good and bad) personally, and I've seen the effects professionally. What we eat
can really change our lives, and you've probably picked up this book because
there is at least a small part of you that thinks this, too. Let's call it your gut.

As a child growing up in a low-income household with a single parent
who worked long hours, I lived on Cap'n Crunch, Pop-Tarts, chocolate milk,
pan-fried steaks, and frozen pot pies—with ice cream for dessert. My family
members suffered from obesity, heart disease, cancer, diabetes, and dementia.
We were the picture of bad health.

Because of an undiagnosed autoimmune disorder that was wreaking
havoc in my body, I suffered for years with childhood illnesses. By the age
of four, I had undergone upper and lower gastrointestinal studies for severe
digestive issues. A few years later, I was hospitalized for mononucleosis, and I
had my tonsils removed. Frequent infections required many courses of antibiotics. If something could go wrong with a kid, it would happen to me.

As a teenager, desperate to escape my family's medical history and my
own health demons, I exercised obsessively. Like many young adults, I thought
if I exercised enough, I could eat whatever I wanted. I continued to live on

1

processed foods, refined sugar, and caffeine. I looked thin and fit on the outside, but I was a mess on the inside.

At the age of twenty-three, I received a devastating diagnosis: thyroid cancer that had metastasized into my lymph nodes.

For eleven years, while my friends were falling in and out of love and studying for exams and starting careers, I endured surgeries and radiation therapy. The treatments and illness came with an array of health challenges, including a serious bout of depression. There were many times when I felt completely hopeless and alone. By the time I was in my thirties, living with thyroid imbalances and having already suffered through so much ill health, I was willing to do *anything* to feel well, including overhauling my diet.

Why my diet? My own health struggles had led me to health care, where I worked as a neurosurgical ICU nurse caring for extremely ill patients. Too often, I was bedside for the consequences and regret that inevitably come with poor lifestyle and food choices—obesity, diabetes, heart disease, cancer, stroke, death. In my experience lifestyle choices always catch up with you at some point—it *is* inevitable. For some people it's in their twenties, as it did for me; for others, it's in middle age. But I was also blessed to witness the unbelievable power of second chances and the miraculous transformations that come from people simply changing how they ate—from reversing diabetes and heart disease to needing to take fewer medications and having renewed energy and health.

So, using the USDA Food Pyramid, I adopted what we all thought at the time was the perfect diet: 6 to 11 servings a day of grains, rice, and pasta; 5 to 9 servings of fruits and vegetables; 2 to 3 servings of meat; and 2 to 3 servings of milk. And I used fats, oils, and sweets sparingly.

Before I knew it, I was back in the hospital to have my gallbladder removed. Blood tests showed I had become insulin-resistant and had high triglycerides, high cholesterol, and high testosterone.

My doctor pulled out his prescription pad to scribble down the names of a myriad of medications I would need to take—perhaps for the rest of my life. Some were to prevent conditions such as osteoporosis and heart disease for which I was at high risk due to the high doses of thyroid medication that I would always have to take. Others were to manage the side effects of the drugs I would be taking. I felt like I was on a perpetual roller coaster of emotions, wired, tired, and anxious, struggling with a racing heart, insomnia, irritability, and decreased sex drive. I needed medication, my doctor explained, because I had been dealt a bad genetic hand. Some people are born unlucky in health, and unfortunately, I was one of them.

Frustrated by my perceived "failures," I was tempted to believe him, give up, give in, take the drugs, and accept my poor health. That's right, I felt like a *failure, a genetic reject.* After all, I was a health professional. I had access to the best medical care and the latest scientific research. Why then was I continuing to struggle with my own health?

But giving up isn't in my nature. It didn't make sense to bombard my body with a laundry list of pills and their unpleasant side effects if there was a chance that I wouldn't have to. Something inside of me said this was the not-so-easy, easy way out. There's that old gut again.

When I insisted that there had to be a better way than giving in to a poly-pharmacy plan for every symptom and risk, I was told that I was "in denial."

That's when I knew that I was going to have to be my own brand of health advocate. I have tremendous respect for doctors who dedicate their lives to trying to heal the sick. Heck, I'm married to one. But I realized that no doctor was going to understand my body or take my health or nutrition as seriously as I would. I had always been a fighter, and I decided this would be the fight of my life, literally.

Over the next ten years, I embarked on a health crusade and nutritional adventure. Unfortunately for me, it meant chasing a few red herrings and falling into a rabbit hole or two. Fortunately for you, I learned a lot in the process and ultimately developed the Omni Diet, which has helped thousands of people lose weight, reverse illness, and change their lives.

THE OMNI DIET

I AM A RESULTS-ORIENTED KIND of lady, and I wanted *extreme* results. So of course, I decided to try an extreme diet first.

In nursing school at a strictly vegetarian university, I had learned about the powerful connection between plant foods and wellness, so I embraced a vegan diet. Knowing that many vegan "meat replacements" are processed and filled with nitrates and fillers, I ditched *all* processed "meats" and fake meat substitutes and refocused my dietary intake on abundant amounts of fresh fruit, dried fruit, vegetables, pasta, whole-grain bread, cracked wheat, barley, rice, and other grains.

Initially, I felt great! My energy soared and my sleep improved. Eliminating processed food and daily super-sized sodas likely had a very positive effect. But within about a month I began to have mid-day energy crashes, eczema appeared on my face, and I had trouble sleeping. After three months, I was eager to see the results of my blood tests. I anticipated a dramatic change for the better. But my blood tests showed that my cholesterol and triglycerides were actually *higher* than they had ever been! I wasn't eating *anything* with cholesterol. Somehow replacing meat with loads of fruit, pasta, bread, and grains actually *increased* my triglycerides and cholesterol. I was worse off than when I had started!

So, as you might expect, I decided to go all-in on the other extreme: a high-protein diet. I cut out all sugar and grains for three months and started eating high-quality, all-natural animal proteins. I was happy to see my cholesterol and triglycerides drop and my energy and focus improve. But by eating mostly protein, I wasn't getting enough essential plant foods. The science is very clear on this, and it's one thing all the experts agree on: Eating *a lot* of fresh plant foods helps lower the risk of heart disease, cancer, diabetes, and other diseases. I needed to increase the micronutrients, phytonutrients, and polyphenols that come from plant foods and minimize the diseases that were part of my genetic makeup.

I'd gone from one extreme to the other, and I *still* wasn't getting the dramatic results I expected. I wanted it all. I wasn't willing to accept an either/or compromise with my health. Caught at a dietary crossroad, my experience was telling me that extreme diets were not the answer. I set out to discover the best of both worlds.

I dared to venture into taboo, uncharted waters: *the middle of the road*! After endless hours of research and thinking about a "bipartisan" approach, I created an eating plan for omnivores that includes animal protein as well as plant foods. The Omni Diet—70 percent whole, plant foods and 30 percent high-quality, lean protein—comprises *all* the foods that have the power to boost health and weight loss, so you aren't forced to choose.

Today, at age forty-three, I am the healthiest I've ever been. My blood sugar, triglycerides, cholesterol, and hormones are all at optimal levels. And I've seen similar results in thousands of people who have followed the Omni Diet. By unleashing and harnessing the full healing power of food, they've reversed illness, altered their genetic destinies, improved their metabolism, balanced their hormones, and lost incredible amounts of weight.

My nursing training made me a stickler for science, so you can be sure that the Omni Diet is built on a solid foundation of scientific research and proven results—not one-sided beliefs and exclusive, one-dimensional food choices. And it's not based on any pop-science nutritional demons or deities. Instead, it provides an ideal way to incorporate into your diet the findings of cutting-edge research, which shows how food can actually turn off certain disease genes and turn on health-promoting genes.

The Omni Diet emphasizes foods that are scientifically proven to

- **Decrease systemic inflammation**
- **Optimize brain function**
- **Offer high-quality, nutrient-dense calories that satiate**
- **Provide maximum quantities and diversity of nutrients**
- **Decrease feelings of hunger and deprivation**
- **Break the chain of food addictions by balancing hormones**
- **Increase energy and youthfulness and feelings of well-being**

The Omni Diet is a carefully designed series of three two-week phases, followed by a maintenance plan that offers a lifetime of healthy living. During each of the three phases, I provide you with meal-planning guidelines and daily menus that feature an exciting variety of easy, delicious recipes along with commonsense advice and simple tips.

I also teach you how to create a supplement plan personalized for *your* specific needs, how to use exercise to magnify the health benefits of your new diet, and how to create a sleep plan that will ensure that you're getting both the quantity and quality of sleep you need for optimal health.

GIVE IT TWO WEEKS

WHENEVER I TALK WITH PEOPLE who want to improve their health and/or lose weight, I tell them this: Just give me two weeks. Simply follow the Omni Diet for two weeks and then let me know if you want to stick with it.

Time and time again, they're hooked. After just fourteen days, they are so thrilled with the changes in their health, mental clarity, energy, vitality, and even the size of their butt and the slimness of their waist, that they joyfully continue with the plan. After six weeks, their new way of eating and living is so ingrained in their psyche that it becomes part of their very identity.

Instead of being addicted to junk food or extreme diets, they're addicted to the incredible feeling of good health and hope that they never thought could be theirs.

When this happens, I'm not the least bit surprised. That's what happened to me—and I bet that after two weeks on the Omni Diet, you'll feel that way, too.

So just give me two weeks. They will change your life.

1

Your History Is NOT Your Destiny

Everyone has a doctor in him or her; we just have to help it in
its work. The natural healing force within each one of us is the
greatest force in getting well. Our food should be our
medicine. Our medicine should be our food.
—HIPPOCRATES

Kathy has had type 2 diabetes for years and has taken medication to help
keep it under control. Although she knew she should stay away from
foods containing sugar and simple carbohydrates, she found it difficult
to resist her cravings. And, although she also knew losing weight would
benefit her health, shedding pounds had always been a struggle.

I MET KATHY AT SADDLEBACK Church in Southern California, where
my husband and I attend services. The church is led by Pastor Rick Warren,
who has inspired millions of followers through his ministry and his bestselling book, *The Purpose Driven Life*. In 2011, he had challenged thousands of parish-
ioners to lose weight and improve their health with a program called the
Daniel Plan. Dr. Mehmet Oz; Dr. Mark Hyman; and my husband, Dr. Daniel
G. Amen, helped motivate 15,000 people to lose more than 125 tons of weight.
I also was deeply involved in the Daniel Plan, teaching nutrition based on
the Omni Diet principles, creating instructional videos, and supplying recipes
and motivational tips.

One Sunday morning, an attractive, middle-aged woman—Kathy—
introduced herself to me.

"Hi, I'm Tana," I responded.

"Oh, I *know* who you are," she said with a big smile. "I've watched your videos on the Daniel Plan Web site. I've made many of your recipes and have followed your tips."

"So, how are you doing?" I asked.

Kathy's smile grew even wider. "I started following the Daniel Plan about ten weeks ago. I had been reluctant to try it because I thought it would be hard. But it's really pretty easy. And I've lost sixteen pounds."

"Congratulations! That's great!" I said. "You must feel wonderful about your weight loss!"

"I do, but that's not what I'm most excited about."

By this time, Kathy was absolutely beaming.

"Once I started the plan," Kathy explained, "I lost all my cravings for sugar within a matter of days! I started eating a much healthier diet, and I no longer had an interest in eating cake, cookies, and all of the other sugary junk that I used to love. My blood sugar began dropping immediately."

"Congratulations! That's fantastic!" I said. Kathy's story reminded me of so many other people I know whose blood sugar and insulin levels had fallen dramatically once they cut out sugar and simple carbohydrate–filled foods, such as bread, muffins, rice, pasta, and anything made with flour.

"There's more to the story," Kathy continued. "This is the best part of all. When I went for a diabetes checkup last week, my doctor told me I no longer have to take diabetes medication. For the first time in years, I'm off my meds! I can't believe it's that simple after only ten weeks!" Seeing the joy on Kathy's face brought tears to my eyes because I know how significant this type of change is in people's lives. She eliminated her need for a very strong daily medication by doing one thing: eating in a new way.

Simply by swapping life-threatening foods for life-supporting foods, Kathy learned to break free from a disease that plagues more than 25 million Americans and is the seventh leading cause of death in the United States. And she did it in only ten weeks! Imagine how much more good health there is in Kathy's future if she continues her new way of eating!

It sounds unbelievable, but it's true. For Kathy and many other people who suffer from chronic illness—such as diabetes, irritable bowel disease, fibromyalgia, rosacea, multiple sclerosis, hypertension, heart disease, depression, and many others—food can be more powerful than medicine.

WITNESS THE POWER OF FOOD

I HAVE NOTHING AGAINST PHARMACEUTICAL drugs—when used appropriately, they play a crucial role in good health. They have the power to save lives. They saved my life! Let me be clear: I am *not* telling you to stop filling your prescriptions! Nor should you feel bad or guilty if you do take medications—I happily take my medication and thank God for it because it helps keep me healthy. The Omni Diet is not an *anti-medication* program. It's an *optimal-health* program.

What I do have a problem with is the indiscriminate use of powerful medication *alone* to manage potentially lethal chronic illnesses *without* proper education about the incredible influence of simple lifestyle modification. A pill may seem like a quick fix, but in my experience managing a chronic illness is almost never that easy. I've worked with thousands of people who have been frustrated to find that their prescriptions are rarely the ticket off the roller-coaster ride of illness, medication, side effects, flare-ups, and really bad days that result from poor health. Medication doesn't give your body everything it needs for health or quality of life. You can think you are doing everything right by following doctor's orders and still feel incredibly sick.

Food can be as healing as a medication. Or, it can be as toxic as a poison. The trick is to harness its amazing power rather than be destroyed by it. By choosing the right foods you, like Kathy, can break some of the bonds of chronic disease. You can positively change the action of your immune system, hormones, genes, and blood sugar. You can help slash your risk of heart disease, diabetes, cancer, dementia, and many other diseases. In many cases, food, along with lifestyle modification, can be as effective as—or even more effective than—pharmaceutical medications. One exciting example is the Diabetes Prevention Program, in which 3,234 women and men with pre-diabetes followed a healthy lifestyle change program that included a diet high in fiber and low in saturated fat, plus regular exercise, or took the diabetes drug metformin. After 2.8 years, the risk for progressing to full-blown, type 2 diabetes was slashed 58 percent in the lifestyle group and just 31 percent with metformin.[1] And *great, healthy* foods don't have all those frightening side effects that you hear so rapidly described at the tail end of pharmaceutical television commercials.

Mother Nature has packed countless powerful benefits into food. It is truly nature's medicine! With the incredible changes you are likely to see with the Omni Diet, you (and your doctor) may discover that you don't need as much medication as you once did. Or you may no longer even need it at all. Even if you do continue to require medication for chronic illnesses, the changes you make as part of the Omni Diet will work with your medication and ultimately boost your energy, vitality, and overall health.

How is it that food—food that may be sitting in your refrigerator at this very moment—can have such a monumental impact on your health, both for better and for worse? What gives food its power? This chapter explains it all. In the pages that follow, I'll tell you about some of the ways that food works as medicine in your body. I'll also explain how the foods I recommend in the Omni Diet will support your health and well-being as you set out to change your health and your life.

COOL THE FIRE OF INFLAMMATION

INFLAMMATION IS YOUR BODY'S WAY of coping with injury or "insult." It is a vital biological response that your body must be able to elicit in the right balance, at the right time. You would never want to eliminate your body's ability to create inflammation, or you wouldn't heal appropriately. But stay with me for a minute.

When you're injured or develop an infection, the many functions of your immune system—both innate (what you're born with) and adaptive (what you acquire during your lifetime from exposure to infection-causing microbes, viruses, and vaccines)—jump into action and set off an acute inflammatory reaction. A cascade of cellular and chemical events occurs: Blood vessels dilate, blood flow to the affected area increases, and pro-inflammatory immune cells and proteins rush to the scene. Nearby tissue becomes swollen, warm, and red as the immune system "inflames" the area and fights to destroy bacteria, eliminate toxins, and clear the way for the healing process to begin.

But injury and infection aren't the only things that trigger inflammation. Environmental toxins, hormone imbalances, emotional stress, excess body fat—especially belly fat—and blood sugar, along with *certain kinds of foods,* also cause inflammation. This kind of inflammation, even though it's low-level, is not helpful, because it is chronic—that is, it stays turned on indefinitely, rather than just being called into action occasionally when an injury or infection occurs.

Over time, chronic, out-of-control inflammation damages your body, rather than healing it. Eventually it can cause or contribute to a range of diseases and conditions, including heart disease, arthritis, gastrointestinal disorders, cancer, Alzheimer's disease, and high blood pressure.

Doctors prescribe anti-inflammatory medications for people with high levels of systemic inflammation. But for many people, the best prescription is a change in diet (the root of the cause), rather than one new medication after another. Relying on multiple medicines to heal a condition that is being caused by, among other things, excessive consumption of inflammation-inducing foods is like putting a Band-Aid over a gunshot wound. It won't help for long. And drugs are not without side effects! Taking pro-inflammatory foods out of the diet and eating more anti-inflammatory foods is a much smarter, healthier approach.

The standard American diet is filled with pro-inflammatory foods. Fast food, sugar, simple carbohydrates, dairy products, trans fats, some animal-derived saturated fats, excess omega-6 fatty acids, and foods that are processed, engineered, or refined promote chronic inflammation. In a small, yet eye-opening 2004 study from the University at Buffalo, a high-fat, high-carbohydrate fast-food breakfast triggered a flood of inflammatory chemicals in nine decidedly unlucky volunteers' bloodstreams. Levels remained elevated until nearly lunchtime, too.[2] When you eat such foods, you're actually injuring your body; in its effort to "heal" from dietary injuries, your body revs up its inflammatory response.

Fortunately, there are many foods that *reduce* inflammation, including fresh vegetables and fruit, fish that are rich in omega-3 fatty acids, nuts, seeds, and certain herbs and spices. They contain compounds that turn down inflammation and lower the strain that it puts on your cells. In a dramatic, recent study, researchers from the University of California, San Francisco, found that good-for-you omega-3 fatty acids can even dial back heightened levels of inflammation after heart surgery, allowing damaged arteries to heal.[3] These and other anti-inflammatory foods are found in abundance in the Omni Diet.

CONTROL YOUR GENES

I OFTEN HEAR PEOPLE AND health-care providers talk about genes like they are an inescapable evil dictatorship controlling our lives; they believe there's nothing you can do about your health because it was determined by your genes. Or, since your mother and grandmother died of a stroke, you will also. Or, poor thing, you're destined to be obese just like the rest of your family. I used to believe these falsehoods, too.

But your genes are not there to ruin your life, or execute the sentence when your time comes. They actually can respond to the choices you make every day. You don't have to sit back and accept the diseases that plague your family. You can fight for your health and actually *change the way your genes behave*.

Your genetic history is not necessarily your destiny.

Let me explain. When you're born, you inherit all of your genes from your parents. Genes are pre-programmed with information that defines what the body has to work with.

Some genetic traits are inescapable—there's nothing you can do to turn your brown eyes blue, short of wearing colored contacts. With eye color, your genes determine your destiny. The same is true with some kinds of conditions, such as Down's syndrome, cystic fibrosis, and hemophilia.

But many genetic factors are not absolute. Some genes *predispose* you to certain health conditions, but external factors can influence whether these genes are expressed in a way that triggers disease. In other words, genetics loads the gun but your environment determines whether or not the trigger gets pulled!

One of those external factors is the nutrients you consume in food and supplements. I'm repeatedly astonished by the simplicity of nature in action. Certain nutrients have the power to influence how a gene is expressed. In other words, if you carry genes that predispose you to, say, type 2 diabetes, the nutrients you consume can help determine whether or not those diabetes genes "turn on"—and if and to what extent you'll actually develop the disease.

Epigenetics is the study of how outside factors affect your genes. Your genome carries all the DNA and instructions for making all the proteins in your body. The epigenome consists of all the chemical compounds (from foods, plants, and environmental influences) that tell your genes when to turn on and how to behave. Researchers have associated changes in the epigenome (the environment your genes are exposed to) to certain types of cancer, autoimmune disorders, mental illnesses, and diabetes. One powerful example is the effect of a compound called indole-3-carbinol, found in cruciferous veggies like broccoli and cabbage, on genes that raise or lower colon cancer risk. Getting more of this good stuff switches off a gene that produces a cancer-promoting protein called survivin and enhances the work of a compound that tells tumor cells it's time to die, according to North Dakota State

University researchers in a 2009 study.[4] The exciting thing about the field of epigenetics is the understanding that altering the environment that influences your DNA can alter your health forever. But there is a responsibility that comes with this knowledge. Many of the chemical exposures that influence the activation or repression of genes occur *years before a child is conceived.* In other words, the choices you make throughout your life can leave a legacy of health or disease for your offspring for generations to come.

The study of how nutrients impact gene expression is known as nutrigenomics. Every day scientists are learning more and more about food's power over genes. A lot of research is being conducted in this exciting new area; we already have plenty of evidence that our diet alters our genetic expression, and that our genes don't have absolute control over our destiny.

Your weight, the food you eat, how much you exercise, sleep patterns, stress management, dietary supplements, environmental toxins, and whether you smoke cigarettes, abuse drugs, or consume alcohol in excess are believed to play a big part in whether certain genes are expressed, or turned on. Amazing, but true. In one headline-grabbing 2010 study from Johns Hopkins University, chronic stress altered gene expression in the brain.[5] Did you happen to notice how many of those factors are in your control?

We're born with our genes, but that doesn't mean we can't control them—in fact, we have more control than we realize!

This information is wildly empowering. In the case of diseases such as type 2 diabetes, heart disease, and some kinds of cancer, just having them in your family doesn't mean you're destined to develop them. Your lifestyle choices are a prime determinant in whether or not these kinds of family diseases "turn on" in you. You can actually affect how your genes are expressed *on a daily basis.*

The food we eat and the lifestyle choices we make impact directly on how our genes function. In fact, the interaction between environmental influences and the chemical compounds that make up your epigenome is constant and ongoing, and it contributes to whether your genes are expressed in a pattern of health or a pattern of dysfunction.

The Omni Diet is built around the foods and lifestyle choices that give you the maximum possible power to influence your genes in a healthy way. Vegetables, fruits, spices, herbs, nuts, and seeds are among the most powerful foods on the planet when it comes to expressing your genes. So, too, are biologically active compounds such as theaflavins and catechins from tea, curcumin from turmeric, and resveratrol from grapes. Nutrition researchers from the University of Navarra, in Spain, found in a 2010 study of 120 people that those who ate the most fruits and vegetables showed dramatic signs of reduced expression of genes that amp up inflammation.[6] There are many other important micronutrients that we will discuss in the pages of this book.

Corey was not a vain man and was more focused on providing for his family than he was on his own physical appearance. At least that was how he saw the 70 pounds of extra weight he was carrying around, until his father began suffering from heart disease, diabetes, and high blood pressure. Corey began to realize that he had a lot in common with his father.

I can't talk about the topic of changing your genetic destiny without telling you about Corey, who participated in one of my Omni Diet classes. After his father had bypass surgery, Corey took his destiny firmly into his own hands and vowed to make changes so he wouldn't go down the same path his father had. Even though he had inherited his genetics from his father, he realized that he could do a lot to be proactive. "Diabetes and heart disease run in my family, and I have been addicted to fatty foods and sweets my whole life," Corey told me. "Now that I have two boys of my own, I am motivated to eat right and be a good example to them."

Corey changed his diet, eliminating all sweetened drinks and juices. He also started to exercise regularly, playing basketball twice a week and walking briskly two days a week. On the weekends, he and his sons go for long-distance bike rides and play soccer, kickball, and baseball in the park.

After following the Omni Diet for twelve weeks, Corey had lost 40 pounds and had gained a new outlook on life. It's a blast to hear how excited Corey is about the changes he's made. "I am glad to be well on my way to a permanent healthy lifestyle that I know will last the rest of my life! It's the first time that I feel I've made a permanent lifestyle change instead of following another temporary diet. I know that I can do this forever because I am eating normally, and I don't crave anything."

Corey is well on his way to altering his genetic destiny. Once you commit yourself to the Omni Diet, you will be, too.

REPAIR YOUR DNA

OUR BODIES ARE MADE UP of an estimated 100 trillion cells. Each cell contains twenty-three pairs of chromosomes (forty-six in total). Every chromosome contains strands of hundreds or even thousands of genes. Overall, each cell in your body is home to about thirty thousand genes. Chromosomes and genes are made of a material called deoxyribonucleic acid (DNA).

The cells in your body are dividing constantly. When cell division occurs, your body makes a copy of the DNA in an old cell and moves it to a new cell. As DNA replicates over and over and over, it can become damaged. Think of making a photocopy from a photocopy, from a photocopy, from a photocopy. Each copy becomes less clear, less like the original, and with more errors. That's how DNA damage happens.

The aging process is tough on DNA. (To see DNA damage and the aging process in action, compare the flawless skin on a child's face to the wrinkles on her grandmother's.) But DNA can also be prematurely harmed by outside forces such as nutritional deficiencies, processed foods, the ingestion of certain drugs (pharmaceutical and recreational), excess alcohol, lack of sleep, radiation, emotional stress, pesticides, sunlight, cigarette smoke, and other environmental toxins.

When we're younger, our bodies are able to efficiently repair damage caused to our DNA. But eventually our genes start to lose their ability to revitalize our DNA. When that happens, aging speeds up and diseases, including the chronic diseases of aging, develop.

Although you can't stop your body from getting older, you can reduce your exposure to things that harm DNA and boost your body's ability to repair DNA when it becomes damaged. Optimal nutrition is the cornerstone of DNA protection. The food choices in the Omni Diet provide exactly the types of vitamins, minerals, and phytonutrients that prevent DNA damage and promote the health and vitality of the genes responsible for DNA repair.

For example, compounds called sulforaphanes, which are found in broccoli and other cruciferous vegetables, boost DNA repair. Many herbs and spices have also shown evidence of preventing DNA damage and aiding in DNA repair. Sulforaphane—released from crucifers when you chew well—protected cells from DNA damage in research conducted recently by scientists at the University of Washington.[7] And the Omni Diet's emphasis on avoiding sugar and other simple carbohydrates and keeping blood sugar levels stable directly benefits your DNA.

Some of the supplements I recommend in chapter 9 make valuable contributions to DNA health. For example, folic acid (also known as folate) is crucial for DNA repair; a deficiency in this B-complex vitamin contributes to the incomplete repair of DNA. Other very important supplements for supporting DNA health include vitamin B12, resveratrol, magnesium, ginseng, alpha lipoic acid, and melatonin. (For details on the science behind these supplements, see chapter 9.)

BATTLE FREE RADICALS

WHEN A CELL CONVERTS OXYGEN into energy, tiny molecules called free radicals are created. When produced in normal amounts, these free radicals work to rid the body of harmful toxins, thereby keeping the body healthy. However, when produced in large amounts (due to poor diet, lack of sleep, excessive exercise, sunlight, pollution, and other insults against the body), free radicals damage cells and tissues and can contribute to heart disease, cancer, cognitive impairment, arthritis, and a host of other diseases.

Antioxidants are nutrients that protect your body from damage due to oxidative stress, which is caused by an overabundance of free radicals. Among the most potent antioxidants are vitamin E, vitamin C, and beta-carotene, which inhibit the overproduction of free radicals or destroy them when they are formed in excess. Studies show that eating foods that are rich in antioxidants—many of which are included in the Omni Diet—helps protect the body from free radicals and prevent the development of oxidative stress–related diseases. Antioxidants are usually found in a plant's pigment (like beta-carotene in winter squash[8]), and to get the greatest range of antioxidants, the Omni Diet chooses a wide variety of plant foods of all colors, from red peppers and yellow squash to blueberries and leafy greens.

BOOST YOUR IMMUNITY— KEEP YOUR PROTECTOR HEALTHY

WHAT IF YOU LIVED IN a dangerous environment where you faced life-threatening situations on a daily basis? If you invested in and relied on a highly trained guard dog to protect you at all times, wouldn't you want him to stay healthy? Would you feed him junk food that you knew would make him sick? Think of your immune system as that guard dog. Your immune system is the most important form of protection you can invest in.

Your immune system (if it is healthy) protects you from all kinds of diseases in a two-step process. First, it recognizes a virus, bacterium, abnormal cell, or other danger. Second, it uses various defense mechanisms to neutralize or destroy the danger. Your skin is a physical barrier that keeps dangers out; your immune cells act like soldiers, patrolling for invading dangers (called antigens) and using antibodies to neutralize them.

As long as your immune system is healthy it works like it's supposed to. But if your immune "guard dog" isn't healthy, it goes mad—it can turn on its owner and attack. That's what happens with autoimmune disorders: The immune system attacks your body instead of protecting it. Once the attack begins, it is difficult to get under control.

Allergies are another example of this kind of biological overreaction. Using a similar analogy, when you have an allergy your guard-dog immune system becomes paranoid and overreacts every time it perceives a threat, unnecessarily launching an all-out fight and wreaking havoc on your body in the form of an allergic reaction.

Food can have a huge impact on the strength and health of your immune system. Both malnutrition (eating too little) and over-nutrition (eating too much) alter immunity. Malnutrition deprives your body of the building blocks it needs to build a healthy immune system. Over-nutrition increases inflammation and oxidative stress, which burden the immune system, making it work too hard. Many people who are overweight are actually *malnourished* as a result of consuming large quantities of "foodlike substances" and processed foods that lack nutritional value—not only are they not giving their bodies the necessary fuel to run a healthy immune system, but the large amount of food they *are* eating is working *against* their immune system, note scientists from China's Beijing Institute of Radiation Medicine in a definitive 2002 review in the journal *Nutrition*.[9]

High blood sugar also harms the immune system, especially in people who are obese. Visceral fat or "belly fat" is the most dangerous fat because it is highly associated with heart disease and diabetes, and it secretes thirty-five different chemicals that increase inflammation and are associated with various disease processes, such as diabetes, cancer, heart disease, dementia, and autoimmune disorders. The list of inflammatory chemicals produced by deep abdominal fat includes tumor necrosis factor, which interferes with healthy blood sugar processing, and resistin, which plays a role in clogging arteries, note researchers from the University of Graz, in Austria.[10] Dealing with all of that is a lot of work for your immune system! But the good news is that as obese people lose weight, their immunity improves.

Eating foods that contain plenty of zinc, selenium, iron, copper, folic acid, and vitamins A, C, E, and B6 can boost immunity. These nutrients are the building blocks that help form healthy cells and improve cell function and cellular communication. Foods that are rich in these nutritional building blocks include seafood, liver, raw cacao, lamb, nuts and seeds, a variety of spices and herbs, green leafy vegetables, red bell peppers, and sweet potatoes. The Omni Diet encourages all of these healthy foods to help keep your immune system in top condition.

Immunity starts in the gut. Something called intestinal permeability is a major source of impaired immunity. This is also known as leaky gut syndrome. When the lining of the bowels is harmed, it becomes permeable—meaning substances that should stay in the bowels can pass out of them. Permeability allows undigested food, bacteria, and waste products to "leak" out of the intestines, which can cause infections, allergies, and digestive problems. Causes of intestinal damage that can lead to intestinal permeability include long-term antibiotic therapy, nonsteroidal anti-inflammatory drug (NSAID) therapy, Crohn's disease, irritable bowel disease, celiac disease, small bowel overgrowth, parasitic infections, food allergies, chronic strenuous exercise, nutritional deficiencies, and excessive sugar intake.

To prevent and reverse intestinal permeability, it's important to eat immunity-enhancing foods. There are plenty of them in the Omni Diet. It's also vital to increase the level of all "good bacteria" in the gut. These bacteria actually help tighten the intestinal "junctions" through which leaking occurs, report researchers from Sapienza University of Rome, in Italy.[11] Probiotics provide these good bacteria, balancing the flora in the gut, and have been shown to be a major player in immune system enhancement, the same researchers and others note. As "good bacteria" begin to repopulate and adhere to the intestinal lining, they compete with the "bad bacteria" (pathogens) for nutrition. As the probiotics consume the nutrients, the pathogens are no longer able to adhere and thrive.

The Omni Diet also avoids foods and drugs that are known to cause intestinal permeability, inflammation, and allergies. Foods that contain sugar, gluten, soy, dairy, and cheap oils (with high levels of omega-6 fatty acids) are the greatest culprits. (I'll go into more detail about this in later chapters.)

[OBESITY: A RAPIDLY GROWING PROBLEM]

Carrying excess pounds is more than just a cosmetic issue—it can have a huge impact on your health. *Belly fat is NOT jolly!* As weight goes up, so do the risks of these medical problems:

- Coronary heart disease
- Type 2 diabetes
- Cancer (especially endometrial, breast, and colon)
- High blood pressure
- High blood lipids, such as cholesterol and triglycerides
- Stroke
- Liver and gallbladder disease
- Sleep apnea and respiratory problems
- Osteoarthritis (degeneration of cartilage and bone in joints)
- Gynecological problems including infertility and abnormal menstruation
- Pregnancy complications (miscarriage, preterm birth, gestational diabetes)

Having excess body fat is dangerous. Fat cells, also known as adipocytes, are mini toxin-manufacturing plants. Adipocytes in visceral fat (belly fat that accumulates around internal organs) produce thirty-five chemicals that lead to increased inflammation, oxidative stress, insulin resistance, and elevated C-reactive protein (which increases inflammation and is a marker and a risk factor for cardiovascular disease).

During the past two decades, there has been a dramatic increase in obesity in the United States. Today, fewer than a third of American adults are of normal weight, more than a third are overweight, and a third are obese, with 6 percent of adults being extremely obese according to the U.S. Centers for Disease Control and Prevention. Among children and adolescents, approximately 17 percent are obese—a threefold increase since 1980.[12]

These numbers are heartbreaking! But know this: Even if you are one of the faces behind those statistics, you *can* lose weight and become healthier and fitter. It doesn't matter if you've tried and failed before. This time, you have the Omni Diet to guide you to a lifetime of good health. You *can* change your weight, your health, and your life.

IMPROVE YOUR BRAIN
FUNCTION AND YOUR MOOD

WHEN YOU EAT FOR OPTIMAL nutrition, you do more than just improve your health. You improve your life. The quality of your diet *directly impacts* the quality of your life. How you perceive the world is heavily influenced by the foods you choose to put in your mouth. Food directly impacts neurotransmitters and thus can have an immediate effect on your mood. But food also has a long-term effect on your well-being. When you eat foods that impact your neurotransmitters and your moods on a regular basis, your diet begins to impact how you think and feel in the long term.

Also, as your weight goes up, the physical size of your brain goes down. Studies have shown that low-quality, high-fat diets and obesity are associated with depression. In a 2013 University of Montreal study, mice were fed a diet high in fat and that led to the mice gaining significant weight; becoming confused; having trouble executing simple, regular routines—such as navigating mazes and performing tasks for food—and showing obvious signs of cognitive decline and depression within twelve weeks.[13] The good news is, at the Amen Clinics, where we have seen tens of thousands of patients from ninety countries, we've found that when people begin to lose weight following an Omni-style diet, most report radical improvement in cognitive function, testing, and mood within eight weeks.

A low-quality diet (think the standard American diet of cheeseburgers, fries, and soda) actually *changes* the chemistry and function of your brain. If you feel lousy, depressed, foggy, tired, and unable to make positive and empowering decisions, it may not all be psychological.

The food you eat has the power to influence six major neurotransmitters in the brain:

SEROTONIN is the "don't worry, be happy" neurotransmitter. It is responsible for mood stability, sleep regulation, appetite control, and social engagement. Serotonin levels go down (sometimes dramatically) at certain times in a woman's menstrual cycle. Being low on serotonin is a common cause of depression and anxiety. If you know someone who gets "stuck" on negative thoughts and can't let go, it could be a sign of low serotonin.

By the way, 90 percent of the serotonin in your body is made in your gut. So if you are suffering from digestive issues and intestinal permeability, you will likely have other issues related to serotonin imbalance. Women, take note: A 2000 study from McGill University in Canada of 11 women and men found that women have a 52 percent lower serotonin production than men do,[14] which could explain why women report twice as much depression as men *and why we crave simple carbohydrates and chocolate.*

People who are naturally low in serotonin—and women whose serotonin levels drop prior to getting their period—often intuitively crave carbohydrate-rich foods such as pasta, bread, and chocolate because carbohydrates raise serotonin levels and increase feelings of well-being. If you're in need of some serotonin-boosting carbs, however, you don't have to reach for refined carbohydrates that trigger inflammation, blood sugar spikes, and high insulin. The Omni Diet includes plenty of complex carbs from plant foods, like sweet potatoes and apples, that will do the trick just as well.

DOPAMINE is the neurotransmitter associated with motivation, emotional significance, relevance, pain, and pleasure. Dopamine-dominant people are usually focused go-getters; insufficient dopamine is associated with attention deficit disorder (ADD), lack of focus, and low motivation.

People with low dopamine are often very impulsive and seek conflict. These are people who say things that no one should hear—they have no filter. Avoiding sugar and refined carbohydrates and increasing lean protein can increase dopamine levels, dramatically improve concentration and judgment, and decrease impulsiveness. Protein-rich foods, such as seafood, poultry, and lean meat, help boost dopamine. This is why high-protein diets that eliminate refined carbohydrates are ideal for people with ADD. However, when people with low serotonin go on a high-protein, low-carb diet, they can quickly find themselves unable to sleep and over-focusing on certain thoughts—especially stressful ones that they can't let go of. The Omni Diet's mix of protein and complex carbohydrates is perfect for those people.

ACETYLCHOLINE is important for learning, memory, and association. Lack of acetylcholine can lead to declining cognitive function and difficulty learning. To stay sharp, the Omni Diet includes foods that optimize acetylcholine, including eggs, salmon, and shrimp.

GABA is an inhibitory neurotransmitter. It is calming, stabilizing, and grounding. GABA-dominant people are well organized and like to keep lists. (We all could use a GABA-dominant person in our lives!) Diminished GABA is associated with depression, bipolar disorder, and mania. Omni Diet foods that are rich in GABA include green tea, broccoli, nuts, and lentils.

GLUTAMATE AND ASPARTATE are excitatory neurotransmitters associated with memory, learning, and pain perception. However, consumed in excess they are potent neurotoxins. The standard American diet is full of foods that contain the amino acids that stimulate these neurotransmitters: the artificial sweetener aspartame, processed lunch meat, sausage, soy, wheat, peanuts, and some preservatives. Having too much of these neurotransmitters damages neurons and causes cell death, and is associated with stroke and diseases such as amyotrophic lateral sclerosis (ALS), autism, intellectual disability, and Alzheimer's disease.

Understanding your brain and simple biochemistry will help you thrive. While we often intuitively reach for foods that satisfy our basic chemical needs and cravings, without education we are left to choose processed, chemical-filled foods that may make us feel better in the short term, but do nothing to nourish our bodies or help us to feel healthier long term. In fact these "anti-nutrition" foods do much to distort your sophisticated hormonal balance and can lead to long-term physical and psychological problems.

HEALTHIER *AND* HAPPIER

THE OMNI DIET OFFERS HIGH-QUALITY, minimally processed nutrition to help ensure that your brain chemistry is synchronized for optimal function. Eat the right food, give your brain the nutrients it needs, and you'll reap a bounty of cognitive benefits: improved mood and memory, stronger cognitive function, laser focus, clear thinking, and a calm, relaxed mind.

The payoff of a healthy diet is not just physical health, but emotional health as well. And it happens quickly: Many people feel sharper and happier within a week or two of starting to follow the Omni Diet. Within eight weeks many people (even those with some of the most challenging lifestyle issues) begin to show dramatic improvement in cognitive function, mood, and decision making.

If you feel lousy, depressed, foggy, tired, and unable to make good decisions, you have a choice: continue to eat a diet that feeds all those negative outcomes, or empower yourself to fight for your health. Starting right now, you can begin to change your diet and your entire outlook on life.

As you learn to eat in a way that truly nourishes your body and your soul, you also begin to perceive yourself in an exciting new way. You will become more confident and emotionally strong. I've seen this time and time again in my classes, especially among women. As participants improve their diet, they feel less isolated, more clear-headed, and better at communicating with others. Some of them discover a healthy self that has been hidden away for many years.

Alicia is one of those women. Before she started the Omni Diet, she did just about anything to avoid confrontation. She's a peacemaker at heart—a good Christian woman who never wanted to rock the boat. When uncomfortable situations arose, she would hold in her emotions and turn to food to help her cope. But a few weeks into my class and her new lifestyle, Alicia began to discover confidence she never knew she had, along with a stronger voice to express herself. One day, a coworker said something untrue about Alicia. Previously she would have let it go and said nothing. But this time she spoke up—she corrected the falsehood and asked her coworker not to say hurtful, untrue things about her. She found her voice and stood her ground in a kind and constructive way.

Alicia beamed as she told her fellow Omni Diet class members about her triumph and described the experience as being "life-changing." For the first time, she realized the connection between her emotions, confidence, and food. Now, she's learning to disconnect those ties and to speak up instead of chowing down.

THE WARRIOR CALL

YOU'RE READING THIS BOOK BECAUSE you want a better present and future. You may want to lose weight—perhaps a great deal of weight—not just to look better, but to circumvent weight-related diseases. Maybe you've been battling an illness or received a medical diagnosis. Maybe you have a family history of health issues you are committed to avoiding. Perhaps you are looking to help someone you love. I know I went looking for the Omni Diet for so many of these reasons.

Many of us enjoy and are good at our jobs. We take care of our families. We're smart. We work hard. And yet we find ourselves discouraged when it comes to our health. We've tried every diet out there. None of them worked— after all the calorie cutting, deprivation, expensive prepared meals, kooky food fixations, and raging hunger—we're right back where we started. And we are frustrated. I hear it over and over: "I have failed every program—how is this one any different?" The self-defeat shows in their eyes. For me it is an exciting moment because *I know the transformation that is about to take place!*

So stop and take a deep breath. The Omni Diet is a plan to make permanent life changes that will stay with you for the rest of your life. You can do this!

I know, you're probably thinking, "I've tried and failed many times before." You aren't a failure—you just never had the right map to get to where you want to go! The Omni Diet is that map. But this time, you're not just going to change your diet. This time, you're going to change yourself—down to the very core of your being. You're not just going to cut a few calories here and add a few minutes of exercise there. You're going to undergo a metamorphosis, discover a new way of looking at life, and become an even better, stronger, healthier version of yourself.

You're going to become a *warrior for your health, a warrior for yourself.*

I am a black belt in tae kwon do. In martial arts, we talk a lot about warriors. Warriors are strong and powerful. They see success as the only possible option—the word "failure" isn't in their vocabulary. They never think of themselves as victims, no matter what life throws at them. Warriors fight to protect themselves and use every possible tactic to defeat their enemies. They are unstoppable and relentless.

You are a warrior for your health. No one will fight for it more than you. No one else can do it but you.

After my cancer diagnosis, everything in my life came to a screeching halt—my career, my relationships, my feeling that I was strong and could do anything I wanted to do. I became so angry, so sorry for myself. I sank into a deep depression. I felt attacked. But the attackers were coming from within my own cells.

I could have rolled over and given in. But instead, I summoned every ounce of power in my being and, with God's help, transformed my anger and fear into a positive energy that fueled a phoenix-like rise from the ashes of poor health. Yes, my inner warrior disappeared for a while, knocked to the mat by cancer. But it was not conquered. It fought and gained strength. Its spirit filled me, and once again, I became a warrior, stronger than ever before.

That is my desire for you. You may feel frustrated or defeated. Your body may seem like your own worst enemy. But channel that inner warrior call for your health. I see people transform every day. I watch with overwhelming pride as the people I work with beat diabetes, overcome obesity, ward off heart disease. . . . These are people, just like you and me, who never believed that they could be so healthy. I've watched these everyday heroes rise through the ranks and earn their "black belts" in health!

Health warriors make big, dramatic changes to their diets and their lives. They walk away from their sedentary ways and exercise with a fighting spirit. They figure out what must be done, and they do it. They commit completely to the tenets of good health—the very core of the Omni Diet—and they transform themselves in ways that they never dreamed possible. With the Omni Diet I will give you the tools to

- **Turn genes on and off**

- **Put the brake on inflammatory processes that scorch your tissues and organs**

- **Annihilate free radical molecules that stress and destroy your cells**

- **Protect your cells' DNA from harm, and repair it when damage does occur**

- **Energize and strengthen your immune system**

I challenge you to join the journey to optimal health. Make the commitment. Educate yourself about the power of food. Transform yourself into the healthiest, best *you* possible. Become a warrior for your health! You won't be alone. I'll be with you every step of the way, explaining what you need to do, showing you exactly how to do it, and helping you understand why it's necessary. I'll be enthusiastically by your side giving you encouragement, advice, and tips. Throughout the book, inspirational Omni Motivation Blasts will give you strategies that will help you change old habits and stay committed. I've created a long list of tried-and-true techniques that will allow you to lean on skill rather than will when temptation strikes.

You have to want it. You have to know your motivation. And you need the formula. Once you get started, you'll see results; and once you see results, your enthusiasm will add exponential power to your progress, like a snowball growing larger as it rolls down a hill. Before you know it you'll begin to feel happier, healthier, and more energetic.

DON'T NEED EASY!

My eight-year-old daughter's favorite movie is *Soul Surfer*, the story of pro surfer Bethany Hamilton. One morning, when Bethany was just a few years older than my daughter, she was surfing in the waters off Kauai. A shark attacked her and tore off her arm in what could very easily have been a fatal accident. Bethany survived the attack.

At first, Bethany felt sorry for herself because it seemed that her surfing days were over. But a mission trip with her church reminded her that even without an arm, she was so much more fortunate than many other people. When Bethany announced to her father that she was determined to go back to surfing, her father told her it wouldn't be easy. "I don't need easy," she told him. "I just need possible."

My daughter is very strong-willed. (I have *no idea* where she gets that from!) I am amazed sometimes by her determination. When anyone tells her something is going to be too hard, she always responds: "I don't need easy! I just need possible!"

Take it from Bethany—and my daughter. What you have to do may not *always* be easy . . . but it is certainly possible. In reality, you'll probably find that the Omni Diet is a whole lot easier than all of the extreme diets you've tried.

2

A Bipartisan Plan for Health

Healing is a matter of time, but it is sometimes also a matter of opportunity.

—HIPPOCRATES

OUR TASTE BUDS HAVE BEEN hijacked! Look around. There are many loud voices telling us what to eat. The loudest, of course, is the food industry. Food manufacturers, restaurants, and retailers use advertising to bombard us with messages about candy, soda, sugary cereal, fried snack foods, and burgers, hawking one unhealthy food after another. Foods in advertisements look so delicious, so mouthwatering, that when we see them on television, on billboards, in magazines, or even on the sides of buses we're left drooling like Pavlov's dogs. That's exactly what the food companies want. They condition us to crave their products, and we shell out billions of dollars to satisfy our cravings.

Food engineers have far more information about the addictive nature of foods on the human brain than the unsuspecting public. They are master manipulators of neuroscience, human behavior, supply and demand. As a society we are only just beginning to see the devastating effects of this irresponsible unleashing of antinutrition Armageddon. Never before in history has society had this problem. Only in the past fifty years or so, with the onslaught of mass media, mass production of food, the ability to supply and store food, and the ability to genetically alter and engineer food, have we become *victims* to the stuff that is supposed to bring vibrant health and sustain life.

The unfortunate result of this vicious cycle of craving creation and momentary satiation is an ugly mess called the standard American diet. With its focus on sugar, unhealthy fats, gluten, artificial flavors, fake fillers, and ingredients that are stripped of their nutritional value, the standard American diet is slowly killing us. It's giving us diabetes, obesity, heart disease, digestive problems, Alzheimer's disease, depression, cognitive decline, autoimmune disorders, and some kinds of cancer. It is making us fat, slow, and dull. And it could shorten your life. In a headline-grabbing 2013 study of 5,350 people, an international team of researchers found that those who ate the "typical Western diet" full of red meat, sweets, fried foods, and refined carbohydrates were 42 percent less likely to age healthfully and more likely to have cardiovascular, metabolic, musculoskeletal, respiratory, mental, and cognitive health problems.[1]

Many of us are wising up. Some of us have diabetes. Others have simply packed on a few pounds. But for one reason or another, we want to eat a healthier diet, to push away the junk and fill our bodies with food that nurtures us, prevents disease, and promotes high-energy health. We are cleaning out our pantries and taking back our taste buds. No more fast food brains and bagel bellies! We want to be conscious eaters who make smart, healthy choices and follow diets that are the best for our bodies.

Once you make the decision to eat healthy and lose weight, it should be simple. Avoid bad food. Eat nutritious food. Right?

This is where things start to get murky. Again, there are people telling you what to eat. This time it's the *health and diet* industry. While their intentions are good, the messages are often contradictory and confusing. In fact, over the last decade or so, the diet industry has become divided between two schools of thought, demanding that people take sides on two extremes of the nutritional spectrum: *Plants v. Protein.*

I've seen people argue about plants versus protein more heatedly than they would debate politics or religion! People who argue stridently on opposite sides of the plants versus protein contest make a Republican-Democrat political debate look like a kindergarten play date. Each side adheres to its philosophy with great rigidity. Each side is dismissive, if not condescending, of the other's prodigious opinions for or against animal foods. Each manages to root out just enough evidence to support its own position.

The result of all this food fighting is nutritional chaos. While diet experts bicker, people who genuinely want to eat a healthy diet and maintain a healthy weight are left to ping pong between polar theories and extreme diets, not knowing *what* to believe, not knowing *what* to eat.

But, as with most things in life, your health and diet are not an either/or proposition. The answer lies not in the polar extremes, but in the reasonable, uncharted middle of the road.

I tip my hat to both plant *and* high-protein diets. Each has some amazing benefits to offer. Plant-based diets are great because they're rich in important phytonutrients and micronutrients that promote heart health and lower the risk of many other diseases. And of course, they are low in the unhealthy saturated fats. High-protein diets are great because they dramatically speed up weight loss, improve energy and focus, limit simple carbohydrates, and help keep blood sugar stable and low. Protein is a peak-performance nutrient that supports mental sharpness and physical stamina.

But neither is *the* best way to eat, and certainly not the *only* way to eat. Healthy people need a wide variety of nutrient-dense, minimally processed foods, including plants *and* protein.

It's time to bridge the gap between meat eaters and vegetarians, weight loss and vibrant health.

The truth is that your body doesn't care about your dietary philosophy. It is practical, like you and me. When it comes to food, your body needs what it needs. We're *omnivores*. Omni means *all*—we need nutrients from *all* of the healthiest sources. We need high-quality protein from a variety of sources, including meat. We need the huge range of nutrients that come from a rainbow of plant foods.

Dr. Loren Cordain, a Paleolithic expert and professor at Colorado State University, performed an in-depth study of 229 hunter-gatherer societies. His results were fascinating: He found that not a single one of the ancient societies he studied ate only plants. This is more evidence that humans are hardwired by nature and by instinct to eat animal protein.[2]

Focusing on the latest food deity while avoiding the most trendy new food demon doesn't serve our bodies well. For optimal health, *we need it all*— the health benefits of some (high-quality) animal protein *and* a lot of (unprocessed) plant foods. Food should not be seen in the light of "demons and deities," but rather as life-giving *fuel*. The Omni Diet focuses on the nutritional science of how food affects your body and your brain, so you can choose the best nourishment.

A DIET WITH EVERYTHING

THE OMNI DIET HAS IT all. It's a simple, science-based plan that provides *both* an abundance of illness-fighting nutrients from whole, living plant foods *and* the perfect proportion of high-quality protein to keep the brain sharp and muscles and organs functioning at peak condition.

The Omni Diet provides the ideal balance of vegetables, fruits, nuts, seeds, fish, and lean meats that give your body *everything* it needs for peak performance, maximum weight loss, and optimal health. Eating a diet that's 70 percent plant foods and 30 percent protein (including animal protein) restores energy, slashes the risk of disease, optimizes brain and hormone functioning, produces dramatic weight loss, and makes the body healthy from the inside out.

Here's how it looks at the table: A huge, raw, multi-colored salad spiked with chunks of avocado and sprinkled with nuts or seeds covers 50 percent of your plate; a lightly cooked plant food such as braised cauliflower with basil sauce fills another 20 percent of your plate, and 3 to 6 ounces of lean protein, such as wild salmon, occupies the remaining 30 percent.

The Omni Diet gives you the best of both worlds—plants and protein—so you don't have to choose between maximum health and dramatic weight loss.

My "bipartisan" Omni Diet is the distillation of an extensive study of nutritional science combined with years of personal and professional experience. Over the course of nearly a decade, I have dedicated my life to expanding my knowledge of nutritional medicine. I have worked with some of the leading "rock star" physicians in the field of functional medicine and nutrition. Recently I was an active part of Saddleback Church's Daniel Plan, one of the largest health efforts ever conducted in a religious organization. The Daniel Plan helped 15,000 people lose more than 125 tons!

Working alongside my husband, Dr. Daniel Amen, whose cutting-edge brain-science programs have broken ground in the understanding of peak brain function, I have seen firsthand how the Omni Diet's 70/30 nutritional balance can reverse illness, modify genetic expression, and accelerate weight loss.

I don't just preach it, I live it. Thanks to the Omni Diet, I am now, at age forty-three, the healthiest I've ever been. My blood sugar, triglycerides, cholesterol, and hormones are all at optimal levels.

The Omni Diet has changed my life and the lives of so many people with whom I have been blessed to connect—and now it can change yours.

The Omni Diet contains a perfect balance of plant foods and protein foods. *Both* are crucial to a healthy diet. It's important to understand why, so let's take a closer look at what protein and plant foods contribute to our health. We'll start with protein. Then I'll tell you about the health benefits that plant foods bring to the table.

Meet Tamara: An Omni Diet Superstar!

At the age of thirty-two, Tamara's health was in shambles. Her joints were swollen. The skin on her knuckles would split and bleed when she changed her baby's diaper. She had shooting pain in her back when she walked up the stairs. Her daily naps were growing increasingly longer, and she was unable to tolerate working or being on her feet for very long. "I felt guilty that I never took my kids to the park to play on sunny days," Tamara confided to me.

Tamara's triglycerides, cholesterol, and blood pressure were very high, and her vitamin D level was dangerously low. Her weight had crept up to 206 pounds. Her markers for inflammation were unexplainably high. Her doctors had no answers for her—tests had ruled out rheumatoid arthritis, celiac disease, Crohn's disease, and irritable bowel syndrome (IBS). Tamara had spent several hours every day in the bathroom with painful diarrhea, *for years*!

After receiving several prescriptions, including one for a statin to help lower her cholesterol, Tamara became desperate. She just didn't want to start taking another medication at age thirty-two! She wanted to be healthy for herself and her children, but she had no idea where to start.

That was when Tamara called me. She had heard about the Omni Diet philosophy and had been resistant to change. But she had hit her breaking point.

After I clearly explained the principles of nutrition to Tamara, she realized that she had been poisoning her body. Once she started getting real nutrition, her body responded immediately.

"I followed Tana's advice, and I figured it would take several weeks before I saw any kind of a difference," Tamara said. "But after just two *days,* my health started to change. I had a normal bowel movement for the first time in years! How could years of suffering appear to be reversed after only a few days of nutritional eating and taking a few supplements?"

Tamara lost 22 pounds in six weeks (with no exercise) and 30 pounds in eight weeks. More important, her lab values changed to completely normal, and the pain in her joints virtually disappeared. "I'm now living with less pain, more rest, and a higher quality of life," Tamara told me. "And this happened almost overnight." Within a year Tamara had lost nearly 60 pounds!

THE MEDICINAL POWER OF PROTEIN

PROTEIN IS A MAJOR PLAYER in the healthy growth and functioning of cells, tissues, and organs throughout your body. Apart from water, protein is the most abundant substance in your body.

Eating protein chases away hunger by balancing the hormones of metabolism. It also causes your body to release the hormone Peptide YY (PYY), which improves sensitivity to leptin, the satiety hormone. Leptin tells your brain when you are full and should stop eating. In a 2005 University of Washington School of Medicine study of 19 people, satisfaction levels soared on a high-protein diet while leptin levels remained stable—a sign of increased leptin sensitivity, the researchers noted.[3]

Protein also stimulates the release of glucagon, note scientists from the Technical University of Munich in a 1989 study that measured levels of this hormone after volunteers ate a protein-rich steak.[4] Glucagon stabilizes blood sugar and prevents energy crashes—the opposite of what insulin does. After eating a protein-containing meal or snack, you feel fuller longer and burn more calories than you do after eating high-carb, sugar-filled foods. I think of protein as medicine you should take in small doses every three to four hours—it belongs in nearly every meal and snack.

Because of how it's metabolized, protein actually speeds up weight loss. Of all the macronutrients, protein requires the most energy to digest. High-protein, low-carbohydrate eating triggers a metabolic state known as ketosis, in which the body burns its own fat for fuel instead of the carbohydrates in food. Ketosis causes the formation of substances called ketones. However, although ketones reduce your appetite, they can also cause bad breath, nausea, gout, kidney problems (in predisposed individuals), and other health issues if elevated long term.

Protein also provides your body with amino acids. Your muscles, skin, hair, many hormones, neurotransmitters, and other body parts all need a reliable and regular intake of essential amino acids for optimal health. Your body can produce *some* of the amino acids it needs, but not all of them—those that can't be manufactured in your body must come from food. These are called essential amino acids, and because your body can't store them for future use, they must be included in your diet on a regular basis.

Plant foods such as nuts, seeds, legumes, and some grains, fruits, and vegetables contain only *some* of the twenty amino acids we need. Fish, poultry,

[HOW MUCH PROTEIN SHOULD *YOU* EAT FOR VIBRANT HEALTH AND LONGEVITY?]

Most people need an average of 45 to 100 grams of dietary protein daily, depending on their size and metabolic demands. That's a big range! To figure out exactly how much *you* should aim for, grab a calculator and follow these steps:

1. The average daily protein intake of a healthy individual should be approximately 0.8 to 1.0 gram of protein per kilogram of ideal body weight. (A kilogram is 2.2 pounds.) So start by figuring out your weight in kilograms: Simply divide your weight in pounds by 2.2.

2. Now, multiply your weight in kilograms by the amount of protein per kilogram. (For myself, I use the higher number of 1.0 gram per kilogram because of my activity level—if you are very active, you can eat extra protein. If you are less active, 0.8 gram per kilogram is sufficient.) This is your daily protein goal.

3. Next, divide this number by the number of meals and snacks you eat throughout the day to determine how much protein you should eat with each meal.

Here's an example for a very active 150-pound person:

1. 150 divided by 2.2 is 68.
2. 68 multiplied by 1.0 is 68.
3. 68 divided by 5 (three meals, two snacks) is 13.6, which you can round up to 14. This means a 150-pound person who eats three meals and two snacks (or five mini-meals) daily should eat about 14 grams of protein with each meal and snack.

and most meats contain *all* of them. The same is true for essential fatty acids, which your body also requires but can't produce on its own.

PROTEIN PROBLEMS

SO, IF SOME PROTEIN IS good, then more is better, right? Wrong! Although high-quality protein is crucial to good health, eating too much of it—or choosing poor-quality protein—can be harmful. Our bodies are simply not designed to effectively process large quantities of protein.

Eating too much protein causes increased oxidative stress and inflammation in the body, which contributes to cellular aging, inefficient DNA repair, and disease. It can be hard on the kidneys and liver, as well. In fact, a 2013 study from the German Institute of Human Nutrition that tracked the diets and health of 2,198 women and men found that while whole grains reduced signs of inflammation, red meat consumption increased an important bloodstream marker for chronic, body-wide inflammation called high-sensitivity C-reactive protein.[5] These organs clean up and eliminate the waste products of protein metabolism—that can be a big job when the diet is high in protein.

SHAKE HANDS WITH PROTEIN

The easiest way to determine how much protein to have at a meal or snack is to use the palm of your hand (minus your fingers) as a guide. If you "shake hands" with protein, you'll get just what you need.

People who make animal protein the cornerstone of their diet often make poor choices about what *kinds* of meat to eat. Rather than choosing the most healthy, high-quality meat, many dieters turn to cheaper processed and cured meats, which often contain excessive amounts of fat, salt, sugar, and fake fillers. They also may buy industrially raised meat, which is higher in palmitic acid (a type of bad saturated fat) than grass-fed meat, according to a definitive 2010 California State University study that compared the fatty-acid profiles of grass- and grain-fed beef.[6] This fat is associated with cardiovascular disease. High-quality animal protein is more expensive than industrially raised animal protein, but it's well worth the investment. What price can you put on feeling great and lowering your risk of illness?

My biggest concern with a high-protein diet is that if you eat excessive amounts of protein, it's nearly impossible for you to get enough of the energy-giving, disease-preventing nutrients that come from whole, living plant foods. There's simply not enough room for these foods in a high-protein diet—especially for someone who is trying to lose weight.

PLANT FOODS: A CORNUCOPIA OF HEALTH BENEFITS

SCIENCE MAKES IT ABUNDANTLY CLEAR that plant foods, especially vegetables, have tremendous health benefits. They provide an enormous array of phytonutrients, enzymes, vitamins, and minerals necessary for good health.

Plant foods prevent and reduce systemic inflammation because they contain many compounds that lower the body's inflammatory response. Excessive inflammation contributes to heart disease, arthritis, gastrointestinal disorders, cancer, Alzheimer's disease, high blood pressure, and many other diseases.

Plant foods also support optimal health at the cellular level. Compounds in plant foods can help repair defects in DNA. That's a big deal, because defective DNA can lead to cancer, chronic diseases, and aging-related health conditions. For example, sulforaphanes found in broccoli and other cruciferous vegetables, and various herbs and spices, such as curcumin, offer natural, powerful support in the process of DNA repair. Plant foods also support healthy apoptosis, the process in which cancer is prevented through programmed cell death. In a recent study from China's Harbin Institute of Technology, researchers found that sulforaphane triggered apoptosis.[7] So did curcumin, a compound found in the spice turmeric, according to a 2006 study by scientists from the University of Texas MD Anderson Cancer Center.[8]

Plant foods also impact the way in which genes are expressed. As we've talked about before, genes actually turn on and turn off as they are influenced by environment, food, drugs, and supplements. Certain genes have the potential to trigger the development of diseases such as diabetes, cancer, and heart disease. If they get "tagged" through a complex process called methylation, they can be switched from healthy genes to disease-producing genes. But the process can also work in reverse, allowing unhealthy genes to begin to express themselves in healthy ways. Methylation is affected to a great degree by the epigenome described earlier. (Remember that the epigenome consists of the chemical compounds from your environment—food substances, drugs, supplements, environmental toxins, and so on—that influence

PLANTS WITH PROTEIN

Most people are surprised to discover that vegetables contain protein, too. For example, minus its water content, spinach is nearly 50 percent protein—a 2-cup serving (85 grams) has 3 grams of protein. Other veggies with a respectable amount of protein include broccoli, kale, cauliflower, bamboo shoots, mushrooms, lettuce, Chinese cabbage, zucchini, and cabbage.

Nuts such as almonds, macadamias, and cashews are also good sources of plant protein. Notice I don't mention peanuts or peanut butter. That's because peanuts are actually legumes, not nuts, and are high in omega-6 fatty acids. But the real problem with peanuts is that they are highly susceptible to contamination during growth and storage, which can lead to infection by the fungus Aspergillus flavus. This fungus releases the toxin aflatoxin, which is a potent carcinogen. If you like peanut butter, try other nut butters instead. Almond butter and cashew butter are much better choices and are delicious spread on veggies for a nutritious snack.

your DNA.) Keeping these genes healthy by keeping your epigenome healthy lowers the chances that they will turn on and allow disease to set in. Many of the compounds in plant foods have been proven to play a part in keeping disease genes turned off.

There is a vast array of phytonutrients in vegetables and other plant foods that boost the health of just about every function and system in your body. Antioxidants help fight harmful free radicals and prevent the development of oxidative stress-related diseases. Plant-plentiful nutrients such as zinc, selenium, iron, copper, folic acid, and vitamins A, C, E, and B6 support a strong, disease-fighting immune system and aid in the vital process of detoxification. Polyphenols have been shown to be cardioprotective (lowering blood pressure, according to a 2013 review from the University of Barcelona,[9] and preventing LDL oxidation, according to nutritional science experts from the University of Connecticut[10]), chemoprotective (scientifically shown to fight many types of cancer), and neuroprotective (with chemical compounds that sequester debris in the brain-associated Alzheimer's disease). All of these vitamins, minerals, and nutrients are found in abundance in plant foods.

Plant foods even boost your brain health. Antioxidants and other nutrients found in plant foods—especially colorful vegetables and fruits—protect the brain from oxidative stress and free radical damage, which helps keep the brain sharp and helps ward off brain diseases and cognitive decline. One exciting example is resveratrol, found in grapes and other types of produce. In lab studies, this compound increased the activity of brain-protecting antioxidants and reduced levels of cognitive impairment, according to biochemists from the University of Maryland School of Medicine.[11]

WHAT'S MISSING FROM PLANT FOODS?

IF PLANT FOODS ARE SO great—and believe me, they truly are—why shouldn't we all be vegetarians? The number one reason is protein. Our bodies need it in a way that plant foods simply can't deliver. Plant foods do contain protein—some are fairly decent sources. But making plant foods your *only* source of protein is a mistake.

Nuts, seeds, some grains, fruits, and vegetables contain only some of the twenty amino acids we need. None has them all. And no plant food contains taurine (except blue green algae, which is a controversial subject), a very important amino acid. But fish, poultry, and most meats contain *all* of the amino acids. This fact alone is a convincing argument that humans were designed to consume at least a modest quantity of animal protein.

To meet all your protein needs with plants, you'd need to know *exactly* which foods contain which amino acids, and *exactly* which amino acids your body needs at various times so they can work together synergistically. Then you'd have to consume a wide variety of unprocessed, plant proteins on a continuous basis.

This would be very, very difficult to do. And it's potentially harmful, because if you made any mistakes, your body would be left without vital amino acids. And you'd still be left with the problem of how to acquire taurine, which is not found in plants at all. Why take risky chances with amino acid bingo when you can get them all wrapped up together in a complete-protein package when you eat meat, poultry, or fish? And it doesn't take a tremendous amount of animal protein to get the job done.

There are other extremely important nutrients found mainly in fish and meat. Key vitamins and minerals, such as iron, zinc, iodine, vitamin A (the direct form), vitamin B12, and vitamin D, are found primarily in animal foods. Our bodies need these nutrients, and can't produce them on their own. It's true that some plant foods contain a *form* of some of these nutrients. For example, plant foods contain beta-carotene, a form of vitamin A. But since beta-carotene needs bile salts to be properly converted to a usable form of vitamin A, some fat must be consumed (since that is what causes your liver to release bile salts). It takes five to six times more beta-carotene in a totally plant-based diet to get the amount of usable vitamin A necessary for great health. (In a 2004 Iowa State University study published in the *American Journal of Clinical Nutrition,* people who ate salads topped with fat-free salad dressing didn't absorb any beta-carotene, while those whose greens were dressed with a full-fat dressing absorbed plenty.[12]) And while zinc can be found in soy, nuts, and legumes (in lesser amounts than in animal protein), it is believed to be less absorbable in these plant foods. The phytic acid in soybeans and other legumes and grains binds to minerals, leading to depletion rather than supplying much-needed nutrition. In addition, grains are very difficult for many people to digest, and as we will see in part 2, can cause a host of health issues (especially when consumed in the amount necessary to obtain enough nutritional value). Vitamin D is another example. While it can be manufactured by the body in the presence of sunlight, it is found only in animal products. It does come in supplement form (which is a good idea when necessary), but it is always best to get as much nutrition as possible from food sources. Since most people don't get much sunlight and wear sunscreen when they are outdoors, animal foods (especially seafood and egg yolks) are the best sources for vitamin D. For all of these reasons, it is essential to eat some animal-based protein—plants just won't fill all of your body's needs.

And don't forget omega-3 fatty acids, in my mind one of the top superstar nutrients. Our bodies need both omega-3 and omega-6 fatty acids. They are both *essential fatty acids,* which means that you need to get them from food or supplements because your body can't make them. But there are key differences between the two: Think of omega-6 as an accelerator—it hastens the creation of inflammation. Omega-3 is like the brake—it decreases inflammation. You need to be able to create inflammation, *sometimes,* in the right amounts and at the right times, such as when you are hurt or sick. However, if it goes too far and inflammation becomes *chronic,* it's like having a slow-burning fire in your body that never goes out. It begins damaging the immune system, arteries, nerve cells, and organs. Ultimately this can lead to heart disease, neurodegenerative diseases like Alzheimer's disease, diabetes, arthritis, autoimmune disorders, asthma, and cancer.

The truth is, you simply can't get optimal amounts of omega-3 fatty acids from plants. Vegans often claim that flax oil is an efficient source of omega-3 fatty acids, but research doesn't back that up. The plant-based omega-3 in flax and flaxseed oil is alpha linolenic acid (ALA)—but only 4 to 21 percent of ALA is converted into more potent eicosapentaenoic acid (EPA) and docosahexaenoic acid (DHA), according to the Linus Pauling Institute at Oregon State University.[13] In addition, flax oil causes inflammation, which isn't good for your body. While there are some algae supplements on the market that show promise, as yet they are inferior to fish sources. (In addition, some algae products have been shown to be toxic for some people.)

Vegetarians get plenty of omega-6 fatty acids, but that actually makes the omega-3 deficiency situation worse, not better. Getting too much omega-6 and not enough omega-3 fatty acids causes harmful inflammation throughout the body. Everyone should be eating fish—or at the very least, taking fish oil supplements. Historically, the human diet contained a ratio of about 1 to 1 or 1 to 2 omega-6 fatty acids to omega-3 fatty acids. Changes to the human diet, and thus human health, happened in stages. Some of these changes were obviously for the good, and some not so good. When farming became possible, people began storing food and domesticating grains. The industrial revolution followed shortly by the farming revolution meant that food could be grown, packaged, shipped, and stored as never before in history. People suddenly had an abundance of food for the first time. Over time advertisers and the food industry answered the call of consumers to make food preparation and storage easier and easier (especially in the United States, where the culture is so focused on convenience).

So what does this have to do with omega fatty acids and inflammation? Well, as food is packaged to maintain long shelf life, preservatives and processed oils are added. These oils, which are high in omega-6 fatty acids, are highly inflammatory. As a result, the composition of our natural diet has gone from a ratio of about 1 to 1 to about 20 to 1 omega-6 fatty acids to omega-3 fatty acids! That is a terrifying shift in a short amount of time.

But let's get back to the question of animal protein in your diet for a moment. Most non–meat eaters tend to supplement their diets with excessive amounts of soy, grains, pasta, and bread. While these foods have been touted as fat-free and wholesome, they can lead to a whole lot of trouble, as we will see in part 2. These foods can lead to high cholesterol or high triglycerides even among people whose weight is in the healthy range. Excessive (and sometimes even moderate) consumption of grains can also damage the intestinal lining, decreasing absorption of vitamins and minerals that are vital for vibrant health and longevity. While an extreme example of this is celiac disease, an autoimmune condition in which the body attacks the intestines in a person who eats gluten from wheat and several other grains, some of these foods cause problems that are not so black-and-white, but rather lie along a continuum. High amounts of soy and grains also trigger systemic inflammation, mental fog, fatigue, and food allergies. These "replacements" for animal protein in a strictly vegetarian diet are not good for your health.

Q: Soy is a plant food that's high in protein—which sounds like a great combination. Is it part of the Omni Diet?

A: Although soy is a major go-to food in both vegetarian and high-protein diets, there are a lot of reasons to avoid it:

- Almost all soy products sold in the United States are made with genetically modified soybeans. (Genetically modified foods have had their DNA altered in some way. Read more about this in part 2: Foods to Lose.)

- Tofu, tempeh, soy milk, and other soy products are heavily processed. While organic tofu and tempeh are not as problematic in small amounts, other foods that contain these products, including soy cheese and meat replacements, contain other ingredients such as processed oils and preservatives that increase inflammation.

- Soy contains high levels of omega-6 fatty acids, which promote inflammation.

- Soy milk contains a significant amount of sugar to mask the intense flavor.

- Soy milk causes the liver to release insulin-like growth factor 1 (IGF-1, a hormone that is similar in structure to insulin), according to a 2002 study from Oklahoma State University.[14] IGF-1 speeds up the aging process. There are over 1,900 studies implicating IGF-1 in hormone-related cancers.

- Soy foods, which contain compounds similar to human estrogen, bind to estrogen receptor sites and may be associated with early puberty in children and may decrease testosterone in men, suggests a 2001 lab study from Brigham Young University.[15]

- Foods made with soy contain unhealthy lectins (more on these later), although tofu and tempeh have fewer than do other soy products because of the fermentation process.

If you do choose to rely on soy for protein be sure to consume organic sources. Small amounts of the whole food (bean) or fermented forms (tofu and tempeh) are best.

IN A NUTSHELL: THE PROS AND CONS OF PLANT-ONLY DIETS AND HIGH-PROTEIN DIETS

Plant-Only Diets

PLANT-ONLY STRENGTHS	PLANT-ONLY WEAKNESSES
Plant foods are an excellent source of nutrients and phytochemicals that promote heart health and reduce the risk of some kinds of cancer and chronic diseases, such as type 2 diabetes.	Plant protein is incomplete; no plant food contains all of the essential amino acids that your body needs.
Plant-only diets include many foods, especially vegetables, that reduce systemic inflammation, a contributor to many chronic diseases.	Plant foods lack certain key nutrients, such as vitamin B12 and zinc, which the body can't manufacture and are found only in animal foods. Most supplements are inferior sources.
The nutrients in plant foods offer strong support for the healthy function of cells and the effective repair of DNA.	Plant foods do not supply adequate omega-3 fatty acids, which are crucial for brain and heart health, reducing inflammation, and other vital health functions.
The nutrients in plant foods lower the chances that genes associated with chronic disease will turn on.	Plant foods can easily deliver too much of omega-6 fatty acids, which trigger inflammation when not in balance with omega-3s.
Antioxidants in plant foods reduce oxidative stress, boost immunity, and contribute to brain health.	Plant-only diets rely too heavily on excessive amounts of soy, grains, pasta, and bread, health-sapping foods that can cause weight gain, carbohydrate cravings, intestinal damage, high cholesterol, high triglycerides, systemic inflammation, and mental fog.

High-Protein Diets

HIGH-PROTEIN STRENGTHS	HIGH-PROTEIN WEAKNESSES
High-protein diets speed up weight loss because protein requires more energy to digest than carbohydrates or fat.	Eating too much protein causes increased oxidative stress, inflammation, cellular aging, poor DNA repair, and disease.
Protein triggers the process of ketosis, which reduces appetite and causes your body to burn fat for fuel instead of carbohydrates.	In the long term, ketosis can cause bad breath, nausea, liver stress, gout, and may contribute to kidney stress.
Getting adequate protein improves energy and focus by fueling optimal brain function.	Excess protein (leading to excessive acid) requires mineral buffers and ultimately leads to leaching of calcium from the bones, which raises risk of osteoporosis and kidney stones.
Protein in the diet helps keep blood sugar low and stable by limiting simple carbohydrates, which can cause blood sugar spikes, inflammation, and a host of other health problems.	An overemphasis on protein limits the consumption of whole, energy-giving, disease-preventing plant foods such as vegetables, fruit, seeds, and nuts.
Eating protein reduces hunger by balancing metabolic hormones that tell you to stop eating and increase feelings of satiety.	Lack of dietary fiber can contribute to constipation and other digestive discomforts, as well as an elevated risk of colon cancer.
Animal protein provides your body with all of the essential amino acids and fatty acids needed for good health.	The need to include large amounts of meat in the diet often leads to the consumption of harmful cured meats and meat from industrially raised animals.

OMNI DIET POSTCARD

"I have learned invaluable information about nutrition, getting healthy, and the reasoning behind it all. I now know what to look for when I am reading labels and making food choices. I am eating healthy foods—*lots* of greens. My eating habits have totally been reinvented. With very little exercise (because I have been recovering from shoulder surgery), I lost fifteen pounds. I am thrilled with how much better and healthier I feel! I still have a long way to go to get down to my goal weight, but I am on my way." —DEBI

THE QUESTION OF CARBOHYDRATES

AMONG HIGH-PROTEIN DIET ADVOCATES, "CARBOHYDRATE" is a dirty word. However, let me be clear: Carbohydrates are not the enemy. They are essential to life. However, we *must* make a distinction between simple carbohydrates and complex carbohydrates.

Simple carbohydrates such as sugar, bread (notice I included *all* bread, not just white bread—more on that later), pasta, white rice, potatoes, and baked goods spike your blood sugar, cause insulin resistance, trigger inflammation, and are low in fiber; most have been completely robbed of their nutritional value by the refining process. Simple carbohydrates provide instant energy. This might sound good, but trust me, it's *really bad*! The instant energy that comes from a blood sugar spike is quickly followed by an insulin spike, leading to a quick drop in blood sugar—which leaves you feeling foggy and craving *more* simple carbs. Simply stated, eating simple carbohydrates and sugar (in any form) keeps you addicted to sugar!

Nobody knows that better than Julie, a member of one of my Omni Diet classes who recently kicked her sugar habit. "I have always eaten fairly healthy (I thought!) but was definitely having too much sugar," Julie told me. However, once she committed to the Omni Diet, she loved the way she felt. "I have much less brain fog now. It's amazing how much clearer my head feels—and my memory is improving as well."

Simple carbs increase triglycerides and low-density lipoproteins (LDL), and decrease high-density lipoproteins (HDL), which is bad for your cholesterol count. Simple carbs can also muffle signals sent by the hunger/satiety hormones ghrelin and leptin, which are responsible for letting you know when to stop eating. The more sugar and simple carbs you eat, the hungrier you will be—simple carbs don't let your body tell itself when it's full, so you keep eating, and keep wanting more, and keep eating, and keep wanting more. . . . In the meantime, you are consuming a lot of *harmful* calories with few nutritional benefits. Simple carbs are not empty calories; they are harmful calories. This is what constitutes a "sweet tooth"!

But here is the good news: Once you let go of sugar, your cravings will subside as well. Within a short time (usually several days) of eliminating sugar and simple carbs, your hormones begin to regulate. Your hunger/satiation signals normalize. You begin to enjoy the taste of real (unprocessed) foods. Fruit tastes sweeter and vegetables more flavorful. You no longer must rely on a lot of salt to bring out the taste of foods. And by eliminating sugar and refined carbs, which contribute to lack of focus and inattention, you have a greater ability to focus on making the healthiest eating choices.

COMPLEX CARBOHYDRATES ARE A WHOLE different ballgame than simple carbs. Complex carbs provide energy more quickly than protein and fats, but in a far more balanced, steady way than simple carbohydrates and sugar. Complex carbohydrates are found in unprocessed plant foods such as vegetables. Generally, foods with complex carbs contain fiber, enzymes, and nutrients, and instead of spiking blood sugar they provide a healthy, steady source of energy, without the dramatic peaks and valleys experienced with simple carbohydrates.

By painting all carbohydrates—rather than just simple carbohydrates—as enemies of good health, anti-carb advocates throw out the baby with the bathwater. If you buy in to the idea that all carbs are bad, you eliminate a food group that contains more life-saving nutrients than any other. The anti-carb philosophy is why most high-protein diets include so few plant foods—because they contain the dreaded *carbohydrates*.

That's a huge mistake!

The Omni Diet makes the distinction that high-protein diets don't: It recognizes the enormous value of complex carbohydrate–rich plant foods while highlighting the harmfulness of sugar and simple carbohydrates.

Vegetarian diets are often high in simple carbohydrates and sugar, and low in protein. This can keep levels of insulin and cortisol chronically elevated, which can lead to rapid aging, muscle wasting, and visceral belly fat (also known as "muffin top"). This explains why many vegans and vegetarians are often soft around the middle even if they are slim.

I recommend eliminating sugar and simple carbohydrates from your diet completely in the beginning, and then consuming *very* small amounts on a long-term basis. This may sound tough, but it's actually a lot easier than you'd imagine. When you stop eating sugar and simple carbohydrates, you'll feel strong cravings at first. But within a couple days, the cravings start to fade away. Really! Once you take *all* bread, *most* grains, white rice, white flour, and sugar out of your diet, and replace them with lean protein, healthy fats, and a lot of whole, fresh vegetables, your carbohydrate fixation will quickly start to disappear. You won't miss those foods because you'll be *adding* so many amazing, delicious foods that you'll enjoy and feel great about due to their incredible capacity to increase energy and fight disease. Instead of being a slave to carb cravings, you'll be actively, energetically boosting your health.

FIBER—THE "INDIGESTIBLE" COMPLEX CARBOHYDRATE

ALTHOUGH IT'S A TYPE OF carbohydrate, dietary fiber is different than simple and complex carbs because it can't be digested by humans. But that doesn't mean it's unimportant—although it moves through your body relatively intact, it plays a dynamic role in optimizing your health.

Dietary fiber helps improve bowel function and reduce the risk of colon cancer. It helps stabilize blood sugar and lower cholesterol. Consuming high-fiber foods—such as broccoli, berries, onions, flax seeds, nuts, green beans, cauliflower, celery, and sweet potatoes (the skin of one sweet potato has more fiber than a bowl of oatmeal!)—makes you feel full faster and longer and helps keep blood sugar low and stable.

Fiber impacts nearly every phase of digestion, starting from your first bite. High-fiber foods generally require longer chewing time, which slows down your eating. This gives the hormones of satiety time to communicate with your brain. In the stomach fiber absorbs water and creates bulk, which can increase the time it takes for food to move out of the stomach. The longer food stays in your stomach, the fuller you feel—and the less likely you are to experience the spikes in blood sugar that occur when food digests quickly and glucose is dumped into the blood. In the small intestines and all the way through to the colon, fiber keeps things moving, yet provides bulk. It's also where the fermentation process begins (a vital process for gut health). Both soluble and insoluble fiber are important in this process.

Soluble fiber (found in foods such as apples, berries, flax seeds, and supplements) provides "food" (prebiotics) to the friendly health-boosting bacteria in your gut. Digestive health is improved when friendly bacteria are well fed and able to crowd out the "bad" bacteria that cause disease and reduce immunity. Friendly bacteria are also responsible for making certain vitamins, such as vitamin K and some B vitamins, and boosting immunity.

Insoluble fiber doesn't provide much benefit in the way of fermentation, but it does work like a broom, helping to keep the intestines cleaned out. It also makes sure that the vital fermented products of the soluble fiber get distributed throughout the entire colon.

With its emphasis on vegetables, the Omni Diet provides significant amounts of both soluble and insoluble fiber. Even so, I believe it's still worthwhile to add fiber supplements to a morning smoothie or afternoon glass of water, particularly when you're just starting out on the Omni Diet, and especially if you are insulin-resistant or have high cholesterol.

DON'T FORGET FAT!

WE CAN'T TALK ABOUT PROTEIN and carbohydrates without considering the impact—good and bad—of dietary fat on health and disease.

Like carbohydrates, fats have been demonized in dietary circles over the past decade or so. For some time, many in the medical establishment thought of all fat as bad fat. The public was told: "If you eat fat you'll get fat." This way of thinking came to a head in the early 1980s, when the fat-free craze took off. The food industry saw a lucrative opportunity and started to exploit it, selling everything from fat-free cheese to fat-free cookies. People gobbled these foods up (even though most tasted pretty disgusting), but to their amazement, they didn't lose weight. In fact, they got fatter.

How could that be?

The food industry's dirty little fat-free secret is that when manufacturers remove fat, they put in its place huge amounts of sugar, salt, and fake food fillers—that was the only way to make fat-free food palatable. The irony is that when compared to full-fat versions, fat-free food often has up to 30 percent more calories, as well as more sugar, more salt, and an ingredient list that requires a biochemistry degree to decipher. Americans thought that by buying fat-free foods they were making healthier choices, when in fact they were getting lower-quality food that was even less healthy than the full-fat original.

That dirty little secret has become America's extra-large dirty laundry! It's no coincidence that obesity rates have skyrocketed since the 1980s. According to data from the Centers for Disease Control and Prevention, about 15 percent

IS FRUIT A SOURCE OF GOOD CARBS OR BAD CARBS?

Fruits are categorized as "good" carbs. However, because of the high sugar content in most fruits, their contribution to health is a bit complicated. Unlike processed foods and simple carbohydrates, such as white bread and table sugar, most fruits contain a significant amount of disease-fighting fiber, vitamins, minerals, and enzymes. But they also contain natural sugar—in fact, the reason fruit juice is not part of the Omni Diet is because of the extreme concentration of sugar at the expense of removing the vital component, fiber. With fruits, the key is to balance the benefits of eating them with the risk of getting too much sugar.

To maintain this balance, I recommend limiting yourself to no more than half a cup (about one serving) of fruit per day for most people in the early phases of the Omni Diet program. The majority of people are addicted to sugar, and large quantities of fruit fuel that addiction. More fruit will be reintroduced after the first phase. Overall, the best fruit choices are organic strawberries, blueberries, raspberries, and blackberries, which have less of an impact on blood sugar, and more nutritional value, than starchy or high-sugar fruits such as bananas and pineapples. Berries also have special brain-health components that help to clean up debris in the brain through a process called autophagy, much like little Pac-Men.

of Americans were obese in the early 1980s; by the early 2000s the rate more than doubled, to 32 percent! The most recent data shows obesity at 36 percent. And it's estimated that at this rate, 42 percent of Americans could be obese by the year 2030, warn researchers from Duke University and the Centers for Disease Control and Prevention.[16] The fat-free movement was one of the worst things to happen to the health and waistlines of this country.

Healthy quantities of healthy fat don't make you fat. They are necessary for heart health, brain health, excellent overall health, and even weight loss. Indiscriminately cutting fats from your diet can dangerously alter your intake of essential fatty acids, such as eicosapentaenoic acid (EPA), and docosahexaenoic acid (DHA). These fats are called essential for a reason—our bodies need them, and the only way to get them is through foods or supplements. The fat-free craze caused a drop in fatty acid intake that resulted in a dramatic increase in heart disease, as well as a devastating rise in the number of athletes who died of sudden cardiac death. By making a conscious effort to eat only fat-free foods, people cut back on the consumption of fatty fish like salmon, nuts and seeds, avocados, and other foods that are naturally high in these disease-fighting, essential fatty acids.

While it's important to avoid fried fats, trans fats, and some saturated fats, cutting way back on healthy fats is harmful, because your body needs them for many crucial functions. Like protein, healthy fats stimulate the release of the hormone PYY, which helps you feel full. Your body also uses healthy fats to store energy, build healthy cells, support proper brain function, prevent oxidative damage and degenerative nerve disorders, and manufacture hormones. Fat is also *required* for your body to absorb and store certain vitamins, minerals, and nutrients (which is why it's a good idea to take nutritional supplements with a meal containing a little healthy fat). And you need a substantial amount of healthy fats (especially omega-3 fatty acids) in your diet (at regular intervals) to prevent the loss of your hard-earned muscles during weight loss.

LIKE WITH SO MANY IMPORTANT topics in the world of optimal nutrition, the enthusiasm for fat-free eating was vastly oversimplified. Let's step back a bit and look at how different kinds of fats impact our health. As with carbohydrates, there are *good* fats and *bad* fats:

OMEGA-3 FATTY ACIDS. This family of fats is definitely good. Omega-3 fatty acids are crucial for optimal health. Your brain needs specific types of essential omega-3 fatty acids, such as DHA and EPA, to function well. These omega-3 fatty acids are found in fish, such as salmon.

Deficiencies in these vital fatty acids have been shown to be associated with cognitive decline with aging, psychological disturbances, depression, mood swings, and neuropathy (tingling in hands and feet). Similarly, these critical fatty acids are necessary for optimal immune response and improving cardiovascular health, joint health, skin quality, vision, and wound healing.

Omega-3 fatty acids are especially important for pregnant women because they contribute to the development of an unborn baby's eyes, brain, and immune system.

UNSATURATED FATS. Unsaturated fats are also considered *good* fats because they contribute to heart and brain health and are essential to decreasing the risk of heart disease, normalizing blood clotting, balancing blood sugar, and decreasing LDL cholesterol. There are two kinds of unsaturated fats: polyunsaturated and monounsaturated. In moderation, both have a place in a healthy diet. Both are found in plant foods such as olive oil and nuts. Both help lower LDL (bad cholesterol) and raise HDL (good cholesterol). But while they offer a lot of nutritional bang for their buck, you need to pay attention to quantity. These fats are calorie-dense, so if you don't pay attention to how much you're eating you can easily double or even triple your intake without even noticing. Doing so can lead you right back to where you started: stuck with a lot of extra pounds to shed.

OMEGA-6 FATTY ACIDS. These fats are necessary, but can be harmful when you eat them in excess, so they're good *and* bad. Omega-6 fatty acids are found in most vegetable oils (soybean, sunflower, safflower, corn, canola), as well as many fried foods, cereals, and whole-grain breads. Omega-6 fatty acids contribute to muscle health, for example. However, eating too much of omega-6 fatty acids is a problem because they cancel out the benefits of omega-3 fatty acids when the ratio of omega-6 to omega-3 is too high.

The optimal ratio is 2 to 1 (omega-6 to omega-3), and not higher than 3 to 1. Most people who eat the standard American diet, which contains high levels of omega-6-rich vegetable oils, have an appalling ratio of up to 20 to 1 or higher. Translated in health terms, this is the inflammatory process at work in your body, putting you at risk for heart disease, cancer, diabetes, and a host of other health problems. A proper ratio of omega-3 fatty acids to omega-6 fatty acids has also been shown to decrease triglycerides and, according to a 2006 report from the Center for Genetics, Nutrition, and Health,[17] to help prevent LDL from oxidizing (which makes it more damaging to arteries).

The best way to balance the ratio is to eat fewer foods that contain omega-6 fatty acids and more that contain omega-3 fatty acids, such as salmon and seaweed. Some plant foods, such as flax seeds and green leafy vegetables, contain alpha linoleic acid (ALA), an omega-3 fatty acid that converts in small amounts to EPA/DHA. However, because there is only about a 5 percent conversion of ALA to EPA/DHA, it shouldn't be considered a reliable source. Grass-fed, free-range meat has about 4–6 percent EPA/DHA and much lower levels of omega-6 fatty acids and saturated fats than factory-farmed meat. You can also help ensure a healthy omega balance by taking fish oil supplements.

SATURATED FATS. These fats can be bad *and* good. While they are commonly known as *bad* fats, the science is still unclear about the overall effect of saturated fats on heart health. This is partially because there is more than one kind of saturated fat and they aren't all particulary equal in the health equation. Here's why:

- Stearic acid is a long-chain fatty acid found in meat and chocolate. Although it is a saturated fat, it has *not* been shown to cause the cardio-vascular problems usually attributed to other saturated fats.

- Lauric acid is a medium-chain fatty acid found in coconut that, although it is saturated, has shown many health benefits. It isn't believed to have the negative effects of other saturated fats. Researchers are continuing to explore the benefits of lauric acid. (Saturated fats from plant sources such as coconut and macadamia nuts are a whole different story than saturated fats from animal foods—I'll explain this in chapter 5.)

- Palmitic acid is also a saturated fat. This is what we think of as *bad* saturated fat because it has a negative impact on cholesterol and heart health. This is the fat that is created in your liver when you eat a high-sugar, high-carbohydrate diet. It also creates the cherished fat "marbling" in the meat of corn-fed cattle.

- Myristic acid is a saturated fat found in most animal fats, butter, and some vegetable oils. There is some evidence that this fatty acid can be detrimental to heart health and should be consumed in small amounts.

Saturated fats have been condemned for years because of the connection between saturated fat consumption and increased cholesterol. However, current research paints a more complicated picture, which requires a more complete explanation. Studies done on the different types of saturated fats have shown varying effects on cholesterol levels and patterns. And simply removing the saturated fats, without adding healthy fats, has not shown an improvement in heart health. A well-respected 2010 analysis of 21 studies by nutrition researchers from the Oakland Research Institute found "no significant evidence" for a link between dietary saturated fat alone and heart disease risk.[18] Some research suggests that the healthiest strategy is to cut back on certain types of saturated fats (especially palmitic acid and myristic acid, which are found in dairy foods and meat, especially factory-farmed meat), and increase consumption of polyunsaturated fatty acids like fish oil, nuts, and seeds. A 2010 University of Cincinnati review of fats and heart disease risk notes higher-than-normal death rates among people who consume higher levels of palmitic and myristic acid, for example.[19]

TRANS FAT. Also known as trans fatty acids, trans fat really is a *bad* fat. In fact, it is the *worst* fat. It raises LDL (bad cholesterol) and lowers HDL (good cholesterol), increases triglycerides, and increases the risk of atheroscle-

rosis (the hardening of arteries) and heart disease, as well as diabetes and inflammation.

There is nothing positive about trans fat. It is found in many processed foods, and is created when unsaturated fats are processed and chemically changed from liquid to solid form. Sources of trans fats include shortening, many margarines, many kinds of commercially prepared fried foods, and many packaged baked goods, including doughnuts, crackers, and snack foods.

Don't get too excited about the generation of trans fat–free foods hitting the shelves. Many aren't really trans-free. According to government regulations, trans fat doesn't have to be listed on a food label if its level is below the legal limit of 0.5 gram per serving. For many baked goods and pastries that are in excess of 5 ounces—remember, a single pastry is often actually several servings, even though most people eat it as one serving—that can translate to 2 or 3 grams of trans fat. Even small amounts of these very unhealthy fats should be avoided.

SEPARATING GOOD FROM BAD

THE OMNI DIET MAKES CAREFUL distinctions when it comes to fat. It includes optimal amounts of healthy fats from fish, nuts, seeds, and avocados, while reducing or eliminating suboptimal or harmful fats (especially industrially raised animal fat, trans fats, and omega-6 fats). But many high-protein diets don't make this distinction. They encourage the wanton consumption of processed, fat-filled animal foods such as cheese, fatty and industrially farmed meats, milk, yogurt, vegetable oils, and processed meats. This just doesn't make sense. Not only are these foods full of bad saturated fat, but they often contain sugar, nitrates, preservatives, and other health-stealing ingredients (we'll talk more about this in part 2). And when you eat them, you have less room in your diet for nutrient-dense plant foods. Human beings are biologically hardwired to seek fatty foods when they are available—a drive that helped us survive during times of famine, but is making us sick and killing us in a fast-food, fried-fat society. That's why it's important to make the distinction between fats that serve you and fats that could harm your health. By eating an abundance of foods that truly are healthy for your body, you crowd out the junk and make it easier to break the addictions fueled by food designers.

The Omni Diet honors our omnivorous nature and encourages you to

[BEST OILS]

Although olive oil and some other oils are nutritious when consumed in raw form, they oxidize and become harmful when heated to high temperatures. When oils reach their smoking point during cooking, they break down, lose nutritional value, and become toxic.

For cooking I usually use coconut, grape-seed, or macadamia-nut oil. These oils have a higher smoking point than olive oil, so they can get hotter without breaking down. Usually you don't even need oil for cooking! Most of the recipes in this book suggest using vegetable broth for sautéing instead of oil. In most cases, it works just as well.

I recommend organic, unrefined, expeller-pressed, and cold-pressed oils. Processing strips oils of all nutritional value, leaving them as nothing more than liquid fat, and not the healthy kind. You can find unrefined oils in most health food stores.

Stay away from flax oil, which many popular diet plans recommend. The ongoing debate as to whether flax oil is a sufficient source of omega-3 fatty acids continues, but thus far the science has failed to prove this idea, and flax *oil* is actually pro-inflammatory. Flax *seeds* are very healthy because they contain lignans, a type of antioxidant. But when the oil is removed from the seed, it becomes pro-inflammatory. Also, while flax oil contains some omega-3 fatty acids, it is higher in omega-6 fatty acids, which negates the positive action of the omega-3s. Flax seeds are great for you, but flax oil? Not so much.

include animal food in your diet. I urge you to eat naturally raised meat only from organic, grass-fed, hormone-free, antibiotic-free animals. Industrialized production of livestock is the mainstream way of producing cattle, pork, and poultry. Factory farming refers to raising industrial animals indoors, with very limited mobility. They are typically fed a mixture of corn, soy, and other grains instead of being allowed to graze on grass and seeds. This unnatural diet makes meat tender and juicy as a result of "marbling," which is what farmers and restaurants want because it allows them to brag about (and charge more for) the superior flavor and texture of their meats. But it also creates toxins that sicken animals and are stored in their fat.

These living conditions are not natural for livestock, and they tend to make them weak and sick. The answer is for producers to pump livestock full of antibiotics to prevent disease, and hormones to make the animals grow large quickly and, in the case of cows, produce freakishly large amounts of milk. It's no surprise that industrially raised animals consume up to 80 percent of the antibiotics used in this country. The corn-fed beef Americans cherish comes at a very high price. In fact, the only *healthy* thing about this scenario is the profit at slaughter time.

When you enjoy the juicy taste of steak marbled with fat from a corn-fed animal, you are ingesting the toxins contained in those fat cells. Think about it: You get the same health-related complications from eating a diet high in sugar and grains (a diet not historically natural to you) that other animals get from eating a diet that isn't natural to them! You get that same lovely marbling on your backside and even "foie gras" (fatty liver). Avoid eating meat that has been fed unnaturally and treated with antibiotics. Choose cage-free, hormone-free, antibiotic-free, *naturally raised* animals and you'll get the protein and nutrients found in meat without all of the excess saturated fat, hormones, and antibiotics that are detrimental to your health.

Wild fish, such as salmon, mahimahi, albacore, shrimp, trout, and tilapia are an excellent source of nutrition. Seafood is one of my favorite sources of protein. I also like eggs (if you don't have food sensitivities) because they are protein-rich, easy to prepare, and easy to pack for on-the-go eating. Be sure to choose cage-free, organic, DHA-enriched eggs from vegetarian-fed chickens.

THE OMNI DIET: THE BEST OF BOTH WORLDS

IT MAY SEEM THAT EXTREME high-protein or strictly vegetarian or vegan eating plans would provide extremely good results. But they don't. Rapid, optimal health gains come from an ideal diet that gives your body the best of protein and the best of plant foods. We are omnivores, and we weren't meant to follow extremes and fad plans that eliminate entire categories of nutritious food that have been the natural, historical sustenance for humans throughout history.

The Omni Diet's 70/30 plan—70 percent plant foods and 30 percent lean protein foods—gives your body all the nutritional support that food can offer to fight illness, prevent disease, optimize brain and hormone function, lose weight, and enjoy peak performance.

I am living proof that your health history, present diagnosis, and genetics don't have to be your destiny. My genetics and my health history say that I should be obese, diabetic, and suffering from the effects of chronic cancer and multiple health issues. But I'm not! The Omni Diet hands thousands of us back our optimism and optimal health.

I explain more about the Omni Diet in the program section of the book. And I provide some easy-to-prepare, mouthwatering recipes using Omni Diet foods. For now, here's a preview of what kinds of foods you'll be eating as you incorporate the Omni Diet into your life:

- Fresh vegetables of all kinds, except white potatoes (and nightshades for some of you)
- Moderate amounts of fruit, especially strawberries, blueberries, raspberries, and blackberries
- Naturally raised lean meat and poultry, and wild-caught seafood
- Eggs
- Raw, unsalted seeds and nuts (I recommend raw nuts and seeds, because roasting nuts and seeds oxidizes their oils and robs them of their health benefits)
- Healthy oils such as coconut oil, almond oil, macadamia-nut oil, grape-seed oil, and olive oil
- Dried beans and lentils in limited amounts
- Fresh and dried herbs and spices, which provide rich nutritional benefits and fantastic flavor
- Super-foods (such as maca root, goji powder, lucuma, and pomegranate) that magnify health-supporting processes

JEANA MAIOCCHI, 44

It's no exaggeration: The Omni Diet changed Jeana's life. For years, she'd been plagued with severe irritable bowel syndrome (IBS), as well as eczema and rosacea, and nothing seemed to help. But within three days of starting the Omni Diet, her symptoms had all disappeared.

"The IBS was ruling my life," Jeana recalls. "I never knew when it would flare up. I'd have horrible stomach pains and be afraid to go out to parties and events. And the eczema—that was like walking around with an itchy sunburn." Though she visited doctor after doctor, there didn't seem to be a solution—until she tried the Omni Diet. But that did the trick—fast. Within three days, her IBS symptoms had disappeared and her skin had pretty much cleared up. "I can't tell you how freeing that was," says Jeana.

And the weight loss? "That was a dramatic side effect!" she says. "I lost 15 pounds the first two weeks and 23 that first month—and in the past year and a half, I've dropped a total of 45 pounds and gone from a size 16 to a size 6. It's been so much fun to wear jeans again!"

For Jeana, the Omni Diet has been a real eye-opener. She learned that many of her health problems were triggered by food—but that didn't mean she had to feel deprived of her favorites. Her motto: Replace, don't erase. Instead of pasta, she'll treat herself to shirataki noodles, and instead of flavored creamers, she'll add a bit of coconut milk and some stevia. "It's not difficult at all," Jeana insists. "And if I'm having dinner out with friends and a piece of cheesecake comes to the table, I'll take one or two bites and be done with it."

Another big turnaround for Jeana: She's become an exercise enthusiast with a 45-minute routine that includes the bike, the elliptical, and some weight lifting. Now she can spend a whole day at the mall or visiting Disneyland with her husband and daughter without the aches and pains she experienced before. She even sleeps better.

When it comes to the Omni Diet, Jeana's a true believer. "It's great waking up in the morning and having so much energy," she says. "I'll never go back!"

PART ONE

FOODS TO CHOOSE

3

[Mimic Calorie Restriction]

(or Eat Like a Gorilla, Not a Mouse)

To eat is a necessity, but to eat intelligently is an art.
—LA ROCHEFOUCAULD

Annette started to gain weight in her twenties. She became a yo-yo dieter, and with each passing year she packed on more pounds. When she started my Omni Diet class, she had been diagnosed with pre-diabetes and weighed in at 326 pounds.

But Annette's weight and health were only part of the problem. What bothered Annette—and interfered with her life the most, at least on a daily basis —was muscle and joint pain that made her feel like an elderly woman even though she was only fifty-five years old.

"My muscles would ache all day. The pain was especially severe when I got out of bed, when I walked, and in the afternoons. I relied heavily on ibuprofen just to get through the day," Annette explained. "I walked like an eighty-year-old. In fact, a friend at work said that when she would see me get up out of my chair so stiffly and then walk bent over, she would say to herself, 'Oh, poor Annette.'"

NOW, NOBODY PITIES ANNETTE ANYMORE. Their sympathy has turned into happiness and admiration. After committing to the Omni Diet

59

as a way of life, Annette underwent an amazing transformation. Just *four days* after starting the Omni Diet, Annette was stunned to discover that her pain had nearly disappeared!

"One morning as I was walking from my car to my office building, I realized that my muscles and joints didn't hurt as much as they usually did," Annette said. "I decided not to take ibuprofen that morning and see how long I could go without it."

Annette didn't need any ibuprofen at all that day, or the next day, or the next day. "I haven't had to take ibuprofen in over two months because my muscle aches and joint pain are gone," Annette told me.

And that's not all: Annette feels better overall, has more energy, and has lowered her blood sugar. "I am much healthier, and I feel joyful. Coworkers are noticing the difference in me. A friend even asked if I had a procedure done on my face. People say my skin looks radiant. Thanks to the Omni Diet plan, I look and feel years younger."

DON'T LET ILLNESS STEAL YOUR YOUTH

LIKE ANNETTE, WE ALL WANT to look younger, feel younger, and fight off age-related decline in our bodies and our health. Trying to discover the fountain of youth has kept scientists and physicians diligently searching for answers throughout history. Unlike the mysterious waters of fables and fairy tales, the fountain of youth is not a magical location that can be found with a treasure map. The fountain of youth lies within our own bodies, and we can use it to stimulate vibrancy and longevity, thanks to a cascade of new discoveries in disease prevention.

The quest to reverse aging and prevent disease has opened the doors to many new scientific discoveries. One of these discoveries is calorie restriction: Significantly reducing calorie intake by as much as 30 to 40 percent—even in people who are not obese—seems to slow the aging process and reduce risk of aging-related illness. When researchers from Washington University School of Medicine in St. Louis measured important markers of heart disease risk in eighteen people who had followed calorie-restricted diets for more than six years and eighteen normal-weight women and men who ate a typical American diet, they found proof. The calorie-restriction group had higher levels of heart-protecting HDL cholesterol and lower levels of heart-menacing LDL cholesterol, triglycerides, blood sugar, and blood pressure. There were also signs that their bodies were more sensitive to the hormone insulin and that levels of body-wide inflammation were also lower.[1]

If I told all my clients that all they had to do is cut 40 percent of their calories, they would likely look for a new coach. This approach has been tried with many diets, and is rarely sustainable long term. When my clients tell me they are afraid they will fail this program just like they have failed other programs, I remind them that it was past programs that failed them! The Omni Diet isn't like other programs. It is designed to provide you with an *abundance* of disease-fighting foods, rather than making you feel deprived. You don't have to cut all those calories out of your diet in order to fight the aging or disease processes. There are ways to make your body *think* you're cutting way back on calories even when you're not. In other words, when it comes to calorie restriction, you can fake it when you can't make it. Changing the way you eat and live can deliver many of the health benefits of calorie restriction *without* your having to eat like a mouse.

I'm getting ahead of myself. Before we talk about how to fake calorie restriction, let's take a brief look at the science behind it. Stay with me—this is fascinating stuff, even if you're not that into science.

About eighty years ago, Cornell University researchers noticed something surprising in their animal laboratories: Research rats that were fed severe food-restricted diets were healthier and developed fewer age-related diseases than lab rats that ate a normal amount of food. The rats that ate a Spartan diet also had longer lives: They lived up to twice as long as the others.[2]

The Cornell researchers wondered: Could a diet that provides all necessary nutrients in as few calories as possible prevent disease and prolong life in animals—and perhaps humans?

The answer seems to be yes. Since that first study, researchers throughout the world have tackled the Cornell question, launching an entirely new area of study looking at "calorie restriction without malnutrition." These calorie-restricted diets provide the vitamins, minerals, and other nutrients that animals need to live, but only as many calories as they need to stay alive. Researchers have fed calorie-restricted diets to all kinds of animals, including fruit flies, earthworms, mice, rats, dogs, and monkeys.

Overall the studies found similar, dramatic results: When animals ate nutrient-rich calorie-restricted diets, they developed fewer age-related diseases such as cancer, obesity, diabetes, autoimmune diseases, and cardiovascular diseases. They also lived longer than those who ate more food.

Once researchers recognized the dramatic positive impact of calorie restriction on animals, they began designing human studies to see if they'd find similar results.

In one of these studies—an ongoing project known as the CALERIE study—volunteers who are of normal weight or slightly overweight are reducing their calorie intake by 25 percent for two years. Along the way, researchers are tracking various biomarkers, which are biological indicators of disease and health, to see whether calorie restriction has any effect on them.

Results from the CALERIE study are only beginning to come in, but so far, the calorie-restricted diet seems to be lowering several disease-risk biomarkers, such as blood pressure, in study participants.[3]

THE DOWNSIDE OF CALORIE RESTRICTION

UNFORTUNATELY, AS THE STUDIES CONTINUE, the results have left scientists hungry for a better solution. Calorie restriction has some significant consequences. The radical calorie restriction required to achieve dramatic results in humans can reduce testosterone levels and lower libido, the CALERIE study found in a 2010 report in the journal *Aging Cell*.[4] It can also reduce bone mass, according to researchers from the Medical College of Georgia,[5] and cause irregular menstruation, reduce muscle mass (which leads to decreased stamina), and result in a lower core body temperature, which can leave people feeling colder than usual. And, although calorie restriction seems to be beneficial for people who are overweight or obese, it may not have the same effect on those who are lean. In fact, there's some evidence that calorie restriction in lean people may actually be harmful.

There's another problem. Restricting calories by 30 percent or 40 percent is not very practical for normal-weight humans. (If you are obese and in the habit of super-sizing everything, however, it may make sense to restrict your calories by 30 percent or more until you can reach a healthier weight.) Calorie restriction is easy for mice in a cage when the meal du jour is a premeasured amount of pellets—they're not making food choices all day, going out to dinner with friends, and being constantly tempted by food advertisements and well-meaning family members who equate home cooking with love.

So what can you do if you want the benefits of calorie restriction without having to severely restrict calories to what feels like a starvation diet?

I know exactly what you can do—but first, I want to tell you a story about a couple of overweight gorillas.

WILD ABOUT COOKIES

BEBAC AND MOKOLO, TWO MALE Western lowland gorillas, live at the Cleveland Metroparks Zoo. At the time of our story, both Bebac and Mokolo were in their midtwenties, which is relatively young—their breed of gorilla can live up to fifty-four years in captivity. Although they were barely into middle age, the gorillas were overweight and had developed heart disease. They also exhibited abnormal behaviors such as regurgitating and reingesting their food and pulling out their hair and eating it. These behaviors are unheard of in wild gorillas—and so is heart disease.

In the wild, gorillas tend to die from things like human poaching and acute illnesses such as pneumonia and E. coli infection. Chronic diseases such as heart disease and diabetes are nonexistent in gorillas living freely in the tropical forests of Sub-Saharan Africa. But among captive gorillas, heart disease is the number one cause of death. This discrepancy has perplexed veterinarians for years.

When Bebac and Mokolo developed heart disease and weight problems, veterinarians analyzed all the aspects of their lives. It soon occurred to them that the difference in the gorillas' diet might be part of the problem.

In the wild, gorillas eat leaves and stems of herbs, shrubs, and vines, as well as a wide variety of fruits, nuts, and seeds. Although they are primarily herbivorous, they also end up eating some of the protein-rich bugs, snails, and spiders found on leaves and fruit. New research also discovered the DNA of monkeys and antelope in the waste of gorillas, suggesting the possibility that they occasionally do ingest some meat. An adult male gorilla eats up to 45 pounds of food daily.[6]

Sadly, the diet for most captive gorillas is more like the standard American diet. Instead of dozens of pounds of wild greens, fiber, and high-quality protein, captive gorillas are commonly fed several servings of "nutritional cookies" made from grains, sugar, and starch.

Things changed at the Cleveland Metroparks Zoo when they decided to replace the cookies with a more wholesome diet of vegetables, fruits, and leafy greens, such as dandelion greens, romaine lettuce, green beans, endive, and alfalfa hay.

Along with a new diet came a change in activity for the gorillas. To get the gorillas moving more, zookeepers scattered the food throughout their habitat, ensuring they would have to forage for their meals rather than being presented with cookies they could gobble up quickly. Instead of munching cookies, the gorillas began to spend up to 75 percent of their day foraging and eating—about the same amount of time they would forage in the wild.

The results of the experiment were breathtaking. Although the wild diet was nearly *double* the calories of the processed cookies, the gorillas *lost* weight. In one year, the gorillas, who weighed 430 and 460 pounds, each lost approximately 65 pounds—around 15 percent—of their body weight. And tests showed *improvement* in heart function for Bebac, and slowing of the progression of heart disease for Mokolo.

The change in diet also ended the gorillas' habit of regurgitating and reingesting their food. Researchers believe they may have done this because the cookies upset their stomach or—even more ominously—that the gorillas regurgitated their food in order to taste the sugar in their cookies again and again. This points to a clear case of sugar addiction, or perhaps an intolerance to foods that are unnatural to gorillas (similar to reactions seen from many processed foods for people). Hair plucking behaviors also became a rare occurrence.

Thinking of the dramatic change in the gorillas, I can't help but consider many of the clients I have worked with who suffer from similar behaviors (uncontrolled hair plucking and regurgitating food). I ponder the question of whether the gorillas were really neurotic, or just being poisoned by the unnatural diet of processed food, grains, sugar, and starch. Similar to the gorillas, people have been demonstrating an increase in chronic diseases and certain unnatural behaviors along with the increase in processed food.

One more interesting note: Veterinarians noticed that Bebac and Mokolo were grumpy and unhappy for about a week after having the sugar-filled cookies removed from their diet. But exactly like the people I coach, they soon got over it, lost their cravings, and then started to get healthy. A week of the grouchiness seems like a minor inconvenience for the payoff of a healthier heart and decreased neurotic behavior.

As a result of the dietary experiment with Bebac and Mokolo, many other zoos in the United States and Canada are changing the way they feed gorillas, hoping for a happy, healthy outcome for their captive gorillas.

Are you willing to make a two-week commitment to see these kinds of changes? You may feel a bit grumpy and fatigued for a few days—and think that sugar is calling your name. But like Bebac and Mokolo, you will soon *get over it and get healthy!*

PICK A SPOT, AND STICK WITH IT

Here's a great way to curb mindless snacking in front of the television, in bed, at the computer, or in the living room. Choose one eating place in your house—the kitchen table is the best place for most people. Make that your one and only eating place for meals and snacks. Having one designated eating spot means that if you want to eat something while you're doing another activity, you have to come to the kitchen and sit at the table to eat. This makes it much easier for you to be fully conscious of what and how much you're eating.

If your chosen eating space has a television nearby, do yourself a favor and turn it off. Watching television while you eat enables mindless snacking and makes fully conscious eating nearly impossible.

EMBRACE YOUR INNER BEAST

WE CAN LEARN A LOT from gorillas. Humans and gorillas share nearly identical DNA and digestive systems. So it's not surprising that when humans eat like gorillas—wild gorillas, that is—we flourish. A gorilla's wild diet is much healthier for people than the standard American diet, which is full of foods that contribute to obesity, heart disease, cancer, and diabetes.

Eating like a gorilla is simple. Don't worry—you don't have to spend hours a day searching for food or eating slugs, nor will you start beating your chest upon adopting this new lifestyle. Your diet is similar to a wild gorilla's when 70 percent of your food comes from whole plant foods—freshly prepared vegetables, vegetable juice, a little fruit, nuts, and seeds—and 30 percent of calories comes from high-quality lean protein. Gorillas don't eat legumes or grains! While grains and legumes have become the cornerstone of the American diet, eliminating some of them and using others as a "condiment" is essential for overall health and longevity (more on this in chapter 7).

In other words, you follow the Omni Diet.

When you eat this way, you get everything your body needs for optimum health: high-quality protein, low-glycemic (low-sugar) carbohydrates, brain-boosting nutrients, disease-fighting greens, and crucial enzymes, phyto-chemicals, and antioxidants.

While eating this way will effectively and *unnoticeably* decrease your caloric intake, it is surprisingly satisfying. By increasing the *volume* of food you eat (veggies are nutrient-dense and calorie-sparse, so you can and *should* eat a lot of them), eating more frequently, and balancing your metabolic hormones (this happens when you minimize sugar intake and eat the right amount of high-quality protein and plant-based foods), your cravings will vanish faster than you imagined possible. You will eat fewer calories without even missing them.

To be crystal clear, the quality of your diet really, *really* matters. When you eat the Omni way, you will notice improved focus, elevated motivation, and loads of energy! The opposite happens when you consume low-quality calories—you damage your health. Eating junk is *not innocuous*! Even if you cut calories, if you eat an anti-nutritious, sugar-filled diet, you will *probably not* lose weight—or if you do, you'll quickly plateau. Many people actually *gain* weight when consuming processed "pseudo food" filled with sugar. And eventually you will most likely begin to see signs of chronic disease from a lack of nutrients and increasing inflammation. In other words, there is no such thing as "empty calories." The term "junk food" is an oxymoron. It's either junk that is driving you toward illness or food that is propelling you toward wellness. Just look around. It doesn't take a brain doctor to see that something is wrong with the way we have been eating!

INSTEAD OF CUTTING CALORIES . . .

SO HOW DID THE GORILLAS get healthier with double the calories? A starvation diet, which is what radical calorie restriction really is, has been shown to improve five essential life processes: It supports DNA repair, slows cellular aging (methylation), improves glucose control, lowers oxidative stress, and lessens inflammation. But calorie restriction isn't the only way. When we manage these five life processes through several other lifestyle factors that have been studied and proven by research (*high-quality* nutrition, exercise, sleep, stress control, and supplements), our bodies get the benefits of calorie restriction without our having to eat like starved laboratory mice. We can eat like wild gorillas! This means a hearty, filling diet, chock-full of powerful, healing nutrients. The Omni Diet is designed to bring about many of the same disease-fighting results as calorie restriction *without cutting way back on calories*. It mimics calorie restriction without the deprivation and the negative side effects of starvation diets. Following the Omni Diet is much more enjoy-

[LONG AND HEALTHY]

Longevity means living a long life. That sounds pretty good, right? Well it is, but living many years shouldn't be our only goal. As a nurse, I've seen lots of very sick people postpone death for many years—but those years are not always very happy or fulfilling. I have worked on a trauma unit, a neurosurgical ICU unit, and a dialysis unit. I have also visited many rehabilitation centers. I know *many* creative ways that can be used to keep people alive for a very long time, often sacrificing *quality* of life. If you have ever seen a patient suffering from blindness, amputations, and stroke caused by the devastating effects of diabetes, or a patient surviving on long-term life support or long-term dialysis with multiple chronic diseases and suffering from severe depression, you begin to rethink the idea of longevity.

What I really want—and what I'm sure you want, too—is to have a long healthspan rather than just a long lifespan. Your healthspan is how long you are able to live in a healthy way, looking and feeling your best, living with passion, and having the greatest possible resistance to disease.

By following the Omni Diet, you set your sights on greater lifespan *and* healthspan—in other words, living a longer, happier, healthier, more energetic life. Isn't that what we all want?

able than dramatically restricting calories because, let's face it, it's more fun and satisfying to eat like a gorilla than a mouse. Instead of insisting that you cut, cut, cut your calories down to the bone, the Omni Diet tells you to eat, eat, eat delicious foods that deliver the same kinds of fantastic results: a wide array of unprocessed, highly nutritious plant foods along with high-quality lean protein, powerful herbs and spices, and some carefully selected supplements. That's right—we can *mimic* significant calorie restriction with high-quality food, longevity super-foods, spices, herbs, and supplements, as well as smart lifestyle choices such as exercise, stress reduction, and getting enough sleep. That's much easier than drastically restricting calories!

The Omni Diet is more than a way to trim your waistline. It is a way of eating and living that combines eating strategies with other factors to positively influence those five crucial life processes. This paves the way for a better, longer, healthier life.

Here's an exercise I do with the people in my Omni Diet class. It's a very effective way to practice the skill of setting and keeping goals, and holding yourself responsible if you don't.

Start by choosing five healthy habits that you can commit to for the next fourteen days. Choose from the list below, or pick your own. They have to be specific, achievable (but not too easy), and good for your health.

1. Exercise one extra day each week
2. Lift weights at least twice each week
3. Drink one extra glass of water daily
4. Eat one extra cup of vegetables daily
5. Write in a food journal every day
6. Find an accountability buddy
7. Talk to your accountability buddy twice a week
8. Pray or meditate for five minutes daily
9. Drink fresh green drinks twice a week
10. Go in the sauna twice a week
11. Write down five things you are grateful for every morning
12. Do "The Work of Byron Katie" on her Web site, www.thework.com, to identify and question your automatic thoughts
13. Mentor someone who wants to improve his or her health
14. List your daily victories in a victory journal
15. Review your goals and values
16. Put up a picture of someone you admire who mirrors your goals

---

OMNI MOTIVATION BLAST

PUT SOME SKIN IN THE GAME

In order to really, truly commit to a new way of eating and living, you've got to have some skin in the game. You can't just say, "I want to change." You have to make specific promises to yourself and identify what the consequence will be if you don't keep your promises. Effective parenting skills usually incorporate some natural consequence for undesirable behavior. Likewise, when your *inner child* is demanding foods that are harmful and the whining begins, giving a few uncomfortable consequences can successfully rein in her temper tantrums. Over time, your inner child will become more disciplined and form good habits.

Next, give your intentions some teeth by adding consequences. What price will you pay for not changing your destructive behavior? What will you pledge to do if you don't keep your promises to yourself? Choose something that is uncomfortable for you, but beneficial in some way, either to yourself or others.

Some consequences that have worked for people in my Omni Diet classes include:

- Donate a certain amount of money to a charity you don't like, but which benefits others
- Work in a soup kitchen for a specified number of hours
- Get up early in order to take the bus to work instead of driving for two weeks
- Choose a service you pay someone else to do—for example, cleaning your house or washing your car—and do it yourself (but pay the service provider anyway)
- Clean your entire basement or garage

Alicia, a woman in one of my Omni Diet classes, took me literally when I suggested she and her classmates put some skin in the game. She chose her five goals and worked at them for fourteen days. She promised herself that if she didn't achieve them, she would "run around the neighborhood without a shirt." We all laughed when she told us her consequence.

Two weeks later, Alicia reported that although she had done a very good job keeping four promises to herself, she fell short on the fifth. So, true to her word, she ran around her neighborhood without a shirt. She quickly reassured us that she had been wearing a sports bra—but for this conservative, modest woman who is *really* uncomfortable showing her body to the world, wearing a sports bra in public was not much different than streaking around naked. The following week she kept her commitments—all five of them.

By the way, Alicia has lost 58 pounds and ran her first half-marathon in just over two hours! She is truly an Omni superstar!

4

The Hidden Power of Herbs and Spices

To comfort the brain, smell chamomile, eat sage, wash measurably,
sleep reasonably, delight to hear melody and singing.

—WILLIAM RAM

BESIDES DELICIOUS, NUTRITIOUS FOOD, THERE are a few secret weapons in the Omni Diet. Herbs and spices are two of those secret weapons. These flavorful foods are among the most powerful health-boosting weapons for fighting disease—and they are a fun, delicious way to add zest to your meals.

We eat for two reasons: for abundant health and sensory enjoyment. Some foods provide one and not the other, but herbs and spices provide *both* nutrition and flavor, balancing wellness and taste in a delicious, win-win way.

When you add a pinch of herbs or a dash of spices to a dish, you mix in deep, delectable flavor. But you also sprinkle on concentrated doses of therapeutic nutrients that boost your health in a variety of ways. Herbs and spices contain so many health-promoting substances that it almost makes sense to store them in the medicine chest rather than the spice rack.

Natural treatments made from herbs and spices have been used around the world since the beginning of time. The seasonings we use in cooking are derived from some of the same plants that our ancestors turned to for comfort and healing.

The therapeutic value of natural plant-based treatments comes from the web of overlapping substances in herbs and spices that have synergistic benefits to the body. Most herbs and spices work on multiple pathways—for example, a single herb may be anti-inflammatory, antibacterial, *and* antiseptic. In contrast, prescription drugs are usually created to treat a single problem and work through only one pathway.

While this chapter is about cooking with herbs and spices rather than a "how to" guide to botanical or herbal supplements, it's worth stopping to think about how these flavorful foods benefit our health. Let's take a sneak peek inside and see which compounds contribute to the super-healing powers of herbs and spices:

- **ANTIOXIDANTS** give herbs and spices the ability to bind to free radicals and to aid in the repair of DNA and the prevention of cancer. Many of the naturally occurring compounds in herbs and spices contain antioxidants.

- **PHYTOALEXINS** are plant compounds that are toxic in high doses, but cancer-preventive in low doses. Think of these as mini chemo agents.

- **POLYPHENOLS** have powerful antioxidant and anti-inflammatory properties. These compounds contribute to the color, flavor, and smell of plant foods.

- **CAROTENOIDS** are a source of antioxidants that are high in vitamin A. Besides being powerful cancer fighters, they are hailed for their immune-boosting abilities.

- **FIBER** such as glucans, glycans, and lignans found in herbs and other plant foods acts as a hormone regulator and immunity booster.

- **ORGANOMINERALS** have antioxidant, anti-inflammatory, and antimicrobial properties.

- **ALKALOIDS** are compounds that contain nitrogen. Some, like caffeine, are psychoactive (meaning that they have the ability to affect brain function, mood, and cognition), while others are antimicrobial and anti-inflammatory by nature.

As you can see, herbs and spices support a plethora of important body functions. In addition to fighting free radicals, preventing disease, and supporting healthy brain function, they taste great and are fun to cook with. Herbs and spices are also a way to help "green-phobic" children get a healthy dose of extra nutrition. Cinnamon, nutmeg, vanilla, and cacao are just a few of the powerful spices that keep kids—and adults—coming back for more. This is why they are a major component of the Omni Diet.

[PLANTS—THE ORIGINAL MEDICINE]

Natural healers believe that giving the body the nutrients it needs in the form of herbal treatments allows the body to self-heal in a holistic way. Herbal treatments have many broad-spectrum health benefits. And, unlike pharmaceutical drugs, which often come with a frightening array of warnings about possible unintended consequences, herbs and spices have minimal side effects that are often limited to rare allergic reactions. They're also relatively inexpensive and they don't require the approval of a health insurer.

Today, people still rely on plant-based preparations as their chief source of medicine in about 80 percent of the developing world.[1] And although they are heavily processed, most of today's medications are derived from plant sources. For example, opium (and many pain medications) comes from poppy seed pods, quinine comes from cinchona bark, and the cancer drug vincristine comes from periwinkle. Even aspirin (salicylic acid), our go-to pain reliever for more than 150 years, was originally derived from willow bark, meadowsweet, and ulmaria.

I've said it before, and I'll say it again: Modern medicine is often miraculous, and it can save lives, especially in acute situations. As a trauma nurse, and as someone who has been ill, I know firsthand how important medications can be when used judiciously. If I were ever in a serious accident, I wouldn't ask for willow bark or grapefruit seed extract. I'd want the most effective medicine available. But it makes more sense, or at least as much sense, to focus on nutritional and lifestyle approaches for *prevention*.

I know that the Omni Diet can fit well into a busy life—after all, I've been fitting it into mine for years! But when I met Kimberly, I realized that a healthy diet and lifestyle are possible for *anyone* who puts her mind to it. I was honored to have Kimberly tell me that my philosophies helped her refine the nutrition plan for her family because she is someone who has always worked diligently to keep her family healthy. Kimberly is such an inspiration. She has nine children—nine!—and she homeschools them all. If anyone has an excuse to be too busy to live a healthy life, it's Kimberly! But nutrition and exercise are important to her, so she's found a way to fit them in.

Kimberly doesn't buy processed food—she hits the grocery store three or four times a week and buys everything fresh. The money she saves on junk food goes toward feeding her children an exceptionally healthy diet—and

EASIER THAN YOU MAY THINK!

Eating well doesn't have to be expensive. Jeana spends just eighty-five dollars a week to feed a family of three. They eat according to Omni Diet principles without breaking the bank. You'll be surprised how much money you save when you stop buying expensive processed food. Be a smart shopper: Look for sales, buy in bulk, and make the rounds of several stores to get the best deals. Check to see if there's an organic community farm in your area—buying a "share" of what's grown is not only a bargain, but a fantastic way to get the freshest, most delicious locally grown produce. And don't forget, it's easy to grow your own herbs from seeds outdoors or even on a sunny windowsill.

When questioned about her shopping skills, Jeana (who has lost more than 40 pounds so far) stated emphatically, "I'm a world-class shopper, but I'd spend more if I had to. I haven't been sick *once* since I started the Omni Diet. My energy is through the roof. I sleep soundly. I no longer suffer from IBS, rosacea, or eczema, and I'm more productive at work. How much money is that worth? And I *know* most people spend a lot of extra money that they don't even think about on coffee drinks and muffins. It's a matter of priority."

she's able to do it on a budget, which tells you something about how costly processed food is. Going to a gym isn't practical for this homeschooling mom, so she leads exercise classes for her kids at home, allowing everyone to get a good workout several times a week.

If you're feeling that you don't have the time or the money to eat well and exercise, take it from Kimberly: If you are busy and on a budget, you can't afford *not* to make your health (and your family's health) a top priority!

HERBS AND SPICES IN THE KITCHEN

MY FAVORITE THING ABOUT THE power of herbs and spices is that they taste great! Cooking with an abundance of them makes great food taste even better; it also makes the Omni Diet more than a diet.

When people come to our home for a meal they don't miss the heavy sauces. They don't even notice that there is no bread and not much starch of any kind on the table, because every dish explodes with the flavor of fresh

(continued on page 76)

[FIGHT PAIN WITH THE OMNI DIET]

A scary new study from the United Kingdom has linked nonsteroidal anti-inflammatory drugs (NSAIDs)—pain relievers like ibuprofen—to a higher risk of heart attacks, strokes, and death from cardiovascular causes, as well as GI problems.[2] Now that you know that, you may be wondering if there's a safer way to soothe your aches and pains.

Relax. According to recent studies, some scrumptious, healthy foods—many of them part of the Omni Diet—actually pack as much pain-fighting power as some pain-relieving drugs do, without the worrisome side effects. Here's a look at some of the tastiest ways to get fast, natural relief for what ails you.

GINGER. Popular as both a spice and a medicine for thousands of years, ginger fights both inflammation and various types of pain. In a recent Iranian study of 120 female university students with painful periods, those who took capsules containing powdered ginger root three times daily for five days had significant drops in both the duration and intensity of their menstrual cramps.[3] And in another study, 43 patients suffering from osteoarthritis of the knee were divided into two groups. Half were treated with a painkiller called diclofenac; the other half were given 4 ounces of ginger extract. At the end of four weeks, those in the ginger group reported pain relief equal to those in the medicine group, but without the adverse effects on their stomach linings.[4] Some easy ways to add ginger to your everyday dishes: Sprinkle some powdered ginger on your veggies, or grate a bit of fresh ginger into stir-fries.

SALMON AND FISH OIL. Foods that are high in omega-3 fatty acids, such as oily fish like salmon, halibut, and tuna, or fish oil supplements, could be just what your aching back needs for relief. Scientists at the University of Pittsburgh studied 250 patients with neck or back pain, treating them with fish oil supplements rather than NSAID pain relievers. After 75 days, 59 percent of them were able to stop taking prescription pain pills; 60 percent reported significant reductions in pain. The scientists reported that omega-3 fish oil supplements "appear to be a safer alternative to NSAIDs" for nonsurgical neck and back pain. Earlier trials have also found fish oil to be as effective as ibuprofen for quelling arthritis pain.[5] For easy ways to add more fish to your menus, try Pan-Roasted Salmon with Vegetables (page 353) or Baked Halibut with Creamed Spinach Sauce (page 358).

PEPPERMINT. Soothing to the digestive system, peppermint oil (taken in capsule form) has been proven effective in several studies for reducing such symptoms of irritable bowel syndrome as cramps, pain, and bloating, with success rates of up to 75 percent.[6] Additionally, dabbing the oil on your temples may help to quell tension headaches. One small study that compared topically applying a 10 percent peppermint oil solution with taking acetaminophen found no significant differences in effectiveness between the two treatments, according to a review article in *American Family Physician*.[7] Have a cup of steaming peppermint tea or add some mint leaves to a fruit salad for a dose of this beneficial herb.

COFFEE. Among the many health perks linked to coffee drinking are weight loss and a reduced risk for diabetes, stroke, and prostate cancer. One of the most surprising benefits of a cup of joe is reduced physical pain, according to scientists at the University of Oslo in Norway. The researchers asked 48 office workers to perform uncomfortable tasks that put strain on their necks, shoulders, forearms, and wrists. Those who drank a cup of coffee beforehand experienced significantly less pain in these areas.[8] And other studies show that coffee in moderate amounts may even help to ward off gallstones. So feel free to have a couple of cups of coffee each day.

EXTRA-VIRGIN OLIVE OIL (EVOO). EVOO contains several potent antioxidants, including a recently discovered one called oleocanthal. It has similar anti-inflammatory and pain-relieving effects as ibuprofen, aspirin, and other NSAIDs, inhibiting production of the pro-inflammatory enzymes COX-1 and COX-2, scientists at the Monell Chemical Senses Center, in collaboration with researchers at the University of Pennsylvania, report.[9] And new research from the University of Louisiana suggests that this compound may also help protect against Alzheimer's disease and other memory-robbing disorders.[10] One of my favorite ways to use EVOO is in Antiox Detox Chopped Salad (page 326) with Simple Shrimp Scampi (page 350).

herbs and exotic spices. Every meal is a tasty, healing creation that leaves our dinner guests feeling *satisfied, light, and energized*. All this is possible because of the versatile power of herbs and spices.

There are no rules to follow when you cook with herbs and spices. I encourage you to make it an exciting journey and to just follow your taste buds. As a nurse who is used to measuring everything carefully, I had a hard time doing this at first. But as I learned to relax and experiment I began to discover wonderful new, healthy, flavor-packed combinations that the entire family loves.

Here are some ways to include them in foods—but use these just as starting points. Be creative and find the tastes you like best.

- Add cinnamon, nutmeg, cacao, vanilla, cardamom, or mint to smoothies
- Toss chopped fresh herbs, such as basil, chives, and cilantro, into salads
- Blend garlic, fresh herbs, nuts, and olive oil to make delicious pesto sauce
- Simmer herbs and spices into soups, stews, and chili
- Sprinkle chopped fresh herbs over grilled meat and fish
- Mix several kinds of spices to make a rub for grilled vegetables
- Blend multiple herbs and spices with a little oil and lemon juice to make marinades for chicken or meat
- Add fresh mint to fruit salad for a surprisingly bright taste twist
- Add fresh ginger and muddled berries to sparkling water for a refreshing summer drink

Cook with fresh herbs when possible, but for convenience, keep dried herbs and spices on hand.

The following herbs and spices are among the most powerful and most delicious. Start making them a part of your recipe repertoire.

BASIL. Few people realize this, but basil is good food for the brain. A potent antioxidant that has been used for medicinal purposes for thousands of years, basil improves blood flow to the brain and enhances overall brain function, report researchers from India's Punjabi University Patiala in a 2011 lab study.[11] Its anti-inflammatory properties also help improve cognitive function and prevent stokes and cancer. In a 2004 lab study from India's Jawaharlal Nehru

University, "Basil leaf extract was highly effective in inhibiting carcinogen-induced tumor incidence," the researchers noted.[12]

Basil also contains generous amounts of vitamin K and calcium, and preserves the integrity of DNA. The essential oils found in basil (like rosmarinic acid) inhibit the growth of disease-causing bacteria such as Staphylococcus aureus (which cause potentially deadly staph infections) and Escherichia coli (E. coli), according to a 2006 study by scientists from Serbia's University of Novi Sad.[13]

BLACK PEPPER. One of the most widely known and traded spices since ancient times, black pepper was used to prevent the growth of bacteria and to preserve meat in hot climates. It enhances absorption of numerous compounds, including curcumin (a powerful antioxidant), and increases hydrochloric acid (stomach acid), which aids in digestion. Researchers from India's St. John's Medical College found in a 1998 study that a compound in black pepper called piperine increases the bioavailability of curcumin—the active ingredient in turmeric—by 154 percent.[14]

CAYENNE PEPPER. The bold taste in cayenne is created by the capsaicin, which is well known for its many health benefits, including preventing ulcers and certain cancers, and relieving pain. It also increases stomach acid, which aids in digestion. Cayenne pepper is loaded with vitamin A carotenoids. It helps fight inflammation, boost immunity, and promote weight loss. Precaution should be taken not to overindulge if you suffer from hypertension.

CHILI POWDER. Made with ground chili peppers, chili powder contains the compound capsaicin, which inhibits inflammation and damage from oxidation. It also may reduce cholesterol and triglycerides, prevent blood clots, lower heart attack risk, boost immunity, lower the risk of prostate cancer, help with the regulation of insulin and blood sugar, reduce nasal congestion and prevent certain types of cancer. A 2011 lab study from Korea's University of Ulsan found that capsaicin reduced blood sugar and switched off genes that fuel inflammation.[15]

CILANTRO. Besides adding great flavor to your salsa, antibiotic chemicals in cilantro appear to help protect your body from food-borne illness such as salmonella. It also contains significant amounts of vitamin K, which supports blood clotting and bone strength. A cilantro extract even reduced blood glucose in a 2011 study from Morocco's Dhar El Mehraz Faculty of Sciences.[16]

CINNAMON. If you want to improve your working memory or your ability to pay attention, try chewing some cinnamon gum (sweetened with xylitol or natural flavoring) or just take a whiff of some cinnamon tea. Research shows that the scent of cinnamon is enough to enhance these functions. In addition, cinnamon helps regulate blood-sugar levels, which improves impulse control, so you are less likely to give in to cravings for cookies, cakes, and candy. Cinnamon also works as an aphrodisiac in men. While it's no substitute for needed diabetes medications and can't replace diet and exercise, cinnamon could help with maintaining healthy blood sugar. In a 2012 Chinese study of 66 people with type 2 diabetes, a cinnamon extract lowered fasting blood sugar levels significantly.[17]

CLOVES. Eugenol is the main compound found in cloves. Eugenol is sometimes used in dentistry because of its analgesic, anti-inflammatory, and antibacterial benefits. It is also thought to offer protection from cardiovascular disease. In a 2012 test-tube study from India's PSNA College of Engineering and Technology, a eugenol extract induced cancer cells to die (a natural, protective process called apoptosis).[18]

CORIANDER. The phytonutrients in coriander may help control blood sugar and lower cholesterol levels. An extract of this seed from the cilantro plant reduced blood fats and blood sugar while cooling inflammation in a 2012 lab study from India's Bharathidasan University.[19] This concentrated form of cilantro contains substantial amounts of manganese, vitamin C, and vitamin K.

CURRY. This popular Indian spice is actually a combination of many different spices, including turmeric, which contains the powerful compound curcumin. A potent antioxidant, curcumin reduces inflammation and helps to prevent and break up the plaques thought to be responsible for Alzheimer's disease. There is also evidence that it offers protection from cancer and supports healthy liver function. There are currently twenty-four published studies listed with the National Institutes of Health reporting the benefits of turmeric and curcumin related to the anti-inflammatory action of these natural chemicals. In a small University of California, Los Angeles, study of people with head and neck cancers, a curcumin extract reduced levels of inflammatory cytokines that promote cancer growth by up to 20 percent.[20]

DILL. Deliciously tart, dill is a natural antibacterial and cancer fighter. And the calcium in dill helps promote bone health. Three compounds in dill—

anethofuran, carvone, and limonene—may show promise against cancer, note researchers from the Minneapolis-based LKT Laboratories, Inc., in a study published in the journal *Planta Medica.*[21]

GARLIC. Although technically a vegetable, I think of garlic as herblike because of its potent flavor. Garlic has been used for medicinal purposes for more than five thousand years. Louis Pasteur confirmed the antibacterial effects of garlic in 1858. Compounds in garlic cause blood vessels to relax and dilate, increasing blood flow to the brain and improving brain function. Eating garlic regularly can help lower the risk of strokes, improve heart health, and boost the immune system's ability to fight off colds and flu. In fact, a study of 146 people from the United Kingdom found that a daily garlic supplement reduced colds by two-thirds and cut the duration of the colds that study volunteers did catch from 5 days to 1½ days.[22]

Allicin is the compound in garlic that performs this antioxidant action. Allicin in garlic is considered by many researchers to be the most potent antioxidant on the planet. Garlic also has insulin-sparing properties, which help to stabilize blood sugar. And it has been shown to decrease LDL (bad) cholesterol and increase HDL (good) cholesterol.

GINGER. An anti-inflammatory agent, ginger may protect against neurodegenerative diseases and reduce oxidative stress that causes brain cells to age and die. Ginger contains natural antiemetic agents to help decrease nausea and vomiting. Scientists from the United Kingdom's University of Exeter concluded in a 2000 report that a ginger compound called 6-gingerol is responsible for this spice's tummy-soothing properties, relaxing

GO EASY WITH SALT

It's best to think twice before shaking salt onto your food. Americans eat about ten times more salt (sodium chloride) than is considered healthy. All this excess salt is associated with endothelial cell stiffness (stiff blood vessels), which ultimately reduces blood flow. It also increases oxidative stress, which can lead to a number of diseases.

Overweight and obese people have an elevated incidence of high blood pressure. Consuming salt raises it even more. Salt also hijacks your taste buds, covering up the delicious natural flavor of foods.

If you do choose to salt your food, use unbleached sea salt or some other salt that hasn't had its minerals removed. Try to use as little as possible, limiting your daily intake of sodium chloride to under 1,500 milligrams.

You might want to try using a potassium-based salt substitute. Studies show that supplementing with about 5 grams of potassium per day and decreasing sodium to 1,500 milligrams per day can improve vascular function, kidney function, and insulin sensitivity and decrease blood pressure, oxidative stress, and inflammation.

THWART YOUR TRIGGERS!

We all have them: foods, situations, people, emotions, memories, even times of day that trigger food cravings. You don't have to be waylaid by triggers. Instead, figure out what triggers your out-of-control eating. Then, make a plan of action you can put in place when (or before) your trigger goes off. Here are some examples of what's worked for me:

- Going to the movies used to be a constant battle for me. My always-on-the-move personality doesn't allow me to sit still without munching on something. It used to be candy and popcorn—but now I plan ahead. I know I'm going to want to eat something—I just can't break the snacking-at-the-movies habit. But now I tuck a bag of nuts, some cherries, or cut-up vegetables and a small container of hummus in my purse, along with a bottle of herbal tea or lemon water. It works!

- Birthday cake—actually, any kind of cake—was another land mine for me. Cake for me was like crack cocaine for a junkie. My addiction is gone now, but when I still had it, I needed a plan or else I'd fall prey to every cake in my path. I made a plan: When I was going to a party where there would be cake, I'd make sure that I ate a snack or meal with protein and some good fat before the party. Protein and fat increase satiety and decrease cravings. I'd also take my own dessert to munch on, such as a piece of dark chocolate. (For more on healthy chocolate choices, see chapter 6.) If I was feeling particularly vulnerable—like if I had PMS—I would

the muscles of the gastrointestinal tract.[23] It is also believed to help lower cholesterol. The antifungal/antibacterial nature of ginger makes it a great treatment for wounds. *Note: Ginger has natural anticoagulant properties, so if you are taking an anticoagulant medication, check with your health-care provider before using ginger supplements.*

MARJORAM. This culinary favorite promotes healthy digestion and can soothe minor digestive upsets. A great source of vitamin K, marjoram has been associated with preventing Alzheimer's disease by decreasing neuronal damage. Besides having anti-inflammatory and antibacterial properties, this sweet-tasting herb is loaded with vitamin C, beta-carotene, vitamin A, cryptoxanthin, lutein, and zeaxanthin (known to protect against age-related leave the party right *after* singing "Happy Birthday," but before the cake was cut. I missed the cake at first, but once I broke my addiction and realized how much better I felt not eating it, I lost interest in what used to be my greatest dietary nemesis.

- Special occasions of any kind can be a challenge when you are starting to get healthy, as Annette, one of my Omni Diet class participants, discovered. She went to a wedding one weekend, and although she thought of having a protein shake before she left her house to curb her appetite at the reception, she wasn't hungry at the time, so she skipped it. "As you can imagine I was so hungry at the reception that I ended up eating some of the unhealthy appetizers!" Had Annette eaten at home, she probably could have easily said no to appetizers. Cheers to Annette for containing the damage, however: "Even though I had some appetizers, I did stay away from the bread, cheese, and crackers. I'm learning!"

- Disneyland is not the happiest place on earth when it comes to eating well. Whenever I go there or to other amusement parks, I always bring my own snacks packed into a cooler.

- I make sure to have healthy snacks with me wherever I go, and I encourage you to have healthy snacks, too. Make a list of healthy snacks that you love, and tape it to your refrigerator so you can be sure never to leave home without the healthy foods you need.

degenerative diseases and cataracts in the eyes). Marjoram also contains compounds that mop up cell-damaging free radicals, according to scientists from Taiwan's Chia Nan University of Pharmacy and Science.[24]

MINT. The oil in mint leaves helps soothe digestive problems such as indigestion and irritable bowel syndrome. Peppermint oil capsules reduced IBS symptoms by 50 percent in one 2007 Italian study.[25] This cooling herb also has antioxidant, anti-inflammatory, and anti-microbial qualities. Healing acne, combating bad breath, and clearing nasal passages related to congestion are just a few of the additional benefits that this tasty herb can offer. Rich in vitamins A, C, B12, thiamin, folic acid, and riboflavin, as well as several important minerals, mint is wonderful for maintaining overall health.

NUTMEG. Like cloves, this aromatic spice contains eugenol (a compound thought to be cardioprotective). It also contains myristicin, which helps to prevent the formation of plaques in the brain that are believed to be responsible for Alzheimer's disease. Chinese medicine recommends nutmeg for the treatment of liver disease. Herbal medicine practitioners often use nutmeg to treat depression and anxiety, and researchers from the William Beaumont Army Medical Center in Texas may have found the basis for this in an anxiety-soothing nutmeg component called myristicin, according to a 2011 lab study.[26]

OREGANO. One of the strongest antioxidants known, oregano protects cells in the body and brain from free radicals that cause premature aging. Oregano is also a source of omega-3 fatty acids, which enhance brain function and offer protection from depression and PMS symptoms. It may also reduce insomnia and relieve migraine headaches. Oil of oregano is a potent antibacterial agent used in treating giardiasis, a parasitic intestinal infection. Oregano compounds can also cool inflammation, say scientists from Spain's Autonomous University of Madrid in a 2010 study.[27]

PARSLEY. The world's most popular herb has been used for its antiseptic properties for centuries. More recently it has been found to contain compounds that may fight cancer by inhibiting tumor formation and fighting free radicals. Parsley may even discourage the formation of blood clots, according to a 2012 study by scientists from Morocco's Mohamed Premier University.[28] Parsley is loaded with vitamins and minerals, promotes heart health, may protect against rheumatoid arthritis, acts as a diuretic and detoxifying agent (which is why it is great to add to green juices when you hit a plateau during weight loss), and increases energy.

Recent studies revealed that the apigenin found in parsley slowed the growth of breast cancer cells in rats. The alkaline nature of parsley helps decrease inflammation in joints, and its high levels of folate make it a great immune booster.

ROSEMARY. The caffeic and rosmarinic acid found in rosemary contribute to its legendary antioxidant and anti-inflammatory properties. In addition, this herb contains betulinic acid and carnosic acid—phytochemicals that fight cancer by revving up nitric oxide activity and encouraging the release of TNF-1 from immune-system cells, Greek researchers found in a 2013 study.[29]

Improved circulation and digestion are a couple of benefits you may enjoy along with the wonderful flavor of this herb. Rosemary also offers protection from cognitive decline associated with dementia and may provide new hope in the treatment of Parkinson's disease.

SAFFRON. In addition to adding a wonderful flavor to soups and other dishes, saffron also wards off depression and improves memory and the ability to learn. There are seven scientific studies that have found this tasty spice to be as effective as medication in warding off depression. In one, published in the *Journal of Ethnopharmacology,* it was as effective as the antidepressant fluoxetine for easing symptoms in 38 people with mild to moderate depression.[30] In addition, saffron helps reverse the loss of sexual desire and function that can be a side effect of conventional antidepressants, report researchers from Iran's Tehran University of Medical Sciences in a 2013 study of 34 women experiencing sexual dysfunction due to the antidepressant fluoxetine.[31] Saffron may also enhance learning, a 2011 lab study from Greece has found, and it could be useful for the treatment of memory impairment thanks to its cell-protecting antioxidants.[32] This prized herb contains carotenoid compounds that boost immune function and ward off cancer.

SAGE. This savory spice boosts memory in healthy people of all ages, and can improve mental functioning in people with Alzheimer's. The ability of sage to boost thinking skills and mood "deserves further attention," note scientists from the United Kingdom's Northumbria University in a 2011 study.[33] The enzymes superoxide dismutase and peroxidase in sage have made it particularly popular with natural healers over the centuries for its effectiveness in fighting bacteria, preventing cancer, aiding digestion, and healing wounds.

THYME. This flavorful spice increases DHA, an omega fatty acid that protects neurons in the brain from premature aging. It is also very high in pyridoxine, which helps keep the neurotransmitter GABA elevatedin the brain, according to a 2011 lab study from Argentina's National University of Córdoba.[34] This may aid in stress reduction. Thyme contains thymol, an essential oil known for its antifungal and antimicrobial properties. Thyme is so densely packed with polyphenols, vitamins, and minerals that it has one of the highest ORAC values of all herbs, according to a recent study from the U.S. Department of Agriculture.[35] (ORAC stands for "oxygen radical absorbance capacity," and is a way of measuring the amount of antioxidant capacity in various foods.)

ALICIA SHINNERS, 37

When is a treat not really a treat? For Alicia, that turned out to be, well, most of the time. "I had a habit of calling everything a celebration," she says. "When my daughter scored a soccer goal or a relative came to town, it was a special occasion that called for ice cream or a chocolate cake. But I finally realized that those treats weren't the exception to the rule but the rule itself. After all, there's always a reason to celebrate *something!* And that's one of the reasons I packed on some extra pounds."

Now, two years later, Alicia has something great to celebrate. On the Omni Diet, she's taken off 30 pounds and learned to look at food through a whole new lens. For her, dieting used to be all about food deprivation. But now she sees it as a way to a healthy life. "For me, it had always been about being skinny," she realized. "But it's not just about appearances. This is the body you have forever, and I just want to take good care of it."

The Omni Diet has taught Alicia dozens of ways to do exactly that. One eating challenge: Stick to her healthy eating plan even though, as the wife of a youth minister, junk food seemed to be on the menu at every event she attended. The solution: Be prepared. Alicia learned to bring along her own snacks. And at church suppers, surveying the table and making the best choices available was a great strategy. "There's always some cut-up fruit or a bowl of nuts," she says.

Alicia, the mother of three children ages ten, six, and three, has recently embarked on a new full-time career as a postpartum doula, helping women ease into life with a new baby. Among her tasks: helping to care for mom and baby, teaching childcare and feeding techniques, and even taking the night shift so the new mother can get some sleep. "In the past," she says, "whenever I had a big change in my life, I'd get derailed from any good eating habits I'd gotten into. But this time was different. To survive such a big change and stay healthy and focused—that's a big accomplishment."

For Alicia, the Omni Diet has been a breakthrough in so many ways— and not all of them are measured on the scale. Her success has given her a boost in confidence and a surge of energy, and buying some new clothes has been fun. "Of course," she adds, "it's nice to get compliments from my husband. When I showed off a new outfit, my husband said to the kids, 'Check out Mom—she's so hot.' That was a really nice moment for me!"

5

Boost Your Diet with Omni NutriPower Foods

How could such sweet and wholesome hours
Be reckoned but with herbs and flowers!
—ANDREW MARVELL

WE GET NUTRIENTS FROM WHOLE foods. And we get them from supplements. But there's another fantastic category of health-giving dietary stars—foods that are far more nutritious than most other foods, boasting supplement-like power. Some people call them super-foods. Others call them neutraceuticals. I call them Omni NutriPower foods, and because of the amazing things they can do for your health, I consider them a critical part of the Omni Diet.

Nutripower foods have been part of the human diet for a very long time. Back when people had no medicines, they turned to food for healing, and passed the folk wisdom of food with curative powers from generation to generation.

As modern medicine developed, many scientists and doctors scoffed at traditional food-based cures. But when open-minded researchers turned their attention to studying these foods in laboratories, they began to discover through science what ancient peoples had long understood: that certain foods have medicinal power.

I encourage you to include nutripower foods in your diet. They offer a variety of health benefits, from reduction of disease risk to blood-sugar control to boosting brain health. Take it from your ancestors: These are some pretty powerful foods.

In this chapter, I describe in detail several of what I consider to be the most essential nutripower foods. I also list some additional super-foods that you may also be interested in. Keep in mind that some individuals should use caution with nutripower foods. For example, women who are pregnant or breastfeeding should avoid them because their effects have not been well studied in that population. And people with certain health conditions should avoid them or use them with caution—I'll give you the details on those warnings later in the chapter. But otherwise, I believe that everyone should follow the wisdom of the past and consider making these nutripower foods part of their healthy diet.

FROM THE TREE OF LIFE: COCONUT OIL

THERE'S A LOT OF MISINFORMATION floating around out there about coconuts. First of all, they're not even nuts, nor are they fruit. They're actually seeds. Second—contrary to popular belief—coconuts are not at all bad for your health. Popular culture has advocated against coconut products because of the high fat content. But they're actually so nutritious that I consider them a nutripower food!

Coconut meat, juice, milk, and oil have nourished people for thousands of years. The coconut palm is often referred to as the tree of life and the Sanskrit word for coconut can be roughly translated as "the food that sustains all life." Traditional cultures have long considered the coconut a symbol (or provider!) of fertility. Coconuts contain ample water, protein, fat, carbohydrates, fiber, vitamins, and minerals for people to live on. (The shell and its fiber can be used for rope, cooking fires, currency, and flotation devices—talk about an all-purpose food!)

Historically, cultures that eat coconut as a major portion of their diet have very low levels of heart disease and other chronic illness. We don't know for sure that coconut can take all the credit for their good health, but many experts believe it plays a major part. Traditional cultures have also valued coconut oil as a medicinal substance, believing that it has the power to cure many kinds of illnesses.

So why has coconut gotten such a bad rap? When food manufacturers get their hands on coconut oil, they commonly put it through a process called

[COCONUT OIL]

WHAT TO BUY: Organic, extra-virgin, cold-pressed coconut oil

HOW TO USE IT: For cooking at high temperatures, sautéing, and in salad dressings and desserts

The Rest of the Coconut

The health benefits of coconut go beyond its oil. Include all of its edible parts in your diet.

COCONUT WATER. The clear, watery liquid inside a coconut is rich in minerals and electrolytes, but contains no coconut oils. Coconut water is great for making smoothies or just as a refreshing drink after a tough hike or workout.

COCONUT MILK. The fluid produced by grating and pressing coconut meat is a rich, white liquid that contains coconut oil. Coconut milk is a great replacement for cream when cooking.

COCONUT MEAT. The white flesh inside a coconut. The soft meat of young Thai coconuts is great for making gluten-free tortilla wraps, smoothies, "ice cream," and many desserts.

COCONUT BUTTER. White, creamy, and spread with the consistency of butter, coconut butter is made of pureed coconut meat and is a nice addition to smoothies. It also makes great desserts and frostings.

hydrogenation—which basically turns it into highly toxic trans fats. Hydrogenated coconut oil is used in all kinds of poor-quality junk food. It's hydrogenated coconut oil that is bad for you—not coconut in its natural, unprocessed form.

Historically, researchers have also been concerned by the saturated fat found in coconut. We know that some of the saturated fat in animal foods is dangerous for the cardiovascular system, and coconut oil does have a high saturated-fat content. But the saturated fat in coconut oil is different than that in animal-based foods. Saturated animal fat links together in chains called *long-chain* fatty acids (LCFA). But the saturated fat in coconut oil forms *medium-chain* fatty acids. The length of the chain makes a big difference in how fat is metabolized. Fats joined in medium chains (also known as medium-chain triglycerides, or MCTs) have a different impact on the body than fats joined in long chains.

MCTs are digested and absorbed immediately through the liver, and are available for quick energy. According to a 1998 review of medium- and long-chain fatty acid metabolism by experts from Canada's McGill University, the body "preferentially" burns the medium-chain type first in the tiny power plants located in every cell in your body.[1] This makes it less likely to cause obesity and high cholesterol. The MCTs in coconut oil have no negative effect on cholesterol levels—in fact, they actually help reduce heart disease risk, note researchers from India's University of Kerala in a 2004 lab study.[2] They also speed up metabolism. In addition, coconut oil has been shown to have many antiviral and antifungal properties.

The coconut got its name from early Spanish explorers who used the word "coco" (which means "monkey face") to describe it. Once it made its way to Europe, the word "nut" was added to its name even though it's a seed, not a nut. Today, coconuts grow in the area around the Pacific, the Indian Ocean, and parts of Africa.

MCTs help the brain, as well. They are quickly converted by the liver to ketones, which serve as backup fuel for our brains and our bodies. In people with dementia, the metabolic system that uses glucose becomes less effective, and so MCTs provide a more accessible fuel to the brain than carbohydrates.

Please note: You should use coconut oil as a nutritional treatment for dementia only under the supervision of a medical doctor.

THE FOOD OF THE GODS: RAW CACAO

MOST OF US THINK OF chocolate in the form of candy bars with a weak, cloyingly sweet, burned-milk taste. But in its raw form, chocolate (cacao) has a bold, deep, earthy taste. It's also an amazing Omni NutriPower food that delivers *many* substantial health benefits.

Raw cacao comes from cacao beans, which are the seeds of the fruit of the cacao tree. (In the United States we spell it *cocoa*.) Unlike most commercially mixed chocolate products, raw cacao contains no additives and has not been processed or roasted.

Cacao contains impressive amounts of antioxidants, which are believed to protect us against cardiovascular disease, premature aging, and some forms of cancer. In fact, ounce for ounce, cacao has more antioxidant power than blueberries, green tea, or red wine. The antioxidants in cacao are known as flavanols.

The science behind cacao and health is strong. In a 2011 analysis of twenty-one studies, Harvard researchers found that cacao consumption was associated

[RAW CACAO]

WHAT TO BUY: **Raw cacao powder and cacao nibs, preferably organic. Be sure the brand you choose has not been treated with alkali (which is known as "Dutch process") and is 100 percent pure, unprocessed, and unroasted.**

HOW TO USE IT: **Add cacao powder to smoothies, tea, and coffee; or use it to make delicious and nutritious sauces for dipping, as well as "haute chocolate." Use cacao nibs as a delicious replacement for chocolate chips in nutritious raw desserts and smoothies.**

with lower blood pressure, healthier blood vessels, and improved cholesterol levels.[3] Studies also have found that cacao consumption can lead to decreased levels of LDL (bad) cholesterol, increased levels of HDL (good) cholesterol, and less plaque in arteries. In a 2007 study from Japan, 25 people had a daily "dose" of about 2 teaspoons of sugar or sugar plus 26 grams of cocoa powder (about the amount in 1 ounce of dark chocolate). After 12 weeks of daily chocolate bliss, the cocoa group saw levels of heart-guarding HDLs rise by 24 percent.[4]

Cacao helps with blood sugar as well. The flavonols in cacao are believed to trigger the production of nitric oxide inside the cells, which helps increase the body's sensitivity to insulin. In a 2008 study from Italy's University of L'Aquila, blood pressure decreased while insulin sensitivity increased when people consumed cocoa rich in these flavonols, also known as polyphenols.[5] In its raw form, cacao is a sugar-free, dairy-free, natural food with a low glycemic index.

Some of the hundreds of plant chemicals in cacao are known for their ability to enhance mood and induce pleasure. One of cacao's components, theobromine, is a mild stimulant similar to caffeine—but it doesn't stimulate the central nervous system as caffeine does, and it doesn't have caffeine's addictiveness. Raw cacao contains virtually no caffeine.

Cacao also contains phenylethylamine (PEA), which releases endorphins in your brain. These are some of the same substances your brain produces when you fall in love. It's not surprising that chocolate has become the international gift of love!

It's only recently that people turned to cacao for its taste. For centuries, it was honored for its medicinal qualities. Aztecs and Mayans drank their cacao in a brew made from cacao beans; they believed it provided strength

LEARN FROM YOUR OWN SUCCESS

Thinking about past success at overcoming bad habits is an excellent way to fuel future success. Try this: Pick a habit that you successfully broke or a negative behavior pattern you were able to change, like when you stopped breaking the bank with daily stops at your local coffee house for extra-large coffee drinks loaded with sugar and milk. Then, analyze it for wisdom you can apply to your current effort to change your unhealthy behaviors. Remember, the fact that you broke at least one bad habit is proof that you can do it again!

While you meditate on your past success, ask yourself these questions:

- When did I realize that I *had* to change?

- What was my leverage? What was one major motivator that propelled me into action (finances, health, love for someone)?

- What had to happen in order for me to succeed?

- What were my beliefs about the challenge I faced?

- What steps were most productive as I worked toward my goal?

- How did I stay focused?

- How much time did I spend trying to change my habit?

- How much dedication did I invest in it?

- Who offered me the most support? Who stood in my way?

- What techniques and skills served me best?

- What techniques and skills were ineffective?

- How did I feel when I broke the habit?

and energy. When Europeans brought cacao home from the Americas, they used it as an all-purpose tonic to treat dozens of health conditions. Europeans referred to chocolate as "the food of the gods."

In the 1900s, chocolate makers began to process cacao with milk, sugar, and other ingredients, draining it of its health benefits and its potent nutrients and transforming it into the food of the fallen gods. When cacao beans are roasted and processed, their essential fatty acids become rancid and take on harmful trans fat–type properties.

NUTRIPOWER FROM PARADISE: MACADAMIA-NUT OIL

IF YOU'VE EVER BEEN TO Hawaii, you've probably had macadamia nuts. Even though they actually originated in Australia, these tree nuts are ubiquitous in the Aloha State—flight attendants hand them out on planes, hotels leave them on your pillow during the evening turndown service, and just about every store sells them.

Macadamia nuts are tasty, but what I really love about macadamia nuts is their oil.

Macadamia-nut oil is packed with nutrients that offer numerous health benefits and reduce the risk of chronic disease. It's also delicious and great for cooking and dressing salads. This versatile oil is even good for your skin!

Let's start with macadamia-nut oil's nutritional profile, which contains the following important components:

- **MONOUNSATURATED FAT.** Macadamia-nut oil is mostly monounsaturated—in fact, it contains a higher percentage of this good kind of fat than any other food.[6]

- **MINERALS.** Potassium phosphorus, magnesium, calcium, selenium, zinc, copper, and iron, which are essential for heart health, restful sleep, DNA repair, detoxification, and improving brain function, to name a few.

- **VITAMINS.** B vitamins, vitamin E, niacin, and folate. Vitamin E is especially important in lowering heart disease risk, because it helps stop plaque from accumulating in your arteries and slowing down blood flow.

- **PHYTOCHEMICALS.** Natural chemicals found in plants that are good for human health, such as polyphenols and flavonols.

- **ANTIOXIDANTS.** These protect our bodies from oxidative stress.

- **PALMITOLEIC ACID.** An omega-7 fatty acid that reduces inflammation, increases the body's sensitivity to insulin, and may help with weight loss. It also contains a small amount of omega-3 fatty acid. Unlike many vegetable oils, it's low in omega-6 fatty acids—that's a good thing, because most of us get too many omega-6 fatty acids.

- **PLANT STEROLS.** These are compounds that help prevent cholesterol from being absorbed into your blood.

All of these powerful nutrients can have a big impact on health. Studies in Australia and Hawaii[7] suggest that the dietary components of macadamias

$$\left[\text{ USING MACADAMIA NUTS }\right]$$

WHAT TO BUY: *Raw* whole nuts, chopped nuts, oil, and nut butter.

HOW TO USE IT: Great for a midday snack (watch your serving size—they are addictive. About ten whole nuts or 1 tablespoon of nut butter is a good amount). Chopped macadamia nuts add crunch and texture to many foods, including salads, and ground nuts make a wonderful crusty coating for fish. Use the oil for sautéing vegetables, cooking at high temperatures, and making delicious salad dressing. The smooth, rich taste of macadamia nuts also makes them a great base for many desserts. The smooth taste of macadamia-nut butter is a wonderful alternative to peanut butter that most children love.

can reduce oxidative stress and inflammation, lower bad LDL cholesterol while maintaining good HDL cholesterol, lower triglycerides, help with weight loss, and lower high blood pressure in people with hypertension. Nutrition scientists from Australia's University of Newcastle found in a 2007 study of 17 men with high cholesterol that a daily helping of these delicious nuts reduced signs of oxidative stress (damage that boosts risk for clogged arteries) and inflammation.[8] In addition to reducing heart disease risk, some lab studies suggest macadamias could help ward off some kinds of cancer. For example, a 2010 lab study from Japan's Jeju National University found evidence that fatty acids of the type found in macadamia nuts may turn off genes that drive the development of skin cancer.[9]

Macadamia nuts originated in Australia, and were consumed for thousands of years by aborigines. Beginning in the 1920s, farmers in Hawaii started raising them as a commercial crop. They are now grown in New Zealand, Brazil, Indonesia, Kenya, and South Africa in addition to Hawaii and Australia.

Macadamia-nut oil is preferable to many other cooking oils because it has a very high smoke point—it can be heated to 425°F before breaking down, so it's good for cooking and sautéing. It's also a perfect oil for salad dressing, because it adds an enjoyable nutty flavor to your greens.

On your skin, macadamia-nut oil is silky and cushiony. Its regenerative properties replace the oils in aging skin, improve skin's elasticity, protect against sun damage, and make your skin look younger and softer. Its antifungal and antibacterial qualities contribute to wound healing; macadamia-nut oil is so good for skin that many high-end cosmetics manufacturers use it as a cornerstone ingredient.

One of my favorite brands is Vital Choice Organic Macadamia Nut Oil, which is available on the Vital Choice Web site (www.vitalchoice.com). Vital Choice also sells fantastic wild salmon and other fish.

Note! Macadamia nuts are toxic to dogs, so keep them away from your four-legged friends.

MEDICINE IN A ROOT: MACA POWDER

THE MACA PLANT GROWS IN the Andes Mountains in Peru. It produces a radish-like vegetable that has been eaten for thousands of years. Its root is ground up to make maca powder.

Maca powder contains a wealth of nutrients and antioxidants, including twenty different fatty acids, amino acids, calcium, phosphorus, vitamin C, several B vitamins, and plant sterols. It also contains glucosinolates and iso-thiocyanates, which are known for their anti-cancer properties.

People use maca powder to

- Enhance sexual function—isothiocyanates are thought to be an aphrodisiac
- Reduce adrenal stress and bring a feeling of balance to the body
- Boost energy and stamina
- Support the nervous system, digestive system, and reproductive system

Animal studies suggest maca powder may work as an antidepressant, improve bone mass, reduce oxidative stress, improve memory, increase glucose tolerance, and improve cholesterol levels. In a 2007 lab study from Palacký University in the Czech Republic, maca boosted blood levels of anti-oxidants and enhanced metabolism of blood sugar and blood fats.[10] Body-builders sometimes take maca powder for its muscle-building properties. And studies show that maca may help improve libido and sexual function for women in menopause as well as for people taking selective serotonin reup-take inhibitor (SSRI) antidepressants , according to a 2008 review by researchers from Massachusetts General Hospital.[11]

Warning: Maca powder is not recommended for pregnant women or people with thyroid conditions because it contains glucosinolates, which can cause goiter.

A BERRY WITH POWER: CAMU CAMU

CAMU CAMU IS A BUSH that grows in the rivers of the Amazon rain forests in Brazil, Colombia, Peru, and Venezuela. Its fruit—small berries with purplish skin and yellow pulp that are a little less than an inch in diameter—has more vitamin C than any other known plant in the world. Camu camu berries have thirty to sixty times more vitamin C than oranges , according to a 2002 Brazilian analysis.[12]

Both the berries and the leaves of the camu camu bush have been used as herbal medicine, but the camu camu berry powder is the easiest to use. The berries are very tart, so eating them whole is not enjoyable. Blending the powder in smoothies or combining it with other ingredients is more appealing to the taste buds. It has earned nutripower status for several reasons:

- The phytochemicals in camu camu fight herpes-related viral infections, such as cold sores, shingles, and genital herpes, according to natural healers. Camu camu contains high levels of ellagic acid,[13] which may have antiviral properties. In fact, camu camu contains more potent anti-herpes phytochemicals than any other known plant, according to well-respected natural healers. When people are infected with the herpes virus, it can lie dormant in the body and become activated when the immune system becomes weakened by stress, emotional strain, certain prescription drugs, poor diet, other infections, or other immunity suppressors.

- Camu camu contains powerful phytochemicals, antioxidants, beta-carotene, calcium, iron, niacin, phosphorus, riboflavin, thiamin, and the amino acids serine, valine, and leucine.

- It helps reduce systemic inflammation.

- Camu camu has antidepressant properties. In some cases, people have been able to wean themselves off prescription antidepressants and take camu camu powder instead—but this should be done only under the supervision of a medical doctor.

- It can help reduce anxiety and panic attacks in people who are prone to them.

WHAT TO BUY: Raw camu camu powder.

HOW TO USE IT: Boost nutrition by adding it to smoothies and raw desserts. It's also a healthy way to add a citrus flavor to poultry.

- A rich emollient, camu camu is sometimes used in South American countries to strengthen and untangle hair.

MYTHOLOGICAL PANACEA BECOMES NATURAL MEDICINE: SEA BUCKTHORN

KNOWN AS THE FOOD OF Pegasus, the mythological flying horse, sea buckthorn is a bush that grows in Europe and Asia. Used in ancient Greece, Tibet, and Mongolia, sea buckthorn has been valued for its medicinal qualities for well over a thousand years.

In today's world, sea buckthorn is held in high regard as much for its nutritional profile as for its medicinal value. The plant's berries are particularly rich in nutrients, including many kinds of vitamins, amino acids, zeaxanthin, lycopene, flavonoids, folic acid, and beta-carotene.

Scientists in China and the former Soviet Union have conducted many studies of the sea buckthorn's juice, oil, and other extractions. They have identified more than 109 biologically active substances that appear to strengthen the immune system and protect against inflammation, radiation, some kinds of cancer, and some kinds of cognitive decline. According to the Web site seabuckthornresearch.com, the berries of this plant are packed with beneficial vitamins, carotenoids, flavonoids, steroids, minerals, enzymes, amino acids, essential oils, and essential fatty acids.[14]

Asian researchers also recognize sea buckthorn as an effective way to treat skin conditions because its oil appears to promote regeneration of the skin. In a 2012 lab study from Korea's Pusan National University, sea buckthorn reduced the effect of ultraviolet light exposure on skin, suggesting that this ancient healer could cut risk for skin aging due to exposure to the sun.[15] Asians use sea buckthorn oil to treat eczema, burns, wounds that don't heal properly, and skin damaged by sun, radiation, and cosmetic laser surgery.

Sea buckthorn also seems to promote the health of mucous membranes,

WHAT TO BUY: Raw powder or oil (be careful not to purchase oil sweetened with sugar).

HOW TO USE IT: Great for making delicious "spritzers" by adding it to sparkling water with a splash (just a *splash*) of pomegranate juice or a few muddled blueberries. The powder is great to add to smoothies and raw desserts.

which makes it a popular choice for the prevention of bleeding gums and disorders of the mucous membranes of the stomach and other organs.

Warning: Sea buckthorn can slow blood clotting, so don't take it within two weeks of surgery and use caution (or avoid it) if you take anticoagulant drugs such as aspirin, clopidogrel, diclofenac, ibuprofen, naproxen, dalteparin, enoxaparin, heparin, warfarin, and others.

DRINK YOUR VEGETABLES: GREEN WATER AND WHEAT GRASS

IN THE PURSUIT OF GOOD health, you can do more than just eat your vegetables. You can drink them, too. Green water, wheat grass, and vegetable smoothies are a convenient way to pack even more nutripower foods into your daily diet.

Green water is an alternative to fresh vegetable juice. It's a form of dehydrated or freeze-dried vegetables. A scoop of "green mix" added to your water is typically the equivalent of about five servings of vegetables. Most green mixes have an extensive list of vegetables and a very high ORAC value. (ORAC is a method of measuring antioxidant capacity—the higher the number, the better.) And it's no wonder. In nature, greens are antioxidant superstars with levels that can outstrip most other vegetables, according to a 2003 Italian analysis.[16]

Green water provides many benefits. Many of the foods in our diet are acidic, and green water and other alkalizing foods help neutralize that acid. It also aids in detoxification. Because it adds substance to water, it helps fill you up, curb hunger, and prevent between-meal snacking.

A daily shot of wheat grass is another great way to add more nutritional vigor to your diet. One ounce has twenty amino acids, ninety-one minerals, and is 70 percent chlorophyll. This power-packed tonic is a great way to get a quick shot of energy and nutrients.

Many pilot studies suggest that wheat grass improves blood flow, digestion, detoxification, and heavy metal chelation. Wheat grass and other green juices are the core of nutritional therapy at many alternative cancer treatment centers.

Don't worry—wheat grass contains no gluten. Wheat grass is a young grass and is picked and juiced before the wheat kernel has formed, therefore it is gluten-free. Once the shaft fully matures and develops the wheat kernels, it is no longer gluten-free. If you have been diagnosed with celiac disease contact your health-care provider before consuming wheat grass or any other green grass supplements.

WHICH IS BETTER, GREEN JUICE OR SMOOTHIES?

The answer is, *both*! Green juice and smoothies each serve an amazing purpose when it comes to your health and I recommend them both for different reasons. Adding greens to your smoothie provides essential fiber. You don't leave any part of the amazing plant behind. Juicing greens extracts the potent alkalinizing tonic, vitamins, and minerals and leaves the fiber behind. Removing the fiber virtually eliminates the digestion time and gives you a big bolus of energy and nutrients. When you blend or crush vegetables with a juicer, you release nutrients from the tough (indigestible) cell walls that are not easily released through chewing. Chewing vegetables releases about 25 percent of the nutrition available. But the process of blending or juicing releases nearly 80 percent of the nutrients from vegetables.

PART TWO

FOODS TO LOSE

6

[A Dozen Ways Doughnuts Can Change Your Life]

Those who think they have no time for healthy eating, will sooner or later have to find time for illness.
—EDWARD STANLEY

CAN DOUGHNUTS CHANGE YOUR LIFE? You bet they can. They changed Tami's life. Or, more accurately, giving them up changed her life. I'll tell you all about Tami (and doughnuts), but first, let's spend a little time on sugar.

I talk about dietary sugar, blood sugar, glucose control, and insulin a lot. One reason for this is because diabetes is such a devastating disease. Type 2 diabetes affects nearly 26 million Americans, or 8.3 percent of the population. Of those, 7 million are undiagnosed. Diabetes is lethal: It is one of the top causes of death in the United States, and is a major cause of heart disease and stroke. It is the leading cause of kidney failure, nontraumatic limb amputation, and new cases of blindness among adults.

Those are the facts. But for me, diabetes has a much more personal side. It robbed me of one of the most important people in my life: my grandmother Abla.

One of my first—and fondest—memories of my grandmother is her large, soft belly. When she cuddled me close, her ample belly and infectious giggles gave me much needed comfort and security. Everything on Abla's four-foot-eleven, 200-pound body was round and soft. I found her plumpness endearing—that is, until I learned that it was killing her.

I used to love the comfort foods that my grandmother would prepare for the two of us. I savored the warm Syrian bread smothered in butter and dripping with honey. (In a pinch we'd substitute tortillas with butter and sugar.) Unfortunately, though, my grandmother also passed along to me some of her unhealthy attachments to food. As a lonely child who was left on her own a lot, I learned quickly that I could comfort myself with the same warm sugary foods that my grandmother ate.

A FRIGHTENING TURN

MY GRANDMOTHER HAD BEEN DIAGNOSED with type 2 diabetes before I was born, and when I was eleven years old, I started administering her insulin shots. She could no longer be trusted to give herself the correct dose because the diabetes had compromised her eyesight. And because my mother worked from early in the morning until long after I was in bed at night, I was the only option.

I practiced giving shots on oranges, which wasn't so hard. But calculating the correct dose of insulin terrified me. Oranges don't die of insulin overdoses, but my grandmother could—miscalculating her insulin could be fatal.

I'm certain that taking care of my grandmother in this way had a huge impact on my decision to become a nurse, and even more on my passion to help people break the bonds to the unhealthy food and lifestyle that keep them hostage to chronic disease, depression, and addiction.

By the time I was twelve years old, Abla was legally blind and had heart disease as well as significant neuropathy (pain, numbness, tingling and ulcerations) in her hands, feet, and eyes. She spent her days staring at the television set in her bedroom, even though she could barely see it.

Diabetes continued to take more and more of my grandmother. Her neuropathy-riddled feet made it a struggle for her to walk—even just to make the journey from her bed to the bathroom. She finally gave in to using a bedside commode. Eventually she couldn't even bathe herself and needed help from my mother or me—a humiliation for such a proud, modest woman. The tips of her toes turned black, sores oozed on her legs, and she sometimes cried from the pain. Had she not died of heart disease, her toes would have had to be amputated. My grandmother had immigrated to America from Lebanon in 1928, when she was eighteen years old. She had experienced significant emotional trauma as a child living in a war-torn country during a time that food was scarce and fear was plentiful. When she arrived in America, she turned to food for comfort. She had not received a formal education, and spoke broken English with a heavy Arabic accent. Although I understood her perfectly, her accent obstructed her communication with others. Regardless of how many times doctors and nurses warned her to stop eating sugar because it was making her diabetes worse, she never seemed to understand. She always kept Lebanese pastries and cookies around, as well as a stash of chocolate in her purse. She continued to eat sweets excessively until she passed away.

Sometimes I think she did understand the risks but chose to ignore them. As her health declined steadily, she turned to the one thing that gave her comfort: food.

A TRAGIC ENDING

MY GRANDMOTHER DIED AT THE age of eighty-four from heart disease brought on by diabetes. Her doctors were surprised that she lived so long, since they had been telling us for decades that she would "not live beyond a year." But those decades were not pleasant or filled with joy and great memories. She lived isolated, in pain, and afraid to change.

My grandmother is a perfect example of the concepts of lifespan versus healthspan. Although she lived a fairly *long* life, her *quality* of life was poor. Her lifespan was pretty good, but her healthspan—her years of health and energy—was not good at all.

I think of my grandmother frequently when I work with people who are trying to improve their health. I wish that her doctors and nurses had pushed harder to help her change the behaviors that took her life. Even more, I wish they had actually taken time to *teach her*!

And, although I understand that her life hit her with blows that I can't even begin to imagine, I also wish that somehow she could have found the strength to turn away from food and look elsewhere for comfort.

It's too late for my grandmother. But unless you are lying in the ICU on life support, it's not too late for you. *Anybody* can take steps to improve their health. *Anyone* with diabetes, pre-diabetes, or a family history of diabetes can make changes that will slow or stop the progression of this awful disease. The best way to start is by getting treatment—and following the Omni Diet.

"I have eaten my way through many of life's changes, generally justifying my poor choices with calling them treats. Then I woke up one day to realize I was passing through years of my life by living from one treat moment to the next, never acknowledging I had made a habit of not taking care of myself. And not only that, but I had passed on these habits to my children who were now living just as unhealthily. This was very sad for me—I knew I had to make some changes. I have had a very long-term committed relationship with sugar, but I am happy to say we have finally broken up. Now the biggest treat I can give myself and my family is to be healthy." —ALICIA

SWEETLY KILLING YOU: TYPE 2 DIABETES

AS MY GRANDMOTHER'S STORY SHOWS, it's hard to overstate the importance of healthy blood sugar control. That's why it plays such a major part in the Omni Diet. You need to control the amount of sugar in your blood in order to control your health.

The best way to control your intake of sugar and simple carbohydrates is to eliminate them from your diet. Giving up sugar and simple carbohydrates is hard for some people. But I believe it's an absolutely crucial step in the quest for optimal health.

If you eat too much sugar and simple carbohydrates in your diet, you will have too much sugar in your blood. And for millions of people, too much sugar in the blood leads to type 2 diabetes, which is one of the leading causes of death and disability in the United States. (When I refer to diabetes, I'm talking only about type 2 diabetes. Type 1 is a different kind of disease.)

When you eat a food that contains carbohydrates, your body breaks them down and converts them to glucose, which elevates your blood sugar. If all is working well and is in balance, your cells, with the help of insulin from your pancreas, use the glucose in your blood for energy.

Simple carbohydrates are found in just about anything white—table sugar, flour, and *nearly all* bread, pasta, and rice (foods that Dr. Steven Gundry refers to as "white poisons")—as well as sugary beverages and fruit juice. All of these foods are converted into glucose very quickly by your body. In contrast, complex carbohydrates—found in fibrous foods such as vegetables, whole fruits, and some whole grains—take longer to break down.

As you digest carbohydrates and glucose and fructose from sugar, the glucose pours into your blood. Glucose from simple carbohydrates enters the blood quickly, causing rapid blood sugar spikes; glucose from complex carbohydrates enters the blood a bit more slowly.

In response to glucose entering the blood, your pancreas secretes the hormone insulin, which pushes glucose into your cells, muscles, and liver to use as energy. (Fructose doesn't need insulin because it goes directly to the liver to be metabolized. Fructose is toxic to the liver—more on that later.)

Insulin resistance and type 2 diabetes begin when your pancreas can't produce enough insulin to keep up with the glucose being launched in your body. If you have type 2 diabetes or insulin resistance, your body is being assaulted by glucose overloads—your body can't muster enough insulin to handle it all. (Having insulin resistance doesn't necessarily mean you have diabetes, but it usually suggests you are well on your way to developing it.) When this happens, it's harder for glucose to enter the cells, so it builds up in your blood, leading to continuous high blood sugar. Over time, excess blood sugar injures the walls of blood vessels throughout the body.

This damage can lead to a long list of health problems, including eye disorders that may lead to blindness, neuropathy (numbness, tingling, and pain) from nerve damage, heart disease, high blood pressure, hearing loss, kidney disease, intestinal damage, gum disease, and more. Recent findings suggest it may also contribute to Alzheimer's disease.

If you think you can't kick your sugar habit, take heart: I've seen even the most sugar-addicted people dump it once they set their minds to it. If Kim can do it, you can, too!

> Although Kim was eating what she thought was a healthy vegan diet, her meals were full of sugar in the form of fruit, pasta, whole-grain breads, legumes, and rice. Kim suffered from mental fog and energy dips. She also admitted to an insatiable sweet tooth.
>
> Kim started following the Omni Diet principles, and within *one week* she had lost her sweet tooth. Her mental fog disappeared, and her energy was improving and staying steady, rather than jumping around all day.

Lifestyle choices can have a huge impact on the prevention and progression of diabetes and metabolic dysfunction. Being overweight or having diabetes in your family doesn't give you an automatic death sentence. You have the ability to dramatically lower your risk. And if you already have diabetes, you can get it under control and limit the damage it does to your body. You

CREATE A MANTRA

Having your own personal mantra—a sentence you can repeat to yourself over and over when you need help getting through a difficult challenge—is an incredibly useful tool. Take some time to create your own mantra. It has to be something meaningful and inspirational, something that speaks to you in a very personal, real way.

I've got a great story about the power of mantras. Ronnette, a gal in one of my Omni Diet classes, was about to turn fifty. She told her friends she didn't want a party, but they went ahead and threw one anyway—complete with a big birthday cake. When they handed Ronnette a slice, she said no thanks. She'd worked very hard to break her addiction to sugar, and she didn't want one piece of cake to set her back. Besides, she really didn't want any cake—amazingly, although she used to crave it, she was happy to do without it.

Despite pressure from her friends, Ronnette didn't give in. She simply focused on her mantra: "I'm fit and fifty, not fat and fifty." For her, that mantra says it all: At this point in her life, being healthy is much more important to her than gorging on cake. Her mantra gave her the strength to stick to her decision, and eventually, her friends backed off.

Ronnette was surprised that her food-pushing friends would be annoyed with her decision to avoid food that was hurting her, but I wasn't. When we take a stand to fight for our health, others can feel that our *good* decisions shine a light on their *harmful* decisions.

may even be able to reduce or get off your medications—I've seen this many, many times in people who follow the Omni Diet.

STOPPING DIABETES IN ITS TRACKS

NOW THAT WE'RE COMPLETELY CLEAR on how excess sugar can harm your body, it's time to get back to Tami and the doughnuts.

Tami is a dynamic woman who was participating in one of my Omni Diet classes. She had type 2 diabetes and has struggled with weight, food addiction, and diabetes for years. She had a previous history with drug and alcohol abuse. When she finally managed to kick those addictions, she turned to food. She was never taught how food affects her hormones, moods, and overall health.

My mantra is different from Ronnette's, but it is equally good at coming to my rescue in difficult situations. I think of myself as a rock, a foundation of good health, an example for others. In spite of my health challenges, I choose to focus on being the strongest I can be and the best leader I can be. So the mantra that works best for me is, "I'm a living example of health and fitness."

Here are some other successful mantras:

- This is how healthy people eat.

- That's not how I eat anymore!

- No food tastes as good as being healthy feels.

- I deserve to take care of myself.

- I can do this.

- I am strong and brave!

- I love my body and want to take care of myself.

- Put down the fork and go for a walk.

- Health is vital to be all God wants me to be.

- My body is a temple, bought with a price.

- I am a warrior for health!

Tami pulled me aside after one of our classes. She told me she wanted to follow the Omni Diet because she was convinced it could help her. But there was one thing she felt she couldn't possibly stop eating: doughnuts. Each morning on the way to work she would stop by her favorite bakery and pick up several warm, fresh-from-the-oven doughnuts. She knew they were full of sugar, simple carbohydrates, trans fats, and empty calories. But the doughnuts were such an enjoyable part of her day that she couldn't even imagine giving them up.

I could see that Tami clearly understood the health and nutrition principles I had explained to her, but I sensed that logic and science were no match for her deep-rooted doughnut dependence. So for the next week's class, I put together a graphic slide show to go along with the lesson plan that I hoped would scare her straight. In a "gentle" (like a pit bull) and loving (as a former ICU nurse I have a reputation to uphold) way I gave her a glimpse of what her future might hold if she continued with her doughnut habit.

A DOZEN WAYS DOUGHNUTS CAN CHANGE YOUR LIFE

DOUGHNUTS FOR BREAKFAST WILL SABOTAGE your health for the rest of your day. Sugar, fat, and gluten are *not* a breakfast of champions. This toxic trio is the breakfast of chronic disease. In fact, starting your day with doughnuts causes insulin to spike, triggers an explosion of inflammation, and shrouds your brain with creativity-robbing fog. It also throws your hormones (insulin, leptin, and ghrelin) completely out of whack, which initiates the craving response that you will battle for the rest of the day.

Doughnuts and other sugary, fatty, glutinous breakfast bombs can damage your health and threaten your life in *at least* a dozen ways:

1. Chronic high blood sugar leads to type 2 diabetes.
2. High blood sugar in people with diabetes can lead to skin ulcerations and nerve damage.
3. Diabetic amputation can result from uncontrolled blood sugar.
4. Diabetes can lead to blindness resulting from retinopathy.
5. Alzheimer's disease is now referred to as type 3 diabetes. It is dramatically increased by obesity, and women are significantly more affected than men.
6. Depression is one of the most common side effects of obesity.
7. Sugar feeds cancer. High insulin is associated with many forms of cancer.
8. Sugar and trans fats lead to elevated cholesterol, high triglycerides, vascular disease, and heart disease.
9. Sugar and trans fats lead to arteriosclerosis and stroke.
10. Sugar causes rapid aging—and wrinkles due to glycation (AGEs).
11. Fructose is toxic to the liver and leads to nonalcoholic fatty liver.
12. Fructose leads to hypertension and gout.

The slide show stunned Tami. Never before had someone explained in such clear, graphic terms what could very well happen to her if she continued to eat doughnuts. Her doctors regularly told her that she needed to "get her blood sugar under control," but that had no real resonance for Tami. Knowing

> "Tana, I recently was waiting for a prescription at Rite Aid and watching old people one after the other shuffling and hunched over, purchasing many prescriptions at the counter. I thought to myself as I was sipping on my coffee with sweetener, which you've said is really bad, that I do not want to end up like them. So I took my coffee and threw it away. I heard your voice in my head saying, 'You will end up like that if you keep eating things that are bad for you.' Your voice is always in my head to do better." —JEANA

that her blood sugar was 160 had no emotional or even practical leverage for Tami because she had no picture to attach the number to.

The next week, Tami reported to me that she hadn't eaten a single doughnut since she watched the slide show and that she didn't think she would ever be able to look at food the same way now that she understood the consequences of what those foods were doing to her body.

Two weeks later, she showed up at class with a huge smile on her face. Since she'd been diagnosed with diabetes six years ago, Tami's blood sugar usually was 150 to 160. But that day at class Tami told me that for the past week her blood sugar had been averaging between 89 and 95—much closer to where it should be. This was a huge drop! Initially, she checked her blood sugar four or five times a day because she thought it was a mistake—she couldn't quite believe it was possible for a change in her diet to affect her blood sugar so quickly.

"Nobody had ever connected the dots for me before this," Tami said. "I had no idea that I was doing such harm to my body with my diet." Following the Omni Diet, Tami kicked her sugar habit and now wouldn't even dream of eating a doughnut. She avoids all sweet foods because she doesn't ever want to be hooked on sugar again.

There was a day, several weeks after her initial revelation, where Tami did have a significant relapse, and rendezvoused with a couple of éclairs. When she came to class, disappointment shone clearly on her face. The first words out of her mouth were, "I failed." We quickly turned Tami's feelings of self-loathing into a powerful learning experience. I reminded her and the rest of the class that it's *impossible* to fail with the Omni Diet. It's a way to change your life forever, and it's all right to start over—repeatedly, if necessary—until you succeed. Failure (I prefer to call it *stumbling*) can be a wonderful motivator once you learn to harness its power.

MAKE IT IMPOSSIBLE TO FAIL!

The people in my classes have all been on diets—*many diets*. Some are significantly overweight. Several are bulimic, and some have gained substantial weight despite having gastric bypass surgery. When they first start my program, many announce that "I'm going to fail this diet just like all the other diets I've tried." I bet there's a pretty good chance that you feel that way, too.

Living under the shadow of failure is a terrible feeling. It interferes with your happiness and gets in the way of making healthy changes. Starting now it's time to face down failure. Failure is no longer an option! As soon as my clients hear this, they begin a radical internal shift.

The Omni Diet isn't a test. There isn't a destination. Therefore you can't fail! If you think of what you're doing as a diet, and you expect to lose x number of pounds in x number of weeks, failure is an option because you may *not* lose x pounds in x weeks. But this is a program to *get control* of your life, to *optimize your health*. Weight loss is the stunning side effect. It's a lifelong journey and every step is a success. *Every time* you grasp a new concept or incorporate a health-promoting habit, you are a winner!

The greatest lessons and learning come from the "not so perfect" times. If you can't give yourself permission to let go of your focus on perfection, you have my permission. If you find you've gotten off track, choose three simple, health-promoting things that you can do quickly (drink a glass of water, call a friend, and go for a walk . . .). Consider this your "make-up" homework that puts you back in the game.

With the Omni Diet, you succeed every time you take a single step toward good health. You're a winner every time you drink a glass of water, go for a walk, do one workout, eat a bowl of broccoli, throw out a bag of chips, ask for support from your accountability buddy, write down your next day's menu, write in your food journal—you get the idea. Even just taking a deep breath, closing your eyes, and reminding yourself that you have committed fully to living a healthier life makes you a success. Remember, when it's this easy to succeed, failure is not an option.

The last time I checked in with Tami she was still on track, keeping her blood sugar controlled and continuing to lose weight. More important, she now understands that the Omni Diet is not something that you "succeed" or "fail" at. It is a healthy, wholesome lifestyle that helps you *thrive*.

IT WON'T HAPPEN TO ME—OR WILL IT?

YOU MAY NOT BE WORRIED at all about diabetes—perhaps your blood sugar levels are perfect.

Or, like 79 million other Americans,[1] you may have pre-diabetes, a situation in which blood sugar levels are above normal, but not yet high enough to be in the diabetes zone. (Pre-diabetes is also referred to as impaired glucose tolerance or impaired fasting glucose.)

If you don't have diabetes, you don't have to cut back on eating sugar or simple carbohydrates, right? Wrong. Even if your blood sugar levels are perfect, there are still many reasons to avoid sugar.

For one thing, when you eat a lot of sugar and simple carbs, your normal blood sugar levels can turn into pre-diabetes—and your pre-diabetes can turn to full-blown type 2 diabetes. This can happen even if you don't have a history of diabetes in your family and you're not very overweight or obese.

The more sugar and simple carbohydrates you eat, the more insulin your pancreas must secrete in order to deal with dietary sugar. This can lead to a situation called hyperinsulinemia. What's wrong with hyperinsulinemia? It's complicated, but I think it's important to understand. So let's give it a try.

All carbohydrates must be broken down to their simplest form of monosaccharides (glucose and fructose) before they can enter the bloodstream and be used for energy. Sugars and simple carbohydrates are broken down easily and quickly; complex carbohydrates take longer, which is why complex carbohydrates are better for controlling blood sugar.

It's important to have just enough glucose for energy, but not so much that you're forcing your pancreas to work overtime pumping out insulin. If you overdose your system on sugar and simple carbohydrates, you keep your body in a chronic state of hyperinsulinemia. Once the liver and muscle cells are full of sugar, the excess carbs are converted to a fat called palmitic acid (PA). PA interferes with the body's response and sensitivity to a hormone called leptin, which is what your gut releases to tell your brain you're full.

Once the insulin can't push any more glucose into your liver and muscles, your liver and muscles become "insulin resistant." Your blood sugar level continues to go higher and higher because there is nowhere for the glucose to be stored. And, because insulin is still present in your blood, your body doesn't get the signal that your cells are full—your body thinks it needs more glucose because of the presence of insulin, and you start craving carbs.

That's right—high blood insulin levels distort your hunger/satiety hormones to the point that you think you're hungry even though you've just eaten. And another one of insulin's jobs is to promote the deposit of fat on your body. So you can see how having a lot of insulin in your system makes it nearly impossible to lose weight.

MORE DESTRUCTION

INSULIN ALSO SIGNALS THE LIVER to make fatty acids, in the form of triglycerides. Eating fat only increases your triglyceride level a little, because when your body perceives the increase, it stops producing its own supply. But the opposite happens when you eat simple carbohydrates. When your liver becomes overdosed with sugar, and is insulin resistant, it becomes very efficient at forming triglycerides. A lot of these triglycerides are processed into VLDL (very low-density lipoprotein), which aids in forming LDL cholesterol. But some of the fat infiltrates the liver, creating a nasty condition called nonalcoholic fatty liver.

At the same time, even though your blood is full of sugar, your body *thinks* your blood sugar is low. It's a vicious cycle. When you have high blood sugar, your body needs insulin. When you have high levels of insulin in your blood, your body craves sugar to prevent hypoglycemia (a dangerous state). Your body thinks this chronic hypoglycemic state is a stress response. The stress hormone cortisol comes to the "rescue" to help increase blood sugar, and starts converting protein from your own muscles into sugar in a process called gluconeogenesis. Cortisol leads to muscle wasting and excess fat deposits around your middle, creating a muffin top of fat that hangs over the waistband. This is visceral fat that accumulates around your organs, and it is very dangerous.

And the sugar roller coaster has only just begun! When fat cells become insulin-resistant, triglycerides go up. Continually forcing your pancreas to secrete more and more insulin can cause your pancreas to function less and less effectively. And the pancreas, already weakened by having to go into constant hyperdrive to produce insulin, becomes very susceptible to oxidative stress, which can cause permanent damage to the very important beta cells in the pancreas. To be clear: *Sugar* leads to elevated triglycerides. And you become very efficient at forming fat from three sources, *sugar, insulin, and cortisol.*

But the ride isn't quite over. As your body is becoming more inflamed, your risk for cancer also increases. Cancer feeds on sugar. Most cancer cells have metabolic needs that are about eight times higher than normal cells', so cancer cells need instant and constant energy—which they get from a sugary diet. Excess insulin levels are also associated with increased risk for many types of cancer, including those of the colon, rectum, pancreas, prostate,[3] and breasts.

When cancer cells develop, our bodies have a much better chance of fighting them when fueled with an anti-cancer diet (such as the Omni Diet) that keeps blood sugar levels low and contains lots of antioxidants and a healthy amount of good fats. Sugary diets may promote breast cancer by boosting levels of insulin-like growth factor (IGF). In a 2007 Italian study, women who ate the most carbohydrates with a high glycemic load—refined and sugary foods that boost blood sugar in a hurry—more than tripled their risk for breast cancer.[4] And in a 2006 Italian study of more than 5,000 women, those who ate the most sweets—cookies, cakes, ice cream, table sugar, honey, jam, and marmalade—were 19 percent more likely to develop breast cancer compared to those who ate the least.[5] But a healthy diet that's not based on these foods has the opposite effect. For example, a diet packed with vegetables lowered risk by 43 percent in a 2005 study of 1,551 women at the University of California, San Diego.[6]

As I've said, your genes are not necessarily your destiny—but your destiny is in your hands! You can take control and make major changes. Just like Tami did.

ALL IN THE FAMILY

HISTORICALLY, TYPE 2 DIABETES HAD been known as adult-onset diabetes, an aging-related disease. But now, more and more children are being

HARNESS THE POWER OF GRATITUDE

Tapping in to gratitude can give you an incredible brain boost that can affect the quality of the decisions you make. The feeling of gratitude literally changes your brain chemistry. Focusing on gratitude increases brain activity, especially in the frontal lobes and cerebellum. The frontal lobes in your brain are responsible for judgment and impulse control and planning. High-performance frontal lobes lead to high-performance decisions, like choosing foods that you know serve you and resisting foods that you know harm you.

In a fascinating study, my husband did brain scans on people to see how gratitude affected brain function. He performed two scans on each person. For the first scan, he asked the subject to focus on the things in life for which she felt grateful. For the second scan, he asked her to think about things that made her angry. The difference was stunning! Feeling grateful had a dramatically beneficial effect on her brain. When she focused on feeling grateful, blood flow increased to the areas of the brain that impact her focus, judgment, and decision-making. When she focused on negative thoughts, the scan showed a drop in her overall brain activity. (Read more about my husband's extraordinary brain research at www.amenclinics.com.)

When you count your blessings, your pituitary gland releases endorphins and other neurotransmitters that contribute to a feeling of well-being in your brain. You can take advantage of these natural mood-boosters simply by thinking about what makes you feel grateful. Write down a list and read it to yourself, or just spend a few minutes meditating on the happiest things in your life. As your sense of well-being goes up, so does your motivation to make healthy choices.

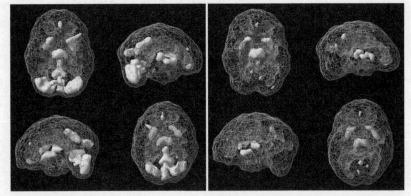

GRATEFUL BRAIN   HATEFUL BRAIN

diagnosed with this dangerous condition. Type 2 diabetes is now the most common chronic disease in Americans under the age of twenty, and it is estimated that one in three children born after the year 2000 will develop type 2 diabetes, according to the Centers for Disease Control and Prevention.[7]

Experts believe several factors are contributing to this epidemic: the huge increase in childhood obesity, low levels of physical activity among young people, and an overabundance of sugar and calories in the foods children eat.

The growing incidence of diabetes in women of childbearing age also seems to be a factor. When a woman develops diabetes before or during pregnancy, her unborn baby is exposed to glucose imbalances in the uterus, which seems to raise the baby's risk of diabetes during childhood and beyond.

The future looks ominous for the next generation if we don't do something to get and keep our children healthy.

The Omni Diet is family friendly. In fact it works much better if the entire family is involved. The earlier you expose your children to a healthy style of eating the easier they will adapt. That's what we've done at my house.

While I don't try to control every bite my daughter, Chloe, takes, especially when she is away from home, I do make sure to provide only healthy food in the house. I refuse to buy sugary, fatty, super-processed "kid food" that will make her sick and fat. (As my friend JJ Virgin says, "exposure equals preference.") I always pack Chloe's lunch (traditional school lunches are truly atrocious, filled with processed simple carbohydrates, bad fats, and salt) and I *educate* her continually about how food affects her body.

On the rare occasion that my daughter pushes back and refuses to eat what is in the house, I don't argue. I simply remind her that there is an abundance of delicious and nutritious food available for her at any time. I am comfortable with her making the decision to miss a meal if she chooses to. Many of my clients are shocked by this statement. Moms are hardwired with a "guilt chip" that makes them feel like bad parents if their children do not eat at least three meals every day—and they will resort to the worst of all "Franken foods" to accomplish this goal if necessary. I know that my daughter will not starve to death. When she is hungry, she will eat.

Although she occasionally complains at home, her friends' parents tell me that at school or on play dates, she proselytizes to their children about making healthier choices. At nine years old, Chloe eats an incredibly healthy diet. And she has more wisdom about how food affects her body than I had when I was thirty.

7

[The Truth about Grains, Dairy, Soy, and Corn]

Tell me what you eat, and I will tell you what you are.

—JEAN ANTHELME BRILLAT-SAVARIN, *THE PHYSIOLOGY OF TASTE*

Jeanine had been struggling with a long string of health problems that interfered with every part of her life. Over the course of several years, she had experienced increasing all-day pain and stiffness in various areas of her body, tendonitis in both shoulders that required hours of physical therapy each week, chest pain, migraine headaches, irritable bowel, insomnia, fatigue, depression, anxiety, and mind fog.

Jeanine had seen many doctors and had undergone many tests. At long last she received a diagnosis: Her doctor pinned her health problems to fibromyalgia. He proposed a three-pronged treatment plan: eight hours of sleep each night, low-impact exercise, and daily pain medication. Jeanine was on board with the sleep and the exercise, but she hoped to find a more natural alternative to medication.

As Jeanine was considering her options, friends invited her to join my Omni Diet class. She referred to this as "God's perfect timing." I have to agree.

When she started on the Omni Diet, Jeanine immediately gave up gluten, refined carbohydrates, salt, sugar, caffeine, and dairy products. She cut back on fruit, ate more berries, changed cooking oils, and made fresh, whole vegetables a major part of her diet.

Jeanine also began taking supplements, including fish oil, vitamin D, and several others targeted to improve mental clarity, sleep, and mobility and to reduce inflammation and pain.

The results were nothing short of amazing. After just a few weeks, most of Jeanine's pain and stiffness disappeared. She slept better and felt more energetic. Instead of feeling groggy and exhausted when she woke up in the morning, Jeanine felt refreshed, alert, and excited to start the day. Jeanine also lost the 15 pounds she had gained while taking a previous medication.

"I had always wanted to learn what to eat and why," Jeanine told me. "With the Omni Diet, I'm getting all the answers I need for my lifelong journey toward good health."

Jeanine's husband got in on the Omni Diet also. He lost 15 pounds, and made his nickname—Dessert King—obsolete. "Family and friends see the difference and want to know more," Jeanine said. "We hope to influence and encourage others to make better choices. With diligence in our decision to stay on the plan with the help of food journaling, accountability, and support, we will have a better life of abundance."

JEANINE'S STORY ILLUSTRATES A CORE principle of the Omni Diet: Some foods have the power to *move us closer to optimal health*, while other foods have the power to *move us away from optimal health*.

In this chapter, I explain which foods should be avoided in the name of good health. And I explain why they have no place in the diet of anyone who's seeking optimal nutrition.

Listen, I know this part of the Omni Diet seems difficult when you first hear it. I know it can be hard to give up favorite foods—I once thought of birthday cake as the eighth Wonder of the World. But once you understand how toxic certain foods can be to your health, it's much easier to break up with them. Once you see how much better you feel without these foods, you start to lose interest in them. What is it called when you can't live without something? Addiction. That's exactly what certain foods do. They create food fog, addiction, and illness.

Think of it the way Jeanine did: Is the taste of bread, milk, and other health-sapping foods so good that you're willing to be in pain every day of your life in order to eat them? For Jeanine, the answer was a resounding no. She would much rather feel energetic, pain-free, and alive than eat foods that make her sick.

When it comes to cutting out foods that compromise your health, knowing *how* they affect your body and *why* you're better off without them is key. Having knowledge fills you with motivation and willpower. That's what I provide in this chapter.

Remember, when a little voice inside you tells you to eat a food that compromises your health, it's a lot easier to silence that voice when you fully understand how perniciously that food behaves inside your body. The toxic foods you are addicted to are *depriving* you of the vibrant health to which you are entitled!

DUMP THE DAIRY

UNLESS YOU GREW UP ON another planet, you've heard that milk "does a body good." You've been told that if you haven't "got milk" you're missing out on something. And you've seen a constellation of movie stars and celebrities smiling at you from beneath their milk mustaches in the pages of glossy magazines.

All these advertising tricks are an attempt to get you to consume a food that your body doesn't need—a food that does a body way more harm than good.

Dairy foods occupy a prominent role in the "healthy" eating patterns recommended by the U.S. Department of Agriculture. The USDA's "My Plate" eating plan (which is a warmed-over update of the flawed food pyramid plan) urges all adults to consume three cups of milk a day or the equivalent in other dairy products such as cheese, yogurt, ice cream, and pudding.

Top nutrition scientists are beginning to recognize what many human intestines have already made clear: Cow's milk is unnecessary in the human diet. Mammals are not designed to drink milk past infancy—and during infancy, they should be drinking milk from their own mother, not a lactating animal from another species.

Many humans have trouble digesting dairy products. After the age of two, fewer than 35 percent of humans produce the enzyme lactase, which is needed to break down lactose (milk sugar) and digest milk, according to

LOVE WHAT YOU HATE

Most people have strong feelings about food. And most food falls into a love or hate category. This often causes nutritional tug of war for my clients. They can't give up doughnuts because they love them. They can't eat vegetables because they hate them. It's so limiting—I urge you to confront your loves and hates. If these food feelings are holding you back, change them! Learn to love what you hate, and hate what you love.

Say you love doughnuts. Think about it: What do you love? The taste, right? Now think about what you can hate about them. Make a list: They raise your blood sugar, they're full of unhealthy ingredients and empty calories, they contribute to weight gain, and they're fried in toxic oil. They cause food fog and addiction. *You love doughnuts, but they don't love you back!*

Maybe you think you hate vegetables. Put that statement to the test. Do you actually hate every vegetable in the world? That's pretty unlikely. So make a list of the vegetables you do like. There may even be a few that you love. And maybe there are some that you don't really care for, but you could probably learn to like them if you gave them a try. Perhaps some tasty herbs and spices would help. Cauliflower is a vegetable that people love to hate, but have you tried cauliflower mashed "potatoes" with garlic? Or lightly steamed and flavored with basil sauce? These foods are worthy of your love. Focus on what's good about them. Think of it that way, and you realize that instead of hating vegetables, you may actually love them.

a 2012 report on lactase persistence from Germany's Johannes Gutenberg University.[1] (People of Jewish, Italian, West African, Arab, Greek, and Asian descent are among those least likely to produce lactase.)

Without lactase in your gut, lactose remains undigested, fermenting in your intestines and causing an array of gastrointestinal symptoms that we refer to as lactose intolerance. (It would really be more accurate to call those few who can easily digest cow's milk "lactase persistent" because not being able to tolerate lactose is actually the norm.) Even if your body can break down lactose, it's still bad news, because it is converted to galactose and glucose, which elevates blood sugar and causes inflammation.

Casein (a protein in milk) is an excitotoxin in the brain. Excitotoxins left unchecked lead to brain inflammation and neurodegenerative diseases. Casein has also been shown to bind to polyphenols found in coffee, tea, berries, and vegetables, rendering these potent nutrients useless. German researchers found in 2007 that while compounds in tea relax arteries, adding milk to tea cancelled the benefits.[2] Casein is also the major "allergenic" protein in cow's milk—the particle that provokes reactions in kids and adults with full-blown milk allergies—Argentinian researchers report.[3]

But what about calcium—don't you need calcium from milk to keep your bones strong and ward off osteoporosis? The answer is yes, you do need calcium. But you are way better off getting calcium from plants. The calcium in milk is not easily utilized by the body, and there's no solid proof that it improves bone strength or prevents bone thinning and osteoporosis. Research with non-milk-drinking Asians has found that Asians get all the calcium they need from plant foods. Osteoporosis rates are much lower in milk-free Asians than in milk-addicted Americans.

Green leafy vegetables, vitamin D supplements, exercise, and increased protein intake are far more effective ways for your body to get the calcium it needs. And unlike these ways of getting calcium, milk doesn't promote weight loss or reduce the risk of cardiovascular disease, either. In fact dairy products are actually associated with an increased risk in acne, prostate cancer, Parkinson's disease, and joint pain.

Here are some more reasons not to drink milk:

- **Pasteurization—the process of heating milk to a high temperature for a short time to kill bacteria—also kills most of the live enzymes that may have made milk slightly worth drinking. While pasteurization is necessary to prevent food poisoning, it renders milk relatively useless, nutritionally speaking. Organic milk is even worse than conventionally produced milk because it requires ultrapasteurization, which kills even more enzymes.**

- **Homogenization, the process of breaking up the fat in milk so it won't separate from the milk, may also break down a substance called plasminogen (found in milk), which may elevate arteriosclerosis risk.**

- **Bovine growth hormones rBST and rBGH are commonly given to dairy cows to increase their milk production. Their presence in the milk you drink stimulates your liver to produce IGF-1 (insulin growth factor). Milk already contains significant amounts of IGF-1, but the addition of these** hormones causes your body to produce even more. Excessive IGF-1 has been strongly associated with cancer of the breast, colon, and prostate.

- Bovine growth hormones are suspected of contributing to early puberty in our children as a result of elevated IGF-1.

- The rBGH given to cows makes them more susceptible to infection, especially mastitis. Infections are treated with antibiotics, which find their way into the milk you drink. Overuse of antibiotics can also lead to the growth of antibiotic-resistant bacteria. Many countries have banned milk from cows that have been treated with rBGH.

GOING AGAINST THE GRAIN

ALMOST WITHOUT FAIL WHEN I explain the downside of grains in a lecture, there are several people who quote scripture from the Bible and assure me that if Jesus ate bread, it must be on the "approved" list of foods. They seem to have a religious attachment to bread! I have nothing but respect for scripture, but I doubt that Jesus was in cahoots with large agribusiness two thousand years ago. So what does the wheat from biblical times and the wheat from today have in common? Absolutely nothing! That's the point. The genetically hybridized grains of today have no resemblance to the pure, wild grains of yesteryear. Yet we're constantly told that whole grains are healthy and nutritious, and that they should make up a large part of our diets. In fact, the USDA's My Plate eating plan advises adults to consume 5 to 8 servings of grains each day.

The fact is that our digestive systems are not designed to process these modern Franken grains, especially as a staple. Before the advent of farming and agriculture, our hunter-gatherer ancestors had access to only small amounts of *wild* grains and ate them sparingly, if at all. It wasn't until the advent of farming around five thousand years ago that grains came on the scene in a big way. But even then farming was hard work—farmers and peasants burned off the excess sugar that the grains they ate dumped into their blood through physical activity.

It's no coincidence that when humans started farming grains (and other crops), evidence of obesity, heart disease, diabetes, and cancer began to show up. We also know that those early people who were overweight and dying of these diseases were (in large part) the aristocracy and the wealthy. With the advent of farming, the people who didn't have to work for their dinner paid for it in a whole new way—with chronic illness.

DON'T ACCEPT FOOD FOR WHICH YOU HAVEN'T ASKED

You're eating a meal with friends or family, and someone offers you food you don't want. You really don't want the food being offered, but you don't want to offend your host. Make one decision instead of hundreds. Instead of grappling with the decision to say yes or no every time you dine with others, make it once. Make the decision that you simply won't accept food you haven't asked for. Period. When someone offers you food you don't want, you'll just say, "No thanks." You don't have to explain, apologize, or make excuses. It's okay just to say no.

It's even worse now that farming is an agribusiness run by corporations that are far more concerned about their bottom line than human health. And, as we'll see, the grain story gets stickier as it unfolds.

So when it comes to diet and scripture, I prefer the story from the Book of Daniel on which the Saddleback Church's Daniel Plan is based. "Daniel then said to the guard whom the chief official had appointed over Daniel, Hananiah, Mishael, and Azariah, 'Please test your servants for ten days: Give us nothing but vegetables to eat and water to drink. Then compare our appearance with that of the young men who eat the royal food, and treat your servants in accordance with what you see.' So he agreed to this and tested them for ten days. At the end of the ten days they looked healthier and better nourished than any of the young men who ate the royal food. So the guard took away their choice food and the wine they were to drink and gave them vegetables instead" (Daniel 1:11-16).

GETTING DOWN WITH GLUTEN

Joan is an educated, highly accomplished career woman. She exercises regularly, has always eaten what she considered to be a healthy diet, and has never been overweight. However, Joan began gaining weight for no apparent reason and was suddenly having trouble getting through the day without the caffeine boost of an afternoon cup of coffee. She also had a nagging and persistent skin rash that left painful sores on her eyelids and back.

Joan was a hard worker, and she was accustomed to being able to achieve whatever goals she set. So she thought that she should be able to push through her health problems, and that to give in to the demands of her body would be to acknowledge weakness—and weakness made her very uncomfortable. But when her symptoms continued to worsen, she began to fear she was developing some form of dementia (which ran in her family).

Joan was desperate to feel like her perky, sharp-witted self again.

Comprehensive blood tests found that Joan had an underactive thyroid condition known as Hashimoto's disease. (Hashimoto's is an autoimmune disease in which your body starts attacking your own thyroid gland.) Fogginess, chronic fatigue, and weight gain are several of many signs of an underactive thyroid. Joan began taking thyroid hormone replacement pills, which helped somewhat—but she still felt foggy, and her unexplained weight gain remained.

When Joan came to me for lifestyle advice, I took a close look at her diet. She was a vegetarian, and grains made up a large part of her diet. I know that there is a strong correlation between Hashimoto's disease and intolerance to gluten, a protein in wheat and some other grains. The protein in gluten (gliadin) closely resembles cells of the thyroid gland. When an allergic reaction is formed against the gliadin protein, the body mistakenly sees the thyroid cells as gliadin, forming a full-fledged attack against the enemy.

With this in mind, I educated Joan about her beloved grains and suggested she eliminate gluten from her diet for a while to see if it helped. Within six weeks she felt better than she had in years! Her brain fog cleared, she lost the weight she had gained, and she felt more energetic than she had in decades.

Not surprisingly, Joan's symptoms would return when she ate gluten, so I recommended that she avoid it as completely as possible, since that is the *only* treatment available. The last time I saw Joan, she told me that when her mental sharpness returned, she completed a master's degree program that she had been struggling with in her gluten-eating days and had received an impressive promotion at work.

THE "GLUE" IN GRAINS

THE WORD *GLUTEN* **COMES FROM** the Latin word for "glue." Gluten is a sticky substance found in wheat, barley (and malt, which is made from barley), rye, kamut, bulgur, and spelt. Gluten is the glue that gives bread dough its elasticity and helps the dough rise and keep its shape; it also gives baked bread its chewy texture. Gluten is found in most commercially made breads, cakes, cookies, cereals, pasta, and many other grain-based products.

You've probably noticed lately that gluten is becoming the latest dietary dirty word. I saw this coming many years ago, when it began to affect me, my daughter, and my sister in a very negative way. The problem with gluten is that it's indigestible. *No one can digest gluten,* yet it pervades the American diet.

Gluten-related health issues are on the rise. Gluten is associated with celiac disease, type 1 diabetes, and Hashimoto's thyroid disease—all of which are autoimmune conditions. Gluten can also trigger flu-like symptoms, psychological disturbances, skin rashes, acne, inflammation, alopecia (baldness), arthritis, and food addiction.

You probably don't think of disease and toxicity when you bite into a slice of bread. But you probably should. We think of bread—especially whole-grain bread—as being a healthy staple of life. But that's just one of the falsehoods we've been convinced of by food manufacturers and government-backed subsidy programs.

Approximately 3 million Americans have celiac disease (formerly known as celiac sprue), a genetic condition in which eating gluten causes an immune reaction that tells the body to attack and destroy villi, the finger-like structures in the small intestines that absorb nutrients from food. Damaged intestinal villi lose their ability to absorb nutrients, leading to vitamin and mineral deficiencies and, in babies and children, a failure to thrive and grow normally.

The number of people with celiac disease has *quadrupled* in the past fifty years. And many experts believe that the number of people with celiac disease is grossly underestimated due to lack of education and poor testing methods.

According to the Center for Celiac Research, an additional 18 million Americans have *gluten sensitivity,* which the center recognizes as a serious health issue. Although gluten sensitivity does not qualify as celiac disease, when people who are sensitive to gluten eat foods with gluten, they can experience celiac-like symptoms.

Gluten sensitivity can lead to over one hundred different symptoms that include (but are not limited to) chronic diarrhea, bloating, flatulence, nausea, abdominal pain, skin rashes, fatigue, and mental fogginess. Gluten sensitivity may even play a role in autism and schizophrenia, note scientists from Italy's Marche Polytechnic University in a sweeping 2013 report on gluten sensitivity published in the journal *Nutrients*.[4] There is simply no health-related reason to eat bread, rolls, pastries, or anything else that contains gluten.

HIDING IN PLAIN SIGHT

TO CUT YOUR TIES TO gluten, you have to do more than just eliminate bread. Gluten is a hidden ingredient in many foods, including some kinds of commercially made soy sauce, barbecue sauce, spice blends, mustard, flavored vinegars, salad dressings, canned soups and broths, and snack foods. It's also

> ### [GLUTEN-RELATED DISEASES: WHAT'S BEHIND THE RISE?]
>
> **More and more people are developing gluten-related health conditions. There are several reasons for this:**
>
> - **Food engineering and hybridization have created wheat that has 14 percent more gluten-containing protein than ancient wheat had.**
> - **There is 40 percent more gluten in today's wheat-based bread than in the bread we ate fifty years ago. In the past, gluten was simply a protein in wheat; now it is separated out of wheat and processed into an ingredient called wheat gluten that is added to bread to magnify chewiness in snacks and other carbohydrate-laden foods.**
> - **We eat more wheat, grains, and gluten-containing foods than ever before. This is due in part to the fat-is-bad craze that pushed bread and pretzels as being better for us than healthy fats and lean meats.**
> - **Babies who are not breastfed are at higher risk for gluten-related symptoms because breastfeeding has a protective effect against gluten.**
> - **Inflammation caused by gluten, and other inflammation-causing foods, is associated with the adhesion and growth of "bad" bacteria, which in turn leads to increased inflammation.**

TESTS FOR CELIAC DISEASE, GLUTEN SENSITIVITY, AND WHEAT ALLERGIES

Are you getting the shaft from eating wheat and other gluten-containing grains? Discovering gluten allergies and sensitivities early can save you from a host of medical problems. There are several kinds of tests that are used for diagnosing gluten-related health problems.

Intestinal biopsy is the gold standard of testing. During a procedure known as an endoscopy, a tiny tissue sample taken from the small intestine is inspected for damage caused by gluten.

A blood test referred to as the celiac panel measures your body's response to gluten. It tests for four antibodies against gluten:

1. tTG-IgA (tissue transglutaminase) is highly suggestive of CD
2. AGA-IgG (antigliadin IgG) is elevated with wheat allergies
3. AGA-IgA (antigliadin IGA) indicates a more serious allergic response
4. Total IGA measures the total reactive response to gliadin in the blood

Stool samples can also be inspected for the presence of gluten-related intestinal antibodies.

The "poor man's gluten test" is simply an elimination plan. If you cut all gluten from your diet and your symptoms go away, that's a pretty good indication that gluten is harmful to you. Keep in mind, however, that even if you have celiac disease, you will test negative for it after following a gluten-free diet for several months. That doesn't mean the disease is gone forever—if you start eating gluten-containing foods again, your symptoms (and positive test results) will return.

in some pretty unexpected nonfood sources, including some medications and even the glue on some lickable envelopes.

It can be difficult to avoid gluten in restaurants, but lately, more and more establishments have been creating gluten-free menus. Even in these restaurants, however, you should question your server, the manager, or the chef about their gluten knowledge. Some think gluten is found only in bread or forget about hidden gluten in menu items—for example, there may be bread crumbs in hamburgers or gluten-containing soy sauce in marinades and sauces.

For people who are sensitive to gluten or who have celiac disease, simply coming in contact with gluten externally might cause dermatological problems.

IDENTIFY "SAFE" RESTAURANTS

Following the Omni Diet means you will learn to be more thoughtful about how to order a meal at restaurants and you will likely become more conscious about where you decide to eat. But that doesn't mean you've got to eat at home for the rest of your life. Most restaurants are happy to accommodate special requests. You will become skilled at communicating your needs.

Start with the establishments in your neighborhood or town. Call during the day, when the kitchen isn't busy. Ask to speak with the chef. Or stop by and talk with the chef in person. Tell him you'd like to dine at his restaurant, but you have special dietary needs. Offer an index card that clearly explains what you do and don't want to eat, along with your name. If it applies, mention that you're a regular customer. You'll be surprised how many chefs are willing to meet their customers' special dietary requests. Some even relish the challenge of going off-menu to create new dishes.

When you arrive for a meal, tell your server (or the manager) to discuss your order with the chef. Be clear and specific: Say something like, "I spoke with Chef Tom earlier about my order. He said he is happy to make me baked salmon and steamed vegetables. Please tell him Mrs. Amen is here."

And don't forget: Be sure to thank the chef (and tip the server nicely) when the restaurant comes through for you. And if a restaurant couldn't be bothered to accommodate you, spread the word among friends and family members who are also on the lookout for safe restaurants.

If you suffer from unexplained eczema, dry skin, acne, or other skin conditions that don't go away when you cut gluten out of your diet, they may be caused by gluten in your cosmetics or bath products. Gluten is a common ingredient in makeup, toiletries, and beauty aids. Cosmetic companies are not required to indicate the presence of gluten on product labels, which makes it nearly impossible to know which products contain gluten. Lipstick, foundation, face powder, body lotion, and lubricants are the main suspects. Not all people with gluten intolerance or celiac disease are sensitive to gluten on their skin, but if you have unexplained skin problems, it's worth it to give gluten-free beauty products a try. To find out if your favorite products contain gluten, call the manufacturer for specific information. Or buy from cosmetic companies that guarantee gluten-free products, such as bareMinerals, Afterglow Cosmetics, Ecco Bella, Lavera Cosmetics, DeVine Lip Shimmers, and Smashbox.

LEAKY AND DANGEROUS

SOME GRAINS, SUCH AS WHEAT (and wheat-related grains), barley, rye, kamut, spelt, oats, rice, buckwheat, and millet, can also trigger a harmful digestive problem known as intestinal permeability, or leaky gut. Researchers from the University Medical Center Groningen in the Netherlands suspect the culprit is a compound called gliadin, which is found in these grains.[5] If you suffer from intestinal permeability, substances in grains you ingest damage your intestines, allowing food, waste, bacteria, viruses, and other toxins to leak out of the intestines and to enter the bloodstream. This damage also prevents the intestines from properly absorbing vitamins, minerals, and other nutrients.

Leakage from the intestines can cause inflammation and can trigger allergies and autoimmune reactions in which the body mistakenly attacks its own healthy tissues. Autoimmune disorders associated with leaky gut include celiac disease, Crohn's disease, rheumatoid arthritis, allergies, multiple sclerosis, lupus, thyroid disease, and pernicious anemia.

Gluten is just one of the components of grains that can threaten intestinal and systemic health. Grains also contain lectins, which are carbohydrate-binding proteins found in a large number of plant foods. In plants, lectins, which can be poisonous to insects, serve as a natural pesticide. They serve as protection for the grain against becoming extinct. When ingested by humans, lectins can cause biochemical changes to the cellular lining of the intestines; these changes contribute to leaky gut, poor absorption of nutrients (including other proteins), and the death of intestinal cells.

Since our bodies can't digest lectins to break them down into amino acids, lectins pass through damaged intestinal lining as whole protein molecules, notes a 1999 review in the *British Medical Journal.*[6] The immune system identifies these protein molecules as foreign invaders that must be neutralized, springs into action, and sets off an antigen/antibody response that can cause inflammation and allergies.

Lectins also strip the intestinal lining of its protective mucus, making it susceptible to infection by H. pylori, a bacterium linked to duodenal ulcers and stomach cancer.

Many foods contain lectins, but some have especially high concentrations of the protein, including wheat, rice, oats, millet, rye, corn, quinoa, dairy,

[CARBS AND CHOLESTEROL]

For most people, eating foods with cholesterol has little impact on raising the level of cholesterol in their blood. Paradoxically, high-sugar foods and processed foods have a much greater impact on raising blood cholesterol than do cholesterol-containing foods. That's right, indulging in brownies and processed, sugary foods is worse for you than eating eggs.

The sugar and simple carbohydrates in many grain products (including bread, white rice, white flour, cakes, and cookies) spike insulin production, which can lead to insulin resistance. What's more, excess sugar is converted to palmitic acid in your liver, which then floods the bloodstream with triglycerides. These excessive triglycerides create the perfect scenario for the processing of VLDL (very low-density lipoprotein), which ultimately contributes to increased production of LDL—the worst, most dangerous kind of blood cholesterol.

legumes (including dry beans and peanuts), soy, and vegetables in the nightshade family—peppers, eggplant, potatoes, and tomatoes.

In large amounts, lectins can be toxic and can lead to many health issues, including insulin resistance, allergy, headache, gastrointestinal disorders, fibromyalgia, dementia, autoimmune disorders, infections, heart disease, migraines, polycystic ovary syndrome, autism, cancer, heart disease, and chronic fatigue.

These symptoms of lectin sensitivity are similar to those of gluten sensitivity, and the two are often confused.

The presence of lectins in legumes is a major reason that I advise consuming legumes like a condiment if you consume them at all. Most of us don't have the enzymes in our guts that are needed to break down the carbohydrates in some beans (especially harder beans such as kidney and navy beans). The phytic acid in beans also hinders digestion and can leach minerals from your body. That's why they cause so much bloating and flatulence. Doesn't it seem that if your body was meant to eat beans and other legumes, you'd have the enzymes necessary to digest and process them? Soaking beans for a minimum of twenty-four hours (preferably forty-eight hours), fermenting them (or consuming them with fermented foods), and sprouting them before eating can help decrease the lectin concentration.

The lectin story is a little mysterious because not all variations of a food type, like beans, pose the same problem. Lentils (a softer bean) don't have the same lectin concentration as other beans. The lectins in tomatoes are found primarily in the seeds, so deseeding helps dramatically. Cooking lectin-rich vegetables and grains *thoroughly* helps to destroy them in some foods. And fermenting foods decreases lectin concentration and neutralizes their effect.

TURNING OVER A NEW LEAF

WHEN I WAS A VEGETARIAN, grains and legumes made up about 30 percent of my diet. When I discovered how detrimental they are, I ditched them and have never felt better. Now, on the rare occasion that I do consume legumes, I make sure they are fresh, soaked overnight, well rinsed (to remove some of the lectins), and thoroughly cooked (to break down the lectins).

I stay away from grains, too, and I avoid gluten in all forms. If you do choose to eat grains, eat them whole and in their natural state rather than having them in processed foods such as bread. Consuming sprouted grains is best. Choose quinoa (which is actually a seed), buckwheat, and amaranth, and consume them as you would a condiment—in very small amounts.

I'm not saying that all grains and legumes are evil and that no one should eat them. Grains and legumes can be a great source of fiber and protein, especially for vegetarians. And not everyone is super sensitive to them. But grains are definitely on the "proceed with caution" list because they can cause so many problems on a larger scale.

Even if you can tolerate them, you risk developing sensitivities to them by eating them in excessive amounts. The bottom line is that they just don't contain as much nutritional value as fruits and vegetables. They're really not worth the trouble they can cause.

NOT SOY WHOLESOME

MODERN COMMERCIAL MARKETING WOULD HAVE you believe that soy is the miracle food that can replace meat and dairy. This is not the case. Although soy does seem to offer some health benefits when eaten in moderation, I believe the disadvantages outweigh the advantages. One of the problems with soy is that we are inundated with it—commercial salad dressings and other products contain soy oil, many processed foods are manufactured with soy protein isolate, and soy chips claim space next to potato chips and other junk snacks on supermarket shelves. Constant exposure to soy can lead to increased sensitivity.

Soy also contains components that are harmful to our health, such as the following:

- A high concentration of lectins (which are more difficult to destroy with heat than in almost any other lectin-containing food).

- Large amounts of omega-6 fatty acids, which in excessive amounts can lead to systemic inflammation.

- Phytoestrogens (plant estrogens) that may or may not contribute to the development of cancer, early puberty in girls, and impotence in men.

- A substantial amount of phytic acid, which is believed to reduce the absorption of vital minerals.

- Soy is not good for blood sugar, either. Like milk protein, soy protein causes the liver to produce IGF-1, which in excess is associated with several kinds of cancer.

CORN: THE KING OF A FAST-FOOD NATION

CORN IS SOMETIMES REFERRED TO as the King of Crops because of its unparalleled abundance in America. I think the King of Chronic Disease would probably be a better title for this overgrown grain. American farmers grow even more corn than soy, and corn derivatives end up in nearly every packaged food. Corn oil, corn syrup, cornstarch, corn alcohol, ethanol, and even corn *gluten* (and many, *many* more corn products) have infiltrated nearly all fast foods, processed foods, pesticides, and even many shampoos, body powder, and other toiletry products.

Corn has the most unhealthy fatty-acid profile of just about any grain. It is very high in omega-6 fatty acids and very low in omega-3 fatty acids, giving it a health-sapping omega ratio. Besides being a breeding ground for twenty-two different fungi, corn is high in aspergillus, a type of mold. Like most grains, corn damages the intestinal lining, creates intestinal permeability, and disrupts blood sugar balance because the lipid transfer protein (protein on the surface of cells in corn) is indigestible for humans. Lipid transfer protein survives cooking and it is linked to corn allergies that produce symptoms such as skin rashes, asthma, swelling of mucous membranes, diarrhea, and vomiting.

Archeological records of Native American and Mayan cultures reveal that when these tribes traded their traditional hunter-gatherer lifestyle for a corn-based diet, they began suffering from malnutrition, osteoporosis, and anemia (caused by phytates in corn that leach minerals such as iron and calcium from the bones and blood). Also, the massive overexposure to corn-containing products leads to food sensitivities and allergies.

What's worse, today's corn doesn't resemble the wild, ancient corn of our

WHAT ARE GM FOODS?

GM foods have had their DNA altered in some way through genetic engineering. This is done for several reasons, such as creating crops that grow faster, are more robust, resist pests and weeds, and can withstand extreme weather conditions.

While GM foods have been sold in stores since about 1996, that's not long enough to give scientists a clear picture of whether genetic modification causes long-term health effects in humans. Recent years have seen a dramatic rise in several health problems, including obesity, type 2 diabetes, allergies, and autism. There's no way to know for sure whether GM foods play a part in any of these conditions.

The most commonly grown GM foods include soybeans, corn, cotton, canola, rice, and alfalfa. The United States is the world's leader in growing GM crops.

Some countries require GM foods to be labeled as such, but the United States does not because the U.S. Food and Drug Administration considers them safe for human consumption. I find this troubling. In the United States, the demand is growing for GM foods to be labeled as such and is sparking referendum votes in some municipalities.

---

ancestors. (The same is true of wheat.) The wild form of corn was classified as a grass. Domestication of corn crops transformed it into a tall stalk that produces grain kernels. Food engineering and hybridization have made even more changes to corn.

Corn gluten is actually used as an herbicide to kill certain seeds and herbs. When other plants die they decompose and serve as a fertilizer to other plants. Not corn! To make matters worse, the pollen from corn, which is spread by wind, kills monarch butterflies (considered a primary species for conservation) and caterpillars that munch on nearby ragweed. The toxic substance in corn that kills butterflies and flying pests is found in Bt-corn (Bt is bacterium Bacillus thuringiensis). Bt-corn is a genetically engineered corn that is used in 85 percent of the crops in the United States.

Corn is everywhere, but that doesn't mean you have to eat it. Although it can be tough to avoid all corn products completely, you can cut way down on it by avoiding processed foods. Simply by following the Omni Diet and preparing meals using recipes from the Omni Diet—which contain no corn products—you'll be able to renounce your citizenship in the corn-fed nation and ensure that corn is not king in your diet.

8

[Wise Up to Sweet Lies and Low-Fat Fibs]

Don't dig your grave with your own knife and fork.

—ENGLISH PROVERB

MANY PEOPLE CHOOSE REDUCED-FAT FOODS and sugar-free drinks, thinking these are healthy alternatives to their fatty, sugary cousins. Nothing could be further from the truth. These "diet" foods contain ingredients that have the potential to spike blood sugar, raise insulin levels, trigger inflammation, harm the liver, raise cholesterol, contribute to hypertension, erode the brain, and even increase the risk of cancer, liver disease, and intestinal problems.

When food manufacturers remove sugar and fat from processed products, they often replace them with harmful additives, chemicals, preservatives, and fillers, none of which has any nutritive value, and some of which are potentially toxic. Ingredient lists in these diet foods often include fake fats, cheap oils, chemical sweeteners, refined sugars, salt, and a huge list of chemicals that sound like they belong in rocket fuel rather than food.

If you've relied on reduced-fat food products and artificially sweetened beverages, it's time to make a seismic shift in the way you eat. Despite manufacturer claims, these foods are not healthy replacements for high-fat, high-calorie, high-sugar foods.

In fact, reduced-fat and artificially sweetened foods are fundamental barriers to weight loss and optimal health.

Toss the reduced-fat cookies. Dump the diet soda. It's time to stop believing the lies and myths surrounding reduced-fat and sugar-free diet foods, and to start eating wholesome, unprocessed foods that provide nourishment instead of harm.

THE FACTS BEHIND ARTIFICIAL SWEETENERS

USING ARTIFICIAL SWEETENERS MAKES A certain amount of sense, philosophically. Sugar tastes good, but is high in calories and terrible for our bodies. So when food manufacturers figured out ways to remove sugar and its calories from foods without taking away the sweet taste, people began to load their grocery carts with artificially sweetened beverages and other products. Chemical sweeteners seemed like the answer to sugar-lovers' prayers.

Americans drink 450 calories a day, twice as many as we did thirty years ago. Sweetened coffee drinks, alcoholic drinks, and super-size sodas have 400 to 700 calories or more. For some people, simply switching to water with lemon can slash substantial calories.

I commend people for making an effort to eat less sugar. But like so many too-good-to-be-true products, artificial sweeteners turned out not to be the panacea people hoped for. Unfortunately, switching from sugar to artificial sweeteners is jumping from the frying pan into the fire. (Just the word "artificial" should tip you off on that.)

Although they are calorie-free, artificial sweeteners are not a benign replacement for sugar. They don't lead to massive reductions in calorie intake or dramatically lower blood sugar levels. They don't even appear to help with weight loss. The great big fat promises made about artificial sweeteners have turned out to be sweet little lies.

For some people, artificial sweeteners turn out to be the cause of mysterious symptoms. That's what happened with Dennis, who took part in one of my Omni Diet classes. Dennis had high blood pressure, migraines, and unexplained nasal congestion. Dennis loved to drink coffee—a lot of coffee—flavored with half-and-half and sugar. As he learned about the negative effects dairy and sugar have on the body, he gave them up. But he didn't like his coffee black, so instead of sugar and half-and-half, he stirred in artificial sweetener and artificial creamer. I was not surprised when he told me that his headaches and congestion got worse.

After a little education Dennis agreed to cut back on coffee. When he enjoyed his favorite brew he opted for coconut milk and stevia instead of all the artificial junk. Much to his surprise his migraines improved, his congestion disappeared, and his blood pressure began to fall.

The past few decades have seen a huge increase in the consumption of artificial sweeteners. Artificial sweeteners or sugar substitutes are used in place of sugar to sweeten foods and beverages. Manufacturers rely on them to sweeten diet soft drinks, sugar-free desserts, gum, gelatin, jellies, fruit juice, yogurt, and nutrition bars. They're also found in sugar-free candies and desserts marketed as being "diabetic-friendly."

Food manufacturers claim these foods are healthy options for people trying to cut back on sugar, control their diabetes, and lose weight. But the facts tell a different story—a story that can be very surprising to people who don't realize the risks they're taking by relying so heavily on these foods. Let's take a look at some of the claims made about the health benefits of artificial sweeteners.

CLAIM: Artificial sweeteners lower insulin levels.
FACT: Artificial sweeteners have actually been shown to *elevate* insulin levels because they send a signal to the brain that "something sweet is coming" even though it's not. So even when they don't elevate blood *sugar,* they can still raise blood *insulin*. In a 2013 study from Washington University School of Medicine in St. Louis, the insulin levels of 20 obese people rose as much as 20 percent after they sipped drinks sweetened with sucralose.[1] Consuming artificial sweeteners on a regular basis can contribute to chronic high insulin, which is harmful to your body and raises risk of heart disease, diabetes, metabolic syndrome, and other health problems.

CLAIM: Artificially sweetened foods and beverages fill you up and satisfy hunger.
FACT: Artificial sweeteners can distort metabolic hormonal messages and *trigger hunger*—but because they provide no calories, your hunger goes unappeased. Unsatiated, your body continues to send hunger signals until you eat something with calories. An aptly titled 2010 Yale University report, "Gain Weight by 'Going Diet?' Artificial Sweeteners and the Neurobiology of Sugar Cravings," notes that like sugar, artificial sweeteners light up areas of the brain associated with pleasure but don't affect areas involved with satisfaction. The result? Cravings and hunger.[2]

CLAIM: Eating artificially sweetened foods helps you lose weight.
FACT: Artificial sweeteners may lower metabolism, leading to *weight gain*. In

research studies, rats fed artificially sweetened foods have been found to have slower metabolisms and greater weight gain than those given sugar-sweetened foods—despite the fact that the rats who ate sugary foods consumed more calories than those who ate artificially sweetened foods. In another, rats that ate saccharin-sweetened yogurt ate more calories and put on more body fat, say researchers from Purdue University. The amazing part? When the scientists measured the animals' core temperatures, they were higher in those that got real sugar but didn't rise in those who got the artificial sweetener—a sign that their metabolism didn't undergo the natural rev-up that happens when we eat.[3] Part of the reason for this is that when people eat sugar-free foods they believe they can consume larger quantities. It's no surprise that as the use of artificial sweeteners has grown in the United States, so has the obesity epidemic.

CLAIM: Artificially sweetened foods satisfy your sweet tooth.
FACT: Artificial sweeteners *contribute to sugar cravings* and sugar addiction because they are so much sweeter than sugar. If you're trying to break your dependence on sugar and simple carbohydrates, drinking diet soda and eating artificially sweetened foods will only sabotage you and keep you hooked on sugar even if you don't eat sugar.

CLAIM: Artificial sweeteners are manufactured in a safe, nontoxic way.
FACT: Some artificial sweeteners are created by chemical processes that require the use of strong chemicals, some of which are known to harm the body.

- Saccharin (brand name Sweet'N Low), which is made through the chemical reaction of anthranilic acid, nitrous oxide, sulfur dioxide, chlorine (a known carcinogen), and ammonia, was linked to bladder cancer in rats in the 1970s. However, later studies did not provide clear evidence of an association between saccharin and cancer in humans. In 2000, saccharin was taken off the U.S. National Toxicology Program's list of human carcinogens. But new research indicates that rodents actually have an enzyme that gives them the ability to metabolize these chemicals better than humans can.

- Sucralose (brand name Splenda) is produced by chlorinating sugar. While this is a simplified explanation, that's basically how it's made. Being a sugar derivative, sucralose has been shown to increase hba1c—a measure of long-term blood sugar levels that looks at the amount of sugar that's glommed on to hemoglobin in the bloodstream. An unpublished British study described in the European Commission's 2000 report on sucralose found that people with type 2 diabetes who consumed

OMNI DIET POSTCARD

"Twelve weeks ago I started this amazing journey that has changed my life for the better. I now know how strong I am, and that I can overpower any obstacle that comes my way. Sugar had become a silent drug that ran through my body. I never realized that yogurt, pasta, diet soda, too much fruit, and artificial pink, blue, and yellow packages could do so much harm. I was addicted to sugar, and I thought I was eating correctly!" —DEBBE

sucralose daily for 6 months saw insulin levels rise.[4] There has also been some concern about the effect of sucralose on the thymus—sucralose may decrease the size of the thymus by up to 40 percent,[5] which can affect immunity. And it has been shown to decrease the amount of good bacteria in the gut by up to 50 percent, while increasing the pH. A 2008 lab study from Duke University Medical Center found that when rats were fed sucralose for 12 weeks, their levels of beneficial bacteria decreased.[6] These studies, conducted on rats, haven't been linked to humans at this time, but still, they raise enough concerns to leave me feeling wary about the safety of sucralose.

CLAIM: Aspartame, the world's bestselling sweetener, is also the safest.

FACT: It is my understanding that, according to the FDA Adverse Event Reporting System, some 75 percent of *all* complaints about food products to the FDA are related to aspartame even though the FDA approved its use more than thirty years ago. And the FDA acknowledges that less than 1 percent of people report side effects they are experiencing. People point to aspartame as the source of memory loss, frequent headaches, depression, gastrointestinal discomfort, violent rages, and abnormal brain function. Although most of this evidence is anecdotal, there is a school of scientific thought that backs it up. For example, Dr. Russell Blaylock, a world-renowned neurosurgeon, has written numerous papers and books about the devastating, neurotoxic effects of aspartame.

Aspartame (brand names NutraSweet and Equal) was approved in 1981 by the FDA. While there has been ongoing debate and contradictory studies about the association of aspartame with cancer, there is no dispute that aspartic acid is detrimental to brain and neurological function.

In my opinion, aspartame is not safe to eat. Natural-healing sources that I have consulted say when aspartame is heated to 89°F during cooking or is destabilized by food processing, it breaks down into phenylalanine, aspartic acid, and methanol—another name for wood alcohol, which is a neurotoxin. Phenylalanine decreases serotonin levels in the brain. Aspartic acid is an excitotoxin associated with brain tumors, multiple sclerosis, epilepsy, chronic fatigue syndrome, Parkinson's disease, Alzheimer's disease, intellectual disability, lymphoma, birth defects, fibromyalgia, and diabetes. Methanol breaks down further into formaldehyde and formalin, potent neurotoxins and known carcinogens, and formic acid, which can cause kidney damage. These are poisons that can't be readily cleared from the body, so they accumulate in it over time.

Think with me for a minute: If aspartame breaks down to potent neurotoxins at 89°F, we have a big problem! Unless you are a vampire your body temperature is about 98.6°F. In other words, there is no *safe* way to consume this substance!

Aspartame has a pH of 4.3, which is very acidic. (The pH scale ranges from 0 to 14, with 7 considered neutral. Numbers below 7 are more acidic; numbers above 7 are more alkaline.) Eating a high-acid diet lowers your body's ability to repair damaged cells and fight genetic mutations.

SUGAR ALCOHOLS: THE GOOD, THE BAD, AND THE UGLY

SUGAR ALCOHOLS CAN BE A good sugar substitute for most people (unless you have Crohn's disease or IBS), although this isn't a black-and-white matter. Erythritol is my favorite sugar alcohol—but before I get ahead of myself, let's take a closer look at the good and bad of sugar alcohols.

THE GOOD: Sugar alcohols occur naturally in many plants and fruits and are now being widely marketed as sugar substitutes. They are neither sugar nor alcohol. But they are carbohydrates—their chemical structure resembles that of half sugar and half alcohol. Sugar alcohols are a decent sweetener (used in moderation) for people with insulin resistance and diabetes. Some of them will raise blood sugar and cause the body to release insulin, but *much more slowly* and not as much as sugar does (except erythritol, which doesn't raise blood sugar or insulin).

THE BAD: Because sugar alcohols are not technically sugar, manufacturers can misleadingly advertise food containing them as "sugar-free." But remember, they still count as a unique class of carbs, which ultimately count as sugar and can lead to insulin resistance if overconsumed. When calculating the amount of "sugar" that these sweeteners contain, take the total carbohydrate count, and divide it in half.

THE UGLY: The body can't digest sugar alcohols easily, which is why they don't spike insulin quickly. They remain in the gastrointestinal tract much longer than sugar—so long that they actually start to ferment. This can lead to bloating, gas, stomach pain, and diarrhea in some people—especially those who have IBS. So I wouldn't suggest consuming a large dessert sweetened with sugar alcohols if you are on a hot date.

Not all sugar alcohols affect people the same way or have the same composition. For example, maltitol tends to cause more GI distress for many people, and it contains a higher level of carbohydrates than some of the others. Xylitol does have a significant calorie and carbohydrate content, but it tends to cause less GI distress for many people and inhibits the growth of dental cavities, which is why it is commonly added to sugar-free gum.

Erythritol is my favorite sugar alcohol to cook with. It comes as crystals that resemble sugar or in a powdered form. It has no calories and doesn't spike blood sugar or insulin. While erythritol causes less GI distress than most other sugar alcohols, it should still be used with caution. People with IBS, IBD, or Crohn's disease should avoid using sugar alcohols, which can trigger a reaction.

On a food label, sugar alcohols are not listed as sugar but are figured into the total carbohydrate tally: Ten grams of sugar alcohols count as 5 grams of carbs. Sugar alcohols are found in manufactured foods such as chewing gum, toothpaste, desserts, and baked goods. To figure out if foods contain sugar alcohols, look for these names on ingredient labels:

- erythritol
- hydrogenated starch hydrolysates
- isomalt
- lactitol
- maltitol
- mannitol
- sorbitol
- xylitol

A SAFER SWEETENER

IF YOU LIKE A LITTLE sweetness in your tea or smoothies, I recommend stevia, which is a much safer option than sugar or artificial sweeteners. While I have a personal bias toward stevia as a sweetener (because it has the least reported problems, and the greatest reported health claims), I must call a spade a spade. Unless you are crushing stevia leaves and using them to sweeten your favorite drink, we're not talking about a totally *natural* sweetener.

The stevia leaf is an herb. Its leaves are ten to fifteen times sweeter than sugar. You can buy stevia plants at nurseries or grow them from seed, and use their leaves as natural sweeteners. That, my friends, qualifies as natural!

You can also buy stevia extract. It is extracted from stevia leaves, which are dried with a water-extraction process. It is refined using ethanol, methanol, and crystallization. It then goes through ultrafiltration and nanofiltration to remove those alcohols. (Be sure the brand you buy has no alcohol remaining in it.) This process doesn't technically qualify as natural. But unlike the process used with aspartame, the alcohols are removed and the end product doesn't decompose to formaldehyde and formalin in your system.

Stevia extract is as much as two hundred to three hundred times sweeter than sugar, so you need only the tiniest amount. If you use too much, you may taste its bitter licorice-like aftertaste. Use it sparingly until you get the hang of it. (My favorite brand is Sweet Leaf.) For many uses I prefer vanilla or chocolate-flavored stevia—it tastes less bitter if you happen to use too much.

Stevia (the leaf) has been used in South America for centuries and in Japan for decades. So far, there's no evidence that stevia is anything but safe. Some early studies (done with the extract) suggested that it might cause genetic damage in the people who consumed it, but the studies turned out to be flawed because the data were mishandled.[7]

Stevia does not impact blood sugar levels the way sugar does, and it does not acidify the system the way toxic sugar substitutes do. There is some evidence to suggest that it may stabilize blood sugar levels, enhance glucose tolerance, and reduce blood pressure[8]—but more research is needed to figure that out for sure.

If you take blood pressure medication or medication for diabetes, use stevia with caution. There is some evidence that it may act synergistically with these medications and could cause hypotension (low blood pressure) and hypoglycemia (low blood sugar).

SUGAR BY ANY OTHER NAME? STILL *SUGAR!*

WHAT WE CALL SUGAR, OR table sugar, is sucrose. (Sometimes it's also called saccharose.) By now I'm sure you understand why sugar is so toxic to your body—it raises blood sugar, causes rapid releases of insulin, is full of empty calories, feeds cancer cells, and causes so many other unhealthy reactions in the body. And although sucrose is only half glucose, it is also half fructose, which as we've already discussed is poisonous to the liver.

In an effort to provide sweet options to the people who choose not to eat sugar, food manufacturers—as well as good-intentioned but misinformed nutrition "experts"—recommend swapping sugar with natural sweeteners such as honey and maple syrup. Don't believe the claims that these sweeteners are wholesome, healthy substitutes for sugar. Whether it comes from a beehive, a maple tree, or any other natural source, sugar is sugar. Sure, these foods are often less processed than table sugar, so you may feel better about using them. But their effect on your blood sugar, insulin, liver, and cholesterol are the same. That said, there are some subtle differences among them.

Here's the scoop on "natural" sweeteners:

HONEY. The sweet nectar made by bees affects blood sugar in much the same way that table sugar does. Like table sugar, it is nearly equal parts fructose and glucose, but almost 18 percent of honey is made up of water. However, it does seem to have minimal health benefits that are not seen with table

---

OMNI MOTIVATION BLAST

TAKE A LEAP OF FAITH

When you first cut sugar out of your diet, you'll miss it. But your taste will change quickly. I know this is hard to believe, but you have to have faith that it will happen. *Within a matter of days,* you'll no longer need refined sugars to satisfy your sweet tooth. You won't need as much salt to flavor foods. The taste of pure, healthy food in its natural state will shine as it inches out from under the shadow of added sugar, salt, artificial flavorings, and fake fats. The nutty, complex flavors and spices and herbs will captivate your taste buds.

Try to be patient while you wait for this transformation to take place. Believe that it will happen, even when it seems that it won't. Soon you'll taste foods in a whole new way, and you'll rediscover the joy of eating.

sugar, because it contains trace amounts of vitamins and minerals and small amounts of antioxidants. But it's easy to get these nutrients elsewhere, so nutrition is not a reason to add honey to your diet.

If you do choose to use honey, I recommend raw, unfiltered, unpasteurized honey because pasteurization kills any live enzymes and nutritional benefits that honey may have. Although it is a natural sweetener, it should be used in very minimal amounts. And it should never be given to children under the age of one year because it may carry the bacteria that cause botulism, which is a serious illness for anyone but can be fatal for babies and people in poor health.

Here are a couple of interesting facts about honey: Some studies have shown it has anti-inflammatory and antibacterial properties[9]—for example, it is sometimes used as a topical wound treatment. Wild honey that is local to your own region may also improve allergies. It contains small amounts of the pollen you are exposed to in your area. Some natural healers say that consuming a small amount—about 1 teaspoon a day (if you are not insulin resistant or diabetic)—acts almost like an allergy vaccine. However, if you have extreme allergies, don't try it.

AGAVE NECTAR. Please don't send me hate mail when you read this—I'm only the messenger. Agave nectar is extracted from the agave plant. Because

As you wean yourself off unhealthy foods, use these super swap strategies:

- Drink green tea or herbal tea with a few drops of stevia instead of coffee. My favorite "comfort drink" is sugar-free, steamed almond milk with a bag of green chai tea and a few drops of cinnamon-flavored stevia. This is a guilt-free "tea latte."
- Use a little light coconut milk in your tea or coffee instead of half-and-half or soy creamer.
- Drink sparkling water sweetened with root beer–flavored stevia instead of diet soda.
- Squeeze lemon or lime or a few drops of lemon-flavored stevia into seltzer, and drink it instead of wine. This is a great drink for parties when you want to have a social drink but don't want to consume alcohol.
- Enjoy almond milk instead of dairy milk or soy milk.
- Replace candy with Brain on Joy bars. They taste exactly like chocolate-almond candy, but they are sweetened with maltitol. This is a great alternative when you have PMS. But they should still be eaten only as an occasional treat. See the source list at the back of the book for online sourcing.
- Replace ice cream with avocado gelato. See recipe on page 386.
- Eat half an apple with almond butter instead of cookies and candy.
- Eat 1/4 cup raw, unsalted nuts and one piece of 70 percent cocoa dark chocolate instead of muffins, candies, and cookies.

of its high fructose content (it varies depending on its source, but it is generally *80 to 90 percent fructose—yikes!*) agave has been hyped as being the best sweetener for people with diabetes. Fructose doesn't cause the same insulin spike reaction as sucrose, so it is often referred to as a low-glycemic sweetener. This is a travesty! Fructose is *toxic* to the liver and ultimately leads to metabolic syndrome, fatty liver, and insulin resistance. Like all sugars—actually, even *more* than all sugars—agave should be avoided or used in very small amounts.

PURE MAPLE SYRUP. Like honey and table sugar, maple syrup is nearly equal parts fructose and glucose. It is also 18 to 20 percent water. Maple syrup has trace minerals and significant amounts of zinc and manganese,

Traditional hunter-gatherer tribes of modern times such as the Aborigines (Australia), Kalahari (Africa), and Pirahã (Amazon River in Brazil) continue to live on wild game, fish, nuts, seeds, and berries. Their diets average between 22 percent and 25 percent of calories from fat. Tribes that have not been Westernized have extremely low rates of chronic disease, showing nearly no evidence of heart disease, diabetes, or cancer. They also demonstrate exceptional physical fitness and low body fat.

Population studies done on Aborigine tribes that shifted from a hunter-gatherer diet to a Western diet show a striking and frightening change. Within a matter of a few short years, Aborigine tribes that had been nearly free of chronic diseases suddenly show the same rate of disease as European, Australian, and Western cultures. A 2006 study from Sweden's Uppsala University found rising rates of heart disease among reindeer-herding Sami people from Scandinavia's far north, possibly due to adoption of a more Western lifestyle.[10]

But probably the most striking paradox regarding fat consumption is seen with the Inuit tribes of Canada and Alaska. The Inuit are famous for a diet consisting of 50 percent to 75 percent fat from whale blubber, seals, and mammals. About 25 percent to 30 percent of their diet is protein. The remaining nutrition comes from the vegetation, vitamins, and minerals found in the stomachs and livers of the animals they consume. Prior to being recently swayed to a Westernized diet, these tribes had virtually no reportable cases of diabetes, hypertension, or heart disease. This sad statistic demonstrates the devastation that the foods found in the standard American diet have on health within a short time. It's not the *healthy* fat that's the problem. The problem is the combination of *processed and fried* fats, drowning in sugar, topped with some artificial fillers and flavors.

so it is slightly preferable to table sugar. But use caution when purchasing maple syrup. Since it is expensive to manufacture, many companies have figured out cheap ways to capitalize on this tasty syrup. Most pancake syrups have *no maple* in them at all—they are primarily made of high-fructose corn syrup and artificial flavoring. That's why they're called *pancake* syrup and not *maple* syrup. Not only do they lack pure maple syrup's minimal health benefits, but they are truly atrocious for your health. Stay away from pancake syrup and use pure maple syrup only in minimal amounts, like all sugars. If you use it, choose grade B maple syrup, which has more trace minerals than grade A has.

FAT-FREE FALLACIES

JUST AS WE'VE BEEN SOLD a load of misinformation about artificial sweeteners, we've been asked to swallow the misleading claims about highly processed fat-free and reduced-fat foods. I'll never forget a couple of yogurt labels I came across a few years ago. One label was for the full-fat version, and the other label was for the fat-free version. True to its claims, the fat-free version had zero fat. But when I read the label I saw that the fat had been replaced with sugars, artificial flavors, and starchy fillers. What was astonishing was that the fat-free version was *50 percent higher in calories* and had *21 grams of additional sugar*! I opted for the 4 grams of extra fat in the regular version.

I wasn't surprised to see that the reduced-fat yogurt had way more carbohydrates than the full-fat version. But I was shocked when I realized that the addition of all that sugar to the reduced-fat yogurt had actually raised its calorie tally higher than that of the full-fat yogurt by 50 percent! Of course, this was back when everyone thought carbohydrates wouldn't make you fat, only fat would make you fat.

This is one of many fat paradoxes I've come across since America jumped onto the reduced-fat bandwagon.

So why did Americans become more obsessed with the idea of eating a low-fat diet than any other country on the planet? It started after the American Heart Association launched a campaign to reduce saturated fat in the standard American diet. The message everyone heard was that they should cut out as much fat as possible from their diets—not just saturated fat, but all fat. Fat was demonized as the cause of heart disease and many other health problems; diets with as little as 5 percent of calories from fat were promoted as being healthy.

The media hyped the message, and of course the advertising industry saw a rich opportunity, and seized it. The Fat-Free Era was born! Eating fat made us fat, and cutting back on fat would make us thin and healthy. Instead of eating fat, we were urged to fill up on fat-free carbohydrates—pretzels, bagels, crackers, and snacks. This advice was based on little more than a vague feeling that since the brain and body use carbohydrates for energy, and because carbohydrates are not fat, we could—and should—eat them in endless quantities. Carbohydrates wouldn't make us fat, the experts said—only fat could make us fat!

Of course, no one actually bothered to check all this out before presenting it as fact, and it backfired in a big, fat way. The single-minded focus on lowering dietary fat caused three huge nutritional problems:

1. Although it's true that certain fats—for example, trans fats and *some* saturated fats—do contribute to heart disease and other conditions, other kinds of fats—such as omega-3 fatty acids and monounsaturated fats—are actually *necessary* for optimal health. They help our heart, brain (which is 60 percent fat), and body function well and protect us from disease. And although it sounds paradoxical, we actually need some dietary fat in order to burn body fat. In addition, extreme low-fat diets are associated with increased risk of depression, suicide, and neurodegenerative diseases.

2. When manufacturers remove fats from foods, they usually replace them with carbohydrates, fake fats, artificial sweeteners, salt, and a long list of other unhealthy ingredients. Instead of whole, natural foods that contained healthy fats, such as avocados, olive oil, fatty fish, nuts, and seeds—foods that we now know are incredibly healthy (and even *essential*)—people were urged to choose highly processed, unnatural foods full of carbohydrates, sugar, and every kind of additive simply to avoid the dreaded f-word.

3. With all the emphasis on fat reduction, people began to think that *reduced-fat* meant *reduced-calorie*, even though many reduced-fat foods actually had as many calories—or even more—than full-fat foods.

The evidence is finally clear: An appropriate amount of healthy fat is not what makes people fat. *Sugar* makes people fat! *Sugar* and simple carbs increase triglycerides, which convert cholesterol to the dangerous, dense form. Not all LDL cholesterol is the same. Big fluffy molecules are less damaging to arteries than small dense molecules. Think of repeatedly throwing a tennis ball at a wall. It doesn't do much damage. But if you repeatedly throw a golf ball at the wall, it begins to cause significant damage in a short time. Well, sugar helps to convert large fluffy molecules of LDL into small dense molecules, which are far more damaging to arteries.

During the all-fat-is-bad fad, Americans gorged on fat-free cookies, drowned their salads in fat-free dressings, gobbled up giant chunks of fat-free cheese (yuck!), and watched movies while noshing on giant tubs of fat-free butter-flavored popcorn. And, while chasing the reduced-fat holy grail, they consumed more carbohydrates, sugar, and calories than ever before.

This triggered a health disaster that is still ongoing. In the early 1980s obesity in America went from 12 percent to 25 percent. That, my friends, is called an epidemic! There was also an increase in sudden cardiac arrest among people who were unknowingly starving their bodies of essential fatty acids in an attempt to eradicate fat from their diets.

Our bodies need healthy fats! Without fat, our bodies can't effectively use fat-soluble vitamins such as A, D, E, and K. Fats also play an important part in the health of your brain function, cellular communication, production of important hormones, skin, hair, body temperature . . . and weight maintenance!

THE OMNI WAY

WHEN YOU'RE ON THE OMNI Diet, you don't eat fake foods foisted on you by the corporate food giants. You don't consume chemical sweeteners that are some food manufacturer's science experiment. You eat whole, natural, nutrient-rich foods that are "manufactured" by Mother Nature, not laboratory workers. Once you break free from your addiction to unnatural food substitutes, you discover and enjoy the natural flavors of foods. You break the bonds of artificial sweeteners and reduced-fat foodlike substances and feast on real foods that you were born to eat. When you leave fake foods behind, your body will thrive and your health will soar.

DO A PERFECTIONISM SELF-CHECK

I have a tendency to be a perfectionist. As a kid, if I scored nineteen out of twenty on a test, all I could think about was the one question I'd missed, not the nineteen I answered correctly. In college, I nearly dropped an entire semester of a class because I received a C on one test. Here's a way to do a perfectionism self-check. On a scale of one to ten, with ten being the best score, rate how well you're doing on the Omni Diet. If you give yourself anything less than a four, I want you to stop and really think about whether that number is accurate. If you really haven't been doing a great job—you don't exercise, you eat candy bars every day, you stay up late watching movies instead of getting adequate sleep—then a low score is probably warranted and you need to be honest about the need to improve. But if you're doing mostly everything right and your score is low, that's a red flag that you're a perfectionist.

During one of my Omni Diet classes recently, I asked the participants to rate their progress on a one-to-ten scale. Then I asked them to share their ratings with the class. We were all shocked to find out that one of the women who was doing an absolutely fantastic job had given herself a two. She commented that since she didn't meet *all* of her goals, she believed she had failed! More than that, she was certain that she would fail this program like all the other programs she had failed in the past. We did some powerful interventions to kill her ANT (Automatic Negative Thought) infestation. She has since lost 18 pounds and continues to do a fabulous job!

If you're a perfectionist, try to work on making your expectations more reasonable. Pay attention to your internal dialogue—are you too hard on yourself when you make mistakes? Do you tell yourself that if you aren't perfect you are a failure? Remind yourself that not only is perfection unattainable, but it's an excuse to fail. Perfectionism keeps people from striving for success. And focus on the fact that being a perfectionist and filling your head with negative self-talk does nothing to empower you—in fact it almost guarantees that you will fail.

PART THREE

HEALTH BOOSTERS

9

Mind the Gap with Dietary Supplements

Mainstream medicine would be very different if they focused on prevention even half as much as they focused on intervention.
—ANONYMOUS

At first glance, Chris looked like someone who had it all: Not only was she gorgeous, but she was fit and trim as well. Her lab numbers were pretty fantastic, too—when I looked at her blood test results, I actually felt envious. She seemed to be in perfect health.

But Chris wasn't as healthy as she looked. Terrible headaches, insomnia, and anxiety had prompted her to go to the Amen Clinics for an evaluation. Brain scans showed an overactive brain. But there was something else—Chris had also developed subtle scaly bumps on the backs of her arms.

I RECOGNIZED THESE BUMPS AS a possible sign of an omega-3 fatty acid deficiency. Lab tests backed up my hunch and showed that Chris was significantly deficient in omega-3 fatty acids.

To make matters worse, her omega-6/omega-3 ratio was way out of balance. When the ratio of omega-6 to omega-3 fatty acids is too high, there's an increase in inflammation and inflammatory diseases because pro-inflammatory omega-6 fatty acids essentially cancel out the benefits of anti-inflammatory omega-3 fatty acids. The optimal ratio is 2 to 1, and not higher than 3 to 1.

Fish oil is the best-known source of the omega-3 fatty acids EPA and DHA. But as a vegetarian, Chris wanted to stay away from fish oil. She had been taking primrose oil, which is erroneously touted as an effective vegetarian source of omega-3s. But it is far inferior to fish oil—as Chris's lab tests showed.

When I explained all this to Chris, she agreed to give fish oil a try. As I expected, her body responded in a very positive way. Within a couple of weeks she felt less anxious, she slept better, her headaches decreased, and the bumps on her arms disappeared. Chris tossed out her primrose oil and jumped onto the fish oil bandwagon for good.

Chris's story demonstrates a very important point: Even if you're eating a healthy diet—and let's face it, there are very few people who eat a perfectly nutritious diet every day—you may not be getting optimal amounts of all of the crucial nutrients your body needs for disease prevention and optimal health.

That's right. Even if you eat 10 servings of organic fruit and vegetables every day, consume proper amounts of lean protein, avoid sugar and other dietary toxins, and drink plenty of water, you may still be short on some important nutrients. (And think of what you're missing if you're not eating that kind of high-quality diet every day!)

Nutritional gaps exist in just about everyone's diet. That's the bad news. But the good news is that nutritional supplements do a fantastic job filling those gaps.

Supplements can't replace a healthy diet—we need a solid nutritional foundation provided by the nutrient-dense foods included in the Omni Diet. They also can't take the place of important health-supporting habits such as exercise, sleep, and stress relief. But supplements can pick up where food leaves off, giving our bodies some of the extra firepower they need to fight disease and protect us from the everyday assaults of the toxins that surround us, such as air pollution and pesticides. Supplements can help reduce inflammation, protect our DNA, fight the oxidative stress caused by free radicals, boost our immune system, improve our moods, and contribute to brain health.

There are a lot of supplements out there—if you've ever walked down the supplement aisle of your local health food store or pharmacy, you know how many choices there are. Even grocery stores sell supplements these days. The key is to know *which* supplements to take and in *what quantity*. Taking the wrong amounts of the wrong supplements is not only a waste of money, but can be harmful to your health.

That's why the Omni Diet includes a clear, two-step approach to supplements that shows you exactly what supplements you should take for maximum effectiveness.

STEP 1. For overall well-being, I recommend that everyone take daily multivitamins, fish oil, vitamin D, magnesium, and probiotics.

STEP 2. For nutritional support that is targeted to your body's own individual needs, I recommend that everyone take supplements that match their *own personal health profile.*

This chapter tells you all about both steps of the Omni Diet approach to supplements. First, you'll learn about why everyone needs those five important supplements for overall well-being. Then, using a specially designed quiz, you can determine which additional supplements you need for personalized, targeted nutritional support. You'll also find out how to select supplements that are safe and effective.

BE AN EDUCATED SUPPLEMENT SHOPPER

IT'S IMPORTANT TO BE FULLY informed about supplements before you take them. Here are some things to know:

SUPPLEMENTS ARE POWERFUL. Compared with prescription drugs and many over-the-counter drugs, supplements have far fewer worrisome side effects. However, supplements are powerful, and some have the potential to cause problems. For example, St. John's wort, which many women take for depression, can alter the effectiveness of birth control pills.

SUPPLEMENTS ARE NATURAL—BUT NOT NECESSARILY BENIGN. Don't assume that because something is natural, it's guaranteed to be safe. After all, arsenic and cyanide are natural substances that are both poisonous. Read labels carefully, and don't be fooled by marketing.

DOSAGE MATTERS. Taking the right amount of supplements is important. Supplements are powerful, and taking too much can be unsafe. Just because some is good doesn't mean more is better.

PREVENTION IS CHEAPER THAN TREATMENT. Supplements are usually cheaper than prescription drugs. However, they're not covered by health insurance, so depending on what kind of policy you have, you may actually pay more out-of-pocket for supplements that *prevent* disease than for medications that *treat* disease. But as a person who has paid the price of being ill, feeling terrible, and experiencing the financial impact of accruing medical bills, I strongly encourage you to consider the price of *not* focusing on prevention. Even if you don't factor in the human cost, the financial cost of developing heart disease, diabetes, obesity, and other chronic health conditions can be devastating, even with good health insurance. It's far less costly to prevent than to treat.

QUALITY VARIES. Ingredient quality can differ among supplement manufacturers, so it's important to buy only from a reliable, trusted supplement maker. The supplement aisle is not the place to be bargain shopping—cheap supplements are likely to be made with low-quality ingredients. When you're buying supplements, try to shop at a store with educated employees. You need expert advice, not uninformed guesswork.

DO YOUR HOMEWORK. Not all supplement claims that you hear about in the media and see in advertisements are true. Dishonest supplement manufacturers use misleading marketing just to sell products. And sometimes, well-meaning but uneducated "experts" push supplements whose effectiveness is questionable. If a claim seems fishy, find out what kind of evidence stands behind it. Please see the sources reference at the back of this book for my supplement picks.

SUPPLEMENTS FOR EVERY BODY, EVERY DAY

FOR OVERALL WELL-BEING I RECOMMEND that everyone take the following five supplements: multivitamin/mineral, fish oil, vitamin D, magnesium, and probiotics.

MULTIVITAMIN/MINERAL

Multivitamin/mineral supplements are the nutritional workhorses. They cover all the nutritional bases, giving you a standard dose of most of the vitamins and minerals you need each day. They set the stage, filling in any diet deficiencies and making sure you're at a good starting point for everyday nutrition. Because these vitamins and minerals provide backup to your body as it faces daily challenges and stresses, helping with mood, mental performance, and energy levels, be sure to choose a high-quality multivitamin/mineral supplement.

FISH OIL

Fish oil contains omega-3 fatty acids. These are essential fatty acids that your body needs but can't make on its own, so it must get them from an outside source. Omega-3 fatty acids are found in fatty fish such as salmon, albacore (white) tuna, mackerel, herring, sardines, lake trout, and halibut. However, it's difficult even for people who love fish to get adequate amounts of omega-3 fatty acids. For this reason, and because omega-3 fatty acids have so many health benefits, I recommend taking an omega-3 supplement every day.

The omega-3 fatty acids in fish oil play a role in brain function, growth, development, and disease prevention. It's never too late to add this essential fat to your diet, via fish or supplements. In one notable Italian study, heart-attack survivors who got 1 gram of omega-3s from fish oil capsules daily slashed their risk for sudden cardiac death in half.[1] Other studies suggest that they:

- Reduce inflammation[2]
- Aid in weight loss[3]
- Protect against cognitive decline and Alzheimer's and are crucial for memory and optimal cognitive performance[4]
- Reduce heart disease risk by lowering cholesterol, blood pressure, and triglycerides[5]
- Prevent and treat atherosclerosis (hardening of the arteries) and lower stroke risk by slowing the development of plaque and blood clots in the blood vessels[6]
- May help lower the risk of macular degeneration[7]
- May help reduce joint pain and stiffness from arthritis[8]
- Protect against depression, ADHD, asthma, and menstrual pain[9]
- May discourage the development of some types of cancer[10]

My recommendation for most adults is to take between 1 and 2 grams of high-quality fish oil a day balanced between EPA and DHA. EPA and DHA are omega-3 fatty acids found primarily in fish. DHA is highly beneficial for brain function. EPA supports many other physical functions in the body. A healthy balance is generally 60 percent EPA to 40 percent DHA (though opinions on this vary among health-care professionals). For people with known inflammatory issues, increase the dose to 3 or 4 grams a day.

The signs and symptoms of essential fatty acid deficiencies are extensive.

SIGNS AND SYMPTOMS OF ESSENTIAL FATTY ACID DEFICIENCY

- systemic inflammation
- impaired brain function
- impaired memory
- arthritis
- asthma
- heart disease
- bumps on back of arms
- dermatitis, dry hair, dandruff
- anxiety and psychological disturbances
- impaired immunity
- tingling in arms and legs
- impaired vision
- depression

Omega-3 and omega-6 fatty acids are essential (must be obtained in the diet or from supplements, because the body cannot manufacture them). Omega-6 fatty acids are abundant in the American diet—too abundant, in fact—but omega-3s (especially EPA and DHA) are sorely lacking. The best source of EPA and DHA is fish oil. Palmitoleic acid (an omega-7 fatty acid) and lauric acid (a saturated fatty acid) are conditionally essential. Conditionally essential means that they need to be supplemented if you are not producing them or if you have increased demand for some reason (such as nutritional deficiency or illness).

VITAMIN D

Vitamin D, which is technically a hormone rather than a vitamin, is a crucial nutrient. Unfortunately, many Americans—even those who eat a good diet—are vitamin D deficient.

Your body gets vitamin D in two ways: via sunlight (the sun's ultraviolet rays must hit your skin in order for your body to manufacture vitamin D) and from a small number of foods, such as fish, eggs, and some mushrooms.

Vitamin D helps your body absorb calcium from foods and balance blood levels of calcium and phosphate, which promotes bone health. When people don't get enough vitamin D, their bones can become brittle and thin and can break more easily. Bone thinning can lead to osteoporosis.

Low levels of vitamin D also interfere with the effectiveness of leptin, the appetite hormone that tells you when you are full.

Vitamin D, which has anti-inflammatory properties, is also crucial for the health of your cells, muscles, and immune system. In one fascinating 2009 analysis of vitamin D studies, researchers from Switzerland's University Hospital Zurich found that getting 700 to 1,000 IU per day even reduced the risk of falls in older people by 19 percent—apparently by bolstering muscle strength.[11] Low levels of vitamin D have been associated with depression, autism, psychosis, Alzheimer's disease, multiple sclerosis, heart disease, diabetes, cancer, the development of body fat, and obesity.[12] If you are overweight or obese, your body may have trouble absorbing vitamin D efficiently. And here's another benefit of vitamin D—it can even help reduce chronic pain in people who suffer from fibromyalgia syndrome (FMS). In a randomized and controlled study of 30 women with FMS, Austrian researchers put half the participants on a 26-week regimen of vitamin D supplements, while the other half were given a placebo. At the end of the experiment, those who took the supplements reported greatly reduced pain levels and less incidence of morning fatigue than those in the placebo group.[13]

The current minimum recommended dose for vitamin D is 400 IUs daily, but most experts agree that this is well below the physiological needs of most individuals and instead suggest 2,000 IUs of vitamin D daily.

Having your blood tested will tell you if your vitamin D blood levels are low. Be sure to ask for the 25-hydroxy vitamin D test, which is more accurate than other vitamin D tests.

About 90 percent of the people we test at the Amen Clinics are seriously deficient in vitamin D. A "normal" vitamin D level in the blood is considered 30 to 100 nanograms per milliliter (ng/mL). However, 30 ng/mL is rock-bottom, and an optimal goal is somewhere between 50 and 80 ng/mL.

The general rule is that for each 10 ng/mL rise in vitamin-D blood level, you need to take a daily vitamin-D dose of 1,000 IUs. So if your blood test shows you're at 20 ng/dL and you want to be at 50, a daily supplement of 3,000 IUs makes sense.

Keep in mind, however, that intestinal permeability, thyroid dysfunction, and other medical issues can cause inefficient absorption of vitamin D. It's not uncommon for people to have to supplement with as much as 5,000 to 15,000 IUs per day in order to get their blood vitamin D levels up to snuff. Also, having darker skin interferes with the body's ability to use the sun to manufacture vitamin D.

MAGNESIUM

Magnesium is a mineral that is essential to good health as it is needed for more than three hundred biochemical reactions in the body. It has been shown to be helpful in calming anxiety and balancing the brain's pleasure centers, which can help reduce cravings. Tests have shown that 80 percent of the population is low in magnesium. Common problems related to magnesium deficiency include chronic fatigue, migraine headaches, anxiety, heart arrhythmia, heart disease, mood changes, and magnified PMS symptoms. Magnesium deficiency results from eating magnesium-depleting foods (such as soft drinks, drinking water with low mineral content, fluoridated water, and nearly all processed foods), and magnesium-depleted foods (including dry-roasted nuts and milled flours that have been stripped of magnesium, as well as vegetables grown in magnesium-depleted soil). The greatest cause of magnesium depletion in our society is the dramatic increase in pharmaceutical drugs that strip magnesium from our bodies—medications such as birth control pills, estrogen replacement therapy, blood pressure medication, cholesterol-lowering drugs, and diuretics.

The typical adult dose of magnesium is 400 to 1,000 mg daily, divided into three doses. If you take calcium supplements, it's best to take them at the same time as magnesium because these minerals work synergistically. The amount of magnesium you take should be about half of the amount of calcium you take.

The calcium contained in a daily multivitamin is usually fine, unless you feel you need additional calcium—for example if you have a history of osteopenia or risk of osteoporosis, or you know your diet lacks adequate calcium. My only caveat is to avoid megadoses of calcium, which may be associated with calcifications in the heart and arteries, leading to increased risk of heart attack and stroke (this is not clearly defined at this time). In a 2013 National Institutes of Health study of 388,229 people, men who took 1,000 milligrams or more of supplemental calcium daily were at 20 percent higher risk of death due to heart-related causes.[14] Instead optimize calcium absorption from food: Be sure you eat plenty of leafy green vegetables; limit your intake of highly acidic foods such as soft drinks, which leach calcium from the bones; and make sure your blood vitamin D levels are high enough (vitamin D improves calcium absorption).

PROBIOTICS

Probiotics are one of my favorite supplements—they are *so* important for good health, especially digestive health. I am not exaggerating when I tell you that some of the people I've worked with believe probiotics have changed their lives by putting an end to years of chronic diarrhea (and the poor sleep that comes with it) and improving irritable bowel disease symptoms.

For Laura, probiotics brought several very welcome health improvements. "They have allowed my body to move into an intestinal rhythm of regular bowel movements," said Laura several weeks into the Omni Diet. "My stomach has gotten noticeably smaller as the inflammation disappeared or at least greatly decreased. Plus, I no longer experience hot flashes. And this may be a strange thing to notice, but my fingernails are now stronger and grow more quickly!"

Studies suggest that probiotics may also help with nongastrointestinal conditions such as eczema and other skin rashes, vaginal infections, and immune disorders; there's also some evidence that they may lower cholesterol and help reduce the risk of some kinds of cancer.[15] In a small but encouraging German study, women who took a daily probiotic for six months even saw levels of good HDL cholesterol increase.[16]

Probiotics bring balance to your digestive system and your entire body. Your digestive system (your gut) contains billions of microorganisms (flora). Some are beneficial, and some are not. You are more likely to be healthy when the beneficial microorganisms in your gut outnumber and outpower the harmful microorganisms (toxins and pathogens). That's where probiotics come in— probiotic supplements help keep your gut flora in a healthy, life-supporting balance, by encouraging the good flora, so it outnumbers the bad flora. (The word "probiotic" comes from Latin: *pro* means "support" and *biotic* means "life.")

Gut flora can be thrown out of balance by many factors, including antibiotics, artificial sweeteners, leaky gut, poor diet, infection, stress, a high-acid diet, and even just the normal changes that occur in your digestive system as you age.

We don't know exactly how probiotic supplements work. However, it may be that the beneficial bacteria and the harmful bacteria compete for survival in your gut, and as with any battle, the more "good" soldiers you have on your side, the more likely you are to win the battle.

We do know that probiotics also stimulate an immune response, sending protective immune cells throughout your body.

Some foods, such as yogurt and fermented vegetables, contain active, live probiotic cultures. In general I don't advocate eating dairy, but a little Greek yogurt or goat's milk yogurt is the one exception for people who *know* they don't have sensitivities to casein and whey in milk. Fermented vegetables such as sauerkraut and kimchi can also add probiotics to your diet, but they can't take the place of probiotic supplements, which contain far greater numbers of bacteria.

There are a few things you should know about probiotic supplements before you start taking them.

- Microorganisms commonly found in probiotic supplements include bifidobacterium, S. thermophilus, L. bulgaricus, L. acidophilus, and L. casei. However, various blends of probiotic supplements contain different strains of microorganisms, so you may want to experiment to find the kind that works most successfully for you. Occasionally people tell me that probiotics did nothing for them, but when I ask them if they switched blends, they usually say no. Gut flora varies by person, so the probiotic that helps some people may not help others.

- One probiotic blend may become less effective over time, so feel free to try new blends after several weeks or months.

- When you start taking probiotic supplements, you may experience a week of bloating, gas, or diarrhea. This is not uncommon. I urge you to hang in there for the seven days or so it takes for your body to adjust to the massive influx of beneficial microorganisms as they colonize in your gut. If symptoms last for more than a week, try switching to a different probiotic blend. But in most cases, symptoms are temporary and are a visible sign that the beneficial microorganisms are shifting your gut flora into a more balanced state and killing off harmful microorganisms.

- Probiotics can be taken with antibiotics, but in order to ensure optimal effectiveness for both, take them several hours apart.

- It's best to choose pharmaceutical-quality probiotics. See the resources section for some of my favorites.

- Probiotic dosages are listed as colony forming units (CFUs). To decide how many CFUs you should take, consult the package directions. Generally I recommend taking a dose of 25 to 50 billion CFUs each day.

SUPPLEMENTS JUST FOR YOU

PERSONALIZING YOUR OWN SUPPLEMENT STRATEGY

Most of us can benefit from a personalized supplement plan. Unfortunately, it can be difficult for anyone who isn't trained in supplement science to wade through the many available options and figure out exactly what they need. In step 2 of the Omni Diet supplement strategy, I recommend a custom-tailored approach that best matches your individual health needs.

I'll make it simple for you.

First, look at the chart below to determine whether you have health conditions that can benefit from certain supplements.

Then, create your very own, personal, just-for-you supplement strategy by using the specially designed Omni Diet Supplement Quiz. The results will tell you exactly which supplements can best target *your* individual health and nutrition needs.

SUPPLEMENTS FOR SPECIFIC HEALTH SITUATIONS

If you have or are at high risk for *certain medical situations,* or if you have lab numbers that are off target, consider taking the following supplements in addition to the ones I will recommend later in the chapter.

CONDITION	SUPPLEMENTS
Inflammation	You're already taking fish oil, which is great for inflammation. You can also take supplements containing turmeric, boswellia, quercetin, rosemary, and ginger. Many proprietary blends contain all or some combination of these. It is generally safe to take them all, or to switch between them, unless you have specific allergies.
DNA health and cancer risk related to oxidative stress, poor detoxification, and malnutrition	Folate, vitamin B12, magnesium, resveratrol, ginseng, alpha lipoic acid, melatonin.
Weak immune system	In addition to probiotics, consider ginseng, cat's claw, echinacea, astragalus, ashwagandha, and vitamins A, C, D, and E.
Diabetes and metabolic syndrome	Vitamin D is essential! In addition, consider chromium chelate and alpha lipoic acid.
Cardiovascular disease risk	Fish oil, magnesium, Coenzyme Q10, taurine, and carnitine.
Sleep irregularities and insomnia	Melatonin, valerian root, magnesium glycinate, PharmaGABA, inositol.
Stress and/or anxiety	Magnesium, Relora, theanine, holy basil, and 5HTP (for obsessiveness).

To take the Omni Diet Supplement Quiz, rate each statement with a score of 1, 2, or 3, using the following guide:

- Give yourself 1 POINT if the statement is USUALLY TRUE.

- Give yourself 2 POINTS if the statement is SOMETIMES TRUE.

- Give yourself 3 POINTS if the statement is USUALLY NOT TRUE.

After you finish each section, add up your points and write your score in the space given.

Part 1: Brain and Memory Power

STATEMENT	RATING (circle one)		
1. I have an excellent memory and can easily recall names and other information.	1	2	3
2. I remember where I leave commonly used items, such as my car keys or my glasses.	1	2	3
3. I am able to focus sharply on tasks that require concentration, such as following printed directions to put together a child's toy.	1	2	3
4. When I listen to people delivering instructions, a speech, a lecture, or a sermon, I find it easy to pay attention to what they are saying and doing, and my mind rarely wanders.	1	2	3
5. I am very good at using logic and reasoning to solve problems.	1	2	3
6. Crossword puzzles and other word games are fairly easy for me, and I enjoy doing them.	1	2	3
7. I rarely find myself craving foods of any kind.	1	2	3
8. I rarely go on eating binges.	1	2	3
9. I find it very easy to avoid alcohol, drugs, gambling, and other potential addictions, and I have never had trouble with substance abuse or high-risk behavior.	1	2	3
10. When difficult situations arise, I am able to deal with them and then put them out of my mind, rather than obsessing over them.	1	2	3

YOUR TOTAL BRAIN AND MEMORY POWER SCORE: _____

Part 2: Craving Control—
Impulsive and Compulsive Behavior

STATEMENT	RATING (circle one)		
1. I rarely find myself craving foods of any kind.	1	2	3
2. I never go on eating binges.	1	2	3
3. I don't starve myself for long periods of time in order to lose weight (anorexia).	1	2	3
4. I don't force myself to vomit after binging (bulimia).	1	2	3
5. I can easily say no to sweet temptations, such as cookies, cake, and candy.	1	2	3
6. I can easily say no to salty temptations, such as potato chips, French fries, and salted nuts.	1	2	3
7. When I'm having a meal at a restaurant with other people and they order rich, fattening foods, it's easy for me to stay focused on my own nutritional goals and order a healthy meal without feeling deprived.	1	2	3
8. I rarely become obsessed with a food that I have chosen never to eat, such as cheeseburgers, ice cream, or crusty French bread.	1	2	3
9. When people around me are drinking cocktails or wine, I'm happy to sip on a glass of seltzer with lemon.	1	2	3
10. I feel so excited about eliminating harmful foods from my diet that I don't think I'll miss my former diet.	1	2	3
YOUR TOTAL CRAVING CONTROL SCORE:			

Part 3: Restful Sleep

STATEMENT	RATING (circle one)		
1. I fall asleep easily at night.	1	2	3
2. I sleep restfully throughout the night.	1	2	3
3. I rarely wake up during the night.	1	2	3
4. I rarely wake up before my alarm goes off in the morning and am unable to go back to sleep.	1	2	3
5. I wake up refreshed in the morning.	1	2	3
6. My sleeping partner says I appear to sleep soundly during the night, rarely waking up, snoring, tossing, turning, shaking, kicking my legs, talking in my sleep, or gasping for breath.	1	2	3
7. I don't rely on coffee or other caffeinated beverages to wake myself up in the morning.	1	2	3
8. I rarely feel tired during the day.	1	2	3
9. I am able to stay focused on lengthy speeches, sermons, and lectures without dozing off.	1	2	3
10. I am able to watch television in the evening without falling asleep.	1	2	3

YOUR TOTAL RESTFUL SLEEP SCORE: _____

Part 4: Comfortable Movement

STATEMENT	RATING (circle one)		
1. I rarely experience unexplained pain.	1	2	3
2. My joints are pain-free.	1	2	3
3. I don't feel sore after gardening, vacuuming, or doing other household chores.	1	2	3
4. I move easily and without discomfort.	1	2	3
5. I rarely wake up with aches and pains.	1	2	3
6. I rarely take ibuprofen and other medications for pain and discomfort.	1	2	3
7. I experience no shoulder, arm, or wrist pain after spending time at the computer.	1	2	3
8. My knees have never felt better.	1	2	3
9. My joints feel no worse on rainy days than on sunny days.	1	2	3
10. When I go to a party, I can dance the night away and feel great the next day.	1	2	3
YOUR TOTAL COMFORTABLE MOVEMENT SCORE:			_____

Part 5: Mood and Emotion

STATEMENT	RATING *(circle one)*		
1. I am even-tempered and calm.	1	2	3
2. Most of the time I feel positive and optimistic.	1	2	3
3. I think of myself as a "glass half-full" person.	1	2	3
4. I rarely feel anxious.	1	2	3
5. I rarely feel depressed.	1	2	3
6. I don't turn to caffeine or alcohol to boost my mood.	1	2	3
7. I rarely go on eating binges to improve my mood and make myself feel better.	1	2	3
8. I rarely find myself craving sugary foods.	1	2	3
9. My mood stays stable and upbeat throughout the month (women) or when situations require me to go longer than usual between lovemaking with my partner (men).	1	2	3
10. I sleep well and am rarely kept awake by feelings of sadness or anxiety.	1	2	3
YOUR TOTAL MOOD AND EMOTION SCORE:			_____

Part 6: Focus and Energy

STATEMENT	RATING *(circle one)*		
1. I don't rely on coffee or other caffeinated beverages in order to be able to focus on my work or other tasks that require concentration.	1	2	3
2. I don't rely on coffee or other caffeinated beverages as an energizing pick-me-up during the day.	1	2	3
3. I wake up feeling refreshed, energized, and excited about the day.	1	2	3
4. My energy levels stay high throughout the day.	1	2	3
5. I am able to focus well on tasks that require concentration.	1	2	3
6. I rarely experience a mid-afternoon energy drop that sends me to the refrigerator or vending machine for a sugary snack.	1	2	3
7. I am able to keep up my stamina and energy during exercise.	1	2	3
8. When I start a task, I stick with it until I complete it.	1	2	3
9. I am the life of the party. I enjoy meeting new people, catching up with old friends, and dancing—even without drinking alcohol.	1	2	3
10. I like to spend time with children—running around, playing games, doing crafts, and feeling like I'm a kid again myself.	1	2	3
YOUR TOTAL FOCUS AND ENERGY SCORE:			

Part 7: Calmness and Relaxation

STATEMENT	RATING (circle one)		
1. When something stressful happens, I'm able to calm myself easily.	1	2	3
2. I rarely lie awake in bed at night feeling stressed about things that happened during the day.	1	2	3
3. I rarely lie awake in bed at night worrying about things that may happen the next day.	1	2	3
4. I rarely wake up during the night in a state of stress or anxiety.	1	2	3
5. I am able to focus on tasks that require concentration.	1	2	3
6. My mind rarely wanders when I am reading or listening to someone speak.	1	2	3
7. When friends and family are stressed and anxious, they turn to me because I am a calming presence in their lives.	1	2	3
8. I have no anxiety-related symptoms, such as headache, digestive issues, libido problems, insomnia, nail-biting, or hair-pulling.	1	2	3
9. At the end of the day, I'm able to unwind and relax easily.	1	2	3
10. When I pray or meditate, I'm able to let go of my worries and settle into a relaxed, calm state.	1	2	3
YOUR TOTAL CALMNESS AND RELAXATION SCORE:			

Now that you've completed the quiz, go back and look at the final scores for each section. In any section where your score is higher than twenty, you can probably benefit from taking supplements that will target that particular set of health issues.

Once you determine which areas to target, use the lists below to determine which supplements you should take. You can purchase them individually at a trusted health food or supplement store. If you prefer to take supplements in already formulated mixes, please see the resource list at the back of the book for suggested supplement mixes from the Amen Clinics.

SUPPLEMENTS FOR BRAIN AND MEMORY POWER
- N-acetyl cysteine (NAC)
- phosphatidylserine
- huperzine A
- acetyl-l-carnitine (ALC)
- vinpocetine
- ginkgo biloba

SUPPLEMENTS FOR CRAVING CONTROL
- N-acetyl cysteine (NAC)
- glutamine
- chromium and alpha lipoic acid
- chocolate and DL phenylalanine

SUPPLEMENTS FOR RESTFUL SLEEP
- melatonin
- GABA
- zinc
- magnesium
- valerian

SUPPLEMENTS FOR COMFORTABLE MOVEMENT
- SAMe (s-adenosyl-methionine)

SUPPLEMENTS FOR MOOD SUPPORT

- 5-HTP
- saffron
- vitamin B5
- inositol

SUPPLEMENTS FOR FOCUS AND ENERGY

- green tea
- choline
- ashwagandha, rhodiola, and panax ginseng (adaptogens)

SUPPLEMENTS FOR CALMNESS AND RELAXATION

- GABA
- vitamin B6
- magnesium
- lemon balm

[LONGEVITY SUPPLEMENTS]

The following supplements are noted for their contributions to longevity:

- alpha lipoic acid
- ashwagandha
- beta-carotene
- black cohosh
- cat's claw
- coenzyme Q10
- fish oil
- folate
- gamma linoleic acid (GLA)
- ginseng
- grape-seed extract
- magnesium
- melatonin
- methionine
- milk thistle
- N-acetyl cysteine (NAC)
- palmitoleic acid
- probiotics
- resveratrol
- SAMe
- selenium
- vitamin B12
- vitamin C
- vitamin D
- vitamin E
- zinc

[MEDICATION EFFECTS AND NUTRIENT DEPLETIONS]

Many medications can cause nutritional depletions. While you shouldn't stop taking necessary medications, you should be aware of potential nutritional pitfalls so you can replace vital nutrients. The following list is credited to James LaValle of the LaValle Metabolic Institute.

- Antacids decrease stomach acid, calcium, phosphorus, folic acid, potassium. Antacids also contribute to small bowel overgrowth, vitamin K deficiency, and low mineral absorption.
- Female hormones decrease folic acid, magnesium, B vitamins, vitamin C, zinc, selenium, CoQ10.
- Antidiabetics decrease CoQ10, vitamin B12.
- Antihypertensives decrease vitamins B6 and K, CoQ10, magnesium, zinc.
- Anti-inflammatories (NSAIDs) decrease vitamins B6, C, D, K, and folic acid, calcium, zinc, and iron.
- Cholesterol-lowering medications decrease CoQ10, omega-3 fatty acids, and carnitine (statins increase oxidative stress, damage mitochondria).
- Antibiotics decrease B vitamins and vitamin K.
- Oral contraceptives decrease B vitamins, magnesium, folic acid, selenium, zinc, tyrosine, and serotonin. Roughly 16 to 52 percent of women taking oral contraceptives experience depression; antidepressants are typically the first-line treatment. Nutritional deficiencies are rarely considered.

A FINAL WORD ON SUPPLEMENTS

AS YOU SETTLE ON A supplement strategy that is best for you—one that includes supplements for optimal health and for the prevention of disease and of health conditions that are of greatest concern to you—always remember that supplements are only a backup to a healthy diet. They cannot replace a nutritious diet, and they can't erase the damage caused by eating processed foods, sugar, unhealthy fats, and excessive calories.

Think of supplements as the cement that strengthens a brick wall. The bricks are the life-giving foods of the Omni Diet—plant foods, lean meats, and healthy fats. Sure, you can build a pretty strong wall by stacking up bricks. But if you cement those bricks together, the wall is sturdier than ever. Add supplements to your Omni Diet eating plan, and you'll be building a robust wall of good health that will help protect you for many years to come.

10

$$\left[\begin{array}{c} \text{The Exponential Power} \\ \text{of Exercise} \end{array} \right]$$

**If we could give every individual the right amount of nourishment
and exercise, not too little and not too much, we would have
found the safest way to health.**

—HIPPOCRATES

IF YOUR DOCTOR OFFERED YOU a medication that would help you
lose weight, lower your risk of numerous life-threatening diseases, boost your
energy, make you look and feel sexier, and possibly even live longer, you'd
most likely insist on getting a prescription and rush to a pharmacy to have it
filled immediately.

There is no such drug. But there is such a treatment! There is something
you can do that will improve your health in just about every way possible without any worrisome side effects: engaging in moderate exercise on a regular basis.

This is no exaggeration. Exercise can do so much for your body that it's
kind of mind-boggling that anyone would choose *not* to exercise. Our bodies
are designed for *movement*!

I'm not talking about grueling, no-pain-no-gain workouts that require
hours at the gym each day. And I'm not talking about running marathons
or becoming a world-class bodybuilder. None of that is necessary to reap the
many benefits of exercise—in fact, research suggests that long bouts of highly
intensive exercise may actually cause more *harm* than *good*. Extreme exercisers
often find themselves suffering from the same problems extreme nonexercisers suffer from. Extreme exercise increases oxidative stress, can damage the
heart, and can cause dangerous heart arrhythmias. Women who overexercise

commonly have amenorrhea (absence of the menstrual period) from having very low body fat.[1] Extreme exercise increases the stress hormone cortisol,[2] disrupts neurotransmitter balance (dopamine, serotonin, and glutamine), and alters healthy immune function.[3] The result can be increased inflammation, chronic fatigue, hypothyroidism, altered sleep patterns, increased risk of autoimmune disorders, and physical injury to muscles, bones, and joints.[4] Extreme exercise, on a regular basis, can even harm your heart, according to a 2012 review of the evidence by researchers from the Mid America Heart Institute of St. Luke's Hospital of Kansas City.[5]

Exercise is so effective that it helps raise fitness levels and lower chronic disease risk *even among overweight or obese people who don't lose weight*. Of course, it's better for people who are carrying around extra pounds to trim down. But even in the absence of weight loss, studies have shown that exercise improves fitness and health. In a 2012 study, extremely overweight people who exercised for just 30 minutes five days a week got a longevity advantage of 2.7 to 3.4 years compared to nonexercisers of the same weight.[6]

One of the most exciting and most immediate benefits of exercise is the energy it gives you. One of the women in my Omni Diet classes e-mailed me after a Zumba workout (an exhilarating dance-fitness class set to pulsating Latin and international music), raving: "I came home last night with so much energy and woke up with lots of energy! I have a whole new perspective now since I know what's going on with my body!"

Exercise is so critically important that it's a cornerstone of the Omni Diet. Exercise actually *magnifies* the benefits of nutritional choices you make as part of the Omni Diet. By combining exercise with all of the other Omni Diet recommendations, you'll speed up weight loss and all of the other potential benefits that await you when you commit to the Omni Diet program.

I explain my Omni Diet Exercise Plan in full detail in part 4 of the book. The Omni Diet Exercise Plan is an effective interval and circuit exercise plan that revs up the metabolism and continues burning fat for up to seventeen hours after a workout ends. Even more important, it is realistic: Just about everyone can do it (even if they're overweight or obese), and it takes as little as thirty minutes a day.

The plan includes a simple-to-follow workout that can be customized for any fitness level, along with specific exercises that are designed to work every part of your body in a surprisingly short amount of time.

Everyone can do the Omni Diet workout—even if you're overweight, obese, or completely out of shape, you can use my interval and circuit workout to

Here are just a few of the benefits of moderate exercise done on a regular basis, according to a U.S. Department of Health and Human Services' definitive 2008 report on physical activity's body-wide perks:

- Faster loss of body fat and body weight
- Less inflammation throughout your system
- Lower levels of cortisol, the stress hormone
- Higher levels of endorphins and other feel-good neurochemicals
- Higher levels of DHEA, the "fountain of youth" hormone
- Better oxygenation in your body's cells, leading to increased energy and improved cellular health
- Improved insulin sensitivity
- Lower risk of diabetes,[7] heart disease,[8] and some kinds of cancer
- More muscle mass
- Higher rate of metabolism
- Increased flexibility and agility
- Greater detoxification through sweat
- Better sleep
- Improved ability to stay calm during stressful situations[9]

OMNI MOTIVATION BLAST

GIVE YOURSELF PERMISSION TO BE SWEATY!

It's hard to find time for exercise. It's even harder when you insist on following every exercise session with a shower, blow-dry, makeup, and a fresh outfit. Make it easier to exercise by skipping all that post-exercise vanity. So what if you're sweaty? Live in your gym clothes! That's what I do—99 percent of the time, I arrive at my Omni Diet classes in the clothes I wore to the gym. Heck, I arrive at meetings, appointments, and school functions in gym clothes. Why not?

After you work out, give your armpits a quick wash, and then get on with your day. Shower, spruce up, and change clothes if you have time, or if you really need to. Otherwise get used to carrying around a stick of deodorant. *I know!* It's not exactly the "country club" image. That's why I don't hang out at the country club. I hang out at the gym! I give you permission to embrace your sweat. S-W-E-A-T is not a four-letter word! Better to be sweaty and healthy than perfectly coiffed and unhealthy.

launch an exercise program that's so enjoyable and doable that you'll be able to use it as a foundation for a lifetime of fitness.

Before you get started, I want to tell you all about how and why exercise benefits your body so much. Knowing this can be a powerful motivator to start exercising and to stick with it.

WHAT HAPPENS WHEN YOU EXERCISE?

WHEN YOU DO MODERATE EXERCISE, you set off a chain of health-boosting physiological responses that benefit you in the short and long term.

YOUR LUNGS BECOME MORE EFFICIENT. When you exercise, cells throughout your body need more oxygen. To get the oxygen you need, you breathe faster and more deeply, pulling greater quantities of air into your lungs. Your lungs take oxygen from the air you inhale and infuse it into your blood, which delivers it to cells that need it. As your blood drops off oxygen it picks up carbon dioxide and other waste products and carries them to the lungs, where you exhale them. Over time, exercise causes your lung capacity to increase in a beneficial way. As you become more fit, your body's ability to use oxygen efficiently during exercise—known as your VO2 max—goes up.

YOUR HEART BECOMES STRONGER. Your heart is a muscle, and like any other muscle, it becomes stronger when it's worked. Your heart must work harder to circulate oxygenated blood throughout your body. Over time, the muscle tissue in your heart becomes stronger, just as your arm muscles become stronger when you lift weights.

YOUR MUSCLES BECOME STRONGER AND BIGGER. Exercise causes very small amounts of damage to your muscle fibers. This damage, which is called microtrauma, sounds bad, but it's actually very good. Your body responds to muscle microtrauma by rebuilding the damaged fibers in such a way that they're stronger than they were before the microtrauma occurred. Over time, this process of damage and repair builds muscle tissue that is denser and stronger.

YOUR IMMUNE RESPONSE IMPROVES. As blood flow increases, so too does the circulation of white blood cells (leukocytes) and other infection-fighting cells throughout your body. It's important to have a strong immune system to fight disease and keep your body strong. Over time, an improved immune response may help prevent some kinds of cancer cells from forming and spreading in your body.

YOUR ADRENAL GLAND LOWERS ITS PRODUCTION OF THE STRESS HOR-MONE CORTISOL. Done in moderation, exercise turns down cortisol production. However, excessive exercise does the opposite—it boosts cortisol levels. Cortisol is a hormone that helps regulate blood pressure, immunity, insulin/blood sugar balance, and the body's response to stress. It also aids in normal wake/sleep cycles. It's important to keep cortisol within normal limits to maintain normal sleep patterns, blood pressure, immunity, and blood sugar balance. Obesity, excessive carbohydrate consumption, chronic stress, and lack of exercise cause elevated cortisol levels. We produce different amounts of cortisol at different times of day. Production is supposed to peak in the morning around the time that you wake up, giving you energy, and should dip later in the evening, hitting a low in the middle of the night (around midnight for most people) to allow sleep. Having too much of it increases inflammation, makes it harder for you to sleep, and increases the fat around your belly. Not having enough leads to fatigue throughout the day and difficulty getting up in the morning.

Chronic high cortisol levels result from long-term exposure to stressful situations, altered sleep cycles, Cushing's syndrome (a rare hormonal disorder), or pituitary or adrenal tumors, which are very rare.

POVERTY OF THE FLESH

Sarcopenia is the loss of muscle mass and strength. Its name, which in Greek means "poverty of the flesh," refers to the degenerative process of aging that typically starts at about age twenty-five. In addition to muscle mass, sarcopenia also affects the endocrine system, joints, bones, and blood vessels.

The action of sarcopenia speeds up when there is a perfect storm of protein deficiency, lack of essential amino acids, diminishing hormones, and a lack of physical activity. Maintaining proper levels of growth hormone and testosterone is critical in the fight against sarcopenia.

The four best ways to keep sarcopenia in control are getting enough protein, cutting back on simple carbohydrates, and getting ample exercise and sleep. These steps help prevent testosterone from dropping while naturally elevating the growth hormone.

The most common cause of low cortisol levels is adrenal fatigue or burnout. (Less common causes include long-term steroid use, Addison's disease—a rare autoimmune disorder—or a pituitary tumor, which is also rare.) If low cortisol levels are caused by chronic stress, this is a bad sign—it means the adrenal glands have been so stressed for so long that they're burning out. This is often referred to as "living with a tiger in the house." Having chronic low cortisol levels is associated with altered memory, increased risk of heart disease, and cancer (immunity becomes altered).

YOUR INFLAMMATION LEVELS DROP. Moderate exercise triggers the release of anti-inflammatory cytokines that help minimize damage caused by inflammation. Studies show that compared with sedentary people, those who exercise regularly have lower blood levels of C-reactive protein, a by-product of inflammation, according to a 2005 review of 19 studies by researchers from the University of Connecticut.[10] Chronic inflammation contributes to many diseases and disorders, including diabetes, heart disease, cancer, joint pain, and obesity. Keeping it in check is important for good health.

JOINT PAIN DECREASES. If you have joint pain caused by inflammation, exercise reduces the inflammatory response, which in turn can reduce pain. Most people experience a decrease in pain caused from arthritis simply by decreasing inflammation.

YOU FEEL LESS STRESSED. When you exercise, your body sends endorphins and other feel-good neurotransmitters and natural substances into your blood. These substances can lower feelings of emotional distress and depression.

YOUR SENSITIVITY TO LEPTIN INCREASES. The hormone leptin tells your body to stop eating when you are full. Exercise increases your body's ability to be better able to receive leptin's satiety messages, so you know sooner when you are full.

YOUR BLOOD SUGAR AND INSULIN LEVELS DROP. Exercise causes your muscles to boost their uptake of glucose from your blood, lowering your blood sugar level. When blood sugar goes down, so does insulin production. Exercise also helps make your body more sensitive to insulin, enabling it to do a better job of moving sugar out of your blood and into your cells.

YOU BURN OFF VISCERAL (BELLY) FAT. Accumulation of visceral fat revs up your body's inflammatory system. Exercising is an excellent way to reduce the fat around your belly and reduce inflammation.

CALORIES *DON'T* MATTER!

I KNEW THAT HEADING WOULD get your attention!

Knowing how many calories there are in the food you eat does matter. But knowing how many calories you burn when you're on the treadmill *doesn't*. That's right—I'm giving you permission to stop watching the calorie count inch up when you're working out. The number of calories you burn during exercise is just not that important.

Let me explain.

One of the questions I am most often asked is this: Which is more important for weight loss—diet or exercise? My answer is . . . both! I know, that's not the answer people are looking for. But I say it because both exercise and diet play such a critical role in weight loss.

If people insist on an answer, I explain that nutrition is about 80 percent responsible for *weight loss,* and exercise is 20 percent responsible for *weight loss.* Many people focus on food. They diet for quick weight loss, and succeed short term. But it rarely lasts because they don't incorporate the benefits of exercise. A better question is: Of the two—exercise and diet—which is most critical for great *health?* In that case, the two are nearly equal. In fact, they are nearly inseparable. When you become truly healthy through a better diet *and* exercise, your weight naturally begins to stabilize to a healthy level. So your major focus should be on *great health.* But let's focus on weight for a moment.

The reason exercise contributes to weight loss is *not* that it burns calories. It does burn calories, of course, but not enough to be that much of an influence in and of itself. The numbers you see on the treadmill or stationary bike can be discouragingly small—jog for half an hour, for example, and you barely burn off the calories in a small salad. But because exercise revs up your metabolism for up to seventeen hours, you continue to burn extra calories long after your workout ends.

So, even if you follow your morning workout with a day spent sitting at your desk, you continue to burn a higher number of calories hour after hour than you would if you hadn't exercised.

Exercise also makes a psychological contribution to weight loss. When you are working out and feeling fit, you feel so good that it's much easier to make smart choices about what you eat. Exercise triggers the release of brain chemicals that boost mood, confidence, willpower, and all of the other emotional factors that help you choose a plate of vegetables over a dish of ice cream. When you feel positive, optimistic, and happy, you don't need to turn to food for emotional support. And the food/exercise connection works the other way, too: When you eat right and start to lose weight, your success fuels your motivation to do other things—such as exercise—that will benefit your health.

In an almost magical way, exercise makes everything else in the Omni Diet work better by increasing insulin sensitivity, improving energy efficiency, improving heart function, decreasing body fat and blood pressure, increasing

TAKE A LESSON FROM YOUR GPS

If you have a GPS (global positioning system) unit in your car, you know what happens when you take a wrong turn: A computer-generated voice instructs you to make your next legal U-turn. It doesn't yell at you, judge you, or call you an idiot. Nor does it tell you that you're a hopeless failure and reprimand you for failing to follow the directions. It simply tells you to make the first possible correction and continue on your journey.

We can learn a lot from those little devices. So many of us beat ourselves up when we make a wrong turn in our diet or exercise plan. We say things to ourselves we wouldn't say to anyone else. Instead of pounding yourself with criticism and self-loathing when you slip up, channel your inner GPS. Don't judge or berate yourself. Just make a U-turn and get back on track.

muscle mass, and helping to balance hormones. Even when exercise doesn't burn a ton of calories, it is a critical component for reversing disease, improving health, and maintaining youth.

Exercise and diet are so interrelated that separating out the benefits of each is a chicken-or-the-egg-type situation. Don't waste time thinking about which is better. Do them both, because they're both great!

HOW EXERCISE CHANGES YOUR GENETICS

EXERCISE MAKES YOU LOOK YOUNGER and healthier. As it turns out, it does the same thing for your genes and your DNA. In fact, exercise can alter the function and expression of your genes.

Being physically active appears to have a positive effect on telomeres, which are the protective DNA caps at the ends of our chromosomes. Picture a shoelace. A telomere is like that plastic thing at the end of the lace that keeps it from fraying.

Telomeres help to protect chromosomes. Telomeres get shorter over time—whenever a cell divides, parts of the telomere drop off. As telomeres get shorter, they are less able to protect the chromosome, leaving it vulnerable to damage. In that respect, telomere shortening is considered part of the aging process. However, telomeres also shorten in response to assaults on

[FAT CELLS, OR FAT *TUMORS?*]

Hopefully the message is clear. Exercise (as well as diet) is vitally important! If that isn't clear enough, think of what fat cells are really doing in your body. Fat cells are like little fat tumors. Yes, it's true: Fat can be lethal. But the good news is that many of the problems associated with excessive body fat (inflammation, diabetes, heart disease, joint pain, mental fog, and so on) begin to clear up quickly when you change your lifestyle.

Our bodies need some body fat to function in a healthy way. But when you have an excessive amount of body fat, you also tend to have too much arachidonic acid (AA), a by-product of systemic inflammation. Since your body doesn't like inflammation, it tries to protect you by storing excess AA in fat cells. As you continue to do the things that caused you to gain all that excess fat—eat a poor diet and live a sedentary lifestyle, for example—your body creates more fat cells to buffer the effects of increasing levels of AA.

Basically, fat cells filled with AA are like toxic little endocrine tumors that will eventually lose the ability to protect you from inflammation. When AA levels get too high and cell death occurs, inflammation speeds up at an alarming rate. This causes a snowballing of detrimental responses, such as higher insulin levels and increased oxidative stress.

You can take steps to stop fat cell growth and proliferation by exercising. Get out there and take a walk, go for a bicycle ride, lift some weights, swim some laps, sign up for a class. Doing anything is better than doing nothing.

your body and your cells, such as poor diet, inactivity, significant stress, and excessive body weight.

As telomeres shorten, so too does their lifespan. When telomeres become very short, the cell dies.

Shorter telomeres on immune cell chromosomes are associated with aging-related diseases such as heart disease, diabetes, osteoporosis, dementia, reduced cognitive function, arthritis, and certain cancers. According to researchers at the University of California, San Francisco, there's strong evidence that shortened telomeres boost the risk of aging and chronic disease.[11] And longer telomeres are associated with healthy aging and overall longevity (except in the case of cancer cells, which have very long telomeres that don't shorten).[12]

Telomere shortening sounds pretty unstoppable. But researchers have discovered that there are ways to lengthen—or at the very least, slow down the shortening of—immune cell telomeres. You probably won't be surprised to hear that some of the factors that can lengthen telomeres include exercise, eating a healthy diet, and reducing stress. These actions appear to increase levels of telomerase, an enzyme that helps protect telomeres from eroding. That's the conclusion of an exciting 2013 study from the University of California, San Francisco, and the Preventive Medicine Research Institute. It found that four healthy habits—a good diet, regular exercise, stress reduction, and plenty of social support—increased telomere length by an impressive 10 percent in men with early stage prostate cancer. In contrast, telomeres shrank by 3 percent in men who did not make these healthy changes.[13]

For example, research has shown that when highly stressed individuals exercised regularly, their telomeres were longer than the telomeres of sedentary people who were also highly stressed.

That's important. Studies suggest that in order to optimize telomere length, you should exercise vigorously (that means breaking a sweat and increasing your heart rate) and often[14]—exactly what the Omni Diet recommends. Losing weight if you're overweight, eating a healthy diet, taking vitamins, reducing stress, and avoiding excess dietary fats (the wrong fats)[15] also seem to help telomere length, and these are all part of the Omni Diet.

BUST THOSE MUSCLE MYTHS!

I AM A HUGE FAN of including strength training in your exercise regimen two or three times a week. Not only does it speed up metabolism and calorie burn, but it does wonderful things for your figure. Let's face it—getting healthy is the goal, but looking younger and sexier is a beautiful benefit.

Unfortunately, there are many myths out there about muscle, muscle building, and strength training. Some people actually refuse to strength train because they believe that if they build muscle, they'll look fat! This is crazy. I want to put that misconception—and all of the other incorrect beliefs about muscle—to rest by telling you the truth about muscle.

MYTH: Strength training causes weight gain.
TRUTH: It's completely false that strength training *for fitness and health* will make you gain weight and become bulky with muscles. Unless you participate in

serious bodybuilding (think Arnold Schwarzenegger), it is highly unlikely that you would gain enough muscle to need bigger clothes—especially if you're a woman. Muscle is lean tissue, and a pound of muscle takes up way less space than a pound of fat. Building muscle will make you look less flabby and more solid (in a very good way), because muscle is 18 percent more dense than fat. When you lose weight and gain muscle you actually look more compact, not bulky.

MYTH: Strength training turns fat into muscle.
TRUTH: Muscle and fat are two different kinds of tissue. Think of a blanket of snow covering a car. No matter how hard you wish, you will never turn a pile of snow into a new Ferrari!

However, when you strength train, you are very likely to lose fat. Here's why: When you strength train, you build muscle. Your body has to rev up your metabolism to maintain that muscle—in fact, meeting the everyday metabolic needs of muscle tissue requires *ten times more energy* than meeting the needs of fat tissue. (A pound of muscle needs 20 calories of energy per day; a pound of fat needs only 2 or 3 calories.) If you don't consume more calories to meet your muscles' need for energy, your body will turn to its energy stores (body fat) in order to give muscles the energy they need. So, as muscle tissue increases, fat burns—provided you don't add calories to your daily diet. Even when you're not moving, your muscle cells burn far more calories than your fat cells. Think of that Ferrari covered with snow. If you turn the engine on, the hood gets warm (metabolism). The snow begins to melt. The faster you rev the car, the faster the snow melts. Also, increasing muscle mass increases sensitivity to insulin, which decreases body fat (by not having excessive insulin in your blood).

MYTH: I am too old to start strength training.
TRUTH: You can begin a strength-training program at any age. When Tufts University researchers taught older women and men how to do simple strength-training routines, the subjects gained muscle, became less frail, improved their mobility and independence, increased bone density, and experienced better quality of life within weeks.[16] That's right, weeks. Muscles respond incredibly quickly to strength training even among the very, very old—so imagine what it can do for you if you haven't yet reached your golden years. Most people begin to lose muscle mass rapidly during their thirties and forties. Strength training for a short amount of time a couple of days a week can stop and reverse this muscle loss.

MYTH: Strength training requires a health club membership and hours of sweating in the gym.

TRUTH: Nothing could be further from the truth. You can strength train in the privacy of your own home in just minutes a day. Armed with nothing more than a couple of inexpensive free weights from a sporting-goods store and the strength-training moves in part 4 of this book, you can do a safe, fast workout. You'll probably break a sweat, but don't worry, you won't be pouring perspiration like the competitive weight-lifters you see on television.

SO, HOW MUCH SHOULD *YOU* EXERCISE?

THE TRICK IS EXERCISING ENOUGH, but not too much. Overworking your body with exercise or any other kind of extreme physical exertion causes more harm than good.

Long bouts of exhaustive exercise can damage your immune response, increase the amount of cortisol and other stress hormones in your blood, increase oxidative stress and inflammation, negatively impact the flow of white blood cells and other infection-fighting cells in your blood, and cause DNA damage.

The stress that marathon runners and other athletic extremists put on their bodies places them at unnecessary risk of injury and other health problems. Doing too much is nearly as bad as doing nothing at all.

Focus on walking during phase 1 of the Omni Diet. To hit your exercise sweet spot—a level that delivers benefits without causing harm—aim for about half an hour (up to an hour if you are already conditioned) of brisk exercise each day. That means walking vigorously enough that you get your heart rate up, but not so fast that you can't talk. (I call this "walking like you're late.")

When you arrive at phase 2, you can start to follow my Omni Diet Workout Plan. It will give you a full-body workout in as little as thirty minutes a day.

I know that getting started on a new exercise routine can seem overwhelming, especially if you have been inactive. But when it comes to exercise, you just have to do it. If you want to improve your health, lose weight, and feel better than ever before, exercise is not optional!

Make exercise fun! Exercise with a friend. Find a sport you can play or a class you can join. The more you can do to make exercise enjoyable, the more likely you are to stick with it.

PART FOUR

THE OMNI DIET PROGRAM

NOW THAT YOU KNOW *WHY* the Omni Diet makes so much sense, you're ready to discover *how* to make it a fundamental part of your daily life. The Omni Diet Program provides all of the step-by-step instructions, practical advice, and heart-to-heart encouragement you'll need to make life-changing improvements in the way you eat, move, and live.

Once you commit to the Omni Diet, you'll begin seeing dramatic results almost immediately. Your energy level and your feeling of well-being will soar, while your weight and your risk factors for a variety of diseases will begin a dramatic decline. Most of my clients notice that they begin to feel better—healthier, stronger, more empowered, and more alive—within a day or two of setting out on the Omni Diet. And it just keeps getting better from there.

The Omni Diet Program is divided into four phases. Phases 1, 2, and 3 guide you through the first six weeks; phase 4 gives you a maintenance plan that will serve as a blueprint for a lifetime of healthy living. The program also includes dozens of super-tasty, super-healthy, easy-to-prepare recipes, along with a shopping list and meal plans that will help you hit the ground running.

By embracing the Omni Diet today, you're taking the first steps toward a healthier, happier, more energetic future!

PHASE 1

[Jump the Canyon]

The gradual process is of no use at all.
—C. S. LEWIS, *THE GREAT DIVORCE*

DURING THE TWO WEEKS OF phase 1, you can look forward to these exciting results:

- Weight loss of up to 10 to 15 pounds, depending on your size and gender (or more if you are very overweight or suffer from extreme inflammation); remember, your focus should be on your health, not the scale—but you can enjoy the fact that radical weight loss is one of the stunning side effects of the Omni Diet

- Disappearance of carbohydrate and sugar cravings within three to seven days

- Reduction of joint pain or swelling in your body as a result of decreased inflammation

- Dramatic improvement in digestion and any digestion-related problems you may have

- Skin that is clearer and noticeably more vibrant

- Improved ability to focus

- Increased energy

As you set out on the Omni Diet, I ask that you take a leap of faith and do something that few other eating plans recommend: jump the canyon and make a whole bunch of changes all at once. The gradual approach, making small, incremental adjustments over the course of weeks or months, is a good way to bring about major behavior change in some parts of your life—but not diet.

Here's why: Like most people who eat the standard American diet, you're probably addicted to refined white sugar, fructose, high-fructose corn syrup, sweeteners, and other simple carbohydrates that turn into sugar soon after you eat them. Giving up foods you're physically dependent upon is difficult. But believe it or not, the easiest, most successful way to break your addiction to sugar is *not* to wean yourself off it a little at a time, but to stop all at once. The best way to shift your diet into the healthiest gear possible is to jump the canyon with both feet. You can't cross a canyon in small steps!

For example, when you eat sugar and other simple carbs, your blood sugar typically shoots up within minutes, stays elevated for a short time, and then plummets. As it falls your body gets an urgent message: Eat *more* sugar and carbohydrates! Then the cravings start all over again.

It's an endless cycle with a terrible ending. Eating sugar makes you *crave* sugar. Eating simple carbohydrates makes you *crave* simple carbohydrates. The only way to break that cycle of eating and craving, eating and craving, is to cut sugar and simple carbohydrates out of your diet completely.

In my experience, most people who follow the Omni Diet lose their desire for carbohydrates and sugar within one to three days. For hard-core sugar addicts, it may take a week. But after that short amount of time, the constant urge to eat sugar and carbohydrates subsides, freeing you from your addiction to a range of foods that are bad for your body in so many ways.

The same goes for all of the health-sapping foods I recommend taking out of your diet, including processed foods, grains, alcohol, gluten, and milk. Jump the canyon! Cut them out all at once and replace them with an entirely new menu of deliciously healthy, nutrient-dense alternatives that will nourish your body in the way it was designed to be nourished.

By eating the right balance of whole, organic foods that are minimally processed and balanced to help you achieve the greatest nutrient density and diversity, you'll get the most bang for your caloric buck. You won't feel hungry or deprived. Instead, like so many people who have followed the Omni Diet, you'll immediately start to feel better than you ever imagined possible.

Phase 1 has six steps. Jump the canyon and conquer them all!

STEP 1: KNOW YOUR NUMBERS

I STRONGLY RECOMMEND SEEING YOUR health-care provider and asking for blood tests that measure your health in various ways. The results of these tests will give you a snapshot of your overall health and clarify which health goals are the most important for you. They can provide a lot of information about cardiovascular disease risk, your inflammation levels, and your body's ability to use blood sugar. They will also allow you and your health-care provider to rule out common health problems, such as thyroid disease and vitamin D deficiency. Not being aware of these deficiencies or imbalances can totally sabotage your success and your health!

The results of your tests may surprise you—even the healthiest people can have unknown issues that are discovered by blood testing. Diseases such as Hashimoto's thyroiditis (the most common form of hypothyroidism, which is also known as "underactive thyroid") can cause fatigue, loss of energy, weight gain, depression, lack of focus, and a range of other health problems, yet it often goes undiagnosed. Getting thyroid imbalances under control makes people feel much better, and it often helps them lose weight more easily.

The Omni Diet changes your body and your health from the inside out. Having your important numbers checked at the start of the program and again after six weeks shows you how much progress you're making. Sure, it's great when the number on the scale changes, but it's fantastic when you have blood test results that prove you're doing more than just losing weight—you're significantly lowering your risk of a range of health problems. In fact, many people who follow the Omni Diet get normal or near-normal lab results after just six to twelve weeks.

Your health-care provider may tell you that you don't need these blood tests. Some providers believe in doing blood tests only when very obvious symptoms of disease appear. I disagree! Wouldn't you rather know the nitty-gritty details about your health *before* you develop a life-threatening disease—when you still have time to prevent it? If your provider balks at blood testing, I encourage you not to take no for an answer (and to consider seeing another provider). Insist on being tested. Or, order your own labs from online sites such as www.saveonlabs.com.

Here are the important numbers you should know:

BODY MASS INDEX (BMI)

A normal BMI is between 18.5 and 25, overweight is between 25 and 30, and obese is greater than 30. You can find a simple BMI calculator on our Web site at www.amenclinics.com.

WAIST SIZE

Fat in the abdomen, which is associated with a larger waist, is metabolically active and produces various hormones that can cause harmful effects, such as diabetes, elevated blood pressure, and altered blood fat levels. Ideally, you want your waist size in inches to be less than half your height. So, if you are 66 inches tall your waist should not be more than 33 inches.

BLOOD PRESSURE

High blood pressure is associated with an increased risk of heart disease and lower overall brain function. (Blood pressure is measured in millimeters of mercury, or mmHg.)

What the numbers mean:

- **120 over 80 (or lower): optimal blood pressure**
- **120 to 139 over 80 to 89: pre-hypertension**
- **140 (or above) over 90 (or above): hypertension**

COMPLETE BLOOD COUNT (CBC)

A CBC is used to check the health of your blood, including red and white blood cells.

CORTISOL

The cortisol test measures the amount of the stress hormone cortisol in your blood.

What the numbers mean:

- **Normal blood: 5 to 23 mcg/dL (morning); 3 to 16 mcg/dL (afternoon)**

Having high cortisol can be caused by something as simple as taking oral contraceptives or lack of adequate sleep to something as complex as a brain tumor. Low cortisol can be related to chronic/severe stress, infection, damage to adrenal glands, or low blood sugar. It's important to have out-of-range lab values checked by a qualified physician.

GENERAL METABOLIC PANEL

This checks the health of your liver, kidneys, fasting blood sugar, and cholesterol.

What the numbers mean:

- **70 to 99 mg/dL: normal**

- **100 to 125 mg/dL: pre-diabetes**

- **126 mg/dL or higher: diabetes**

HEMOGLOBIN A1C (ALSO REFERRED TO AS HBA1C)

This test shows your average blood sugar levels over the past two to three months and is used to help diagnose diabetes and pre-diabetes.

What the numbers mean:

- **Less than 5.7 percent: normal**

- **5.7 to 6.4: pre-diabetes**

- **6.4 or higher: suggests diabetes**

VITAMIN D LEVEL

Low levels of vitamin D have been associated with obesity, depression, cognitive impairment, heart disease, reduced immunity, cancer, psychosis, and all causes of mortality. Have your physician check your 25-hydroxy vitamin D level.

What the numbers mean:

- **30 to 100 ng/dL: healthy**

- **50 to 100 ng/dL: optimal**

- **Over 100 is generally considered too high**

THYROID HORMONE LEVELS

Abnormal thyroid hormone levels are a common cause of forgetfulness, confusion, lethargy, and other cognitive symptoms in both women and men. Having low thyroid levels decreases overall brain activity, which can impair your thinking, judgment, and self-control, and make it very hard for you to feel good. Low-thyroid functioning can make it nearly impossible to manage weight effectively. Medication can get thyroid hormone levels back in balance.

What the numbers mean:

- **TSH (thyroid stimulating hormone): normal level is between 0.350 and 3.0 IU/mL**

- **Free T3: 300 to 400 pg/dL**

- **Free T4: 1.0 to 1.80 ng/dL**

- **Thyroid antibodies (TPO): 0 to 34 IU/mL**

Make an appointment with a physician if your thyroid numbers are too high (a sign of Hashimoto's disease, an autoimmune disorder that causes hypothyroidism) or too low (a sign that you have an overactive thyroid, also known as hyperthyroidism).

C-REACTIVE PROTEIN

The C-reactive protein is a measure of inflammation. The most common reason for an elevated C-reactive protein is metabolic syndrome or insulin resistance. The second most common is some sort of reaction to food— either a sensitivity, a true allergy, or an autoimmune reaction (as occurs with gluten). It can also indicate hidden infections. A healthy range is between 0.0 and 1.0 mg/dL.

HOMOCYSTEINE

Elevated levels (more than 10 micromoles/liter) in the blood have been associated with damage to the lining of arteries and atherosclerosis (hardening and narrowing of the arteries) as well as an increased risk of heart attacks, strokes, blood clot formation, and possibly Alzheimer's disease. They are also a marker of inflammation.

FERRITIN

This is a measure of iron stores that increase with inflammation and insulin resistance. Normal levels for females: 12 to 150 ng/mL. Normal levels for males: 12 to 300 ng/mL.

FREE AND TOTAL SERUM TESTOSTERONE LEVEL

Low levels of the hormone testosterone, for men or women, have been associated with low energy, cardiovascular disease, obesity, low libido, depression, and Alzheimer's disease.

Normal levels for adult males:

- **Total: 280 to 800 ng/dL**

- **Free: 7.2 to 24 pg/mL**

CREATE A PATTERN INTERRUPT

Although cravings become less frequent and less intense as you move forward on the Omni Diet, they still occur sometimes, usually when you least expect them. It's wise to always have a plan! A "pattern interrupt" is a strategy that shifts your focus away from whatever triggered your craving. Make a list of simple distractions that can be quickly executed when a craving strikes. Some good options include going for a walk, taking the dog out, drinking a tall glass of water, eating a plate of veggies, calling a friend, reorganizing a drawer, or even just going for a drive. If you're home, simply getting out of the house (and away from your temptation) usually does the trick.

If you can't kick the craving and you decide to eat the food, do it with consciousness and enjoyment, rather than guilt and self-criticism. Follow the three-bite rule and savor each bite. Then get rid of whatever's left and move forward. Taking three mindful bites is better than going on a mindless binge.

Normal levels for adult females:

- Total: 6 to 82 ng/dL
- Free: 0.0 to 2.2 pg/mL

LIPID PANEL

This measures levels of HDL ("good" cholesterol), LDL ("bad" cholesterol), and triglycerides (a form of fat).

Optimal levels:

- Total cholesterol: less than 200 mg/dL
- HDL: greater than 60 mg/dL
- LDL: less than 100 mg/dL
- Triglycerides: less than 100 mg/dL

Don't forget to take your measurements (waist-to-height ratio), weigh yourself, and snap a "before" photo. You'll repeat this step in six weeks and be amazed by how much you've changed!

STEP 2: PURGE YOUR PANTRY

IF YOU EAT THE STANDARD American diet, your kitchen cabinets, refrigerator, and freezer contain foods that are terrible for your health and your weight. The best thing you can do for yourself and your family is to do a clean sweep of your entire kitchen and get rid of all the foods that sabotage your health. Doing so makes it easier for you to make conscious eating decisions. It helps prevent impulsive, mindless snacking as you change your eating patterns. When you purge your pantry, you make one decision—not to have unhealthy foods in your house—rather than *dozens* of decisions throughout the day to avoid foods that are sitting in your kitchen.

Here's a list of what to toss. Refer back to earlier chapters for details about why these foods don't belong in a healthy kitchen.

- The majority of processed foods (crackers, cookies, jelly, popcorn, frozen dinners, syrup, ketchup, processed meats, and most jarred, canned foods). Most contain a lot of unhealthy fat, sugar, artificial sweeteners, and other ingredients that you'll be avoiding. Read package labels; be especially aware of any product that has more than five ingredients or contains ingredients with chemical-sounding names you can't pronounce.

- All foods that contain high-fructose corn syrup, sugar, artificial sweeteners, soy, trans fat, and hydrogenated fat (soda, ice cream, syrup, candy, condiments, processed lunch meat, bread, potato chips, and crackers).

- Vegetable oils. As I explain in chapter 3, vegetable oils such as corn oil, safflower oil, canola oil, and soy-based oils are not healthy choices.

- Cereal, rice, and other grain-based foods (including all processed cereal, instant oatmeal, wheat, barley, rye, and corn).

- Bread, pasta, and other foods that contain gluten.

- Fruit juice. Even if it's 100 percent fruit, juice causes unhealthy blood sugar spikes. It is also fructose, which is toxic to your liver.

- Foods that contain genetically modified ingredients.

- Foods that contain milk, cheese, or other dairy products.

- Cookies, cakes, candy, and other sweets.

- Condiments such as ketchup, barbecue sauce, and mustard, which are usually packed with sugar, salt, and artificial ingredients. Soy sauce contains gluten, (usually) soy, and excessive sodium. Mustard that is gluten-free and sugar-free can stay.

- Jams, jellies, and pancake syrup. They are pure sugar. Most pancake syrup contains no maple syrup at all! It is high-fructose corn syrup and artificial flavoring.

- Alcohol.

STEP 3: STOCK UP ON STAPLES

NOW THAT YOUR PANTRY IS cleansed of unhealthy processed foods, you have plenty of space for whole, nutritious foods that boost your health and provide your body with the vitamins, minerals, antioxidants, and anti-inflammatory compounds it needs for excellent health and peak performance. Head to the grocery store, health food store, and farmers' market and stock up on the following:

- Vegetables of all kinds (except white potatoes). Purchase fresh, organic produce when possible.

- Small amounts of fruit. The best choices are organic strawberries, blueberries, raspberries, and blackberries, which have less of an impact on blood sugar and more nutritional value than starchy fruits such as

[NUTS AND SEEDS IN THE RAW]

Nuts and seeds increase satiety, boost omega-3 fatty acids, and prevent gluconeogenesis, the conversion of muscle to glucose during weight loss. I recommend eating raw nuts because the oil in nuts becomes oxidized when roasted. On the rare occasion that you eat roasted nuts, try to eat dry roasted over oil roasted. Oil roasting is similar to deep frying and adds trans fats. In a nutshell, eating roasted nuts eliminates the benefits of eating the nuts in the first place, and adds harmful peroxides and trans fats.

As for salt, it is unnecessary because Americans already get too much salt in their diets. At first, unsalted seeds and nuts may seem bland, but stick with them—you will soon discover that the nuts' and seeds' own flavor is much more interesting when it's not hidden by salt.

Try to choose tree nuts over peanuts (which are actually legumes). Peanuts, which complete the growth process underground, are easily contaminated. They have been shown to be very high in the fungus aflatoxin, which is a potent carcinogen. Peanuts are also higher in omega-6 fatty acids than most tree nuts.

bananas. You will only be eating about ½ cup of berries or one piece of fruit per day through the first phase.

- Lean meat, fish, and poultry. Great sources of protein include wild salmon, tuna, herring, skinless chicken and turkey, lamb, and lean beef. Buy meats that are grass-fed, free-range, hormone-free, and antibiotic-free.

- Eggs. Choose cage-free, organic, DHA-enriched eggs from vegetarian-fed chickens.

- Raw, unsalted seeds and nuts. Be sure to choose raw nuts and seeds, because roasting nuts and seeds oxidizes their oils and robs them of their health benefits.

- Healthy oils such as coconut oil, almond oil, macadamia-nut oil, grape-seed oil, and olive oil.

- Dried beans and lentils (in limited amounts).

- Fresh and dried herbs and spices, which provide rich nutritional benefits and fantastic flavor. It's best to cook with fresh herbs, but dried herbs work in a pinch. (See chapter 4 for a full list of healthy herbs and spices.)

- Pure Wrap coconut wraps.

- Lots of travel-size storage containers, ice packs, and coolers for packing leftovers and on-the-go lunches and snacks.

STEP 4: WALK AS IF YOU'RE LATE

EXERCISE IS A CRUCIAL PART of the Omni Diet, and we'll focus on it in detail in phase 2. For now, walk at least thirty minutes a day. To be sure you're getting your heart rate up, walk briskly—as if you're late for an appointment. If you currently engage in regular exercise, continue your program. Be sure to move your body *at least* four days per week.

STEP 5: CALCULATE YOUR CALORIE GOALS—OR NOT!

IF YOU FOLLOW THE OMNI Diet closely, eating a balanced 70 percent plant/30 percent lean protein diet, you don't have to bother counting calories. The calories will take care of themselves! In essence, I've done most of the work for you.

[GO ORGANIC]

Organic fruits and vegetables cost more, but if you can possibly afford them, they're worth buying. If money is tight, buy organic when you're choosing produce that tends to have high amounts of pesticide residue. I recommend following the advice of the Environmental Working Group (EWG). The EWG, a nonprofit environmental advocacy group, has compiled a list of the "dirty dozen" fruits and vegetables with the most pesticide residue and the "clean 15" with the least pesticide residue. It has also ranked the pesticide residue typically found on fifty-three kinds of fruits and vegetables. For more information, check out the EWG's shopper's guide at www.ewg.org/foodnews/.

The EWG dirty dozen: apples, celery, sweet bell peppers, peaches, strawberries, imported nectarines, grapes, spinach, lettuce, cucumbers, domestic blueberries, and potatoes. (Green beans and greens such as kale may also contain pesticide residue of special concern.)

The EWG clean 15: onions, sweet corn, pineapples, avocado, cabbage, sweet peas, asparagus, mangoes, eggplant, kiwi, domestic cantaloupe, sweet potatoes, grapefruit, watermelon, and mushrooms.

To reduce exposure to pesticides in nonorganic produce, wash it well and remove peels. In meats, fish, and poultry, cut away any visible skin and fat, where pesticide levels may be higher. When you can't get fresh organic produce, choose organic frozen produce over canned.

If you buy organic produce, it's best to leave the skin on. In produce such as carrots, sweet potatoes, and cucumbers, most of the vitamins are found just beneath the skin. And the skin is a good source of fiber. However, if you choose nonorganic produce, remove the skin, because that's where pesticides collect.

[SHOULD I TAKE SUPPLEMENTS AS PART OF THE OMNI DIET?]

Yes. Each day during phase 1 and phase 2, take a multivitamin, fish oil capsules (1 to 2 grams total), vitamin D (at least 2,000 IUs), magnesium (400 to 1,000 mg, divided into three doses per day), and probiotics (25 billion to 50 billion CFUs). Many people need other supplements as well. See chapter 9 to learn more about supplements and take a quiz that guides you as you customize your own personal supplement strategy.

If you're someone who likes to play with numbers, go ahead and calculate your daily calorie goals. Most women need 1,800 to 2,000 calories a day to maintain their current weight; most men need 2,200 to 2,500. To lose a pound of weight a week, you need to cut (by eating less) or burn (by exercising more) a total of 500 calories daily (I want you to do both). But don't go below 1,200 calories per day.

Following the formula in this program, most women will consume 1,400 to 1,600 calories a day. Men will consume 1,600 to 2,000. Because of the quality of the calories, this ends up being a *large volume* of food. Very few people who follow the Omni Diet complain of feeling hungry. Often, it's the other way around—people have trouble adjusting to eating every three to four hours because they are not hungry enough.

To find out more about how many calories you need each day, use the handy calorie calculator on the Amen Clincs' Web site, www.amenclinics .com/cybcyb.

STEP 6: PLAN YOUR MEALS

NOW IT'S TIME TO START planning your meals. For the next two weeks, you're going to eat a 70/30 diet: Seventy percent of your calories will come from plant foods, and 30 percent will come from protein foods. Healthy fats will come from the plant and protein foods you choose.

During this first phase of the Omni Diet, you'll eat no grains, sugar, breads, white flour, or simple carbohydrates of any kind. This will help you kick your dependence on sugar and focus on the super-nutritious foods that will fuel your body in an entirely new, entirely healthy way. If you have digestive issues (IBS, Crohn's disease, constipation, diarrhea) or autoimmune disorders, fatigue, or general malaise, eliminate all legumes until phase 2. Pay attention to how you feel and whether your symptoms change—legumes may be causing or worsening them.

It's best to sit down each evening and write down the next day's menu— or spend time on the weekend planning and shopping for a week's meals. That way, you can make sure you're eating all of the right things in the right amounts.

As you plan your meals, keep in mind that the building blocks of the Omni Diet are protein, healthy fats, and complex carbohydrates.

Protein curbs hunger, helps keep blood sugar stable, prevents energy

Here are some other healthy foods to keep on hand:

- Hummus, salsa, and guacamole for dipping raw vegetables
- Shirataki, soy-free noodles (instead of pasta: my favorite brand is Miracle Noodle)
- Unbleached sea salt (instead of bleached table salt) to be used in *very small* amounts
- Salt substitute (potassium chloride), which is a great substitute for many people on a low-sodium diet
- Unsweetened almond milk or hemp milk (instead of cow's milk)
- Coconut oil, grape-seed oil, macadamia-nut oil, and almond oil
- Almond, macadamia-nut or cashew butter instead of peanut butter
- Goji berries
- Raw, shaved coconut
- Vegan protein powder (sugar-free and sweetened with stevia)— Olympian Labs makes a great-tasting pea protein
- Flax and chia seeds
- Hemp seeds and hemp-seed oil
- Freeze-dried greens
- Earth Balance (butter substitute) or ghee
- Tamari sauce
- Coconut milk
- Liquid stevia sweetener (various flavors) instead of sugar
- Raw, unsweetened cacao (not commercial cocoa)
- Raw cacao nibs

crashes, boosts concentration, helps with weight loss, and provides the necessary building blocks for brain health. Best sources include fish, skinless poultry, eggs, raw nuts, and seeds. Legumes are a good source of protein, but eat them in moderation, and eliminate them altogether if you are symptomatic, meaning you suffer from gastrointestinal upset, skin rashes, fatigue, bloating, flatulence, eczema, congestion, or brain fog. You'll also get protein from some vegetables, such as broccoli and spinach.

Keep these protein guidelines in mind as you plan your meals:

[CAN I DRINK COFFEE AND OTHER CAFFEINATED DRINKS ON THE OMNI DIET?]

It's fine to have one cup of coffee per day (regular size—about 5 to 6 ounces, not a gallon-size Thermos) as long as you drink it before noon. Coffee contains a substance (kahweol) that is considered a super-food, with powerful antioxidant benefits. It's the caffeine that is controversial. For people who metabolize caffeine slowly in the liver (these are people who are usually sensitive to medications), caffeine can have detrimental effects on the heart and blood pressure. For people who metabolize caffeine quickly in the liver (it takes an elephant tranquilizer to knock them out), caffeine does not have the same detrimental effect. However, caffeine does constrict blood flow to the brain and can affect sleep patterns, so it should be consumed only in small amounts and early in the day. Organic coffee is best, as nonorganic coffee is known to contain low levels of arsenic.

If you are a diehard coffee lover, try water-processed decaf or "half-caf" for your afternoon cups.

Green tea is another great alternative. This super-food has been shown to be a powerful antioxidant, and three cups of green tea daily has been shown to have a positive effect on DNA. Be careful not to drink it too late in the afternoon because it does contain caffeine (but less than coffee).

Adding dairy to coffee and tea has been shown to neutralize the healthful antioxidant effects of these drinks. The casein in dairy products binds to the antioxidants and renders them useless. Try a little coconut milk instead.

- 30 percent of your day's calories should come from protein-rich foods.

- Women should eat protein portions of 3 to 4 ounces, or 15 to 20 grams, with each meal.

- Men should eat protein portions of 4 to 6 ounces, or 20 to 25 grams, with each meal.

- Be sure to eat a portion of protein at least four times a day, or every three to four hours.

- Never go longer than four hours without a portion of protein.

Healthy fats help you feel satiated, help your body absorb some nutrients, help you fend off oxidative damage and degenerative nerve disorders, and aid in brain health, hormone synthesis, and cholesterol reduction. Best sources include avocados, tree nuts, seeds, fatty fish such as salmon, and healthy oils such as coconut oil, macadamia-nut oil, and extra-virgin olive oil.

Complex carbohydrates provide energy to your body and brain. Best sources are vegetables, vegetables, and *more vegetables,* as well as fruit in small amounts. Although grains also contain complex carbohydrates, I recommend avoiding them completely during this phase of the Omni Diet. In later weeks you can use them in small amounts if they don't bother you, but for now, it's best to hold off until you've broken your addiction to sugar and simple carbohydrates.

Keep these complex carbohydrate guidelines in mind as you plan your meals:

- **70 percent of your daily calories should come from complex carbohydrates.**

- **Aim to eat 9 cups of vegetables each day. That's right—9 cups. It sounds like a lot, but if you include some at each meal and snack, you'll hit that goal.**

Now, let's look at individual meal planning. First, I'll give you some ideas about what to include in each meal. I don't want you to depend on me for your meals—I want you to eat foods you enjoy. But I will give you two weeks of daily menu suggestions using some of the recipes in this book. These menu ideas should help you figure out exactly how to tailor the Omni Diet to your own individual taste.

BREAKFAST

The old saying is true: Breakfast really is the most important meal of the day. Be sure to eat within an hour of waking up. Research shows that people who eat breakfast every day maintain weight loss better than those who skip their morning meal. A 2002 National Weight Control Registry study of the success secrets of 2,959 people who had lost weight and maintained their new, healthier weight found that 80 percent eat breakfast.[1] Just don't have a simple carb–heavy breakfast. A breakfast of vegetables, healthy fat, and protein balances blood sugar, increases focus, stimulates the hormones associated with satiety, and gives you the mental clarity to make better food decisions all day long. It gives you massive amounts of energy and laser-like focus when you need it most, and it helps prime your hormones to keep cravings at bay later in the day.

Each day, your breakfast should include the following:

- Protein: 3 to 4 ounces for women, 4 to 6 ounces for men
- Healthy fats: approximately 9 or 10 grams (100 calories) from coconut, avocado, flax, eggs, or other healthy source
- Complex carbohydrates: 2 cups of nonstarchy green veggies and ½ cup berries or 1 piece of fruit. You can also add the ingredients suggested in the smoothie recipes, which have been carefully created for you.

LUNCH

Never allowing yourself to get too hungry is one of the keys to success when you are trying to improve your eating and lose weight. When you go too long without food, your blood sugar plummets, your thinking gets foggy, and you become much more prone to make impulsive food choices that are not healthy. Make sure you eat a lunch that includes vegetables, protein, and healthy fats in order to keep your blood sugar stable and your metabolism revved.

Each day, your lunch should include the following:

- Protein: 3 to 4 ounces for women, 4 to 6 ounces for men
- Healthy fats: 10 to 13 grams (90–120 calories), which is equal to about 1 tablespoon olive oil, 1 tablespoon nuts, or 2 ounces avocado
- Complex carbohydrates: 1 cup mixed green salad with 1 cup of mixed veggies

SNACKS

The word "snack" usually conjures up thoughts of junk foods such as candy, cookies, or chips. Forget that. Smart snacks play a crucial role in a healthy diet. These mini-meals help keep blood sugar stable, prevent impulsive eating, keep your metabolism in high gear throughout the day, and give you the fuel you need to concentrate from morning until night. Sensible snacking fights mid-morning fatigue, mid-afternoon carb cravings, and mindless evening grazing.

Each day, plan to eat two or three snacks—good times to snack are mid-morning, mid-afternoon, and late-afternoon. Each snack should include the following:

- Protein: 1–2 ounces (equal to about 2 tablespoons hummus or guacamole or a slice of turkey, or 2 tablespoons whole, raw nuts)
- Healthy fats: 3 to 15 grams
- Complex carbohydrates: 2 to 3 cups raw or lightly steamed veggies

DINNER

The evening is a wonderful time to spend with family and friends cooking and eating an enjoyable, nutrient-packed meal. Your dinner menu can include a healthy protein such as fish or poultry, some lightly cooked vegetables, and a huge salad. Don't forget the fresh herbs and spices, which add deep flavor and important nutrients. Adding the rich flavors of herbs and spices also helps to minimize cravings for heavy sauces.

Remember, eat like a gorilla: Salad with a rainbow of raw veggies, a little fruit, and some nuts and seeds is the "human food" that best matches the gorilla's diet. Add some protein such as fish or meat and you've got a complete meal. Dress salads with 1 tablespoon of healthy oil mixed with either balsamic vinegar or lemon juice and the herbs and spices of your choice.

If you're starving when dinnertime rolls around, you may need to add in an extra afternoon snack. Try a cup of soup such as Shirataki Spinach Soup (page 343) or one of the other snacks I recommended previously.

Each day's dinner should include the following:

- **Protein: 3 to 4 ounces for women, 4 to 6 ounces for men**

- **Healthy fats: 15 to 20 grams (1 tablespoon olive oil, seeds, and avocado on salad, plus minimal amount of oil for cooking)**

- **Complex carbohydrates: 2 cups mixed greens with chopped veggies for salad, plus an additional vegetable dish—3 to 4 cups total**

DESSERT

During phase 1, I suggest minimizing desserts to help crush your cravings. If you really want something sweet, I recommend one piece of extra-dark

IF YOU FAIL TO PLAN, YOU PLAN TO FAIL!

I believe in that 100 percent. Making healthy changes in your diet is so much easier when you plan ahead. The better prepared you can be, the more likely you are to stick with the program.

One of the secrets of Omni Diet success is to take a few minutes each evening to write down what you plan to eat the next day. That way, you won't be making decisions on the fly about what to eat for each meal. You'll know exactly what and how much to eat.

Here are some tips for effective planning:

- Have plenty of travel-size storage containers on hand, and keep them in a convenient location in your kitchen. Immediately pack leftovers in the containers so you have a good supply of healthy ready-to-eat foods.

- Always have an ice chest ready for on-the-go meals and snacks. Having a good supply of meals and snacks helps keep you out of the drive-thru line.

- Stock your kitchen with healthy foods (veggies, hummus, nuts, and seeds) packed in snack-size portions.

- Set aside time each week to draw up a grocery list, plan the week's meals, go shopping, and do prep work such as washing and cutting vegetables. When you shop, don't deviate from your list.

- When you prepare meals, make extra so there's plenty of left-overs.

- Always carry nuts and seeds in your purse so you can keep yourself from getting too hungry if you're delayed.

- Set aside a few minutes each evening to plan your next day's menu.

- If mornings are rushed, pack your lunch and snacks the evening before.

- When you're invited to someone's house for dinner, tell them you'll bring a big salad. That way, you know there'll be something for you to eat—and you'll be spreading the word about healthy food by showing others how delicious a nutrient-packed salad can be.

organic chocolate, another smoothie, or half an apple with almond butter. Or have ½ cup of Fresh Berries with Macadamia-Nut Sauce (recipe on page 380) as an acceptable treat. Eating dessert replaces one of your five "meals," unless you only eat *one* piece (½ ounce) of dark chocolate.

In future weeks, there will be more room for desserts in the Omni Diet.

WATER

Your body needs water in order to process protein and prevent dehydration, so as you increase your protein intake with the Omni Diet, you must make sure you're drinking enough water. I recommend drinking half your body weight in ounces—for example, if you weigh 160 pounds, drink 80 ounces of water daily. Do not exceed 100 ounces of water daily.

Staying hydrated helps you in some other ways, too. Your brain is

OMNI DIET POSTCARD

"While losing fifteen pounds is a very exciting start, what I value most are the tools I have gained to be healthy, feel better, live longer, and be the best I can be. I am also so grateful that the foods actually taste great!" —RONNETTE

80 percent water. Keeping your brain hydrated helps optimize brain function. Water helps your body process and flush out the toxins that are released when you lose weight and burn stored body fat. Staying hydrated also helps prevent overeating. Often when people think they're hungry, they're actually thirsty. Drinking 16 ounces of water before a meal or snack helps you eat less and still feel satiated.[2]

SAMPLE MENUS:
TWO WEEKS TO JUMPSTART YOUR NEW LIFE

THIS TWO-WEEK SAMPLE MENU WILL help you get started on your journey to success. The recipes for each meal are found in the back of this book. As this healthy, energizing menu shows, there are as many options as there are days in a year if you mix and match meals.

Keep in mind this sample menu is just a suggestion. Many of these recipes are versatile enough that you can adapt them according to what you like. As for the portion sizes, if you need to increase your calorie count a bit, add another half portion to one or two of the meal items. Men may need to double the portion sizes on some meal items.

Phase 1, Week 1 Success Menu

	BREAKFAST	SNACK	LUNCH	SNACK	DINNER
DAY 1	Brain-Smart Start Smoothie	¼ cup raw almonds or sunflower seeds	Heirloom Tomato Salad	2 cups mixed veggies with 2 tablespoons Traditional Hummus	Serrano Chile Shrimp, Harmonizing Vegetable Soup, and simple mixed green salad
DAY 2	Pacific Coast Scramble	Homemade Super-Food Protein Bar and ½ cup mixed berries *or* 1 piece of fruit	Seared Ahi with Cucumber Salad	Large mixed green salad, with 3 ounces hard-boiled egg or other protein, 1 tablespoon raw seeds, and 1 tablespoon olive oil and lemon juice	Sizzling Chicken Kabobs with Rainbow Chard Slaw
DAY 3	Very Omega Cherry Smoothie	1 hard-boiled egg and 2 cups raw veggies with 2 tablespoons Guacamole for dipping	Simple mixed green salad with Herb-Marinated Chicken and 1 tablespoon olive oil and balsamic vinegar	2 tablespoons raw nuts or seeds	Macadamia-Crusted Mahimahi, Pan-Roasted Brussels Sprouts, and Shirataki Spinach Soup
DAY 4	Brain-Smart Start Smoothie	2 cups of raw vegetables + ¼ cup Guacamole	Peaceful Asian Pear Salad with shrimp	Tasty Turkey Wrap	Free-Range Bison Meatloaf, Cauliflower Garlic Mashed "Potatoes," Amazing Raw Creamed Spinach
DAY 5	Chocolate-Covered Strawberry Smoothie	1 hard-boiled egg and celery with 1 tablespoon almond butter	Brain-Boosting BBQ Chicken Salad	2 cups raw vegetables with 2 tablespoons Traditional Hummus, Guacamole, or salsa for dipping	Spice of Life Chicken with Roasted Beet Salad and 2 cups steamed vegetables
DAY 6	Cinnamon-Spice Stabilizer	2–3 cups chopped veggies with Split Pea Hummus	Tasty Turkey Wrap	1 apple and ¼ cup raw nuts or seeds	Crowd-Pleasing Cioppino, Sautéed Collard Greens, and Antiox Detox Chopped Salad
DAY 7	Seafood Omelet for Super Focus with ¼ cup blueberries	¼ cup raw nuts or seeds and 1 small piece of fruit	Stay-Sharp Chard Salad	1 sliced tomato with avocado (about 2 tablespoons)	"Spaghetti" with Turkey Meatballs, steamed broccoli, and Cool Kale Salad with Cilantro Dressing

Phase 1, Week 2 Success Menu

	BREAKFAST	SNACK	LUNCH	SNACK	DINNER
DAY 1	Green Tea Berry Blastoff	Celery with 2 tablespoons raw almond butter	Asian-Fusion Chicken Salad	Simple mixed green salad with sunflower seeds and 1 tablespoon olive oil and lemon juice	Pan-Roasted Salmon with Vegetables
DAY 2	Antioxidant Energizing Smoothie	2 cups raw vegetables with 2 tablespoons Baba Ghanoush	Get Smart Mahimahi Burger wrapped in romaine lettuce	¼ cup raw nuts and seeds and 2 cups veggies with salsa	Savory Lubia Rose Stew, Stay-Sharp Chard Salad, and Yellow Beans with Tomatoes
DAY 3	Brainy Breakfast Burrito	Homemade Super-Food Protein Bar and 1 piece of fruit or ½ cup berries	Snappy Mango Chicken Salad	1 hard-boiled egg and 2 cups chopped veggies with Guacamole (2 tablespoons)	Shrimp Chowder and Red, White, and Blue Salad
DAY 4	Brain-Smart Start Smoothie	2 cups raw vegetables with ¼ cup Guacamole	Peaceful Asian Pear Salad	Tasty Turkey Wrap	Free-Range Bison Meatloaf, Cauliflower Garlic Mashed "Potatoes," and Amazing Raw Creamed Spinach
DAY 5	Super Surprise Frittata	Omni Grainless Granola Protein Bar and 1 piece of fruit or ½ cup berries	Turkey Burger	Celery with 2 tablespoons raw almond butter	Seared Ahi with Guacamole, Tana's Smooth Sweet Potato Soup, and Magnificent Mind Cucumber Mint Salad
DAY 6	Chocolate-Covered Strawberry Smoothie	1 sliced tomato with 2 tablespoons avocado	Hearty Chicken Stew	Devil-Less Eggs	Roasted Vegetable Salad, Pan-Seared Salmon, and Cream of Broccoli Soup
DAY 7	Benedict-Style Poached Eggs with kale or steamed spinach	2 cups veggies with 2 tablespoons Traditional Hummus or Split Pea Hummus	Guiltless Chicken Breast Tenders, kale, and Harmonizing Vegetable Soup	½ cup berries with ¼ cup Go Well Trail Mix	Healthy Turkey Chili and Rainbow Chard Slaw

PUTTING IT ON THE PLATE:
MY TYPICAL DAY ON THE OMNI DIET

I DON'T JUST FOLLOW THE Omni Diet—I live it. And I enjoy it! Every day I eat a variety of delicious, healthy foods. My menu is a bit less complex than the sample menus—I'm on the run most days, and it's easier for me to eat simply, with a focus on vegetables and easy-to-carry meals. At my house, the special meal of the day is dinner, and I make sure there's enough food so that I automatically have lunch made for the next day. That saves me a lot of time. Here's a look at a typical day of eating for me:

6:30 A.M.

BREAKFAST. Within an hour of waking up, I have a Brain-Smart Start Smoothie made with ½ cup of organic berries or cherries, ⅛ avocado, 1 cup of spinach, and 1 cup kale or chard (which I can't even taste), a scoop of dried greens, 4 to 8 ounces of coconut water or unsweetened almond milk, 16 ounces of water, 15 to 20 grams of protein powder, and a few drops of stevia. I also add a few super-foods such as bee pollen, aloe vera gel, or raw cacao. After my smoothie, I have a cup of green or herbal tea.

10:00 A.M.

MID-MORNING SNACK. A hard-boiled egg and a green juice; 16 ounces of water with fresh-squeezed lemon juice.

12–12:30 P.M.

LUNCH. 2 to 3 cups of raw, chopped veggies with 2 tablespoons hummus, baba ghanoush, or salsa; 2 to 3 ounces of lean protein (usually tuna, salmon, or shrimp), and 1 tablespoon chopped, raw almonds or walnuts; 16 ounces of water with lemon.

2:00 P.M.

MID-AFTERNOON SNACK (optional—if I'm hungry). A homemade Super-Food Protein Bar (page 323); 16 ounces of water.

4:30 P.M.

LATE-AFTERNOON SNACK.

OPTION 1: Amazing Apple-Cinnamon Chicken Salad; water with lemon.

OPTION 2: If I am on the run, I have another Brain-Smart Start Smoothie with ½ apple, ½ grapefruit or pear, ½ carrot, ½ cucumber, one scoop of dried greens, 10 to 15 grams of protein powder, and 1 tablespoon flax or pumpkin seeds; 16 ounces water with lemon.

[TAKEOFF TIPS]

Keep these strategies in mind as you plan your meals each day:

- Eat breakfast within an hour of waking up.
- Eat every three to four hours, having a meal or snack five or six times a day.
- Limit foods that are overcooked. Instead, opt for as many raw and lightly cooked choices as possible.
- Shake hands with protein. You can use the palm of your hand to determine a good portion size for protein foods. A 20–40 gram serving of meat or fish is about the size and width of the palm of your hand (minus your fingers).
- Never allow yourself to become too hungry. Be sure to eat every three to four hours, and always include protein and healthy fats in each meal.
- If you are going to go off plan and splurge, do it with lean protein and healthy fat, *not carbohydrates!* This will help to give your brain the signal that you are satisfied, unlike simple or starchy carbs, which will make you hungrier.
- If you are eating every three to four hours and you still feel hungry, increase your intake of raw or lightly cooked (nonstarchy) vegetables—they're "green light" foods, and you can have as much as you want. Keep in mind that fruit, with its high concentration of fructose (fruit sugar), raises blood sugar and insulin levels and therefore should be limited to one or two servings a day.
- Instead of bread, use lettuce wraps for sandwiches and burgers.
- Always plan ahead. Do your menu planning, shopping, and food preparation in advance—it's great if you can use one day each week to prepare for the following days. Pack your lunch and have plenty of healthy snacks on hand, along with an ice chest that's ready to go whenever you leave the house. The better prepared you can be, the more likely you are to stick with the program. As the saying goes, if you fail to plan, you plan to fail.
- When you're preparing meals, cook extra and pack leftovers for the next day's lunch.
- Always have fresh avocados handy for guacamole.
- In restaurants, don't let the waiter leave bread on the table.
- Have a delicious list of alternatives handy for the things you might crave.

[MAKE SMOOTHIES YOUR GO-TO FAST FOOD]

Smoothies are my favorite example of a perfectly balanced meal. They're a convenient, delicious way to optimize nutrition and enjoy a tasty, refreshing raw meal of protein, healthy fat, phytonutrients, vitamins, minerals, fiber, and other fabulous nutrients. And they're great when you're in a hurry—think of them as the Omni Diet's fast food.

If you've never made smoothies before, I recommend you give them a try. Before you know it, you'll wonder how you lived without them! Here are some tips for making sensational smoothies:

- Use a high-powered blender. It doesn't have to be expensive, but it's best if it's high-powered. Vitamix is great, but expensive. Blendtec is also a great product.
- Play with the ingredients and be creative, but pay attention to sugar and calorie content. Make sure to include at least 1 tablespoon of healthy fat and 20 to 30 grams of protein. The recipes I provide are a balance of protein, healthy fat, and an abundance of micronutrients and phytonutrients.
- Use pure coconut water, which is a natural electrolyte-rich "sports drink," as a smoothie base. If you like to add ice to your smoothies, freeze coconut water in an ice cube tray and toss coconut cubes into the blender.
- Add soluble fiber to increase feelings of fullness and satiety, and to aid with bowel health. Inulin is a prebiotic (food for the good bacteria in your gut). Glucomannan increases bulk, balances blood sugar, and has been shown to improve cholesterol profiles.
- Add in super-foods such as bee pollen, aloe gel, maca root powder, acai, pomegranate, camu camu, lucuma, and goji powder, many

7–7:30 P.M.

DINNER. 1½ cups shredded spaghetti squash or shirataki noodles topped with tomato-basil sauce containing 2 to 3 ounces of lean protein (shrimp or ground turkey); a large green salad with 1 tablespoon olive oil dressing; 1 to 2 cups steamed broccoli; 1 cup of caffeine-free herbal tea with a few drops of stevia.

of which are believed to have antioxidant or anti-inflammatory properties.

- Add freeze-dried greens—my favorite brand is Vibrant Health Green Vibrance, which contains probiotics and a lot of fruit and vegetable extracts. I also like the chocolate flavor from Amazing Grass. I buy it at my local health food store. When choosing powdered greens, be sure they do not contain gluten.

- Raw greens contribute lots of fabulous nutrients to smoothies, but they have a tart taste that can take some getting used to. If you are sensitive to the taste of raw greens, start with a small amount, and gradually increase the amount you add as you acquire a taste for them. Your goal should be four parts greens to one part fruit. You can also add a teaspoon of raw honey (if you are not insulin-resistant) to soften the bitterness of the greens, but once you get used to it, cut back and eventually eliminate your use of sweeteners other than stevia.

- Raw cacao is one of my favorite smoothie ingredients—it is the pure form of cacao before it has been processed. It is loaded with antioxidants and phytonutrients, and adds fun flavor. You can find it in most health food stores.

- Add 1 or 2 teaspoons of coconut butter or almond butter to add the appropriate amount of healthy fats, soften the taste of the greens, and add a creamy texture to a smoothie.

- 1 tablespoon of flax, hemp, or chia seeds adds additional fiber and plant-based proteins. These ingredients are high in omega-3 fatty acids and contain potent cancer-fighting properties. Do not use flax oil—it contains inflammatory omega-6 fatty acids and loses most of its anti-cancer benefits during processing.

MOST PEOPLE FIND THAT THEY are not able to consume this much food after the first couple of weeks (when cravings disappear). Eliminate a snack if this happens. And remember, the meals are supposed to be small.

PHASE 2

[Pump It Up]

We must all suffer from one of two pains, the pain of
discipline or the pain of regret!

—JIM ROHN

DURING THE TWO WEEKS OF phase 2, you can look forward to these
exciting results:

- Weight loss of 5 to 15 pounds (15 to 30 pounds all together, depending
  on your size and gender)

- Increased muscle mass

- Decreased body fat—during phase 2, people really start noticing a difference in their appearance

- Dramatic improvement in energy and focus

- Radical improvement of memory and cognitive function

- Significant changes in personal motivation, accountability, and feelings
  of excitement

- Increasing comfort with your new way of eating, which becomes easier
  and more natural as new routines form into habits

YOUR STRATEGY

During phase 2, you continue the 70/30 eating strategy you started in
phase 1—70 percent of your calories from plant foods, and 30 percent from

protein-rich foods. To help you know exactly how to design your phase 2 daily menus, I'll give you specific guidelines and a two-week sample menu plan featuring recipes from this book.

You'll also ramp up your exercise. During phase 1, you walked briskly for 30 minutes a day. Now you'll add easy, effective muscle-building, fat-burning exercise routines that will jump-start your fitness level and your weight loss.

GET STARTED

First we'll talk food; then I'll tell you how to pump up your fitness with the Omni Diet Exercise Plan.

STEP 1: PLAN YOUR MEALS

MEAL PLANNING CONTINUES TO BE key as you start phase 2 of the Omni Diet. Plan your meals by the day or week so you can be sure you're getting the right amount and the right kinds of food. Keep your kitchen well stocked with fresh, whole foods from the grocery store, health food store, and farmers' market. And continue to think ahead when you're preparing meals—whenever possible, make extra and pack it up for easy grab-and-go lunches and snacks.

Calorie goals are the same as in phase 1, but it's good to look at where you might be able to refine your program. You can't keep doing the same thing and expect the same results. As you lose dramatic amounts of weight (if that's your goal), you will need to "up your game" if you want to continue losing. I am not an advocate of starvation diets, so I don't recommend slashing calories to a dangerous level. But I do recommend taking a serious inventory of your food consumption and increasing daily exercise during phase 2.

In my experience, clients forget or begin to relax on portion sizes after a couple of weeks, and old habits begin to sneak back in. Although you are less likely to crave sugar, you still have some work to do on breaking old habits, creating new ones, and changing your psychology. This is the time to be *the most vigilant!*

If you're not already keeping a food journal, start now. Journaling cures "food amnesia," a phenomenon that nearly everyone I work with has. Yes, the two bites of your daughter's French toast—with syrup—count. It all adds up. Writing down everything you eat in a food journal helps you become more aware of what and how much you're eating. It also allows you to pinpoint

(continued on page 218)

KEEP A FOOD JOURNAL

Writing down everything you eat in a food journal is an incredibly good way to understand your own eating patterns—and an incredibly effective tool for Omni Diet success.

I know, I know. You don't feel like keeping a journal. You've got enough to do without having to keep track of every morsel that goes into your mouth. I get it—keeping a journal takes time. But let me tell you: It's worth it. Research shows (as does nearly every successful long-term program) that keeping a food journal is a critical tool for changing eating behavior.

"A food journal is one of the easiest ways to keep track of what you're eating," says Anne McTiernan, a researcher at Fred Hutchinson Cancer Research Center who recently published a study about the effectiveness of food journaling.[1] "If you write it down, it seems more real. If you don't, it's so easy to pretend to yourself that you didn't eat that much."

Keeping a food journal was an incredibly eye-opening experience for Mari, who has struggled with eating disorders since she was a teen. When she started following the Omni Diet, Mari thought she was doing everything right, but she wasn't losing weight. That didn't stop her from continuing her new way of eating because she was experiencing other wonderful benefits: She felt better and was excited that she finally understood exactly how food and health were connected. Even more important, the Omni Diet was helping Mari stay "sober" with food and change her disordered eating patterns for the first time in many years. Still, she would have liked to be losing weight.

I recommended she keep a food journal. Like many people, Mari was reluctant to do this at first. But I convinced her, and it made a big difference. Writing down everything she ate, Mari realized that she hadn't been measuring her portion sizes correctly and was not sticking to a helpful meal schedule. Also, it showed her how many calories she took in by unconsciously having a bite here and a nibble there. What she thought were normal eating patterns were actually patterns that were sabotaging her success.

Thanks to her food journaling, Mari lost 17 pounds. She looks incredible, is making great progress with her eating disorder, and has more energy than ever before. "Now I come home and have energy for my family," Mari reported. "They have their mommy back."

Like just about everyone who keeps a food journal, Mari learned first-hand that writing down your meals and snacks forces you to be completely aware of (and accountable for) the food choices you make. It is the best treatment I know for a very prevalent condition known as "food amnesia"—forgetting when you eat a few bites of your child's breakfast or polish off the dinner leftovers that were supposed to be the next day's lunch, which can add hundreds of calories to your diet each day.

Any kind of journal works—a notebook, your phone, even just a piece of paper taped to the refrigerator. Keep it simple: Whenever you eat something, write down the time, the food, and the portion size. And jot down some other relevant notes as well, such as what events or situations preceded the meal or snack, whether you were stressed or had PMS, whether you were eating in response to a craving, and anything else that might be relevant. It really doesn't take long at all.

After a week of keeping a food journal, go through it and see what you notice. Usually, strong patterns pointing to unhealthy eating jump right out at you. For example, you may see that you make poor snack choices in the evening while you're watching TV. Or you may notice hunger at 3 P.M. sends you off to the vending machines at work.

Once you know and understand your negative eating patterns, you can devise solutions. If you like to eat in the evening, rearrange your meals to make room for an extra evening meal or snack. If you're very hungry at 3 P.M., shift some of your dinner calories to mid-afternoon and be sure to have healthy snacks close at hand. Once you know your weak points, you can address them in a healthy way.

Don't worry—you don't have to keep this up forever (although some people do because it helps them so much). Keeping a food journal for even just a couple of weeks can help cure food amnesia and give you valuable information about your eating habits.

problems in your diet— not only *what* you are eating, but *when.* Journaling will help you identify the negative pattern. If you are slipping up every night right before dinner at the same time, you may need to eat dinner a bit earlier. Or if you are finding yourself tempted at work by the junk on your colleague's desk, start bringing a healthy snack that you can enjoy instead. Checking your food journal can tell you how to adjust your next day's menu. Use whatever kind of journal you like—a notebook, a page taped to the refrigerator, your datebook, an online journal, or your phone. But keep the journal handy, and keep the pages together.

Journaling is not something you will need to do forever. It is a tool to help you increase conscientiousness, to help you change the bad habits that took years to develop.

The good habits you implemented in phase 1 should continue:

- Eat breakfast within an hour of waking up.

- Limit foods that are overcooked; opt for as many raw and lightly cooked choices as possible.

- Measure your portions.

- If you are tempted to indulge in food not on your menu—which you should be less likely to do, now that you've broken your sugar addiction—do so with healthy fat and protein, not carbohydrates.

- Never allow yourself to become too hungry. Be sure to eat every three or four hours, having a meal or snack five or six times a day, and always include protein and healthy fats in each meal.

- If you do feel hungry, increase your intake of raw vegetables in meals and snacks.

- Continue to limit fruit to no more than one or two servings a day; the best choices are strawberries, blueberries, and blackberries, which have less of an impact on blood sugar than starchy fruits such as bananas.

- Always, always, always plan ahead!

Breakfast, lunch, dinner, and snacks should be the same size and calorie count as phase 1. However, there's more room for dessert during phase 2 of the Omni Diet—but not the sugar-filled, fat-laden "treats" that the food industry has convinced Americans to eat. The fact is, you can make delicious desserts without butter, sugar, white flour, and a processing factory. Now that you've broken your addiction to sugar and simple carbohydrates, you're reactivat-

Homemade protein bars (grain-free, gluten-free) make a great snack, and they are quick and easy to make. I've included a simple, delicious recipe for protein bars that you can whip up in no time. While commercial protein bars are not my first choice, they are good in a pinch. Sometimes I carry them when I'm traveling and am unable to plan meals as effectively as usual. If you buy protein bars, be sure to read labels carefully, because many are loaded with sugar.

ing your taste buds. Now you can start to enjoy the taste of naturally sweet, unprocessed foods that satisfy your sweet tooth and reflect the Omni Diet's nutritional principles.

If you choose to have dessert, it counts as a meal or snack. Make sure you factor it into your daily plan. These delicious treats should be eaten in *small portions*! I don't want you ruining all of the hard work you have done and reactivating your sweet tooth.

SAMPLE MENUS

THIS TWO-WEEK SAMPLE MENU WILL help you keep up the momentum you built during the first two weeks of the Omni Diet. As with previous menus, the recipes in these menus are found in the back of this book.

Continue to adapt the menus according to what kinds of foods you like. And continue to adjust portion sizes based on your daily calorie needs.

Phase 2, Week 1 Success Menu

	BREAKFAST	SNACK	LUNCH	SNACK	DINNER	DESSERT
DAY 1	Peach Fuzz Fantastico Smoothie	¼ cup raw almonds or sunflower seeds	Amazing Apple-Cinnamon Chicken Salad	2 cups mixed veggies with 2 tablespoons Traditional Hummus	Snapper with Tomato Caper Sauce, Harmonizing Vegetable Soup, and South of the Border Salad Cups	Goji Nut Truffles (1 to 2 pieces, but don't make them huge! Use only 2 tablespoons honey)
DAY 2	Herb Garden Frittata	Homemade Super-Food Protein Bar and ½ cup mixed berries	Seared Ahi with Cucumber Salad	Large mixed green salad with 3 ounces hard-boiled egg or other protein, 1 tablespoon raw seeds, and 1 tablespoon olive oil and lemon juice	Tomato Curry Chicken with Saffron and Rainbow Chard Slaw	1 piece extra-dark, organic chocolate (½ ounce)
DAY 3	Very Omega Cherry Smoothie	1 hard-boiled egg and 2 cups raw veggies with 2 tablespoons Guacamole for dipping	Simple mixed green salad with Herb-Marinated Chicken and 1 tablespoon olive oil and balsamic vinegar	2 tablespoons raw nuts or seeds	Macadamia-Crusted Mahimahi, Pan-Roasted Brussels Sprouts, and Shirataki Spinach Soup	Avocado Gelato Square
DAY 4	Clear Start Breakfast Burrito	Pumpkin Protein Bar and 1 piece of fruit *or* ½ cup berries	Get Fit Chicken, Fennel, and Orange Salad	2–3 cups raw veggies with 2 tablespoons Traditional Hummus, Guacamole, or salsa for dipping	Cedar Plank Salmon, Roasted Beet Salad, and Braised Cauliflower with Basil Sauce	Dessert Smoothie

	BREAKFAST	SNACK	LUNCH	SNACK	DINNER	DESSERT
DAY 5	Chocolate-Covered Strawberry Smoothie	Celery with 2 tablespoons raw almond butter	Spinach and Strawberry Salad with Pecans and Shrimp Cocktail	2 cups raw vegetables with 2 tablespoons Traditional Hummus, Guacamole, or salsa for dipping	The Best Beef Stroganoff with Roasted Beet Salad and 2 cups steamed vegetables	Fresh Berries with Macadamia-Nut Sauce
DAY 6	Cacao Mint Madness	2–3 cups chopped veggies with Split Pea Hummus	Tasty Turkey Wrap	1 apple and ¼ cup raw nuts or seeds	Crowd-Pleasing Cioppino, Sautéed Collard Greens, and Antiox Detox Chopped Salad	1 piece extra-dark, organic chocolate (½ ounce)
DAY 7	Omni-Style Crepes	¼ cup raw nuts or seeds and 1 small piece of fruit	Stay-Sharp Chard Salad	1 sliced tomato with avocado (about 2 tablespoons)	Bison London Broil, steamed broccoli, and Cool Kale Salad with Cilantro Dressing	Fabulous Fruit Fondue (2 pieces)

Phase 2, Week 2 Success Menu

	BREAKFAST	SNACK	LUNCH	SNACK	DINNER	DESSERT
DAY 1	Mango Passion Smoothie	Celery with 2 tablespoons raw almond butter	Ahi and Tana's Smooth Sweet Potato Soup	Simple mixed green salad with sunflower seeds and 1 tablespoon olive oil and lemon juice	Simply Delicious Pan-Seared Trout and Cucumber Salad	Goji Nut Truffles
DAY 2	Antioxidant Energizing Smoothie	2 cups raw vegetables with 2 tablespoons Baba Ghanoush	Salmon Burger wrapped in romaine lettuce	¼ cup raw nuts and seeds and ¼ cup frozen grapes	Lentil Lamb Stew, Stay-Sharp Chard Salad, and Yellow Beans with Tomatoes	Magnificent Cacao "Nut" Macaroons (1–2 pieces)
DAY 3	Sausage in Green Blankets and steamed spinach	Homemade Super-Food Protein Bar and 1 piece of fruit or ½ cup berries	Rainbow Quinoa Salad with Chicken	Low-carb protein bar	Shrimp Chowder and Red, White, and Blue Salad	1 piece extra-dark, organic chocolate (½ ounce)
DAY 4	Brain-Smart Start Smoothie	2 cups raw vegetables with ¼ cup Guacamole	Almond Chicken Chopped Salad	Tasty Turkey Wrap	Dr. Amen's Quick and Tasty Pork Chops, Cauliflower Mashed Garlic "Potatoes," and Amazing Raw Creamed Spinach	Frozen Banana
DAY 5	Southwestern Huevos	Homemade Super-Food Protein Bar and 1 piece of fruit or ½ cup berries	Turkey Burger	Celery with 2 tablespoons raw almond butter	Baked Halibut with Creamed Spinach Sauce, Tana's Smooth Sweet Potato Soup, and Magnificent Mind Cucumber Mint Salad	Mulberry Ball
DAY 6	Chocolate-Covered Strawberry Smoothie	1 sliced tomato with 2 tablespoons avocado	Hearty Chicken Stew	Devil-Less Eggs	Pan-Roasted Salmon with Vegetables and Cream of Broccoli Soup	Chocolate Coconut Ice Cream
DAY 7	Benedict-Style Poached Eggs with kale	2 cups veggies with 2 tablespoons Traditional Hummus or Split Pea Hummus	Brain-Fit Fajitas and Harmonizing Vegetable Soup	½ cup berries with ¼ cup Go Well Trail Mix	Turkey Bolognese and Rainbow Chard Slaw	Pumpkin Protein Bar

[A RAINBOW OF ANTIOXIDANTS]

Be sure to include plenty of colorful antioxidant foods in your daily diet—they protect your body from oxidative stress. Eating from the rainbow ensures you are getting micronutrients and phytonutrients, which boost the antioxidant level in your body and help keep your body and brain young and healthy.

Some of the best include:

- apples
- arugula
- basil
- beets
- berries (blueberries, raspberries, strawberries, acai berries)
- bok choy
- broccoli
- Brussels sprouts
- cabbage and kohlrabi
- carrots
- cauliflower
- chicory
- chives/onions/leeks
- citrus fruits
- collard greens
- daikon
- garlic
- grapes
- green beans
- horseradish
- kale
- lettuce
- mangoes
- melon
- noni juice
- peaches
- pears
- peas
- peppers
- pomegranates
- pumpkin and squash
- red radish
- spinach
- spices such as cardamom, cinnamon, cloves, and oregano
- tomatoes
- turnips

STEP 2: EXERCISE SMARTER

IF SOME EXERCISE IS GOOD, more is better—and a huge amount is best of all, right? Wrong! That's a myth so many people have bought into. Not only is it untrue, but it's destructive. It stops people from getting optimal exercise results because they don't have hours a day to spend in the gym that they think they need.

Here's the truth about exercise: It is incredibly valuable for many reasons, which I explain in chapter 10. But you don't have to run marathons or become a world-class bodybuilder to benefit from exercise. You can attain optimal fitness in far less time than you might imagine. Success comes from exercising smarter, not necessarily harder.

The key is to train well without overtraining. Doing too much aerobic exercise decreases muscle mass, increases cortisol secretion, and depletes your organ reserves. Organ reserve refers to the "cushion" you have (to function beyond ordinary needs) in case of illness or accident. The most effective and healthiest form of exercise is shorter in duration and higher in intensity.

My Omni Diet Workout is the smartest way to exercise because it concentrates highly effective moves into a program that works your entire body. It combines interval training with weight training for maximum benefits in the shortest time. It can be done at home, in the gym, or even in a hotel room when you're on the road. You can adjust its intensity according to your current fitness level, and increase intensity as you become stronger.

Before you get started, keep two things in mind. First, if you have a medical condition or if you've never engaged in regular exercise, be sure to get your doctor's approval before you start. Second, once you first start exercising, you may find that you feel so good that you overdo it. Try to hold back—the best, fastest way to achieve results is not to overtrain but to train at optimal levels.

YOUR WORKOUT SCHEDULE

For best results, follow this exercise schedule:

- **Mondays, Wednesdays, and Fridays:** Strength train for about 40 minutes a day using the Omni Strength-Training Workout.

- **Tuesdays and Thursdays:** Interval train for 30 minutes (20 minutes if you're a beginner) a day using the Omni Interval Training Workout.

- **Saturdays:** Interval train or take a leisurely 30-minute walk.

- **Sundays:** Rest and rejuvenate.

THE OMNI INTERVAL TRAINING WORKOUT

INTERVAL TRAINING COMBINES MODERATE EXERCISE with bursts of intensity. When you do interval training, you work at a moderate pace, go all out at a high intensity for a short period of time, and then return to your initial moderate pace. After giving yourself some time to recover, repeat your high-intensity burst of activity.

For example, you may alternate three minutes of brisk walking with one minute of sprinting. Or on a bicycle, you may alternate several minutes of comfortable pedaling with a brief burst of intense pedaling. You can do interval training indoors on a treadmill, stationary cycle, or other cardiovascular gym machine, or outdoors while walking, jogging, or cycling.

Let your fitness level determine your pace. Train for 20 to 30 minutes, but no longer. Begin with a moderate pace for 3 minutes, followed by a burst of maximum exertion for 30 seconds to 1 minute. Then repeat. Try to burst at least four times during an interval workout.

If you are just starting to exercise and are overweight, your pace for interval training may be a slow walk. If you're already in good shape, you may be sprinting uphill. Either one is okay. Start where you are, and work up from there.

If you're a beginner or if you have any medical conditions, I advise using a heart-rate (HR) monitor. You can get a decent one for about twenty-five dollars. Using an HR monitor helps you regulate your workouts and prevents you from exercising too intensely. Once you're in shape, you won't need it as much.

THE OMNI STRENGTH-TRAINING WORKOUT

STRENGTH TRAINING BUILDS LEAN MUSCLE tissue. As I explain in chapter 10, increasing lean muscle revs up your metabolism and boosts calorie burn even when you're not exercising. Why? Because maintaining muscle requires ten times more energy than maintaining fat. Building lean muscle tissue also helps prevent osteoporosis and bone loss.

I recommend doing the Omni Strength-Training Workout three times a week, on Mondays, Wednesdays, and Fridays. Plan about 40 minutes per session.

Other than comfortable clothes and sneakers, this workout requires little or no exercise equipment. If you can afford it, buy some dumbbells, also known as free weights. It's nice to have a workout bench, but if you don't, you can use a chair or bed. And as I mentioned, an HR monitor can be helpful.

Exercise is most effective when the intensity level causes your heart to beat at specific rates, depending on the kind of exercise you're doing. To determine your optimal heart rates for various activities, follow these steps:

- For your maximum heart rate (MHR), subtract your age from 220. If you are fifty years old, for example, your maximum heart rate is 170.
- For your target heart rate (THR), multiply your MHR by 0.6 (60 percent) for strength training, 0.7 (70 percent) for cardiovascular training, and 0.85 (85 percent) for interval training.
- Check your HR monitor while you're working out. If your HR is too high, slow down a bit. If it's too low, push a little harder.
- Never let your heart rate exceed 85 percent of your MHR.
- If you have health problems, talk with your health-care provider about the right target heart rates for you.

When you do your strength-training exercises, be sure to rest between sets until your heart rate reaches about 60 percent of your maximum heart rate. This is your target heart rate. (See the Best Beats box for details on determining target heart rates.) As you begin to increase your strength and endurance, you will naturally decrease the amount of rest time between sets.

Special thanks to Brad Davidson from Stark Training for his help in designing a safe introductory workout that can be done anywhere. For more information on Stark Training and Brad Davidson, visit www.starktraining.com.

Split Squats (Lunges)

You get a lot of bang for your buck with split squats, which target all the big muscles in your legs, including the calves, hamstrings, quadriceps, inner and outer thighs, hips, and glutes (buttocks). That's a lot of muscles to work with one simple move.

SPLIT SQUAT START POSITION   **SPLIT SQUAT END POSITION**

1. Start by standing with your feet hip-width distance apart.

2. Step your left foot back about two feet so you are resting on the ball of the left foot. Make sure your front foot is completely flat on the floor.

3. Slowly bend both knees and lower your body into a lunge so your left knee is almost touching the ground and your right knee is in line with or slightly behind your right toes. Keep your torso upright rather than leaning forward.

4. Come back to standing with your feet hip-width apart.

5. Do 15 to 20 reps on each side.

   - If you are a beginner or feel unstable in this stance, you can do split squats without moving your feet. Simply lunge on one leg and come back to standing.

   - If you are more advanced, you can alternate legs with each repetition.

   - For the most advanced version, do walking lunges while carrying dumbbells.

Dumbbell Single Arm Rows

If you've ever leaned over to pick something up off the floor, you've done a single arm row. Rows may look like they're targeting your arm muscles, but they actually strengthen the muscles in your back. Start with 5- to 10-pound weights if you're a woman, and 10- to 15-pound weights if you're a man.

SINGLE ARM ROW START AND END POSITION   **SINGLE ARM ROW MID-POINT POSITION**

1. Start with your left knee and left hand on a bench (or couch or bed) and your back parallel to the floor. Your torso will hover above the bench with your back as flat as a table. Hold a free weight in your right hand, making sure it is in alignment with your right shoulder.

2. Bend your right elbow as you slowly pull the weight toward you, making sure you don't hunch your shoulder up toward your ear.

3. Do 10 to 12 reps.

4. Switch sides so your right knee and right hand are on the bench/couch/bed and the weight is in your left hand.

5. Do 10 to 12 reps.

Bridge with Alternating Leg Lifts

This is a great exercise to tone and tighten the glutes (buttocks) without the risk of hurting your back.

BRIDGE START POSITION

BRIDGE MID-POINT POSITION

BRIDGE END POSITION

1. Start by lying on your back with both your knees bent and your feet flat on the floor. Allow your arms to rest on the ground at a 45 degree angle from your torso (this is for support and to aid in balance).

2. Push your weight into your heels and lift your hips up toward the ceiling.

3. Really squeeze your abs and slowly lift your right foot about 6 inches off the ground. Slowly lower your foot back to the ground. Lift your left foot about 6 inches off the ground. (To make this exercise more difficult, extend the leg you are lifting straight out.)

4. Perform 15 to 20 lifts on each leg.

Chest Press

This upper-body move targets the chest muscles. Use 5- to 8-pound weights if you're a woman and 12- to 15-pound weights if you're a man.

CHEST PRESS START AND END POSITION

CHEST PRESS MID-POINT POSITION

1. Lie down on the bench on your back with your feet on the floor and your knees bent.

2. Holding your dumbbells, put your arms out to your sides and bend your arms at a 90 degree angle to the floor.

3. Lift the weights straight up toward the ceiling, keeping your hands in alignment with your shoulders. Exhale as you lift.

4. Bend your elbows and lower the weights in a slow and controlled motion back down to the starting position.

5. Do 10 to 12 reps. If you can do more than 12 reps easily, the weight isn't heavy enough. If you can't do 10 reps, switch to lighter weights.

Plank Rolls

This move may look like it focuses on your arms, but it also targets your core muscles, which are essential for having a strong abdomen and healthy back.

PLANK ROLL START POSITION

PLANK ROLL MID-POINT POSITION

PLANK ROLL END POSITION

1. Lie facedown on the ground and rest your forearms on the floor so that your right hand is near your left elbow and your left hand is near your right elbow.

2. Lift your body up so you are supporting your body weight on your forearms and your toes.

3. Pull your abs in and hold your body straight without letting your backside pop up in the air or letting your middle sag down toward the ground. Hold this position for 8 seconds.

4. Keeping your right arm bent, twist your body to the right so your right side is facing the ceiling. Don't let your hips sag down toward the ground. Hold this position for 8 seconds.

5. Twist back down to the start position. Hold this position for 8 seconds.

6. Keeping your left arm bent, twist your body to the left so your left side is facing the ceiling. Don't let your hips sag down toward the ground. Hold this position for 8 seconds.

7. Start with 2 to 4 reps (1 rep = facedown, right, and left position). Eventually, work up to 12 reps.

Bird Dog

This is one of the safest and most-effective core exercises to strengthen the muscles that protect the spine.

BIRD DOG START POSITION

BIRD DOG MID-POINT POSITION

BIRD DOG END POSITION

1. Start on your hands and knees. You want your hands to be in alignment with your shoulders and your knees to be in alignment with your hips perpendicular to the floor. Make sure your eyes are looking straight at the ground and try really hard to keep your head in a flat line with your back parallel to the floor.

2. Slowly lift your right hand off the ground and extend it forward at a 45 degree angle. At the same time, lift your left knee off the ground and extend your left leg out straight behind you.

3. Hold both limbs off the ground for 5 seconds and then place your hand and knee back on the ground.

4. Now repeat with your left hand and right knee.

5. Do 4 reps per side. Eventually, work up to 10 to 12 reps on each side.

THE OMNI DIET FOUR-WEEK WORKOUT

USING THE MOVES IN THE previous pages, I've created a sample two-week routine that builds strength and endurance in the shortest time possible. Remember, the following strength-training exercises should be performed every other day: on Mondays, Wednesdays, and Fridays. On alternating days do cardiovascular training with bursting.

Here's how to read the following workouts. These include "supersets," which means you do one exercise (for example, A1), rest for the recommended number of seconds, do a second one (A2), rest, then go back to the first (A1). Do all sets of A1 and A2, then move on to the B exercises and the C exercises.

SAMPLE TWO-WEEK WORKOUT

A1. SPLIT SQUATS

WEEK	SETS	REPS	REST (SECONDS)
1	2	15–20	120
2	2	15–20	100

A2. DUMBBELL SINGLE ARM ROWS

WEEK	SETS	REPS	REST (SECONDS)
1	2	10–12	120
2	2	10–12	100

B1. BRIDGE WITH ALTERNATING LEG LIFTS

WEEK	SETS	REPS	REST (SECONDS)
1	2	15–20	120
2	2	15–20	100

B2. CHEST PRESS

WEEK	SETS	REPS	REST (SECONDS)
1	2	10–12	120
2	2	10–12	100

C1. PLANK ROLLS

WEEK	SETS	REPS	REST (SECONDS)
1	1	1 each (hold 8 seconds)	100
2	2	2 each (hold 8 seconds)	90

C2. BIRD DOG

WEEK	SETS	REPS	REST (SECONDS)
1	1	2 each (hold 5 seconds)	100
2	3	3 each (hold 5 seconds)	90

[WARM UP, COOL DOWN]

It's essential that you begin any workout routine with a proper warm-up and range-of-motion (ROM) routine. Keep your warm-up simple: Begin by walking or riding an exercise bike at low resistance for 5 to 10 minutes. This will increase your body temperature and your heart rate in a gentle way.

Next, do some ROM exercises such as head rotations, shoulder rolls, small arm circles, gentle side bends, forward bends, hip rotations, knee rotations, hamstring stretches, calf stretches, etc. You get the idea. Always move gradually and comfortably and increase your range of motion without any bouncy movements. All of your movements and stretches should be done in a manner that is smooth and gentle. This prepares you for more intense exercise.

After every workout, take 5 to 10 minutes to do a proper cool-down. Take a slow walk or ride a stationary bike with very little resistance. This allows you to bring your heart rate down in a gradual and gentle manner.

For example, your Week 1 workout would go as follows:

A1. Split Squat	15–20 reps	rest 120 seconds
A2. Dumbbell Single Arm Row	10–12 reps	rest 120 seconds
A1. Split Squat	15–20 reps	rest 120 seconds
A2. Dumbbell Single Arm Row	10–12 reps	rest 120 seconds

Be sure to allow your heart rate to return to slightly above normal between each set.

B1. Bridge with Alternating Leg Lifts	15–20 reps	rest 120 seconds
B2. Chest Press	10–12 reps	rest 120 seconds
B1. Bridge with Alternating Leg Lifts	15–20 reps	rest 120 seconds
B2. Chest Press	10–12 reps	rest 120 seconds

Be sure to allow your heart rate to return to slightly above normal between each set.

C1. Plank Rolls	1 each	rest 100 seconds
C2. Bird Dog	2 each	rest 100 seconds
C1. Plank Rolls	1 each	rest 100 seconds
C2. Bird Dog	2 each	rest 100 seconds

Be sure to allow your heart rate to return to slightly above normal between each set.

As your fitness level improves, you may want to add exercises that engage multiple major muscle groups, such as push-ups and pull-ups. Or you may want to add bursting segments into your strength-training workout by doing calisthenics, squat-thrusts, or running on stairs between sets of strength-training moves. Just make sure your heart rate comes back to target level before starting a new set.

PHASE 3

Relax Your Way to Better Health

We don't see things as they are, we see them as we are.

—ANAÏS NIN

DURING THE TWO WEEKS OF phase 3, you can look forward to these exciting results:

- Weight loss of up to 5 to 10 pounds (20 to 40 pounds altogether, depending on your size and gender). People who are extremely obese or who begin with excessive inflammation may experience more weight loss.

- Normal or near normal lab values. Within six weeks, most people see decreases in cholesterol, triglycerides, blood pressure, and markers of inflammation; vitamin D and certain hormone levels often change even in some of the unhealthiest beginners.

- Although sleep actually improves early on, by this phase people are sleeping soundly.

- As a result of decreased weight and inflammation, sleep apnea usually subsides.

- Skin takes on a youthful glow.

YOUR STRATEGY

In phase 3, you continue the 70/30 eating strategy you've been following for four weeks—70 percent of your calories from plant foods, and 30 percent from protein-rich foods. You also continue the exercise regimen you started in phase 2, increasing your intensity as you become more fit. Keep up with the other Omni Diet healthy habits, as well—taking supplements, drinking lots of water, getting enough sleep, and exercising daily.

Now that you've gotten accustomed to the Omni Diet, there is room for some extra flexibility. The Omni Diet is part of your life, and you've kicked your addiction to sugar, so you can enjoy an occasional planned (and sometimes, unplanned) treat without feeling guilty. That's why I recommend the 90/10 rule: If you follow the Omni Diet 90 percent of the time, you can be *a bit* more relaxed with your food choices 10 percent of the time. By now you should be able to be more conscious about these choices, even when choosing non-Omni foods.

You can also reintroduce small amounts of grains and legumes, but instead of piling them on your plate like you probably did in the past, you'll use them more like condiments that complement the lean protein, healthy fats, and large amounts of vegetables in your meals. Many people notice such a positive change in the way they feel that they don't want to add these foods back in at all—and that's great!

Speaking of being relaxed: In phase 3 we'll add in another facet of the Omni Diet— getting enough sleep. That's right—on the Omni Diet, you can sleep yourself thin! Earlier in the book we discussed *why* sleep is so important, but now we'll talk about *how* you can design a sleep schedule that gives you optimal health benefits and fits your busy life. To help get you started, I'll provide a two-week sleep plan that will guide you to healthier, more satisfying sleep that will leave you feeling fully energized every day.

Phase 3 is also a good time to do the supplement quiz in chapter 9 (if you haven't already done so) to create your own personalized supplement strategy.

At the end of phase 3, it's a good idea to follow up with your health-care provider so you can "know your important numbers" again after six weeks on the Omni Diet. If you followed the plan closely, you should see significant improvements in your numbers. For some people, health insurance will dictate that you wait twelve weeks for a follow-up evaluation. Either way, you should be pleasantly surprised by the results.

LET'S GET STARTED. FIRST WE'LL talk food; then I'll show you how to optimize your sleep with the Omni Diet Successful Sleep Plan. Finally we'll talk about what to expect when you have your blood work repeated at the end of phase 3.

STEP 1: MAKE 90/10 YOUR GOLDEN RULE

LET'S FACE IT: LIFE DOESN'T occur in a vacuum. There will be days that you forget to pack a lunch. Or you may choose to sample a meal prepared by someone else for a celebratory event. With the 90/10 rule, that's okay.

To clarify, I *do not* advocate setting aside an entire day every week for you to "go off your diet" and eat anything and everything you see. While many programs suggest this, I have yet to see it work well for anyone long term. There are several inherent problems with this thinking.

1. I have seen people eat up to *four thousand* calories of sugar and fat in hours just because they have designated one day a week for that purpose. This can sabotage the entire week of dedication and sweat.

2. If you can't wait to go off your program, it means you haven't committed to real change in your lifestyle, and you are still thinking of the program as a restrictive punishment rather than a path to good health.

3. Even a one-day gorge on unhealthy foods can trigger the process of inflammation in your body.

4. Binging on sugary foods can reignite your sugar addiction. Planning a day of cheating with high-sugar foods is like sending a drug addict into a crack house for one day. It is foolish and sets you up to fail.

So how does the 90/10 philosophy work? It is a little extra room built in to your program so you can enjoy the social aspect of life. Also, there may be times you have less-than-optimal choices due to travel or other circumstances. You should still avoid trigger foods and foods that cause trouble with your health. For example, I couldn't take even a bite of any kind of cake, pastry, or doughnut for many months because it would trigger major cravings. I knew that if I indulged, I would soon find myself hiding in a dark corner of a doughnut shop, licking frosting off waxed paper! Now, after years of clean eating, I find most of those foods repulsive. On the rare occasion that

OMNI DIET POSTCARD

"In these last twelve weeks I have changed my diet and way of thinking, and have never felt better in my life. I now feel good saying, 'I don't eat that anymore.' I like your 90/10 rule, that if you do choose to eat 'non-Omni food' once in a while, you just go right back to the way you were eating and in a couple of days you will feel better." —VIKI

FOLLOW THE THREE-BITE RULE

If after careful consideration you decide to eat something off plan, follow the three-bite rule. Think about it: The majority of enjoyment comes from the first three bites—after that, your taste buds start getting bored, and you're no longer getting the bang-for-the-buck that came with the first three bites.

As you have your three bites, be fully present and conscious so you can really concentrate on enjoying the food. (I'm talking three average-size bites, not three elephant-size bites.) Then, after three bites, throw the rest away. Don't keep it in your house. I guarantee that you'll get far more pleasure from three fully mindful bites than you would from a giant portion gobbled up impulsively and thoughtlessly! Plus, when you take just three bites, you won't have to face the very unpleasant aftertaste of regret.

I take a bite of cake, I have no desire for more. The key is, I only take a *bite*.

There may be times that you forget to take your prepacked daily food bag with you, and you have to make the healthiest choices possible. Or you may be attending an event that doesn't allow you to bring in food of any kind. (By the way, if you are diabetic, lactose intolerant, gluten intolerant, or have special dietary needs, you must be allowed to bring your food with you unless the venue can accommodate your needs.) Birthday parties, weddings, and amusement parks are other places that you may find yourself wanting to relax *a little* as you celebrate a special occasion. My suggestion is to plan ahead and not be caught off guard. Here are a few ways to do that:

- Make the decision to have *one* food that is not on your Omni Diet plan that day. Don't use the excuse that since you made one unhealthy choice, you might as well eat lousy for the entire day and then resume your program the following day. This rarely works for people and makes it much harder to get back on track. On average, it takes about three days to feel well and lose your cravings again after *only one day* of gorging on sugar and fat.

- Be brutally honest with yourself about your addictions. If you know that you are still vulnerable to relapse, give yourself a couple of more weeks before loosening the reigns. I had total control over food like pasta, burgers, fries, and even most sugary foods after about four weeks.

However, it took about three months to develop absolute control over my most serious trigger foods. Most of my clients report the same.

- Scout out healthy lunch alternatives in your area in advance for the times that you find yourself without your lunch bag.

- Make the healthiest choices possible from the selection available.

- When you do make the decision to indulge, make it a conscious decision, and enjoy the moment. Don't feel guilty. Then, get back on track immediately.

- Afterward, reflect on how the non-Omni choice made you feel. Usually when I make a decision to eat food that doesn't serve me, I don't feel great. Being aware helps me to be truthful with myself about how much I miss certain foods.

- On the rare occasion that you make an impulsive decision, don't beat yourself up about it. That won't help you at all. If you make a mistake, turn around and get back on track without judgments, criticisms, or anger.

Phase 3, Week 1 Success Menu

	BREAKFAST	SNACK	LUNCH	SNACK	DINNER	DESSERT
DAY 1	Omni Oatmeal	¼ cup raw almonds or sunflower seeds	Blueberry Tarragon Chicken Salad	2 cups mixed veggies with 2 tablespoons Traditional Hummus	Simple Shrimp Scampi, Mindful Minestrone Soup, and Pan-Roasted Brussels Sprouts	Goji Nut Truffles
DAY 2	Pacific Coast Scramble	Homemade Super-food Protein Bar and ½ cup mixed berries	Serrano Chile Shrimp	Large mixed green salad with 3 ounces hard-boiled egg or other protein, 1 tablespoon raw seeds, and 1 tablespoon olive oil and lemon juice	Cashew Cream Squash with Turkey and Roasted Peppers and Rainbow Chard Slaw	Magnificent Cacao "Nut" Macaroon
DAY 3	Very Omega Cherry Smoothie	1 hard-boiled egg and 2 cups raw veggies with 2 tablespoons Guacamole for dipping	Simple mixed green salad with Herb-Marinated Chicken and 1 tablespoon olive oil and balsamic vinegar	2 tablespoons raw nuts or seeds	Macadamia-Crusted Mahimahi and Tana's Smooth Sweet Potato Soup	Fresh Berries with Macadamia-Nut Sauce

	BREAKFAST	SNACK	LUNCH	SNACK	DINNER	DESSERT
DAY 4	Clear Start Breakfast Burrito	Homemade Super-Food Protein Bar and 1 piece of fruit or ½ cup berries	V-8 Macho Gazpacho on the Go	2–3 cups raw veggies with 2 tablespoons Traditional Hummus, Guacamole, or salsa for dipping	Cedar Plank Salmon, Asian Citrus Pear Salad, and Succulent Roasted Sweet Potatoes	Omni Apple Cobbler Square
DAY 5	Chunky Chocolate Monkey Smoothie	Celery with 2 tablespoons raw almond butter	Spinach and Strawberry Salad with Pecans and Shrimp Cocktail	2 cups raw vegetables with 2 tablespoons Traditional Hummus, Guacamole, or salsa for dipping	The Best Beef Stroganoff with Roasted Beet Salad and 2 cups steamed vegetables	Dessert Smoothie or 1 piece extra-dark, organic chocolate (½ ounce)
DAY 6	Sunrise Surprise Smoothie	2–3 cups chopped veggies with Split Pea Hummus	Tasty Turkey Wrap and gluten-free tabouleh	1 apple and ¼ cup raw nuts or seeds	Poached Sea Bass in Tomato Broth, Herbed Garden Vegetables, and Antiox Detox Chopped Salad	Avocado Gelato Square
DAY 7	Gluten-Free Blueberry French Toast	¼ cup raw nuts or seeds and 1 small piece of fruit	Stay-Sharp Chard Salad	1 sliced tomato with avocado (about 2 tablespoons)	"Spaghetti" with Turkey Meatballs, steamed broccoli, and Cool Kale Salad with Cilantro Dressing	Fresh Berries with Macadamia-Nut Sauce

Phase 3, Week 2 Success Menu

	BREAKFAST	SNACK	LUNCH	SNACK	DINNER	DESSERT
DAY 1	Brain-Smart Start Smoothie	Celery with 2 tablespoons raw almond butter	Asian-Fusion Chicken Salad	Simple mixed green salad with sunflower seeds and 1 tablespoon olive oil and lemon juice	Poached Tilapia with Saffron Sauce, Sautéed Collard Greens, and Breaded Zucchini and Squash	Goji Nut Truffles (1–2 pieces)
DAY 2	Chocolate-Covered Strawberry Smoothie	2 cups raw vegetables with 2 tablespoons Baba Ghanoush	Salmon Burger wrapped in romaine lettuce	¼ cup raw nuts and seeds and ¼ cup seeded grapes	Savory Lubia Rose Stew, Stay-Sharp Chard Salad, and Yellow Beans with Tomatoes	Fresh Berries with Macadamia-Nut Sauce
DAY 3	Feel-Good Eggs Ranchero	Homemade Super-Food Protein Bar and 1 piece of fruit or ½ cup berries	Rainbow Quinoa Salad with Chicken	Omni Grainless Granola Protein Bar	Shrimp Chowder and simple green salad	1 piece extra-dark, organic chocolate (½ ounces) or Mulberry Ball
DAY 4	Brain-Smart Start Smoothie	2 cups raw vegetables with ¼ cup Guacamole	Peaceful Asian Pear Salad	Tasty Turkey Wrap	Roasted Rack of Lamb, Warm Spinach Asparagus Salad with Quinoa, and Red, White, and Blue Salad with 1 tablespoon olive oil dressing	Pumpkin Protein Bar
DAY 5	Super Surprise Frittata	Omni Grainless Granola Protein Bar and 1 piece of fruit or ½ cup berries	Turkey Burger	Celery with 2 tablespoons raw almond butter	Hawaiian Blackened Tuna with Mango Salsa, steamed broccoli, and Antiox Detox Chopped Salad	Fabulous Fruit Fondue
DAY 6	Chocolate-Covered Strawberry Smoothie	1 sliced tomato with 2 tablespoons avocado	Chicken Lentil Soup	Devil-Less Eggs	Ginger Glazed Salmon and Creamy Asparagus Soup	Dessert Smoothie or 1 piece extra-dark, organic chocolate (½ ounce)
DAY 7	Berry Nutty Breakfast Quinoa	2 cups veggies with 2 tablespoons Traditional Hummus or Split Pea Hummus	Guiltless Chicken Breast Tenders and Harmonizing Vegetable Soup	½ cup berries with ¼ cup Go Well Trail Mix	Healthy Turkey Chili and Magnificent Mind Cucumber Mint Salad	Frozen Banana

[SUPER-FOODS THAT FOSTER LONGEVITY]

The following foods, herbs, and spices are nutritious for many reasons, but one of their claims to fame is that they contribute to longevity. If they're not already part of your dietary repertoire, consider adding them.

- avocado
- basil
- cardamom
- cinnamon
- cordyceps and reishi mushrooms
- cruciferous vegetables such as broccoli, kale, collards, cabbage, cauliflower, and bok choy
- curcumin
- curry
- garlic
- green leafy vegetables such as spinach, collards, turnip greens, chard, and mustard greens
- green tea
- marjoram
- olive oil, coconut oil, macadamia-nut oil
- omega-3-rich seafood such as salmon, tuna, and halibut
- oregano
- papayas
- raw nuts
- rosemary
- saffron
- sage
- seeds (flax, chia, hemp, sunflower, pepita, etc.)
- thyme
- turmeric

STEP 2: SLEEP YOUR WAY TO BETTER HEALTH

SLEEP IS A CORNERSTONE OF long-term brain health and vibrant energy. It also plays a surprising part in weight control. Many studies have shown that chronic failure to get enough sleep increases the risk of being overweight or obese. A 2006 Case Western Reserve University study of more than 68,000 women found that risk for a major weight gain was 30 percent higher for those who logged less than five hours of sleep per night and 12 percent higher for those getting less than six.[1] You should get at least seven hours of sleep per night.

Sleep restriction lowers levels of leptin, the hormone that tells you to stop eating when you're full. When leptin is low, your brain receives the message that you should eat more, even if your body doesn't actually need more calories. Not getting enough sleep also increases levels of the hormone ghrelin, which promotes appetite. And levels of orexin, a neurotransmitter that increases food cravings, also go up in people who don't sleep enough.

Being overtired interrupts healthy glucose metabolism, making your body more resistant to insulin. Over time, the increased demand on the pancreas from insulin resistance can compromise beta-cell function and lead to type 2 diabetes.

Lack of sleep is also linked to high blood pressure, heart attack, and increased risk of car accidents, depression, and substance abuse. And you don't need scientific research to tell you that when people are exhausted they become forgetful, inattentive, and irritable.

When you feel refreshed and rested, you feel energized, think clearly, and are much more likely to make smart choices about eating and exercising.

TWO-WEEK SUCCESSFUL SLEEP PLAN

DURING THE NEXT TWO WEEKS, I want you to focus on improving your sleep. If you have been following the Omni Diet closely, you may already have noticed a dramatic improvement in your sleep patterns. If not, now's the time to find out why sleep eludes you, and ways to improve it.

During the first week of the Successful Sleep Plan, work on assessing your sleep and making whatever changes are necessary to improve it. During the second week, focus on reducing stress, which can interfere with good health by day and night. Once you start reducing stress and improving your sleep, you'll see a big difference in your mood and your health twenty-four hours a day.

WEEK 1: ASK YOURSELF: WHAT IS KEEPING YOU AWAKE?

- **DO YOU HAVE SLEEP APNEA?** This is a sleep disorder that causes abnormally long breathing pauses or very soft, shallow breaths during sleep. If you do, take it seriously, because it lowers the amount of oxygen your body and brain get. Sleep apnea is more common in overweight and obese people. If you have sleep apnea due to excess weight, you may be noticing a dramatic improvement in quality of sleep as you lose weight. Sometimes, sleep apnea is the result of structural issues such as septal deviation, large uvula, or small airway. If you have symptoms of sleep apnea, you should see a health-care provider who specializes in sleep disorders.

- **DO YOU TAKE MEDICATIONS THAT INTERFERE WITH SLEEP?** Take an inventory of medications and supplements that may be keeping the sandman at bay. Antihistamines, asthma medications, steroids, and anticonvulsants can interrupt sleep. Consult with your health-care provider to look for options that won't impact your sleep. The conditions for which these medications are prescribed can be exacerbated by exhaustion, so getting enough sleep may reduce your need for meds. Supplements such as green tea, rhodiola, SAMe, and ginseng, which boost energy and focus, can interfere with a good night's sleep if taken too late in the day. Limit these supplements to morning and early afternoon use if you have trouble sleeping.

- **ARE YOU HOOKED ON CAFFEINE?** Caffeine is one of the primary culprits for robbing people of precious sleep. Try to limit coffee to one cup per day. Avoid caffeinated drinks after noon. And read labels—caffeine is sometimes an unexpected ingredient in foods and medicines.

- **DO YOU DRINK ALCOHOL?** Many people drink alcohol to induce relaxation and sleep, but it actually does the opposite. Alcohol can cause a hypoglycemic rebound reaction that leads to sleeplessness. Avoid it for a while and see if your sleep improves.

- **ARE YOUR HORMONES OUT OF BALANCE?** Hormone fluctuations in women, especially during pregnancy and menopause, are classic sleep disruptors. Comfort measures and smart sleep hygiene (see the twelve tips provided in the following section) can help during pregnancy. Menopausal women should consider seeing a hormone specialist to help soothe their sleep.

- **DO YOU HAVE A MEDICAL CONDITION?** Thyroid disease, congestive heart failure, chronic pain, and many other conditions disrupt sleep and can have long-term detrimental health ramifications if left untreated. Make sure you're getting the medical care you need so problems are diagnosed and properly treated.

- **DO YOU WORK ODD HOURS?** Shift work (nights and odd hours) can wreak havoc on overall health and well-being. If you are a shift worker, do your best to keep your schedule consistent so you can at least adjust to one time schedule. Take sleep hygiene seriously, and consider melatonin supplements.

- **DO YOU GIVE YOURSELF ENOUGH TIME FOR SLEEP?** This is crucial. You can't get eight hours of sleep every night if you go to bed at midnight and get up at six in the morning. Make sure there's enough time in your schedule for a good night's sleep.

- **IS YOUR BEDROOM SLEEP-FRIENDLY?** Light, sound, electronics, mattress comfort, temperature, and a host of other factors can cause tossing and turning. Look around at your sleep space, identify any road-blocks to sleep, and correct them.

NOW, FIX IT: TWELVE WAYS TO SLEEP EASY

SOMETIMES, SOLVING A SLEEP PROBLEM is as simple as changing the temperature in your bedroom or choosing a different bedtime routine. For a better night's sleep, give these twelve tips a try:

1. **KEEP IT DARK.** Eliminate all light by using room-darkening shades and a non-lighted alarm clock, or wear an eye mask.

2. **STAY ON SCHEDULE.** Waking up and going to sleep at varying times can disrupt your circadian rhythm. Try to stay on a regular schedule, and avoid daytime naps.

3. **POWER DOWN.** Shut off the computer, television, and other electronic devices at least an hour before bedtime.

4. **SOAK IN A BATH.** Sprinkle lavender oil in the water to relax half an hour before bed.

5. **BLOCK OUT NOISE.** Keep your room quiet or use ear plugs.

6. **BE STILL.** Avoid strenuous exercise at least three hours before going to sleep. Intense exercise increases blood flow to the brain and can be overstimulating.

7. **RELAX.** Listen to guided meditation, soothing music, or guided hypnosis on your iPod.

8. **TURN ON WHITE NOISE.** A fan, soft music, or a white-noise machine can create just enough sound to lull your busy brain to sleep.

9. **ENJOY A SOOTHING TONIC.** Increase levels of the sleep-regulating hormone serotonin with chamomile tea or warm almond

milk with a teaspoon of honey, a teaspoon of cocoa powder, and a few drops of chocolate-flavored stevia.

10. MAKE LOVE. Having an orgasm helps create a feeling of overall well-being, and bonding with your partner helps decrease anxiety and stress.

11. GET UP. If you can't fall asleep or you wake up in the middle of the night and can't get back to sleep, don't stay in bed tossing and turning. Get up and go to another room for a short time. Read a soothing book or listen to a guided relaxation exercise; then give sleep another try.

12. WRITE IT DOWN. Keep a pen and paper next to your bed, and if your racing mind wakes you up, write down your thoughts for next-day consideration.

WEEK 2: MANAGE STRESS

WE ALL EXPERIENCE STRESS FROM time to time. But when stress becomes a *way of life,* it can overburden the body. Chronic stress causes damaging chemical and hormonal reactions. When your body constantly produces too much of the stress hormone cortisol, it triggers increases in blood sugar and belly fat as well as changes in your metabolism. Another hormone, norepinephrine, can cause blood pressure to go up and can aggravate attention-deficit disorder.

SPECT scans of the brain of someone who's meditating compared with scans of someone who's stressed show dramatic differences in blood flow and neurotransmitter activity. Chronic stress lowers brain activity, which increases your vulnerability to depression, anxiety, impulsiveness, and illness. It compromises your health and contributes to weight gain and buildup of belly fat, which is especially lethal because it surrounds and impacts the health of vital organs in the core of your body. Cutting down the stress in your life—and developing good coping skills to help you deal with stresses that you can't control—is good for your health *and* your weight.

A DOZEN DE-STRESSORS

THERE ARE MANY NATURAL AND effective ways to reduce stress. Here are just a few:

1. MOVE YOUR BODY. Moderate exercise balances stress hormones, increases endorphins (feel-good chemicals in the brain), and

helps to channel energy in a positive direction. In fact, exercise is the most powerful tool I can recommend for combating stress. The more stress or frustration I feel, the more I take it out on my weights. I also practice martial arts, which is great for focusing the mind. (And truth be told, there is nothing quite like kicking the heck out of a big padded guy or breaking boards to let off a little steam. I highly recommend it!) Remember, moderate exercise helps reduce cortisol and can make you feel less tense, but excessive or intense exercise on a regular basis can increase cortisol levels. So be sure to have a balanced approach to exercise.

2. **KEEP A JOURNAL.** Writing about your stressors and possible solutions can trigger positive thinking and open your mind to new possibilities.

3. **PRACTICE SAYING NO.** People—especially women—often feel guilty about saying no to the many demands made on them. But spreading yourself too thin causes stress to you and the people you love. If it's hard to say no, say "Let me think about it." This gives you time to make the best decisions.

4. **SURROUND YOURSELF WITH POSITIVE, HEALTHY PEOPLE.** A study at the University of Pittsburgh revealed that people tend to adopt thoughts and habits of the people around them, and that spending time with unhealthy people can actually shorten your lifespan.

5. **LOOK FOR SHORTCUTS.** I hate shopping, but I have a friend who loves it. So she shops for me, and I repay her with a gift of some kind. I also shop through an online retailer with a simple return policy. Sometimes shortcuts cost more, but they're worth it if they free you up to be more productive.

6. **PRACTICE RELAXATION SKILLS.** Visualization, meditation, biofeedback, and other relaxation skills improve feelings of well-being, dramatically increase blood flow to the brain, activate the prefrontal cortex (the part of the brain associated with judgment and impulse control), and help you feel less stressed. Use a CD or book to guide you.

7. **USE HYPNOSIS.** This is a controversial subject for some people. While I can appreciate this, I have to tell you that hypnosis is an extremely powerful tool. If you are uncomfortable with the idea of someone making "suggestions" to your subconscious, I would recommend making sure you know and trust the person hypnotizing you. I had my husband make me a hypnosis CD for peak performance when I was training for my black belt. I would fall asleep listening to it the night before my classes. I noticed a

When you're eighteen, you're worried about what everyone else is thinking about you.

When you're forty, you don't give a heck what anyone else is thinking about you.

When you're sixty, you realize no one has been thinking about you at all. They have been too busy thinking about themselves!

dramatic difference in my athletic ability and focus after listening to the CD regularly.

8. **PRAY—AND LISTEN.** Studies show that prayer and meditation actually activate the front part of your brain, which is responsible for judgment, forethought, and impulse control. I think of prayer as a time to talk to God and meditation as a time to listen to God. I usually spend a few minutes each morning doing both. Since I have trouble just being still and quiet and focusing on "nothing," I pick one powerful word that I want to manifest for the day, and I use it to guide my prayer and meditation. This helps me focus and prevents me from getting that chaotic feeling I call "monkey mind."

9. **KILL THE ANTS!** This is a technique my husband developed to eliminate the "automatic negative thoughts" that come into your mind and steal your joy. Negative thinking has an oppressive effect on the brain and can decrease impulse control. Kill your ANTs by writing down your negative thoughts, working to restructure them so they're positive—or neutral—instead of negative. For help with this, go to the Kill the ANTs room at www.theamensolution.com.

10. **BE GRATEFUL.** Every morning, write down five things for which you are thankful. The simple act of focusing on gratitude reduces stress and changes the chemistry in your brain.

11. **SAY IT TILL YOU FEEL IT.** An incantation is a set of words or a phrase that you repeat to yourself over and over for calmness and focus. I do this while I drive and play my favorite music. As corny as it sounds, incantations help reset your thinking and inspire accountability. I say things like, "I am a living example of health and fitness." I repeat it until I start to *believe and feel* it!

12. **REACH OUT TO FAMILY, FRIENDS, AND COMMUNITY.** Humans need to bond—we are not designed to be alone. Spending enjoyable time with family, friends, or groups with whom you share

[CHANGE YOUR NEGATIVE THINKING]

The Work of Byron Katie is one of my favorite tools for changing negative thinking. In her book *Loving What Is*, Katie elegantly uses four simple questions to help readers discover who they would be without their "story." Here are the four questions, and you can download helpful (and free) worksheets at www.thework.com. This effective tool can be used for any negative thought.

- Is it true? If the answer is yes . . .
- Can I absolutely know that it's true (beyond any doubt)?
- How do I feel when I have that thought? (Is there a stress-free reason to hold on to the thought? How do I treat others, myself . . . ?)
- Who would I be without the thought (if I could never think that thought)?

Once you answer the four questions, turn the thought around to its opposite, as shown in the following example.

NEGATIVE THOUGHT: "I hate my body because I'm fat."

QUESTION 1: Is it true that I hate my body? *Yes*

QUESTION 2: Can I absolutely know it's true, without question? *Well, no. I don't always hate my body. I don't want to die, so I must not completely hate it.*

common values is important to your sense of well-being because it provides love, support, a feeling of connection, and a sense of accountability.

STEP 3: REVISIT YOUR IMPORTANT NUMBERS

AT THE END OF PHASE 3 it's great to have your lab work repeated. Some health insurance won't cover it after just six weeks, but if yours does, consider taking a second look at your numbers. Tracking your progress in this way is a powerful motivator. It's very rewarding to see your numbers correlate with your newfound energy. Many people who follow the Omni Diet see their numbers tracking back toward normal within six to twelve weeks.

Your important numbers will also reveal if there is something beyond diet that you should address with your doctor.

QUESTION 3: **How do I feel when I have the thought?** *Sad, depressed, angry, embarrassed, ashamed, introverted, irritable, alone . . .*

Is there a stress-free reason to hold on to the thought? *Of course not.*

QUESTION 4: **Who would I be without the thought?** *Free! Present! I would not feel trapped in a body I don't like. I would enjoy going out with friends. I would be grateful for my health and what my body does for me. I would not be embarrassed to go out and enjoy life without worrying about what other people are thinking.*

Now, turn the thought around with three examples:

1. I don't hate my body. I have nice eyes, my hair is pretty, sometimes I feel really good about myself when I dress up.
2. I love my body. I am grateful for my health, my body has taken good care of me, even though I haven't always taken good care of it, etc.
3. I hate the way I feel and the way I treat my body when I don't take the time to take care of myself. I feel fat and tired when I don't take care of myself, then I use caffeine, sugar, and lousy food to "medicate" myself.

Now, ask yourself if the turnarounds are true or truer than the original thought. *Yes!*

[A NOTE ABOUT PLATEAUS]

When you make any type of dramatic change to your daily eating regimen, your body eventually will adjust, and you may hit a plateau. This is common with typical fad diets. But unlike fad diets, the Omni Diet takes human biology into account and recognizes that plateaus are often a normal process in a healthy weight-loss program. This means that you should not equate plateaus with failure. Instead, use them as an opportunity to make an honest assessment of where you are in your program. If you have been following the Omni Diet principles and you suddenly hit a plateau, it could mean several things:

- Initially you may have lost weight rapidly as a result of detoxification. When you reduce your intake of toxins, your body responds by decreasing inflammation. Eventually, it stabilizes and weight loss will take on a slower, steadier pace. Don't be discouraged—this is healthy!

- Plateaus sometimes occur as a way for the body to adjust to the rapid loss of toxins from the fat cells. Since fat cells store toxic material, your body needs time to clear the waste away. You can override this natural process and "diet" through it, but you will likely put the weight back on, and then some. Instead, increase your water intake, consume more greens or green drinks, and participate in activities that cause you to sweat a little more, such as exercise and saunas. Plateaus usually last for only a week or two.

- If you have lost a significant amount of weight and you have been eating a lot of animal protein, it may be time to adjust your program and decrease your intake of animal protein a bit, replacing it with more wholesome choices. You will still need to get regular "doses" of protein throughout the day, but in smaller portions. Also, consider eating more vegetable sources of protein.

- Go back to the basics of what makes the Omni Diet so successful. Are you slipping back into old habits? Many times when I speak with people at this critical juncture, I question them repeatedly about what they are doing differently. They often say they haven't changed anything. But by about the third time I ask, they suddenly remember the chocolate cake they ate on the weekend, the popcorn at the movies, the hot dog at the picnic . . . you get the idea. When you hit a plateau, pull out your food journal and start measuring and writing down everything you eat. A couple of extra bites here and there can really add up.

- Review your exercise regimen. Sometimes a weight-loss plateau coincides with an exercise plateau—it may be time to push your workouts up a notch.

PHASE 4

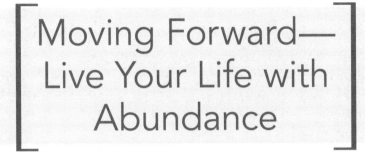

Moving Forward— Live Your Life with Abundance

There is no passion to be found in playing small—in settling for a life that is less than the one you are capable of living.

—NELSON MANDELA

THE LAST PHASE OF THE Omni Diet never ends—it's a maintenance plan that you'll use as a blueprint for healthy eating as you live your life. As you go forward with your commitment to the Omni Diet, you can enjoy these valuable benefits:

- Continued weight loss until you reach a healthy goal weight.

- Continued improvement in your health and your lab values. If they haven't returned to normal already, you'll see further positive changes in cholesterol, triglycerides, blood pressure, markers of inflammation, vitamin D, and certain hormone levels.

- If it hasn't already happened, you may see chronic health conditions such as high blood pressure and insulin resistance decrease or disappear completely.

- Continued improvements in energy levels, focus, sleep quality, and overall quality of life.

- A steady increase in your fitness level and lean tissue mass as you continue to follow the Omni Diet exercise plan and shed body fat.

- Greater feelings of attractiveness and increases in your libido.

Most people who follow the Omni Diet are hooked on its amazing, dramatic results and stay on it for life. They feel younger, healthier, more energized, and more attractive than they have in years or even decades. Fabulous results make it relatively easy for them to stick with the Omni Diet.

But it does require a commitment. Maintaining your adherence to the principles we've covered in this book and that you've incorporated into your life during the past six weeks is crucial. As you've likely seen, you can make tremendous changes to your body and your health in six weeks. However, you can't maintain those changes unless you maintain your commitment to the changes you've made.

During the Live with Abundance phase, you'll continue eating 70/30 for 90/10—in other words, you'll get 70 percent of your calories from plant foods and 30 percent from protein-rich foods, and you'll stay true to the Omni Diet 90 percent of the time. You'll also continue to

- **Follow your exercise regimen, increasing your intensity as your fitness level goes up**
- **Maintain your supplement routine**
- **Get regular sleep**
- **Continue to check in on your important numbers annually**
- **Drink plenty of water**
- **Plan your meals in advance**
- **Carry healthy snacks and meals with you when you're on the road or traveling**
- **Use the Omni Diet recipes**

I also urge you to become an Omni Diet mentor. This is one of the best possible ways to stay committed to the Omni Diet and your goal of proactively pursuing a healthy, energized, happy life. The people I've worked with who have had the greatest success have mentored other people as they've learned to embrace the Omni Diet's health-supporting life changes.

Not only does mentoring help someone else achieve their health goals, but it gives you a support system and someone to whom you can be accountable. Once you've mastered the Omni Diet, share it with someone you care about—a spouse, parent, coworker, or friend.

The best way to mentor a friend or partner is to lead by example. As you become healthier, people notice and will ask questions. They are drawn organically to your increased energy and sense of well-being. Tell them about the changes you're making and the improvements in your health. Then reach out to them in some of the following ways:

- Invite them to join you for daily walks
- Fill your kitchen with whole, high-quality, nutritious food and invite guests over to enjoy delectable, healthy meals
- Share delicious Omni Diet snacks with coworkers
- When having a party, serve Omni Diet foods or ask your caterer to prepare a menu that meets Omni Diet specifications
- When you are invited to friends' homes, bring along a delicious Omni dish or snack
- Always be positive and upbeat about your progress, but don't preach or push—people often need time to gather the courage to change

OMNI DIET POSTCARD

"I am so proud to share that I have lost fifteen pounds and definitely inches, too. My large thirty-five-inch waist is working its way down, as well. I haven't measured myself lately, but I'm very comfortable in clothes that I haven't worn in a long time. For me it's been about learning to eat. No one ever taught me about nutrition. It's just as important as history and math, but here I am at forty-four learning about nutrition for the first time. Now I'm choosing foods that give energy and nutrients to my body and brain. I'm no longer in a battle with food. I eat to live, not live to eat. Freedom is mine!" —MARI

JASON STUBER, 34

Remember that George Clooney movie *Up in the Air*? That's the one where Clooney's character, Ryan, works for a company whose reps travel back and forth across the country, breaking the news to downsized employees that they're being let go. Ryan's goal in life: to rack up 10 million frequent flyer miles.

Sometimes Jason Stuber, 34, feels a little bit like Ryan. A communications technology consultant, he's on the road 250 days a year, and his travels take him all over the globe. That makes healthy eating a major challenge and weight gain just about inevitable. "I'd grab fast food at the airport and room service at the hotel, and when I finally got home, all I'd want to do was order a pizza and lie on the couch in front of the TV."

But newly single, weighing in at 240 pounds, and concerned about his cholesterol, Jason knew that he had to make some changes. That's when the Omni Diet came along. He started on Thanksgiving of 2011, and by Valentine's Day he was down to 203—and he's still going strong.

First things first: He cleaned out all of the junk foods from his cupboards, tossing all the snack cakes, chips, and other processed foods. Then he learned about healthy substitutions. And finally, he learned to make the gym his friend.

"Life got really simple," Jason says. "I learned that even at the airport, I could order grilled salmon or chicken and ask for lots of extra vegetables. If all they had was a sandwich, I'd take it apart, skip the bread, and just munch on the protein and the veggies. I work out first thing in the morning and come out of the gym actually craving eggs and kale!"

For Jason, the Omni Diet isn't so much a diet as a whole new way of life. "I feel lighter, more energetic, and much more focused," he says. "This has been a fantastic turnaround."

Conclusion: The Omni Way

The definition of insanity is doing the same thing over and over and expecting different results.

—UNKNOWN

OFTEN OUR GREATEST CHALLENGES LEAD to our most valuable learning opportunities—and our most gratifying victories.

My very first client presented me with the most complicated challenges of my professional career. Although she was a young woman, she had the medical history of an elderly, chronically ill ICU patient. Her health problems included recurrent cancer, an autoimmune disorder, insulin resistance, polycystic ovary syndrome, gallbladder disease, high cholesterol, unexplained digestive issues, diarrhea, eczema, acne, mood swings, and dramatic fluctuations in her energy levels. She had been given nine different prescriptions. "Wired and tired," my client was fed up.

In order to become well, she needed to go in a completely new direction. It just didn't make sense for her to stick to the same-old diets, medical regimens, and treatments. I didn't want her to become a "frequent flyer," as we referred to the chronically ill patients who returned month after month to the ICU. Every time these patients turned up, we'd administer the same treatment, and send them home. Unless they made big lifestyle changes—which few did—we could count on them to keep returning to the ICU until their bodies couldn't take it anymore.

My first client's lab results, which were terrible for a woman of her age, were not surprising. Take a look:

LAB TEST	LAB RESULT
Total cholesterol (mg/dL)	265 (high)
HDL (mg/dL)	60 (good)
LDL (mg/dL)	205 (very high)
Triglycerides (mg/dL)	275 (high)
Blood pressure (mm/Hg)	118/76 (normal)
Vitamin D (ng/dL)	20 (low—sign of inflammation)
Fatty acid ratio	22.0 (high—sign of inflammation)
CRP (mg/L)	4.2 (high—sign of inflammation)
Hemoglobin A1c (percent)	5.8 (high—insulin resistant)
Fasting glucose	99 (high normal—not optimal)
Testosterone (ng/dL)	Total: 78 (high) Free: 8.2 (high)

Most of the clients I see who have a medical history and lab numbers like these are morbidly obese, depressed, diabetic (or close to it), taking a long list of prescription drugs to treat each of their chronic illnesses, and taking even more medications to help them manage medical side effects as well as risks and complications that *could* occur.

This client had seen the best doctors and had tried the most advanced medical treatments for her conditions. If she hadn't, I would likely have thought she was beyond the scope of my coaching expertise and would have referred her to a highly qualified physician—remember, she was my first client. But she had been down that conventional-medicine road, and she was still terribly unwell. She wanted a *new lifestyle and a new way of living!* She wanted to *live with energy and passion!*

After ninety days of living the Omni way she had turned her health and her life around. She continued to manage a lifelong chronic condition responsibly with *some* daily medication prescribed by a physician. But she eliminated (with her doctor's help) the need for an *excessive* list of prescriptions. And she improved all of her lab numbers. Today, her lab numbers are fantastic, as the chart below shows:

LAB TEST	ORIGINAL LAB RESULT	LAB RESULT AFTER NINETY DAYS ON THE OMNI DIET	TODAY
Total cholesterol (mg/dL)	265 (high)	201 (normal)	190 (excellent)
HDL (mg/dL)	60 (good)	81 (excellent)	80 (excellent)
LDL (mg/dL)	205 (very high)	120 (a little high, but coming down *without* medication)	110 (nearly ideal)
Triglycerides (mg/dL)	275 (high)	78 (normal)	56 (excellent)
Blood pressure (mm/Hg)	118/76 (normal)	105/64 (excellent)	104/65 (excellent)
Vitamin D (ng/dL)	20 (low—sign of inflammation)	58 (normal)	72 (excellent)
Fatty acid ratio	22.0 (high—sign of inflammation)	2.8 (normal)	1.7 (excellent)
CRP (mg/L)	4.2 (high—sign of inflammation)	0.5 (normal)	0.2 (excellent)
Hemoglobin A1c (percent)	5.8 (high—insulin resistant)	5.6 (normal)	5.4 (excellent)
Fasting glucose	99 (high normal—not optimal)	90 (getting better)	85 (excellent)
Testosterone (ng/dL)	Total: 78 (high) Free: 8.2 (high)	Total: 55 (normal) Free: 3.2 (normal)	Total: 33 (excellent) Free: 2.0 (excellent)

More important than my client's lab values were the changes in her quality of life. Today she is healthy, happy, and full of energy. She is living her life with purpose and passion!

By now you've probably figured out the identity of my first client: me. I was my own greatest professional challenge. But that challenge led me to the most important learning opportunity of my life. In fighting for my own wellness, I won the ultimate victory: optimal health. And I learned firsthand that just because you have challenges doesn't mean you can't optimize the hand you've been dealt.

Sometimes clients who are very unwell think I can't possibly know what they are going through. But when I share my very personal (and sometimes uncomfortable) life story, they know that I understand their challenges.

In sharing my story—and the stories of other Omni Diet fans—with you, I sincerely hope that you find inspiration and hope. So many of us have found optimal health with the Omni Diet —I know that you can, too!

PART FIVE

OMNI RECIPES

Brain-Smart Start Smoothie SERVES 2

½ cup frozen organic blueberries

½ cup frozen cherries

⅓ banana

8 ounces pure coconut water or unsweetened almond milk

1 large handful baby spinach (about 1½ cups) (I promise you can't taste it, but you can adjust the amount initially until you get used to it, if necessary)

2 chard leaves or 1 small cucumber

2 tablespoons hemp seeds, shelled

1 tablespoon coconut butter

1 tablespoon goji powder

1 scoop vanilla, or berry-flavored, sugar-free pea protein powder (sweetened with stevia) (use 2 scoops for large men)

1 tablespoon freeze-dried greens (Green Vibrance is one of my favorite brands)

1 dropperful berry- or vanilla crème–flavored liquid stevia

OPTIONAL
soluble fiber
maca powder
bee pollen
aloe gel

1. Add all ingredients to blender bowl.

2. Turn blender on low at first, then increase speed.

3. Add additional almond milk or coconut water as needed to achieve desired consistency.

4. Pour into two large glasses and serve cold.

NUTRITIONAL INFORMATION PER SERVING

305 calories ▪ 25g protein ▪ 30.4g carbohydrates ▪ 7.6g fiber ▪ 14.2g sugar ▪ 11g fat 4.9g saturated fat ▪ 0.0mg cholesterol ▪ 288mg sodium

Very Omega Cherry Smoothie SERVES 2

1 cup organic pitted cherries, frozen

8 ounces almond milk, unsweetened

1 cup baby spinach

2 to 3 kale leaves

¼ cup raw pecans or other nuts

1 tablespoon chia seeds

1 scoop sugar-free vanilla protein powder (I prefer pea or rice protein sweetened with stevia) (use 2 scoops for large men)

1 tablespoon freeze-dried greens

1 dropperful vanilla crème–flavored liquid stevia

OPTIONAL

fiber

bee pollen

aloe gel

1. Add all ingredients to blender bowl.

2. Turn blender on low at first, then increase speed.

3. Add additional water or almond milk as needed to achieve desired consistency.

4. Pour into glasses and serve cold.

NUTRITIONAL INFORMATION PER SERVING

320 calories ▪ 25g protein ▪ 29g carbohydrates ▪ 8g sugar ▪ 9g fiber ▪ 16g fat 1g saturated fat ▪ 0.0mg cholesterol ▪ 129mg sodium

Mango Passion Smoothie SERVES 2

½ cup fresh mango, seeded, and roughly chopped

½ banana, chopped

½ cup baby spinach leaves

2 kale leaves

1 handful ice

1 scoop freeze-dried greens

2 tablespoons flax seeds

1½ teaspoons coconut butter

2 scoops vanilla-flavored pea protein powder (sweetened with stevia)

2 packets mango-flavored stevia

8 ounces unsweetened almond milk or coconut water

8 ounces cold purified water (add water for desired consistency)

OPTIONAL

1 tablespoon prebiotic soluble fiber

2 teaspoons maca root powder

1. Place all ingredients in a blender bowl.

2. Mix for about 30 seconds. Do not over-blend.

3. Pour into two large glasses and serve.

NUTRITIONAL INFORMATION PER SERVING

255 calories ▪ 25g protein ▪ 47g carbohydrates ▪ 10.2g fiber ▪ 13.3g sugar ▪ 6.5g fat
2.5g saturated fat ▪ 0.0mg cholesterol ▪ 335mg sodium

Sunrise Surprise Smoothie SERVES 2

½ pink grapefruit, peeled
1 large orange, peeled
1 carrot, unpeeled
1 cup iceberg lettuce
1 tablespoon hemp seeds
1 tablespoon raw sunflower seeds
1 scoop sugar-free vanilla protein powder
1 tablespoon freeze-dried greens
1 dropperful orange-flavored liquid stevia
handful of ice cubes

OPTIONAL
fiber
bee pollen
aloe gel

1. Add all ingredients to blender bowl.

2. Turn blender on low at first, then increase speed. Blend until smooth.

3. Add additional water or almond milk as needed to achieve desired consistency.

4. Pour into glasses and serve cold.

NOTE: For the protein powder, I prefer pea or rice protein sweetened with stevia.
Use 2 scoops for large men.

NUTRITIONAL INFORMATION PER SERVING

273 calories ▪ 25g protein ▪ 32g carbohydrates ▪ 7g fiber ▪ 4.25g sugar ▪ 7g fat
1g saturated fat ▪ 0.0mg cholesterol ▪ 62mg sodium

Peach Fuzz Fantastico Smoothie **SERVES 2**

This recipe requires iced tea. I prefer oolong or white tea. Prepare tea in advance and refrigerate.

1 ripe peach, pit removed
2 tablespoons chia seeds
1 scoop freeze-dried greens
¼ cup coconut milk
½ cup baby spinach
1 small cucumber, peeled and chopped
2 scoops vanilla-flavored pea protein powder (sweetened with stevia)
2 dropperfuls vanilla- or peach-flavored stevia
8 ounces coconut water and 8 ounces filtered water
handful of ice

OPTIONAL
2 teaspoons maca powder
1 tablespoon prebiotic soluble fiber

1. Place all ingredients in a blender bowl.

2. Mix for about 30 seconds. Do not over-blend.

3. Pour into two large glasses and serve.

NUTRITIONAL INFORMATION PER SERVING

285 calories ▪ 25g protein ▪ 34.4g carbohydrates ▪ 12.3g fiber ▪ 10.5g sugar ▪ 8.8g fat
3.6g saturated fat ▪ 0.0mg cholesterol ▪ 413mg sodium

Chocolate-Covered Strawberry Smoothie **SERVES 2**

1 cup organic strawberries, frozen
¼ avocado (about 2 tablespoons)
8 ounces unsweetened almond milk
1 cup baby spinach
1 tablespoon sunflower seeds
1 scoop sugar-free chocolate protein powder (use 2 scoops for large men)
1 tablespoon freeze-dried greens
1 dropperful chocolate-flavored liquid stevia

OPTIONAL
1 teaspoon raw cacao, unsweetened (found in health food stores)
fiber
bee pollen
aloe gel

1. Add all ingredients to blender bowl.

2. Turn blender on low at first, then increase speed.

3. Add additional water or almond milk to achieve desired consistency.

4. Pour into glasses and serve cold.

   NUTRITIONAL INFORMATION PER SERVING

   235 calories ▪ 25g protein ▪ 22g carbohydrates ▪ 9g sugar ▪ 7g fiber ▪ 9g fat
   1g saturated fat ▪ 0.0mg cholesterol ▪ 124mg sodium

Chunky Chocolate Monkey Smoothie SERVES 2

This is a favorite with children and a great way to introduce them to greens and raw food. Start out using only avocado. As your children get used to drinking smoothies try adding a small amount of spinach. They will likely never notice.

    1 slightly green banana
    ¼ avocado (about 2 tablespoons)
    8 ounces almond milk, unsweetened
    ¼ cup raw macadamia nuts or almonds
    1 tablespoon raw coconut, unsweetened and shaved
    1 scoop sugar-free chocolate protein powder (I prefer pea or rice protein
        sweetened with stevia) (use 2 scoops for large men)
    1 tablespoon freeze-dried greens
    1 to 2 teaspoons raw cacao, unsweetened
    1 dropperful chocolate-flavored liquid stevia
    handful of ice cubes

    OPTIONAL
    1 tablespoon raw cacao nibs, unsweetened
    fiber
    bee pollen
    aloe gel

1. Add all ingredients to blender bowl.

2. Turn blender on low at first, then increase speed. Blend until smooth.

3. Add additional water or almond milk as needed to achieve desired consistency.

4. Pour into glasses and serve cold.

   NUTRITIONAL INFORMATION PER SERVING

   328 calories ▪ 25g protein ▪ 32g carbohydrates ▪ 8g fiber ▪ 7.5g sugar ▪ 14g fat
   2g saturated fat ▪ 0.0mg cholesterol ▪ 113mg sodium

Cacao Mint Madness SERVES 2

2 tablespoons raw coconut, unsweetened and shaved (or the meat of one coconut)

½ slightly green banana

½ apple

2 tablespoons raw macadamia nuts or almonds

8 ounces pure coconut water, unsweetened

4 to 5 fresh mint leaves

1 cup iceberg lettuce or spinach

1 scoop sugar-free chocolate protein powder (I prefer pea or rice protein sweetened with stevia) (use 2 scoops for large men)

1 tablespoon freeze-dried greens

1 teaspoon raw cacao, unsweetened

1 dropperful chocolate-flavored liquid stevia

handful of ice cubes

OPTIONAL

1 tablespoon raw cacao nibs, unsweetened (they taste like chocolate chips)

fiber

bee pollen

aloe gel

1. Add all ingredients to blender bowl.

2. Turn blender on low at first, then increase speed.

3. Add additional water or almond milk to achieve desired consistency.

4. Pour into glasses and serve cold.

NUTRITIONAL INFORMATION PER SERVING

289 calories ▪ 25g protein ▪ 31g carbohydrates ▪ 5g fiber ▪ 5g sugar ▪ 4g fat 2g saturated fat ▪ 0.0mg cholesterol ▪ 50mg sodium

Cinnamon-Spice Stabilizer SERVES 2

Being focused and energized throughout the day requires that you keep your blood sugar balanced. The best way to do that is by starting the day off with a healthy breakfast and eating small meals every three or four hours. The spices in this smoothie do more than taste great. They help stabilize blood sugar and improve attention. The healthy fats will help sustain you longer, and they contain omega-3 fatty acids.

  1 large unpeeled apple, chopped
  2 tablespoons avocado (about ¼ of an avocado)
  ½ cup baby spinach
  2 tablespoons shelled hemp seeds
  2 scoops rice or pea protein (sweetened with stevia)
  1 teaspoon cardamom powder
  1 teaspoon cinnamon
  ¼ teaspoon nutmeg
  2 cups unsweetened almond milk
  1 cup purified water
  handful ice cubes

  OPTIONAL
  1 tablespoon prebiotic soluble fiber
  1 dropperful vanilla-flavored stevia

1. Place all ingredients in a blender bowl.

2. Mix for about 30 seconds. Do not over-blend.

3. Pour into two large glasses and serve.

  NUTRITIONAL INFORMATION PER SERVING
  300 calories ▪ 25g protein ▪ 32.2g carbohydrates ▪ 7.7g fiber ▪ 10.4g sugar ▪ 8.6g fat
  0.9g saturated fat ▪ 0.0mg cholesterol ▪ 162mg sodium

Green Tea Berry Blastoff SERVES 2

This recipe requires preparation of the iced tea in advance. Prepare green tea according to directions and refrigerate.

⅓ cup frozen organic blueberries

⅓ cup frozen organic blackberries

⅓ cup frozen organic raspberries (you can substitute one or both kinds of berries for another)

½ cup spinach

2 kale leaves, about ½ cup, chopped (discard the thick stalk, and use only the leafy portion)

2 tablespoons chia seeds

1 scoop freeze-dried greens

2 scoops vanilla-flavored pea or rice protein (sweetened with stevia)

2 tablespoons raw almonds

1 dropperful vanilla- or berry-flavored stevia

16 to 20 ounces cold green tea

purified water as desired

OPTIONAL

1 tablespoon prebiotic soluble fiber

1. Place all ingredients in a blender bowl.

2. Mix for about 30 seconds. Do not over-blend.

3. Pour into two large glasses and serve.

NUTRITIONAL INFORMATION PER SERVING

305 calories ▪ 25g protein ▪ 26.7g carbohydrates ▪ 11.2g fiber ▪ 6.6g sugar ▪ 14.3g fat 5g saturated fat ▪ 0.0mg cholesterol ▪ 240mg sodium

Antioxidant Energizing Smoothie SERVES 2

This recipe requires iced tea. I prefer oolong or white tea. Prepare tea in advance and refrigerate.

½ cup fresh pomegranate seeds (in season)—use any fresh, organic berry in place of pomegranate if necessary

½ cup frozen strawberries or other berries of your choice

½ cup baby spinach leaves

2 kale leaves torn from stalk (discard the thick stalk, and use only the leafy portion)

1 scoop freeze-dried greens

2 tablespoons chia seeds

1 tablespoon coconut butter

2 scoops vanilla-flavored pea protein powder (sweetened with stevia)

1 to 2 dropperfuls vanilla- or pomegranate-flavored stevia

16 ounces iced tea

8 ounces cold purified water (add more purified water for desired consistency)

handful of ice

OPTIONAL
2 tablespoons pomegranate powder (found in health food stores)

1 tablespoon prebiotic soluble fiber

1. Place all ingredients in a blender bowl.

2. Mix for about 30 seconds. Do not over-blend.

3. Pour into two large glasses and serve.

NUTRITIONAL INFORMATION PER SERVING

270 calories ▪ 25g protein ▪ 32.2g carbohydrates ▪ 10.9g fiber ▪ 6g sugar ▪ 10.6g fat 4.8g saturated fat ▪ 0.0mg cholesterol ▪ 250mg sodium

Omni Oatmeal SERVES 4

Oatmeal is almost as American as apple pie. This protein-packed version makes for a better-balanced breakfast choice. And thanks to the cinnamon, it can also enhance your attention and help regulate blood sugar levels, which may help curb your cravings.

- 1 cup steel-cut (not instant) oats
- 2 tablespoons ground flax seeds
- 3½ cups water
- ¼ cup protein powder (sweetened with stevia)
- 1 cup almond or rice milk
- ½ cup blueberries
- ½ small apple, chopped
- 10 drops vanilla crème–flavored liquid stevia (optional)
- cinnamon
- 2 tablespoons chopped raw walnuts

1. In a medium saucepan, mix oats, flax seeds, and water. Bring to a boil. Cover, reduce heat to low, and simmer, stirring occasionally, for 45 to 50 minutes, or until the oats are soft and the mixture is creamy.

2. When oats are cooked, mix in protein powder.

3. Stir in almond milk, blueberries, and chopped apple. Add stevia as needed.

4. Sprinkle with cinnamon.

5. Ladle into bowls.

6. Top with chopped walnuts.

NUTRITIONAL INFORMATION PER SERVING

222 calories ▪ 20g protein ▪ 31g carbohydrates ▪ 8g fiber ▪ 5g sugar ▪ 5g fat 1g saturated fat ▪ 0.0mg cholesterol ▪ 64mg sodium

Berry Nutty Breakfast Quinoa SERVES 4

1 cup almond milk, unsweetened

1 cup water

1 cup quinoa, rinsed

1 tablespoon Earth Balance butter substitute

4 drops vanilla-flavored stevia (optional)

1 cup fresh blueberries

1 cup fresh strawberries, sliced

½ teaspoon ground cinnamon

¼ cup chopped raw walnuts

OPTIONAL

1 tablespoon unsweetened pea protein powder

1 teaspoon pure maple syrup for drizzling

1. In a medium saucepan over high heat, combine almond milk, water, and quinoa. Bring to a boil. Reduce heat to medium low. Cover and simmer until most of the liquid is absorbed, about 15 minutes.

2. Add Earth Balance, pea protein, and stevia (if desired) and stir well.

3. Remove the saucepan from heat and let stand for 5 minutes.

4. Stir in blueberries, strawberries, and cinnamon.

5. Top with walnuts, drizzle with syrup, and serve warm.

NUTRITIONAL INFORMATION PER SERVING

252 calories ▪ 7g protein (protein powder adds approximately 12g protein)
32g carbohydrates ▪ 5g fiber ▪ 5.75g sugar ▪ 11g fat ▪ 1g saturated fat
0.0mg cholesterol ▪ 76mg sodium

Pacific Coast Scramble **SERVES 2**

I love using leftover salmon or wild smoked salmon for this dish. Vital Choice sells a variety of high-quality wild fish. Their canned fish is wild, contains only extra-virgin olive oil and a little sea salt, and they don't line their cans with bisphenol A (BPA) (a common problem with canned foods), a synthetic estrogen that has been linked to many health conditions. Vital Choice products can be purchased online at www.vitalchoice.com.

- 1 tablespoon grape-seed oil
- ½ shallot, minced, or ¼ cup chopped red onion
- 8 egg whites (preferably organic), beaten, or 2 eggs plus 4 additional egg whites, beaten
- 8 ounces wild salmon, mackerel, or small cooked shrimp (or combination of your choice)
- 1 teaspoon fresh oregano (optional)
- 1 teaspoon fresh basil (optional)
- 1 cup baby spinach
- ½ roma tomato, sliced
- ¼ avocado, diced
- ¼ teaspoon sea salt (optional)
- pepper to taste

1. Heat oil in a large skillet over medium heat. Add shallots and sauté for 2 minutes.

2. Add egg whites to the skillet and allow to set for about 30 seconds. Stir with a spatula.

3. Add your choice of seafood and herbs. Mix with spatula until seafood is warmed, but eggs are not yet thoroughly cooked.

4. Add spinach. Mix in with spatula and finish cooking, about 1 minute. Remove the skillet from heat.

5. Place tomato slices on bottom of two plates.

6. Divide egg and seafood mixture evenly and place on top of tomatoes.

7. Top each scrambled egg with avocado. Add sea salt and pepper as desired.

NUTRITIONAL INFORMATION PER SERVING

291 calories ▪ 43.9g protein ▪ 5.9g carbohydrates ▪ 0.8g fiber ▪ 2.1g sugar ▪ 9.7g fat 0.8g saturated fat ▪ 230mg cholesterol ▪ 558mg sodium

Seafood Omelet for Super Focus SERVES 2

1 teaspoon coconut oil

1 teaspoon ginger, minced

4 scallions, chopped (I use both the white and green parts)

5 medium-size shrimp, peeled, deveined, and halved lengthwise

5 medium-size scallops

2 whole eggs

2 egg whites

white pepper, to taste

2 teaspoons Earth Balance butter substitute or raw organic butter

½ cup bean sprouts

1 chive, chopped

OPTIONAL

1 grapefruit, halved

1. In a skillet, heat oil over medium heat. Add ginger and scallions, and sauté for 1 minute.

2. Add shrimp and scallops, and cook for 1 more minute. Set aside.

3. In a small bowl, whisk eggs and egg whites, and season with pepper.

4. Heat a medium skillet over medium heat and lightly coat with Earth Balance butter substitute or butter. Pour eggs into the skillet. Lift edges frequently to allow uncooked portion to flow underneath. Flip the omelet over and finish cooking, approximately 1 minute.

5. Transfer eggs to a plate, top with cooked seafood and with bean sprouts. Garnish with chives. May serve with half a grapefruit.

NUTRITIONAL INFORMATION PER SERVING

325 calories ▪ 24g protein ▪ 6g carbohydrates ▪ 2g fiber ▪ <1g sugar ▪ 24g fat
11g saturated fat ▪ 249mg cholesterol ▪ 338mg sodium

Super Surprise Frittata SERVES 4

2 teaspoons coconut oil or grape-seed oil

2 scallions, finely chopped

½ red bell pepper, minced

2 garlic cloves, minced

2 tomatoes, diced

1 tablespoon fresh thyme, chopped, or 1 teaspoon dried thyme

1 tablespoon fresh marjoram, chopped, or 1 teaspoon dried marjoram

8 ounces cooked chicken breast, diced or shredded, or cooked turkey, steak, or meatloaf—any precooked meat will do

sea salt and pepper, to taste

1 cup baby spinach leaves

8 eggs (organic, mega-3), lightly beaten

½ avocado, thinly sliced

1. Preheat oven to broil and set rack on lowest level.

2. Heat oil in a medium skillet over medium-high heat. (Use a skillet that will fit in the oven and has an oven-safe handle.) Add scallions and red bell peppers, and cook for about 2 minutes.

3. Add garlic, tomatoes, thyme, marjoram, and chicken (or other meat), and sea salt and pepper, if desired. Cook for about a minute.

4. Add spinach to the skillet and cook for another minute. Do not allow spinach to bunch together.

5. Add eggs to the skillet. Using a spatula, stir the mixture until the eggs begin to set, but are still runny.

6. Put skillet in the oven for 4 to 5 minutes, until the frittata becomes firm and fluffy.

7. Transfer cooked frittata to a plate. Cut into quarters and serve each piece topped with two slices of avocado.

NUTRITIONAL INFORMATION PER SERVING

312 calories ▪ 31.9g protein ▪ 7.9g carbohydrates ▪ 3g fiber ▪ 3.4g sugar ▪ 16.7g fat 4.3g saturated fat ▪ 420mg cholesterol ▪ 198mg sodium

Herb Garden Frittata SERVES 2

You will notice that this recipe and many others call for Real Salt. I love this brand of salt, which is pure, and has no additives, chemicals, or heat processing. It is healthier for you than regular table salt.

2 whole eggs (organic, omega-3)
4 egg whites (organic)
2 teaspoons ghee or coconut oil
¼ cup finely chopped red onion
½ cup asparagus tips
2 garlic cloves, finely chopped
2 handfuls spinach leaves
1 teaspoon chopped fresh rosemary
1 teaspoon chopped fresh thyme
1 tablespoon chopped fresh basil
Real Salt and pepper, to taste
1 vine-ripened tomato, thinly sliced

1. Preheat oven to 350°F. Whisk eggs and egg whites in a bowl and set aside.

2. In a small nonstick pan, heat 1 teaspoon ghee or oil over medium heat. Sauté onion and asparagus for about 2 minutes, until softened. Add garlic and sauté for another 2 minutes. Add spinach to pan for 2 minutes.

3. Remove onion, asparagus, and garlic from pan. Place on dish and set aside.

4. Add 1 teaspoon ghee or oil to pan. Pour egg mixture into pan. As egg mixture begins to set, add onion, asparagus, spinach, herbs, Real Salt and pepper (if desired), and garlic mixture to eggs, but do not scramble. Allow mixture to set in a nice round shape, about 5 minutes.

5. Transfer skillet to oven for 5 minutes, or until frittata is light golden brown.

6. Place frittata on plates and top with tomato slices.

NOTE: For a vegan option, use 8 ounces of firm tofu (equivalent of 4 eggs) or about 8 ounces tofu. If substituting egg product with tofu follow same steps above but use tofu in step 4. Crumble tofu and cook until slightly browned. Continue with steps 5 and 6. The "frittata" will not have the same set look that eggs do, but the flavor will be delicious.

Dried spices may be substituted. However, for the health benefit as well as flavor, you should try to use fresh herbs. If using dried herbs, use no more than 1 teaspoon of each.

NUTRITIONAL INFORMATION PER SERVING

133 calories ▪ 15g protein ▪ 12g carbohydrates ▪ 2g fiber ▪ <1g sugar ▪ 4g fat
2g saturated fat ▪ 372mg cholesterol ▪ 258mg sodium

Omni-Style Crepes SERVES 4

TOPPING INGREDIENTS

1 cup fresh organic strawberries, cleaned and stems removed

½ cup full-fat coconut milk from can (skim cream from top after refrigerated) (optional)

2 tablespoons erythritol or xylitol (optional)

2 teaspoons ground cinnamon (optional)

1 cup fresh organic blueberries, cleaned

2 tablespoons unsweetened carob chips

BATTER INGREDIENTS

½ cup almond meal or coconut flour

½ cup all-purpose gluten-free flour

2 tablespoons flaxseed meal

2 tablespoons erythritol or xylitol

1 teaspoon baking powder

5 egg whites

1 cup plain unsweetened almond milk or rice milk

1 teaspoon pure vanilla extract

TOPPING PREPARATION

1. Put strawberries in a high-powered blender. If desired, put coconut cream in blender with strawberries. Puree until the strawberries become a smooth sauce. Pour sauce into a squeeze bottle (cake decorator), or just put in a dish, cover, and set aside.

2. If desired, mix erythritol (or xylitol) and cinnamon to sprinkle later.

CREPES PREPARATION

1. In a large mixing bowl, combine the dry ingredients first: the almond meal, flour, flaxseed meal, erythritol, and baking powder.

2. Add the egg whites, almond milk, and vanilla. Using a handheld electric mixer at medium speed or a whisk, beat until batter is smooth. Do not allow to rest for long, as the flax tends to thicken the batter over time. For best results, the batter should be thin.

3. Use a non-teflon, nonstick crepe pan or skillet over medium heat. Pour a little less than ¼ cup of the batter into the pan (just enough to cover the pan with a *thin* layer), tilting the pan with a circular motion so that the batter coats the pan evenly. Cook the pancake for about 1 minute, until the bottom is golden brown. Loosen with a spatula, turn over, and cook the other side for about 30 seconds. It's all right to use your hand to help turn it. Remove the crepe and set aside on a plate, then repeat with the remaining batter.

4. Place crepe on a plate for serving. Put a line of blueberries down the center. You may choose to put a dollop of the strawberry sauce down the center as well, reserving enough of the sauce to garnish the top later. Roll the crepe. Repeat with all the remaining crepes.

5. When the crepes are assembled, place them back in the pan, four or five at a time, for about 30 seconds/side. When thoroughly warmed, remove and place two to a plate, and decorate the top of each plate with a generous serving of the strawberry sauce. Squeeze bottles lend themselves to great designs. Otherwise, spoon about a tablespoon over each crepe.

6. If desired, sprinkle 4 or 5 carob chips across the top of each crepe. Kids *love* this! It gives the illusion of decadence.

7. Sprinkle a generous amount of cinnamon/erythritol mixture across the entire plate. Serve quickly while crepes are warm.

NOTE: Crepes made with almond meal and gluten-free flour are heavier and a little trickier to turn. If you have trouble, try using a little nonstick spray on your skillet. These crepes are worth the effort. They taste great and are much healthier!

NOTE: Stack the crepes on a plate as you finish them. As you get better at making them, you may choose to make two at a time! You may also use parchment paper between them to prevent sticking and to keep them warm if you choose, or you can quickly reheat them before serving (as restaurants do).

BATTER NUTRITIONAL INFORMATION PER SERVING

179 calories ▪ 10.5g protein ▪ 21.95g carbohydrates ▪ 4.25g fiber ▪ 1.1g sugar
9.5g fat ▪ 0.6g saturated fat ▪ 0.0mg cholesterol ▪ 235.75mg sodium

STRAWBERRY/BLUEBERRY TOPPING NUTRITIONAL INFORMATION PER SERVING

31.7 calories ▪ 0.48g protein ▪ 7.8g carbohydrates ▪ 1.85g fiber ▪ 5.75g sugar
0.15g fat ▪ 0.0g saturated fat ▪ 0.0mg cholesterol ▪ 2.55mg sodium
Adding the coconut milk will add about 100 calories

Benedict-Style Poached Eggs SERVES 2

SAUCE INGREDIENTS

2 egg yolks (organic)

2 tablespoons plain coconut milk

1 tablespoon hot purified water

1 tablespoon lemon juice, or to taste, depending on desired tartness

⅛ teaspoon (or a pinch) cayenne pepper

2 tablespoons Earth Balance butter substitute (use the one made with olive oil instead of soy), melted and hot

EGGS INGREDIENTS

grape-seed oil for greasing

2 eggs (organic, omega-3 added)

2 thick slices turkey breast meat or a slice of Canadian bacon (organic, nitrate-free, hormone-free, antibiotic-free)

4 large chard leaves or kale leaves, or 1 cup spinach

1 cup mixed berries

OPTIONAL

1 teaspoon gluten-free Dijon mustard

⅛ teaspoon sea salt

2 slices gluten-free Ezekiel bread or tortillas

SAUCE PREPARATION

1. In a blender bowl, place all ingredients for sauce (including mustard, if desired), except for Earth Balance. Blend for 10 seconds on high setting.

2. With the blender running on high, slowly pour in melted Earth Balance in a steady stream.

3. Pour entire mixture into a small saucepan and heat over low heat for 4 to 5 minutes, stirring regularly while eggs are cooking. Sauce will thicken as you stir.

EGG PREPARATION

1. The easiest way to poach eggs is in an egg poacher. Fill the bottom of the egg-poaching pan with ½ inch of water and bring to a boil.

2. Grease the egg cups with a small amount of grape-seed oil.

3. Crack eggs and place into egg cups from egg poacher. Be careful not to break the yolks.

4. Place egg cups in poaching pan, within frame.

5. For soft yolks, boil for 2 minutes. For firm yolks, boil for 4 minutes. Set aside.

6. If you choose to serve with Ezekiel bread, toast bread and place one slice on each plate.

7. Quickly heat turkey breast in pan or microwave for a few seconds.

8. Stack greens neatly on each plate (or on top of bread).

9. Place one slice of turkey breast or ham on top of greens.

10. Place one egg on top of turkey breast.

11. Spoon sauce over eggs, dividing evenly between plates, with a sprinkling of salt if desired.

12. Place ½ cup of berries on each plate.

NOTE: To poach eggs without a poacher: Fill a small saucepan halfway with purified water and bring to a boil. Reduce heat slightly. Cooking one egg at a time, crack the egg into a small cup. Lower cup to water level and gently release egg into the water. Use a spoon to guide the egg whites back toward the yolk. Cook for about 4 minutes each. Use a slotted spoon to remove eggs from water. You may choose to add a teaspoon of vinegar to the water to help the egg whites congeal.

NUTRITIONAL INFORMATION PER SERVING

333 calories ▪ 21g protein ▪ 13.3g carbohydrates ▪ 2.7g fiber ▪ 7.3g sugar ▪ 16.3g fat 9.1g saturated fat ▪ 393mg cholesterol ▪ 718mg sodium

Feel-Good Eggs Ranchero SERVES 2

Did you know that eggs are good-mood foods? They increase dopamine and acetylcholine. These neurotransmitters boost attention and memory. So when you start your day with eggs, it can put a little extra spring in your step. Personally, I love this meal because of the balance between protein and carbs.

2 teaspoons coconut oil
2 shallots, chopped
1 garlic clove, minced
½ cup red or kidney beans, soaked overnight and cooked, or canned beans
¼ teaspoon cumin
½ teaspoon paprika
½ teaspoon garlic salt (optional)
pepper, to taste
2 whole eggs
2 egg whites
2 cups baby spinach (or 2 gluten-free tortillas)
2 tablespoons fire-roasted salsa

1. In a medium skillet, heat 1 teaspoon coconut oil over medium heat. Sauté shallots and garlic for 3 minutes.

2. Add beans, cumin, and paprika, and season with pepper, as desired. Cook beans for 4 minutes, stirring frequently. Set aside and keep warm.

3. Beat eggs and egg whites in a bowl. Heat the rest of the coconut oil in a small skillet and cook eggs until opaque. Season with salt and pepper.

4. Place the spinach on a plate. Top with beans and eggs, and serve with salsa.

NUTRITIONAL INFORMATION PER SERVING
351 calories ▪ 22g protein ▪ 30g carbohydrates ▪ 4g fiber ▪ <1g sugar ▪ 19g fat
13g saturated fat ▪ 387mg cholesterol ▪ 405mg sodium

Southwestern Huevos SERVES 2

2 flax wraps or 2 gluten-free rice flour tortillas (optional)

2 cups baby spinach leaves

2 teaspoons grape-seed oil

¼ cup chopped onion

2 garlic cloves, chopped

1 cup black beans, soaked and cooked

½ teaspoon chili powder

½ teaspoon cumin

¼ teaspoon black pepper

¼ teaspoon sea salt

8 egg whites (organic)

½ cup fresh salsa

½ avocado, sliced

1 tablespoon chopped cilantro

1. If you are using rice tortillas or flax wraps, heat them in a pan and place them on two plates, then arrange the spinach on top.

2. Heat 1 teaspoon oil in medium pan over medium heat. Add onion and garlic, and sauté for about 1 minute.

3. Add black beans, chili powder, cumin, pepper, and salt, if desired. Cook for about 3 minutes. Place contents of pan into a bowl and cover to keep warm.

4. Add the rest of the oil to the pan, making sure there is enough to prevent sticking, then add egg whites and cook omelet-style or scrambled.

5. Divide eggs evenly and place onto each plate over the greens.

6. Spread half of the bean mixture onto each plate, over the greens.

7. Top with ½ cup salsa on each plate and top with avocado and cilantro.

NUTRITIONAL INFORMATION PER SERVING

323 calories ▪ 25.1g protein ▪ 34.4 carbohydrates ▪ 11.4g fiber ▪ 4.9g sugar ▪ 11g fat 1.4g saturated fat ▪ 0.0mg cholesterol ▪ 740mg sodium

Brainy Breakfast Burrito SERVES 2

2 whole eggs
4 egg whites
1 teaspoon coconut butter
1 leek, cut in half moons (white part only)
1 garlic clove, minced
¼ cup chopped red bell pepper
¼ cup sliced crimini mushrooms
¼ cup chopped broccoli
4 romaine/iceberg lettuce leaves or 2 coconut curry wraps (I like Pure Wraps)
2 tablespoons salsa
¼ avocado, sliced

1. In a small bowl, whisk eggs and egg whites.

2. In a medium skillet, heat coconut butter over medium heat.

3. Add leek and garlic to the skillet, and sauté for 1 minute.

4. Add bell peppers, mushrooms, and broccoli to the skillet, and cook for 2 to 3 minutes.

5. Add eggs to the skillet, and stir until cooked through.

6. Spread each with 1 tablespoon of salsa, divided egg mixture, and top with sliced avocado. Roll up and serve immediately.

NUTRITIONAL INFORMATION PER SERVING

311 calories ▪ 16g protein ▪ 25g carbohydrates ▪ 7g fiber ▪ <1g sugar ▪ 19g fat
3g saturated fat ▪ 213mg cholesterol ▪ 218mg sodium

COCONUT CURRY WRAPS (BY PURE WRAP) NUTRITIONAL INFORMATION

70 calories ▪ 0g protein ▪ 9g carbohydrates ▪ 1g fiber ▪ <1g sugar ▪ 3g fat
2.5g saturated fat ▪ 0.0mg cholesterol ▪ 240mg sodium

Clear Start Breakfast Burrito **SERVES 2**

2 whole eggs

4 egg whites

2 teaspoons grape-seed oil

¼ onion, chopped

1 garlic clove, minced

¼ cup chopped red bell pepper

¼ cup sliced crimini or shiitake mushrooms

¼ cup chopped broccoli florets

4 large romaine or iceberg lettuce leaves, or coconut curry wraps (I like Pure Wraps)

1 tablespoon salsa

¼ avocado, diced

1. Whisk the eggs and egg whites in a small bowl.

2. Heat grape-seed oil in a medium nonstick skillet over medium heat.

3. Add onion and garlic. Sauté for 1 minute.

4. Add bell pepper, mushrooms, and broccoli. Cook for 2 to 3 minutes.

5. Add the eggs and stir until cooked through.

6. Double up romaine leaves to be used as two burrito wraps.

7. Divide eggs evenly and place in wraps. Spread with salsa.

8. Top with avocado. Roll wraps to secure.

NUTRITIONAL INFORMATION PER SERVING

248 calories ▪ 16g protein ▪ 9.4g carbohydrates ▪ 3.9g fiber ▪ 3.2g sugar ▪ 10.6g fat
2.6g saturated fat ▪ 186mg cholesterol ▪ 239mg sodium

Sausage in Green Blankets SERVES 4

1½ teaspoons coconut oil
½ organic green apple, diced
½ yellow onion, diced
2 garlic cloves, minced
1 pound ground chicken (free-range, antibiotic-free, hormone-free)
1 tablespoon fresh oregano
1 teaspoon sage
1 tablespoon rosemary
1 teaspoon allspice
¼ teaspoon black pepper
1 tablespoon pure maple syrup (optional)
½ teaspoon sea salt (optional)
16 large iceberg or romaine lettuce leaves

1. Heat 1 teaspoon oil in a large skillet over medium-high heat. Add apple and onion and sauté for 3 minutes.

2. Add garlic and sauté for another minute. Remove from pan and allow to cool.

3. Mix chicken and remaining ingredients, except lettuce, in a large bowl. When cool enough, add apple mixture to chicken and mix well with hands. Be sure ingredients are well blended.

4. You may choose to form sausages into patties or links. Mixture should make about 8 patties or links (patties work better with iceberg, and links with romaine).

5. In the large skillet, add ½ teaspoon more of coconut oil. Heat to medium and add patties or links. Reduce heat slightly. Cook for about 3–4 minutes each side, until browned.

6. Remove the sausage from heat and allow to cool for a couple of minutes. Add sea salt, to taste.

7. Wrap sausage in lettuce leaves.

NUTRITIONAL INFORMATION PER SERVING
211 calories ▪ 20.8g protein ▪ 8.2g carbohydrates ▪ 2.4g fiber ▪ 4.1g sugar ▪ 11.3g fat
4.2g saturated fat ▪ 98mg cholesterol ▪ 76mg sodium

Gluten-Free Blueberry French Toast SERVES 2

2 eggs
2 egg whites
⅛ teaspoon cinnamon
2 slices gluten-free bread
2 teaspoons coconut oil
½ cup organic blueberries
2 tablespoons pure organic maple syrup

1. Whip eggs, egg whites, and cinnamon in a bowl large enough to put bread in without breaking it.

2. Soak each piece of bread on each side on a tray for at least 2 minutes. (Gluten-free bread tends to be dense and firm.)

3. Heat oil in a large pan over medium heat. Add bread to pan when pan is hot. When the egg coating the bread begins to cook and brown slightly, turn and cook on the other side. Repeat until egg appears completely cooked.

4. Prepare two plates. Place one piece of French toast on each plate.

5. Top each piece of French toast with ¼ cup of blueberries and 1 tablespoon of maple syrup. Serve hot.

NUTRITIONAL INFORMATION PER SERVING

295 calories ▪ 14.2g protein ▪ 33g carbohydrates ▪ 3g fiber ▪ 12g sugar ▪ 12.5g fat
5.5g saturated fat ▪ 186mg cholesterol ▪ 133mg sodium

Heirloom Tomato Salad SERVES 4

1 pound heirloom tomatoes, or a variety of seasonal tomatoes from local farmers' market (I love black and yellow tomatoes), sliced

¼ cup chopped parsley

1 tablespoon small capers

¼ cup sliced kalamata olives

1 pound sliced turkey breast (cage-free, hormone-free, antibiotic-free)

DRESSING INGREDIENTS

2 tablespoons balsamic *fig* vinegar (found at most health food stores) or sherry vinegar

¼ teaspoon sea salt

freshly ground black pepper

1 teaspoon minced garlic

1 teaspoon *herbes de Provence*

¼ cup olive oil

1. Arrange colorful sliced tomatoes artfully on a platter, alternating colors.

2. To make the dressing, in a small bowl whisk together the vinegar, salt, pepper, garlic, and *herbes de Provence*. Slowly drizzle in the olive oil, whisking the whole time to create an emulsion.

3. Scatter the parsley, capers, and olives evenly over the tomatoes.

4. Drizzle the dressing over the tomatoes.

5. Roll the turkey and place around the platter.

NUTRITIONAL INFORMATION PER SERVING

290 calories ▪ 18g protein ▪ 1.4g carbohydrates ▪ 2g fiber ▪ 3g sugar ▪ 15g fat 1.8g saturated fat ▪ 30mg cholesterol ▪ 405mg sodium

Peaceful Asian Pear Salad SERVES 4

¼ cup grape-seed oil
1 teaspoon honey
½ teaspoon Dijon mustard
1 tablespoon apple cider vinegar
salt and pepper, to taste
8 cups arugula
1 Asian pear, cored and thinly sliced
¼ cup pecans
1 pound (16 ounces) cooked shrimp

1. In a small bowl, whisk together the grape-seed oil, honey, mustard, and vinegar.

2. Season with salt and pepper, then set aside.

3. On a large plate, arrange arugula and top with pear and pecans.

4. Drizzle the dressing over the salad when ready to eat.

5. Top with shrimp and serve.

NUTRITIONAL INFORMATION PER SERVING

321 calories ▪ 25g protein ▪ 7g carbohydrates ▪ 2g fiber ▪ 3.8g sugar ▪ 19g fat
2g saturated fat ▪ 172mg cholesterol ▪ 193mg sodium

Spinach and Strawberry Salad with Pecans SERVES 4

2 tablespoons balsamic vinegar
1 teaspoon raw honey
¼ cup olive oil
salt to taste
3 cups baby spinach
1 cup sliced strawberries
¼ cup pecan halves or chopped pecans

1. In a small bowl, mix balsamic vinegar and honey.

2. Slowly whisk in olive oil. Season with salt. Refrigerate until ready to serve.

3. Spread spinach on plate, and top with strawberries and pecans. Drizzle with balsamic vinaigrette and serve.

NUTRITIONAL INFORMATION PER SERVING

176 calories ▪ 2g protein ▪ 8g carbohydrates ▪ 3g fiber ▪ 3.4g sugar ▪ 16g fat
3g saturated fat ▪ 0.0mg cholesterol ▪ 21mg sodium

Stay-Sharp Chard Salad SERVES 4

3 cups shredded chard
1 cup shredded green cabbage
4 tablespoons dried blueberries
1 tablespoon hemp-seed oil
½ avocado, diced
½ cup chopped cilantro
2 tablespoons fresh lime juice
¼ cup coconut milk
salt and pepper, to taste
2 tablespoons hemp seeds
1 tablespoon chopped fresh basil
16 ounces chopped cooked chicken breast

1. In a large bowl, mix chard, green cabbage, and blueberries.

2. In a blender bowl or small food processor, place hemp-seed oil, avocado, cilantro, lime juice, coconut milk, salt, and pepper. Blend until smooth.

3. Toss the dressing with chard mixture in the large bowl.

4. Sprinkle with hemp seeds and basil, and mix well.

5. Marinate in refrigerator for 1 hour.

6. Top with chicken when ready to serve.

NUTRITIONAL INFORMATION PER SERVING

191 calories ▪ 6g protein ▪ 20g carbohydrates ▪ 7g fiber ▪ 1g sugar ▪ 11g fat
1g saturated fat ▪ 1mg cholesterol ▪ 256mg sodium

Seared Ahi with Cucumber Salad SERVES 2

This quick and nutritious meal is one of our favorites. It is perfectly satisfying.

4 Persian cucumbers, thinly sliced
½ avocado, diced
1 tablespoon olive oil
2 teaspoons chopped dill
1 shallot, finely chopped
1 teaspoon fresh lemon juice
salt and pepper, to taste
1 lime, juiced
2 garlic cloves, minced
2 teaspoons grated fresh ginger
1 teaspoon honey
2 ahi tuna steaks (4 to 6 ounces each)
2 teaspoons coconut oil
3 cups mixed greens

PREPARATION FOR CUCUMBER SALAD

1. In a medium bowl, combine cucumber, avocado, olive oil, dill, shallots, and lemon juice, and season with salt and pepper.

2. Cover and refrigerate for 30 minutes.

PREPARATION FOR TUNA

1. In a medium bowl, mix lime juice, garlic, ginger, and honey.

2. Season tuna with salt and pepper. Place fish in lime marinade, cover, and refrigerate for 15 to 30 minutes.

3. In a skillet, heat coconut oil over medium heat. Sear tuna for 1 to 2 minutes on each side, depending on how rare you prefer. Remove tuna from the skillet and slice into ¼-inch-thick slices.

4. Place mixed greens on plates, add cucumber salad, and top with the tuna.

NUTRITIONAL INFORMATION PER SERVING

361 calories ▪ 31g protein ▪ 20g carbohydrates ▪ 7g fiber ▪ 7g sugar ▪ 13g fat
6g saturated fat ▪ 50mg cholesterol ▪ 60mg sodium

Shrimp over Watermelon Mint Salad SERVES 4

GRILLED SHRIMP
4 wood or stainless steel skewers (pre-soak wood skewers for 30–60 minutes prior to grilling)
1 pound jumbo shrimp, 20 to 24, deveined
2 teaspoons olive oil
½ teaspoon paprika
½ teaspoon garlic powder
½ teaspoon Old Bay Seasoning
juice of 1 lime

DRESSING INGREDIENTS
2 tablespoons extra-virgin olive oil
2 tablespoons macadamia-nut oil
½ teaspoon gluten-free Dijon mustard
½ teaspoon fresh minced garlic, or ¼ teaspoon garlic powder
⅛ teaspoon cumin
¼ teaspoon sea salt
2 to 3 tablespoons fresh lime juice
1 to 2 teaspoons raw honey (optional)

SALAD INGREDIENTS
6 cups mixed greens
½ cup fresh mint leaves
1 Persian cucumber, thinly sliced
2 cups watermelon cubed into 1-inch pieces
¼ cup pine nuts

1. Preheat grill to medium heat.

2. Place shrimp in large Ziploc bag. Drizzle oil over the shrimp to coat. Sprinkle with paprika, garlic powder, Old Bay, and lime juice. Seal and shake the bag until the shrimp are coated evenly.

3. Place shrimp on wooden skewers. Put on grill, cooking until shrimp tails turn white, 2 to 3 minutes. Flip and cook for 1½ to 2 minutes more (depending on size).

4. Mix olive oil and macadamia-nut oil together in a small bowl. Set aside. In a small bowl, combine mustard, garlic, cumin, salt, lime juice, and honey. Drizzle oil into spice mixture in a slow steady stream, whisking continuously. Cover dressing and refrigerate until ready to use.

5. Put mixed greens, mint, and cucumber in a large bowl and toss well with half of the dressing to coat *lightly*. Add more if necessary. Store remaining dressing in the refrigerator for up to 1 week.

6. Divide salad evenly and place on plates. Scatter watermelon and pine nuts over lettuce mixture.

7. Place skewers over salad and serve.

SALAD NUTRITIONAL INFORMATION PER SERVING

170 calories ▪ 25g protein ▪ 12.24g carbohydrates ▪ 3.08g fiber ▪ 5g sugar ▪ 8.8g fat 0.7g saturated fat ▪ 59mg cholesterol ▪ 268.1mg sodium

DRESSING NUTRITIONAL INFORMATION PER SERVING (NOTE RECIPE MAKES 8 SERVINGS)

71.13 calories ▪ 0.0g protein ▪ 2.56g carbohydrates ▪ 0.25g fiber ▪ 2g sugar ▪ 7.01g fat 1g saturated fat ▪ 0.0mg cholesterol ▪ 56.5mg sodium

Rainbow Quinoa Salad with Chicken SERVES 6

1 cup red quinoa
¼ cup olive oil
2 tablespoons fresh lemon juice
zest from 1 lemon
salt and pepper, to taste
½ cup pomegranate seeds or ¼ cup dried cranberries
4 scallions, chopped
1 yellow pepper, thinly sliced
1 cup baby spinach
1 cup garbanzo beans, rinsed and drained (always soak overnight and cook thoroughly; only use canned beans in a pinch)
½ cup fresh basil, chopped
3 cups baked or grilled chopped chicken breast (hormone-free, antibiotic-free, free-range)

1. Rinse quinoa well. Combine quinoa with 2 cups water in a medium pot and bring it to a boil over high heat. Reduce heat, cover, and simmer for 20 to 30 minutes or until water is absorbed and quinoa is fluffy. Remove from heat and let cool.

2. In a small bowl, mix olive oil, lemon juice, lemon zest, salt, and pepper. Set aside.

3. In a large bowl, mix quinoa, pomegranate seeds, scallions, yellow pepper, baby spinach, and garbanzo beans.

4. Stir in basil and toss with prepared dressing.

5. Top with chicken.

6. Serve chilled or at room temperature.

NUTRITIONAL INFORMATION PER SERVING

371 calories ▪ 28g protein ▪ 39g carbohydrates ▪ 6g fiber ▪ 0.25g sugar ▪ 12g fat 1g saturated fat ▪ 49mg cholesterol ▪ 183mg sodium

Get Fit Chicken, Fennel, and Orange Salad SERVES 4

I typically advise people to avoid drinking fruit juice because it is so high in sugar, but the very small amount of juice used to flavor the dressing in this recipe adds very little sugar. It is preferable to consume a tiny amount of fresh juice in a salad dressing than to have the refined sugar that is used in so many processed dressings.

3 oranges
3 tablespoons grape-seed oil
½ teaspoon honey
½ teaspoon lemon zest
salt and pepper, to taste
2 fennel bulbs, cut in half and thinly sliced
2 cups cooked chicken breast

1. Peel oranges with a small knife, removing as much pulp as possible without damaging the fruit.

2. Holding each orange over a bowl to catch the juice, run a knife between the membranes. Segment orange, lifting the juicy part of the fruit out of the membrane with the knife. Squeeze the rest of the juice from what is left in the membrane into a small bowl. Measure out 2 tablespoons juice and set aside.

3. In a small bowl, mix grape-seed oil, orange juice, honey, and lemon zest. Season with salt and pepper. In a medium bowl, mix the fennel, sectioned orange pieces, and dressing.

4. Cover the bowl, refrigerate, and allow to marinate for 1 hour.

5. Top with chicken just before serving.

NOTE: This dish can be prepared a day in advance. You can also replace the chicken with cooked shrimp or halibut.

NUTRITIONAL INFORMATION PER SERVING

290 calories ▪ 21g protein ▪ 19g carbohydrates ▪ 5g fiber ▪ 8g sugar ▪ 15g fat
1g saturated fat ▪ 49mg cholesterol ▪ 116mg sodium

Amazing Apple-Cinnamon Chicken Salad SERVES 2

2 boneless, skinless chicken breasts (4 to 6 ounces)

salt and pepper, to taste

2 tablespoons Vegenaise

1 teaspoon apple cider vinegar

½ teaspoon cinnamon

1 medium apple, chopped

¼ cup raisins

2 tablespoons chopped pecans

4 cups lettuce or other greens

1. Preheat the grill to medium-high heat.

2. Season chicken with salt and pepper.

3. Cook chicken 7 to 10 minutes on each side or until the juices run clear. Let cool.

4. In a medium bowl, mix Vegenaise, vinegar, and cinnamon.

5. Dice chicken into large chunks.

6. Add chicken, apple, raisins, and pecans to dressing mixture.

7. Toss gently to coat. Season with salt and pepper, if needed.

8. Refrigerate for 2 hours. Serve on a bed of your favorite greens.

NUTRITIONAL INFORMATION PER SERVING

239 calories ▪ 22g protein ▪ 25g carbohydrates ▪ 4g fiber ▪ 11g sugar ▪ 11g fat
2g saturated fat ▪ 49mg cholesterol ▪ 107mg sodium

Brain-Boosting BBQ Chicken Salad SERVES 4

1 lime, juiced

¼ cup fresh orange juice

3 garlic cloves, minced

½ teaspoon onion powder

1 tablespoon chopped fresh sage

1 tablespoon chopped fresh thyme

½ teaspoon salt

¼ teaspoon pepper

2 boneless, skinless chicken breasts, 4 ounces each (free-range, hormone-free, antibiotic-free)

1 tablespoon olive oil

2 tablespoons fresh lime juice

1 tablespoon chopped cilantro

1 red bell pepper, chopped

½ cup chopped celery

½ cup black beans, soaked overnight and cooked thoroughly or drained and rinsed canned beans, in a pinch

1 avocado, cut into chunks

3 scallions, chopped

salt and pepper, to taste

4 cups mixed greens

1. In a small bowl, combine lime and orange juice, garlic, onion powder, sage, thyme, salt, and pepper.

2. Put chicken in a plastic bag. Pour in lime and orange juice mixture. Turn chicken to coat, and refrigerate for at least 3 hours, up to 24 hours.

3. Preheat the grill to medium-high heat.

4. Remove chicken from plastic bag. Grill the chicken for 5 to 7 minutes on each side or until chicken is no longer pink in the center. Slice.

5. In a large bowl, mix olive oil, lime juice, and cilantro.

6. Add red bell pepper, celery, black beans, avocado, and scallions to the bowl. Season with salt and pepper.

7. To serve, place greens on each plate and top with chopped veggie-and-bean mixture and slices of the grilled chicken.

NUTRITIONAL INFORMATION PER SERVING

226 calories ▪ 16g protein ▪ 18g carbohydrates ▪ 11g fiber ▪ 1.5g sugar ▪ 14g fat 2g saturated fat ▪ 21mg cholesterol ▪ 332mg sodium

Sesame Kale Salad with Chicken SERVES 6

½ pound organic kale

1½ teaspoons raw honey

½ teaspoon sea salt

½ teaspoon ground pepper

4 tablespoons extra-virgin olive oil

1 tablespoon sesame oil

¼ cup golden raisins

2 tablespoons toasted sesame seeds

¼ cup roughly chopped raw pecans

3 cups chopped grilled or baked chicken (free-range, hormone-free, antibiotic-free)

1. Tear or cut kale leaves and place in a large salad bowl.

2. In a small bowl whisk together honey, salt, pepper, and olive and sesame oil. Whisk until well blended.

3. Toss raisins, sesame seeds, nuts, and dressing with kale in the large bowl. Refrigerate for 30 minutes prior to serving.

4. Serve salad on plates and top with chicken.

NUTRITIONAL INFORMATION PER SERVING

316 calories ▪ 26g protein ▪ 16g carbohydrates ▪ 1.9g fiber ▪ 2g sugar ▪ 16g fat
2.6g saturated fat ▪ 39.6mg cholesterol ▪ 175mg sodium

Almond Chicken Chopped Salad SERVES 6

DRESSING INGREDIENTS

2 tablespoons fresh lemon juice

grated zest and juice of 1 orange

1 teaspoon chopped rosemary

½ teaspoon sea salt (optional)

1 teaspoon raw honey (optional)

½ cup extra-virgin olive oil

SALAD INGREDIENTS

6 cups organic mixed seasonal greens

¼ cup chopped dates

½ cup raw almonds, whole

1 cup *very finely* diced jicama

1 pound chopped baked or grilled chicken breast (free-range, hormone-free, antibiotic-free)

1. Whisk all dressing ingredients except oil. While whisking, pour in oil in a slow stream to create an emulsion. Chill until ready to serve.

2. Place greens in a large salad bowl.

3. Toss greens with half of dressing. (Try to coat the salad with only a very small amount of dressing, but drizzle more as necessary.) Store the rest of the dressing in an airtight container in the refrigerator for up to 1 week.

4. Mix in dates, almonds, and jicama.

5. Top with chicken and serve.

SALAD NUTRITIONAL INFORMATION PER SERVING

198 calories ▪ 14g protein ▪ 16.8g carbohydrates ▪ 6.1g fiber ▪ 8.5g sugar ▪ 9.7g fat
0.85g saturated fat ▪ 20.6mg cholesterol ▪ 32.5mg sodium

DRESSING NUTRITIONAL INFORMATION PER SERVING

134.8 calories ▪ 0.2g protein ▪ 2.25g carbohydrates ▪ 0.4g fiber ▪ 0.3g sugar ▪ 14g fat
2g saturated fat ▪ 0.0mg cholesterol ▪ 0.0mg sodium

Blueberry Tarragon Chicken Salad SERVES 6

1 cup lentils, rinsed, soaked overnight

1 to 2 cups water, or low-sodium vegetable broth

1 bay leaf

1 teaspoon coconut oil

¼ cup diced sweet onion

1½ cups organic blueberries, rinsed

2 teaspoons apple cider vinegar

½ teaspoon sea salt

1 to 2 tablespoons dates, fresh, pitted

1 tablespoon fresh tarragon

fresh zest from 1 small lemon

1 teaspoon fresh lemon juice

½ cup water

8 ounces baby spinach

1 cup roughly chopped raw walnuts

1 pound baked or grilled chicken breast, chopped into 1-inch pieces (free-range, hormone-free, antibiotic-free)

1. Combine lentils, water or broth, and bay leaf. Bring to a boil. Simmer for 15 to 20 minutes, or until the lentils are soft. Check occasionally to see if more water is needed. Don't let lentils get dry.

2. Drain. Discard the bay leaf. Set the lentils aside and let cool.

3. Heat coconut oil in a skillet over medium heat. Sauté onions until lightly brown. Let cool.

4. Place onions and coconut oil in a blender. Add ½ cup of the blueberries, the apple cider vinegar, sea salt, dates, tarragon, lemon zest, lemon juice, and water. Blend until smooth. Chill.

5. For the salad, toss lentils and spinach together. Arrange spinach mix on plates. Top salad with chicken. Garnish with the remaining 1 cup of blueberries and the walnuts.

6. Drizzle dressing over the salad.

NUTRITIONAL INFORMATION PER SERVING

210 calories ■ 9.2g protein ■ 13.7g carbohydrates ■ 5.4g fiber ■ 4.2g sugar ■ 14.4g fat 2.0g saturated fat ■ 6.8mg cholesterol ■ 143mg sodium

Snappy Mango Chicken Salad SERVES 6

1 teaspoon minced garlic

1 teaspoon minced fresh ginger

¼ cup chunky almond butter

¼ teaspoon ancho chile powder

3 tablespoons seasoned rice vinegar

1 tablespoon tamari sauce

1½ ounces water

2 cups stemmed, thinly sliced diagonally snap peas (slicing looks nice, but leave them whole if you need to save time)

1 cup grated carrot

2 cups halved, sliced cucumber

1 cup shirataki noodles rinsed and boiled for 3 minutes (or you may prefer kelp noodles)

1 cup peeled, diced mango

6 cups baby greens

3 cups baked or grilled chicken (hormone-free, antibiotic-free, free-range)

¼ cup slivered raw almonds

1. In a small bowl, combine garlic, ginger, almond butter, chile powder, rice vinegar, and tamari sauce. Add water. Whisk until smooth.

2. In a large bowl, mix together the snap peas, carrot, cucumber, noodles, and mango.

3. To serve, arrange salad greens on a serving plate. Top the salad with snap pea mix.

4. Drizzle with dressing.

5. Top with chicken and sprinkle almonds on top.

NOTE: Purchase high-quality precooked chicken or turkey to use in a pinch.

NUTRITIONAL INFORMATION PER SERVING

240 calories ▪ 22g protein ▪ 15g carbohydrates ▪ 3.3g fiber ▪ 6.95g sugar ▪ 8.8g fat 0.8g saturated fat ▪ 13.9mg cholesterol ▪ 238mg sodium

Asian-Fusion Chicken Salad SERVES 4

This recipe requires marinating the chicken for at least 1 hour, and up to 24 hours.

INGREDIENTS FOR MARINADE

¼ cup sesame oil

¼ cup macadamia-nut oil or grape-seed oil

2 garlic cloves, minced

½ shallot, minced (about 1 tablespoon)

1 tablespoon finely chopped fresh ginger

¼ cup rice vinegar

¼ cup low-sodium chicken broth

2 tablespoons low-sodium tamari sauce

2 tablespoons fresh lemon juice

½ teaspoon red curry powder

4 boneless, skinless chicken breast halves (free-range, hormone-free, antibiotic-free)

INGREDIENTS FOR DRESSING

⅓ cup olive oil

2 teaspoons low-sodium tamari sauce

3 tablespoons fresh lemon juice

1 to 2 teaspoons raw honey

INGREDIENTS FOR SALAD

8 cups mixed greens

½ organic pear, sliced

¼ cup fresh, organic pomegranate seeds

1 tablespoon black sesame seeds

1. Whisk all marinade ingredients except chicken together in a mixing bowl.

2. Put chicken in a Ziploc bag and pour marinade over the chicken. Remove air from the bag and seal. Refrigerate for at least a half hour before cooking. Remove from refrigerator 30 minutes before cooking and let stand.

3. Preheat grill to medium-high heat. Grill chicken until cooked through, about 4 to 5 minutes per side. Remove from grill and set aside.

4. In a small bowl, whisk together olive oil, tamari sauce, lemon juice, and honey.

5. Arrange greens on 4 plates. Place pear slices around sides. Sprinkle pomegranate seeds over the salad. Drizzle each salad with about 1 tablespoon of dressing.

6. Slice chicken breast into thin slices and place them on each salad.

7. Sprinkle sesame seeds over the top of each salad.

NOTE: Raw, unfiltered honey is not appropriate for children under two years of age. Use pasteurized honey in recipes that will be fed to children under the age of two.

NUTRITIONAL INFORMATION PER SERVING

305 calories ▪ 30.2g protein ▪ 19.1g carbohydrates ▪ 4.1g fiber ▪ 8g sugar ▪ 12g fat
5.5g saturated fat ▪ 73mg cholesterol ▪ 580mg sodium

V-8 Macho Gazpacho on the Go SERVES 8

I love this recipe because it is quick and simple. I even love it for breakfast. You can make it the night before, or you can make it early in the morning and it's ready for lunch. Adding protein powder makes it a complete meal. Otherwise, be sure to add some lean protein to your meal.

1½ pounds yellow tomatoes, quartered
1 cup peeled, seeded, and chopped cucumber
1 cup chopped yellow bell pepper
½ large sweet onion, chopped
½ cup fresh-squeezed orange juice
1 ounce extra-virgin olive oil
½ ounce white balsamic vinegar
½ ounce fresh lime juice
1 teaspoon minced garlic
1 serrano pepper, seeded and minced (optional)
½ teaspoon sea salt (optional)
½ teaspoon freshly ground black pepper (optional)
¼ cup unflavored pea protein
½ cup diced avocado, from 1 large avocado
1 ounce Cilantro Oil (optional) (see opposite page)

1. Place a fine mesh strainer over the top of a bowl. Squeeze tomatoes over the top of the strainer, discarding seeds and keeping the tomato meat. Reserve the juice and chop tomato meat.

2. In a blender, combine tomato, cucumber, and bell pepper and blend until smooth.

3. Add reserved tomato juice, onion, orange juice, oil, vinegar, lime juice, garlic, and serrano pepper, if using. Blend until smooth. Add salt and black pepper, if desired.

4. Cover and refrigerate for 2 to 3 hours before serving.

5. Blend in protein powder just before serving.

6. Ladle into bowls and sprinkle with avocado.

7. Drizzle about a teaspoon of cilantro oil over the top of each bowl for flavor and garnish, if desired.

NUTRITIONAL INFORMATION PER SERVING

236 calories ▪ 3g protein (protein powder adds 5g to 8g protein per serving) 18g carbohydrates ▪ 6g fiber ▪ 5g sugar ▪ 16g fat ▪ 2g saturated fat 0.0mg cholesterol ▪ 129mg sodium

Cilantro Oil

1 cup cilantro, packed
1 cup extra-virgin olive oil
⅛ teaspoon all-purpose seasoning

1. Bring 1 quart of water to a boil. Dunk cilantro in hot water for about 5 seconds. Remove cilantro from water and rinse with cold water immediately (this is called blanching). Squeeze water from cilantro. Place cilantro and olive oil in a blender. Blend until smooth. Season with all-purpose seasoning mix.

2. The oil keeps 1 week in the refrigerator or 3 months in the freezer.

NUTRITIONAL INFORMATION PER SERVING

196 calories ▪ 7g protein ▪ 18g carbohydrates ▪ 6g fiber ▪ 0.5g sugar ▪ 10g fat 2g saturated fat ▪ 0.0mg cholesterol ▪ 129mg sodium

Ahi Sweet Potato Stew SERVES 2

1 tablespoon coconut oil
2 small onions, chopped
2 garlic cloves, minced
1 green bell pepper, cut lengthwise into thin slices
1 jar roasted sweet red peppers, or 2 roasted red bell peppers, diced
1 tablespoon chopped fresh tarragon
1 yellow squash, cubed
1 sweet potato, cubed
1 cup no-salt-added vegetable broth
½ cup low-sodium tomato sauce
1 pound ahi, cut into bite-size 1-inch cubes

1. Heat oil in a large pan over medium heat. Add onions and cook for 2 minutes.

2. Add garlic and green peppers and cook for 3 more minutes.

3. Add diced red peppers and tarragon and cook for 2 to 3 minutes.

4. Add squash, sweet potato, vegetable broth, and tomato sauce. Bring to a boil, then reduce heat to low for 5 minutes.

5. Add ahi and cook for another 3 to 5 minutes or until ahi appears cooked. Ahi may be eaten rare, if desired. Be careful not to overcook it.

6. Ladle stew into bowls and serve hot.

NUTRITIONAL INFORMATION PER SERVING

468 calories ▪ 60.5g protein ▪ 35.7g carbohydrates ▪ 8g fiber ▪ 16.7g sugar ▪ 8.6g fat 6.4g saturated fat ▪ 88mg cholesterol ▪ 223mg sodium

Hearty Chicken Stew SERVES 6

2 tablespoons grape-seed oil

2 celery stalks, chopped

1 onion, chopped

2 garlic cloves, minced

4 cups no-salt-added chicken broth

1 teaspoon Italian seasoning

1 tablespoon chopped fresh sage

1 tablespoon chopped fresh thyme

1 tablespoon chopped fresh basil

3 sweet potatoes, peeled and cubed

1 cup chopped green beans

1 cup chopped zucchini

2 cups white beans, soaked overnight and cooked

1½ to 2 pounds diced cooked boneless chicken (white or dark meat), follow recipe for Herb-Marinated Chicken (page 314)

sea salt, to taste

1. Heat oil in a large pot over medium-high heat. Sauté celery, onion, and garlic for 3 to 5 minutes or until soft.

2. Add broth. Bring to a boil.

3. Add Italian seasoning, herbs (or you may use any of your favorite herbs), and sweet potatoes. Reduce heat and simmer for 20 minutes.

4. Add green beans, zucchini, white beans, and chicken. Simmer 15 minutes. Add sea salt, if desired.

5. Ladle stew into bowls and serve hot.

NUTRITIONAL INFORMATION PER SERVING

443 calories ▪ 51.6g protein ▪ 35.8g carbohydrates ▪ 7.6g fiber ▪ 6.4g sugar ▪ 69.7g fat 1.9g saturated fat ▪ 112mg cholesterol ▪ 525mg sodium

Kale and Chicken Soup SERVES 8

2 tablespoons grape-seed oil

1 large red onion, cut into 8 wedges, then halved again

2 large tomatoes, quartered

1 sweet potato, cut into 1-inch cubes

2 cups sliced shiitake or crimini mushrooms

6 garlic cloves, peeled

½ teaspoon sea salt (optional)

½ teaspoon pepper (optional)

1 tablespoon chopped fresh thyme

1 tablespoon chopped fresh marjoram

6 cups no-salt-added vegetable broth

4 cups chopped kale

½ teaspoon white pepper

½ teaspoon chili powder

3 cups chopped cooked chicken breast (free-range, hormone-free, antibiotic-free)

¼ teaspoon Bragg's Liquid Aminos (optional)

1. Preheat oven to 375°F.

2. Lightly oil a large cookie sheet with a couple teaspoons of the oil. Spread onion, tomato, sweet potato, mushrooms, and garlic on cookie sheet and brush vegetables with remaining oil on both sides. Sprinkle with sea salt and pepper, as desired.

3. Bake for 30 to 40 minutes or until vegetables are lightly browned and tender. Turn over the vegetables once after 20 minutes. Remove from oven. Set aside mushrooms and sweet potato.

4. Place garlic, onion, tomato, thyme, and marjoram in a food processor. Pulse until mixture is creamy and smooth.

5. Transfer vegetable puree to a large pot and heat over medium-high heat.

6. Add vegetable broth, kale, white pepper, and chili powder. Bring to a boil. Reduce heat and simmer uncovered for 20 to 30 minutes.

7. Add sweet potato, mushrooms, chicken, and Bragg's Liquid Aminos, if using, to pot, stir, and heat through, for about 5 minutes.

8. Ladle soup into bowls and serve hot.

NUTRITIONAL INFORMATION PER SERVING

164 calories ▪ 19.2g protein ▪ 11.9g carbohydrates ▪ 4.7g fiber ▪ 5.3g sugar ▪ 3.9g fat 0.4g saturated fat ▪ 37mg cholesterol ▪ 137mg sodium

Chicken Lentil Soup SERVES 8

- ¼ cup no-salt-added vegetable broth (preferably), or 1 tablespoon refined coconut oil
- 4 celery stalks, cut into ½-inch pieces
- 1 carrot, cut into ½-inch pieces
- 1 red bell pepper, chopped
- 2 onions, chopped
- 2 garlic cloves, minced
- 6 cups purified water
- 6 cups no-salt-added vegetable broth
- 2 cups red lentils
- 1 tablespoon finely chopped fresh marjoram (optional)
- 1 tablespoon finely chopped fresh sage (optional)
- 1 teaspoon garlic salt (optional)
- ½ teaspoon curry powder
- ½ teaspoon ground cumin
- 1 tablespoon lemon pepper
- 1 teaspoon pepper
- 2 cups chopped cooked chicken breast (hormone-free, antibiotic-free, free-range)
- 1 tablespoon fresh lemon juice

1. In a large soup pot, heat vegetable broth or refined coconut oil. Add celery, carrot, peppers, onion, and garlic, and cook for about 5 minutes.

2. Add water and vegetable broth to pot. Stir in lentils. Cover and bring to a boil. Reduce heat and simmer, stirring occasionally, for about 25 minutes.

3. Stir in marjoram, sage, garlic salt, curry, cumin, lemon pepper, and pepper. Simmer uncovered for about 20 minutes, or until lentils fall apart and the mixture thickens. Add chicken during the last 5 minutes.

4. Stir in lemon juice.

5. Ladle soup into bowls and serve hot.

NUTRITIONAL INFORMATION PER SERVING

251 calories ▪ 24g protein ▪ 37g carbohydrates ▪ 8.9g fiber ▪ 1.2g sugar ▪ 3.2g fat
1.6g saturated fat ▪ 49mg cholesterol ▪ 125mg sodium

Shrimp Cocktail SERVES 2

The problem with shrimp cocktail is the sauce. It is loaded with sugar (or even high-fructose corn syrup)! However, it is easy to make your own brain-healthy sauce, and ditch the sugar. Or try an alternative for summer parties: mango salsa. Yum!

½ cup no-salt-added sugar-free tomato sauce
2 tablespoons horseradish (gluten-free)
¼ teaspoon lemon juice
ice cubes
8 jumbo prawns, cleaned, deveined, and cooked

1. In a small bowl, mix tomato sauce, horseradish, and lemon juice. Blend well.

2. Place a few ice cubes in the bottom of 2 dessert bowls.

3. Arrange prawns around the rims of the dessert bowls, with tails pointing outward.

4. Put ¼ cup cocktail sauce in a small sauce dish and place in the center of the prawns.

5. Serve cold.

NOTE: Try blending several tomatoes in the blender to make your own tomato sauce!

NUTRITIONAL INFORMATION PER SERVING
58 calories ▪ 1.6g protein ▪ 7.2g carbohydrates ▪ 3g fiber ▪ 2.4g sugar ▪ 3.3g fat
0.5g saturated fat ▪ 0.0mg cholesterol ▪ 27mg sodium

Serrano Chile Shrimp SERVES 4

1 cup quinoa
¼ cup vegetable broth, or 2 tablespoons grape-seed oil for sautéeing
4 garlic cloves, thinly sliced
3 serrano peppers, sliced in thin rings (if you don't like spicy, slice the chiles in half and remove the seeds, then dice)
1½ pounds jumbo shrimp, 20 to 24 count, peeled, deveined
1 teaspoon all-purpose seasoning, such as Spike
½ cup chopped cilantro
¼ cup fresh lime juice
1 pound baby spinach

1. In a medium pot, cook quinoa in water according to package instructions.

2. Meanwhile, heat broth or oil in skillet over medium heat. Sauté garlic and serrano peppers till tender, about 1 minute.

3. Add shrimp. Sauté until shrimp are pink and cooked through, about 3 minutes.

4. Add the all-purpose seasoning. Turn off heat. Add cilantro and lime juice.

5. Just before removing quinoa from heat, add baby spinach and blend into quinoa. Remove from heat immediately. Only leave on long enough to wilt spinach slightly, 1 to 2 minutes.

6. Put quinoa/spinach mixture on a platter and arrange shrimp over the top. Drizzle the sauce over the entire dish.

NUTRITIONAL INFORMATION PER SERVING

251.8 calories ▪ 17.35g protein ▪ 38.4g carbohydrates ▪ 5.6g fiber ▪ 3.9g sugar
3.9g fat ▪ 0.2g saturated fat ▪ 483.5mg cholesterol ▪ 288mg sodium

Get Smart Mahimahi Burgers with Pineapple Salsa SERVES 4

4 mahimahi fillets, 4 ounces each
1 tablespoon grape-seed oil
lemon pepper, to taste
1 cup fresh diced pineapple
½ cup diced red bell pepper
2 tablespoons minced fresh cilantro
2 tablespoons minced shallots
salt and pepper, to taste
large romaine or iceberg lettuce leaves or 2 gluten-free buns, split in half

1. Preheat the grill to medium-high heat.

2. Brush fillets with oil and sprinkle with lemon pepper.

3. Grill fillets for about 5 minutes per side or until mahimahi flakes easily when tested with fork.

4. Meanwhile, mix pineapple, red bell pepper, cilantro, and shallots in a bowl and season with salt and pepper.

5. Serve fillets on lettuce leaves with pineapple salsa.

NUTRITIONAL INFORMATION PER SERVING (WITHOUT BUN)

257 calories ▪ 27g protein ▪ 30g carbohydrates ▪ 5g fiber ▪ 4g sugar ▪ 5g fat
4g saturated fat ▪ 40mg cholesterol ▪ 336mg sodium

Salmon Burgers SERVES 4

This recipe is great with leftover salmon! If using leftover salmon, cut cooking time for salmon by 2 to 3 minutes to avoid burgers becoming dry. Adjust spices and herbs according to what is in the leftover salmon.

- 1 pound wild salmon fillet, roughly chopped
- ½ cup roughly chopped red bell pepper
- 2 celery stalks, cut in 2-inch pieces
- ½ onion, roughly chopped
- 2 garlic cloves
- 1 egg (organic, omega-3)
- 1 teaspoon fresh lemon juice
- 1 tablespoon low-sodium tamari sauce (unless salmon is from leftovers and already flavored)
- 1 tablespoon unchopped fresh dill (optional)
- 1 tablespoon coconut oil
- 8 large iceberg lettuce leaves or 2 Ezekiel gluten-free buns
- 1 tablespoon Vegenaise
- 1 tablespoon gluten-free Dijon mustard
- 4 large tomato slices

1. In a large food processor, combine salmon, bell peppers, celery, onion, garlic, egg, lemon juice, tamari sauce, and dill. Chop until thoroughly mixed and salmon and vegetables reach a fine consistency, but are not mushy.

2. Remove from processor and place in a medium bowl. Form mixture into 4 patties of equal size.

3. Heat oil in a large skillet over medium-high heat. Place patties in the hot skillet and cook for about 5 minutes on each side (turning after 2 minutes per side), or until patties reach desired doneness.

4. Place 4 lettuce leaves on 4 plates. If using buns, place half a bun on each plate.

5. Remove salmon patties from heat and place on a plate until they cool slightly. After a couple of minutes, place patties on lettuce wraps.

6. Add Vegenaise and mustard to one side of each patty and top with a tomato slice. Place remaining lettuce leaves on top of burgers and wrap to secure.

NUTRITIONAL INFORMATION PER SERVING

288 calories ▪ 132 calories from fat ▪ 31.3g protein ▪ 5.4g carbohydrates ▪ 1.4g fiber 2.4g sugar ▪ 14.9g fat ▪ 4.8g saturated fat ▪ 127mg cholesterol ▪ 220mg sodium

Teriyaki Salmon Bowl SERVES 2

This dish is traditionally eaten with rice, but you can easily make it a grain-free dish by serving the salmon over shirataki noodles and greens.

    4 teaspoons tamari sauce
    1 tablespoon rice vinegar
    1 teaspoon grated ginger
    1 teaspoon honey
    1 garlic clove, minced
    ¼ teaspoon cayenne pepper
    2 salmon steaks (4 to 6 ounces each)
    1 tablespoon sesame oil
    1 teaspoon gluten-free Dijon mustard
    2 tablespoons chopped fresh cilantro
    1 cup cooked shirataki noodles
    ½ cup grated carrots
    ¼ cup chopped scallions
    6 to 8 cups baby spinach or bok choy

1. Preheat oven to 400°F.

2. In a medium bowl, mix tamari sauce, vinegar, ginger, honey, garlic, and cayenne pepper.

3. Place salmon steaks in a baking dish and cover with marinade.

4. Refrigerate for 15 to 30 minutes.

5. In a large bowl, mix sesame oil, mustard, and cilantro.

6. Stir in shirataki noodles, carrots, and scallions. Set aside.

7. Remove salmon from the refrigerator and roast for about 15 minutes, or until fish flakes with a fork. Cut salmon into cubes.

8. Meanwhile, steam spinach in a steamer basket for about 5 minutes, or until completely wilted. Drain well.

9. In bowls, put steamed spinach on bottom, layer with shirataki noodle mixture, and top with salmon.

NOTE: To make shirataki noodles, drain water from bag and boil in filtered water for 3 minutes.

NUTRITIONAL INFORMATION PER SERVING

439 calories ▪ 36g protein ▪ 38g carbohydrates ▪ 12g fiber ▪ 4.3g sugar ▪ 18g fat
3g saturated fat ▪ 80mg cholesterol ▪ 373mg sodium

Tasty Turkey Wrap SERVES 4

It doesn't get easier than this when you are on the run.

2 tablespoons olive oil

1 teaspoon fresh lime juice

2 tablespoons chopped fresh cilantro

salt and pepper, to taste

2 cups mixed baby greens

½ pound roast turkey breast, sliced (free-range, antibiotic-free, hormone-free)

4 gluten-free tortillas, romaine or iceberg lettuce leaves, or coconut curry wraps (I like Pure Wraps)

2 tomatoes, sliced

1 small avocado, sliced

1. In a large bowl, combine olive oil, lime juice, cilantro, salt, and pepper.

2. Add baby greens and mix well.

3. Divide turkey among tortillas or lettuce leaves.

4. Top with baby greens, tomatoes, and avocado.

5. Fold the wrap over about 1 inch on two opposite sides, and then roll up completely. Slice in half diagonally and serve.

NUTRITIONAL INFORMATION PER SERVING

223 calories ▪ 10g protein ▪ 9g carbohydrates ▪ 4g fiber ▪ <1g sugar ▪ 18g fat 3g saturated fat ▪ 24mg cholesterol ▪ 492mg sodium

Turkey Burgers   SERVES 6

- 4 celery stalks, cut into 2-inch pieces
- 1 small onion, chopped
- 2 garlic cloves
- 2 tablespoons whole sage leaves (about 8 to 10 leaves)
- 1 tablespoon whole fresh marjoram
- ½ teaspoon sea salt (optional)
- 1½ pounds lowest-fat ground turkey breast (free-range, hormone-free, antibiotic-free)
- 1 egg (organic, omega-3)
- 2 teaspoons grape-seed or coconut oil
- 12 large iceberg lettuce leaves, or 3 Oroweat Sandwich Thins (100 calorie), or gluten-free buns
- 1 large tomato, sliced
- 1 avocado, thinly sliced
- 6 teaspoons Vegenaise (optional)
- 6 tablespoons Dijon mustard (optional)

1. In a food processor, process celery, onion, garlic, sage, marjoram, and sea salt. Process until onion and celery are finely chopped but not mushy.

2. In a medium mixing bowl, mix turkey with egg.

3. Add celery mixture to turkey and mix until well blended.

4. Form turkey into 6 patties.

5. Heat oil in a large skillet over medium heat.

6. Cook turkey patties in batches for about 5 minutes on each side, or until cooked through and browned on the outside.

7. Remove patties from skillet and place on a plate as the rest finish cooking. Cover to keep warm.

8. Double lettuce leaves and place on plates.

9. Place turkey burgers on lettuce wraps.

10. Top with tomato and avocado. Place Vegenaise and mustard next to each burger.

NOTE: If using Oroweat Sandwich Thins, try having an open-faced burger, with lettuce on top.

NUTRITIONAL INFORMATION PER SERVING

241 calories ▪ 23.7g protein ▪ 6.5g carbohydrates ▪ 3g fiber ▪ 2.4g sugar ▪ 13.9g fat 3.3g saturated fat ▪ 115mg cholesterol ▪ 118mg sodium

Herb-Marinated Chicken SERVES 6

This recipe is best if marinated for a minimum of 2 hours in advance, and can be marinated for as long as 24 hours.

  1 tablespoon fresh rosemary
  1 tablespoon fresh thyme
  1 teaspoon fresh sage leaves
  6 garlic cloves, peeled
  1 teaspoon sea salt, or as desired for low-sodium diet
  ¼ teaspoon black pepper
  ¼ cup fresh-squeezed lemon juice
  ¼ cup grape-seed oil
  8 skinless chicken breast halves (hormone-free, antibiotic-free, free-range)

1. Place rosemary, thyme, sage, and garlic in a food processor and chop until all ingredients are finely minced. If you don't have a food processor, you can chop all ingredients by hand.

2. Transfer herb mixture to a small mixing bowl.

3. Add sea salt, pepper, lemon juice, and grape-seed oil to a bowl and whisk until marinade is well blended. Set aside.

4. On a nonporous cutting board, lightly pound chicken breasts (for tenderizing). Do not over-pound and make them too thin.

5. Pour marinade mixture into a bowl or baking dish large enough to hold all the chicken. Add the chicken to the mixture, making sure that all chicken is coated with marinade.

6. Cover and refrigerate for a minimum of 2 hours and up to 24 hours.

7. Heat grill to medium-high heat.

8. Grill chicken until it is cooked through, turning every 2 minutes. Cooking time may vary, but is usually about 3 to 4 minutes per side. I prefer using a knife and making a small cut into one piece to verify that chicken is cooked through but not overcooked. You may also use a meat thermometer to test that the internal temperature reaches 160°F.

NOTE: This tastes great using chicken thighs as well.

NUTRITIONAL INFORMATION PER SERVING
208 calories ▪ 26.9g protein ▪ 1.5g carbohydrates ▪ 0.2g fiber ▪ 0.2g sugar ▪ 9.9g fat ▪ 1.5g saturated fat ▪ 73mg cholesterol ▪ 646mg sodium

Guiltless Chicken Breast Tenders SERVES 4

1 teaspoon sea salt

½ teaspoon pepper (optional)

½ teaspoon garlic powder

1 cup almond meal (or gluten-free flour), or you may grind almonds finely in the food processor

1 pound chicken tenders (free-range, hormone-free, antibiotic-free)

1 egg, lightly beaten (organic, omega-3)

1. Preheat oven to 375°F.

2. In a bowl, mix sea salt, pepper, garlic powder, and almond meal and blend well with a fork.

3. Dip the chicken pieces in the egg, coating both sides. Immediately dredge in the almond meal mixture, covering both sides completely.

4. Place chicken on a baking sheet. Cook for about 12 minutes, being sure to turn chicken over after 6 minutes.

NOTE: Chicken tenders will not be crispy. If you are used to fried chicken tenders, you may want to finish with one more step: Heat 2 teaspoons of coconut oil in a large skillet over medium-high heat. When skillet is hot, add half of the baked tenders to the skillet. Cook for about 30 to 60 seconds per side, depending on desired crispiness. Remove tenders and repeat process for remaining chicken tenders. Allow to cool for several minutes if serving to children.

NOTE: Consider serving with a honey mustard sauce. Mix 1 tablespoon of gluten-free mustard with 1 teaspoon of raw, unfiltered honey. Raw, unfiltered honey is not appropriate for children under two years of age. Use pasteurized honey in recipes that will be fed to children under two.

NUTRITIONAL INFORMATION PER SERVING

306 calories ▪ 21.3g protein ▪ 39.4g carbohydrates ▪ 4.3g fiber ▪ 1.5g sugar ▪ 7.0g fat 4.1g saturated fat ▪ 93mg cholesterol ▪ 529mg sodium

Brain-Fit Fajitas SERVES 6

3 tablespoons grape-seed oil

1 tablespoon ground cumin

½ teaspoon paprika

1 teaspoon chili powder

½ teaspoon Real Salt

¼ teaspoon pepper

2 garlic cloves, minced

½ small eggplant, peeled and diced

1 zucchini, sliced

1 yellow squash, sliced

1 red bell pepper, thinly sliced

1 yellow onion, diced

1 cup black or pinto beans

½ cup cilantro, chopped

2 ripe avocados, pitted, peeled, and mashed (guacamole-style)

2 vine-ripened tomatoes, cut into wedges

3 cups shredded lettuce or cabbage

1 head romaine lettuce, whole leaves separated, or coconut curry wraps
(I like Pure Wraps)

SALSA INGREDIENTS

1 small onion, cut into quarters

2 garlic cloves, cut in half

¼ cup chopped cilantro

1 lime, juiced

½ to 1 jalapeño, roughly chopped (remove seeds unless you like it *really* hot!)

one 28-ounce can whole tomatoes

1 teaspoon hot cayenne pepper

1 teaspoon Real Salt (optional)

½ teaspoon pepper (optional)

1. Preheat oven to 400°F. Lightly oil two cookie sheets with ½ tablespoon grape-seed oil each.

2. In a small bowl, mix together the remaining oil, cumin, paprika, chili powder, salt, pepper, and garlic.

3. Place eggplant, zucchini, squash, bell pepper, and onion on cookie sheets and lightly brush the vegetables with oil mixture.

4. Place the cookie sheets in the oven and roast for 20 to 25 minutes, or until the eggplant is tender. Be sure to turn vegetables at least once.

5. Heat beans and place in serving bowl.

6. Arrange vegetables separately on a serving platter and serve hot. Place avocado, tomatoes, and shredded lettuce on a serving tray.

7. Serve warm vegetables, cold vegetables, salsa, and beans together.

8. Put either lettuce or coconut wraps on a plate to serve with fajita filling.

SALSA PREPARATION

1. Place onion and garlic in food processor and pulse several times until onion is coarsely chopped, but not overprocessed.

2. Add cilantro, lime juice, jalapeño, tomatoes, and cayenne pepper.

3. Process until salsa is desired consistency but not mushy.

4. Add salt and pepper to taste.

NUTRITIONAL INFORMATION PER SERVING, INCLUDING SALSA

260 calories (without tortillas) ▪ 13g protein ▪ 24g carbohydrates ▪ 3g fiber
3.6g sugar ▪ 19.5g fat ▪ 0.25g saturated fat ▪ 0.0mg cholesterol ▪ 888 mg sodium

NUTRITIONAL INFORMATION FOR SALSA PER SERVING

30 calories ▪ 1g protein ▪ 7g carbohydrates ▪ 2g fiber ▪ 2g sugar ▪ 0.0g fat
0.0g saturated fat ▪ 0.0mg cholesterol ▪ 570mg sodium

Guacamole SERVES 16, ABOUT 2 TABLESPOONS PER SERVING

2 ripe avocados, peeled and pitted
¼ cup finely chopped red onion
2 tablespoons finely chopped fresh cilantro
1 tablespoon fresh lime juice
½ ripe tomato, seeded and diced
½ teaspoon sea salt (optional)

1. In a medium bowl, mash avocado with a fork until smooth. Some chunks are fine, if you like chunky guacamole.

2. Add remaining ingredients and mix well. Serve cold.

NOTE: Do not add tomatoes if you are not serving guacamole right away. Refrigerate guacamole without tomatoes and add them just before serving. Tomatoes will release water and make the guacamole wet.

NUTRITIONAL INFORMATION PER SERVING

61 calories ▪ 0.8g protein ▪ 3.9g carbohydrates ▪ 2.5g fiber ▪ 0.6g sugar ▪ 5.3g fat
0.7g saturated fat ▪ 0.0mg cholesterol ▪ 3mg sodium

Traditional Hummus SERVES 16

2 cups garbanzo beans, soaked and cooked
3 garlic cloves
2 tablespoons tahini paste
2 tablespoons extra-virgin olive oil
½ cup baby spinach (optional)
¼ cup lemon juice
¼ teaspoon sea salt (optional)
½ teaspoon paprika for garnish

1. In a food processor, combine beans, garlic, tahini, olive oil, and spinach.

2. Blend until smooth.

3. Add lemon juice and sea salt. Process until mixture is completely smooth and creamy. Garnish with the paprika.

NUTRITIONAL INFORMATION PER SERVING

64 calories ▪ 1.9g protein ▪ 7.7g carbohydrates ▪ 1.4g fiber ▪ 0.1g sugar ▪ 3g fat
0.4g saturated fat ▪ 0.0mg cholesterol ▪ 127mg sodium

Split Pea Hummus SERVES 16, 2 TABLESPOONS PER SERVING

This is a fabulous-tasting alternative to regular hummus, which is made with garbanzo beans. Raw veggies and hummus are one of my favorite snacks, but I prefer not to overindulge with too many legumes, as they can irritate the intestinal lining. In general, the greener the plant, the fewer lectins and less phytic acid it contains. So peas do not have the same irritating effect as other legumes—but don't overdo it.

    1 cup dry split peas
    2½ cups purified water
    1 bay leaf
    2 tablespoons olive oil
    2 garlic cloves, minced
    2 tablespoons tahini paste
    ½ cup fresh lemon juice
    ¼ teaspoon sea salt (optional)

1. Place split peas, water, and bay leaf in a medium pan. Bring to a boil. Cover, reduce the heat, and simmer for 40 minutes or until the peas are tender and liquid is absorbed, stirring occasionally. Remove bay leaf.

2. In a food processor place cooked peas, olive oil, garlic, and tahini. Process until well blended.

3. Add lemon juice and salt. Process until smooth and creamy.

NUTRITIONAL INFORMATION PER SERVING
42 calories ▪ 1.4g protein ▪ 3.4g carbohydrates ▪ 1.1g fiber ▪ 0.5g sugar ▪ 2.7g fat 0.4g saturated fat ▪ 0.0mg cholesterol ▪ 39mg sodium

Baba Ganoush SERVES 4

2 eggplants
1 garlic clove, chopped
1 tablespoon lemon juice
2 tablespoons tahini
½ teaspoon Real Salt
½ teaspoon cumin
2 tablespoons extra-virgin olive oil

OPTIONAL
1 tablespoon pine nuts
3 to 4 olives

1. Poke eggplants with fork on all sides and then grill eggplants until charred on all sides.

2. Scoop out insides of eggplants and put into blender with all the other ingredients. Blend until smooth and creamy.

3. Place into decorative serving bowl. Top with pine nuts or olives, if desired.

NUTRITIONAL INFORMATION PER SERVING
76 calories ▪ 2g protein ▪ 11g carbohydrates ▪ 4g fiber ▪ 0.1g sugar ▪ 4g fat
1g saturated fat ▪ 13mg cholesterol ▪ 285mg sodium

Go Well Trail Mix SERVES 6

¼ cup raw cashews
¼ cup raw slivered almonds
¼ cup raw walnuts
¼ cup raw cacao nibs
2 tablespoons goji berries, unsweetened
2 tablespoons shaved coconut, unsweetened

1. Mix all ingredients well and store in an airtight container until ready to consume.

NUTRITIONAL INFORMATION PER SERVING
137 calories ▪ 4.2g protein ▪ 5.6g carbohydrates ▪ 4g fiber ▪ 2.8g sugar ▪ 8.9g fat
2.5g saturated fat ▪ 0.0mg cholesterol ▪ 12mg sodium

Devil-Less Eggs SERVES 6

12 eggs (organic, omega-3)
1 tablespoon gluten-free Dijon mustard
½ teaspoon onion powder
½ teaspoon garlic powder
¼ teaspoon cayenne pepper
2 tablespoons flax- or hemp-seed oil

OPTIONAL FOR GARNISH
¼ teaspoon paprika
1 tablespoon finely chopped fresh chives

1. Place eggs in a large pot with just enough water so the eggs are fully covered. Don't fill the pot all the way. Bring the water to a boil, then turn the heat off and let the eggs sit in the hot water for 12 minutes (no longer).

2. Fill a large bowl with ice water. Remove the eggs and place in ice water for a couple of minutes, until eggs are completely cool.

3. Peel eggs, being careful not to damage the whites. Cut eggs in half lengthwise.

4. Gently remove the yolks without damaging the whites. If you squeeze lightly, the yolk should pop out. Make sure you do this over a bowl.

5. Arrange egg-white halves directly on a serving platter. Set aside.

6. In a medium bowl, mash egg yolks, mustard, onion powder, garlic powder, cayenne, and flax-seed oil with a fork or rubber spatula until the mixture is smooth and creamy.

7. Use a melon scooper or a small spoon to scoop the mixture back into the egg-white halves in equal amounts.

8. Sprinkle with paprika and/or chives, if desired. Serve immediately or refrigerate until ready to serve.

NUTRITIONAL INFORMATION PER SERVING
184 calories ▪ 12.7g protein ▪ 3.7g carbohydrates ▪ 0.1g fiber ▪ 2.8g sugar ▪ 12.6g fat ▪ 2.8g saturated fat ▪ 350mg cholesterol ▪ 200mg sodium

Omni Grainless Granola Protein Bars SERVES 16

These delicious bars can be made in advance and hold up well when stored in the refrigerator. If you are not allergic to eggs, you may choose to cut fat in half and increase the protein by eliminating the cacao butter and adding 4 egg whites.

2 tablespoons cacao butter
½ cup raw pumpkin seeds
½ cup walnuts or cashews
½ cup shredded (raw, unsweetened) coconut
½ cup almond meal
¼ cup chocolate-flavored pea protein (sweetened with stevia)
½ cup raw sunflower seeds
1 teaspoon cinnamon
¼ teaspoon cloves
½ teaspoon ginger
1 teaspoon pure vanilla extract
2 tablespoons macadamia-nut oil
1 teaspoon grape-seed oil
¼ cup honey
¼ cup erythritol
2 tablespoons 70-percent cacao, nondairy chips (or unsweetened carob chips)
2 tablespoons dried goji berries or mulberries

1. Preheat oven to 350°F.

2. In a small saucepan, melt the cacao butter over low heat.

3. Using a food processor, grind the pumpkin seeds, nuts, and coconut until you achieve the texture of a coarse flour. Place mixture in a large bowl.

4. Add almond meal, protein powder, sunflower seeds, cinnamon, cloves, and ginger to the bowl. Mix. The mixture will be thick, so you may need to use your hands to mix it thoroughly.

5. Add vanilla, oil, and cacao butter. Mix well with a fork or rubber spatula.

6. Add the honey and erythritol and mix well.

7. Fold in chips and berries and mix well.

8. Lightly grease a 13x9-inch baking pan with grape-seed oil (or use a nonstick baking pan). Press the mix into the pan until it is even on all sides. Bake for 10 to 15 minutes or until lightly golden.

NUTRITIONAL INFORMATION PER SERVING

158 calories ▪ 6g protein ▪ 12g carbohydrates ▪ 2g fiber ▪ 5g sugar ▪ 12g fat
3g saturated fat ▪ 0.0mg cholesterol ▪ 33mg sodium

Super-Food Protein Bars SERVES 12

½ cup cacao butter
½ cup raw cashews, finely chopped
½ cup raw almonds, finely chopped
¼ cup mulberries
2 tablespoons hemp seeds or flax seeds
½ cup coconut butter
2 tablespoons lucuma powder
½ cup pea protein (sweetened with stevia)
1 teaspoon cinnamon
½ teaspoon nutmeg
2 tablespoons raw, unfiltered honey
¼ cup goji berries
1 tablespoon maca root powder (optional)

1. Melt the cacao butter in a small saucepan over low heat.

2. In a food processor, combine half of the cashews and half of the almonds, all of the mulberries, hemp seeds, coconut butter, lucuma powder, protein powder, cinnamon, and nutmeg.

3. Remove cacao butter from heat and add honey to the saucepan.

4. Slowly pulse nuts and powder mixture in food processor while adding the melted cacao butter and honey in a steady stream. The mixture will form a dough-like texture.

5. Remove dough from processor and place in a bowl. Add remaining nuts, goji berries, and maca root powder, if desired. Dough should be very thick. However, if it is too thick to mix, add 1 tablespoon of water at a time until the mixture combines, but remains very thick.

6. Press dough into a 13x9-inch baking dish and refrigerate for at least 1 hour.

7. Cut into bars.

NOTE: For chocolate protein bars, either use chocolate protein powder or add 2 tablespoons of cacao powder in step 5.

NUTRITIONAL INFORMATION PER SERVING

189 calories ▪ 7.5g protein ▪ 8.8g carbohydrates ▪ 2.2g fiber ▪ 3.4g sugar ▪ 14.7g fat 7.8g saturated fat ▪ 0.0mg cholesterol ▪ 9.3mg sodium

Pumpkin Protein Bars SERVES 24

one 15-ounce can organic pumpkin
¼ cup light coconut milk
2 tablespoons macadamia-nut oil
1 teaspoon vanilla extract
5 egg whites
¼ cup raw honey
½ cup erythritol
¾ cup almond meal
¾ cup all-purpose gluten-free flour
¼ cup flax meal
¼ cup vanilla-flavored pea protein (sweetened with stevia)
2 teaspoons baking powder
1 teaspoon baking soda
1 tablespoon pumpkin pie spice

COCONUT CREAM FROSTING
2 cups fresh coconut meat from young Thai coconuts
¼ cup raw honey
½ cup unsweetened almond milk (use more as needed to blend)

1. Preheat the oven to 350°F.

2. Using a handheld electric mixer at medium speed, beat together the pumpkin, coconut milk, oil, vanilla, egg whites, honey, and erythritol until smooth.

3. In a separate bowl mix dry ingredients: almond meal, flour, flax meal, protein powder, baking powder, baking soda, and pumpkin pie spice.

4. Combine dry ingredients with wet ingredients. Using the electric mixer, mix on medium-to-high speed until thoroughly combined and the batter is smooth. Spread the batter into a greased jellyroll 10½x15-inch baking pan. Bake for 20 to 25 minutes. Let cool completely before frosting and cutting into bars.

TO MAKE THE FROSTING

1. Crack coconuts with a meat cleaver. Drain coconut water into a jar and save for smoothies!

2. Using a spoon, scrape all coconut meat out of the shell. The younger and fresher the coconut, the softer the meat and the less milk you will need for mixing.

3. In a high-powered blender, mix coconut meat and honey and ½ cup of the almond milk.

4. Add almond milk slowly to avoid making the frosting too thin. It will be difficult to mix at first. Mix until very thick and creamy. This can take several minutes.

5. Refrigerate frosting until you're ready to frost bars.

NOTE: If you decide not to use frosting, you can add ½ cup unsweetened carob chips to the batter. Reserve a few chips to scatter over the top.

NUTRITIONAL INFORMATION PER SERVING

72 calories ▪ 3.3g protein ▪ 12g carbohydrates ▪ 1g fiber ▪ 3.5g sugar ▪ 3.6g fat
0.5g saturated fat ▪ 0.0mg cholesterol ▪ 108mg sodium

FROSTING NUTRITIONAL INFORMATION

69 calories ▪ <1g protein ▪ 5.4g carbohydrates ▪ <1g fiber ▪ 4g sugar ▪ 5.5g fat
4.9g saturated fat ▪ 0.0mg cholesterol ▪ 1.2mg sodium

Antiox Detox Chopped Salad SERVES 4

1 green apple, cored and diced
½ cup pomegranate seeds
2 cups finely chopped kale
4 cups mixed greens
½ cup chopped raw walnuts
2 Persian cucumbers, thinly sliced
¼ cup extra-virgin olive oil
2 tablespoons red wine vinegar
½ teaspoon turmeric
1 garlic clove, minced
1 teaspoon xylitol or raw, unfiltered honey (optional)
1 avocado, diced

1. In a large salad bowl, combine apple, pomegranate seeds, kale, mixed greens, walnuts, and cucumber.

2. In a small bowl, combine olive oil, red wine vinegar, turmeric, garlic, and xylitol or raw, unfiltered honey, if using. Whisk until well blended.

3. Combine with salad mixture and toss well.

4. Divide evenly among 4 plates.

5. Top with avocado.

NUTRITIONAL INFORMATION PER SERVING

209 calories ▪ 5.8g protein ▪ 23.9g carbohydrates ▪ 8g fiber ▪ 10.9g sugar ▪ 10g fat
3.6g saturated fat ▪ 0.0mg cholesterol ▪ 42mg sodium

Magnificent Mind Cucumber Mint Salad SERVES 6

1 bunch mint, stems removed
1 bunch parsley, stems removed
2 cucumbers, minced
1 red bell pepper, finely chopped
6 scallions, minced
4 tomatoes, seeded and finely chopped
½ cup fresh lemon juice
¼ cup olive oil
½ teaspoon Real Salt
½ teaspoon paprika

1. Finely mince mint and parsley by hand or in food processor, if preferred.

2. In large mixing bowl, blend minced herbs with cucumber, bell pepper, scallions, and tomatoes.

3. Add lemon juice, olive oil, salt, and paprika.

4. Toss and serve.

NUTRITIONAL INFORMATION PER SERVING

130 calories ▪ 2g protein ▪ 12g carbohydrates ▪ 3g fiber ▪ 0.48g sugar ▪ 9g fat
2g saturated fat ▪ 0.0mg cholesterol ▪ 205mg sodium

Herbed Garden Vegetables SERVES 4

1 red bell pepper, chopped
2 cups cauliflower, cut into florets
1 zucchini, sliced
1 cup broccoli florets
1 cup sliced crimini mushrooms
1 yellow onion, cut in half moons
2 garlic cloves, minced
1 tablespoon fresh lemon juice
1 teaspoon chopped fresh thyme
1 tablespoon chopped fresh basil
¼ cup olive oil
salt and pepper, to taste

1. Bring water to a full boil in the bottom of a covered steamer. Add red bell pepper, cauliflower, zucchini, broccoli, mushrooms, and onion to the steamer, making sure water does not cover the vegetables.

2. Cover and steam for 3 to 5 minutes. Do not overcook. Vegetables should remain crisp.

3. While vegetables are steaming, mix garlic, lemon juice, thyme, and basil in a large bowl.

4. Whisk in olive oil. Season with salt and pepper, as desired.

5. When vegetables are ready, transfer them to the large bowl with the dressing and toss to coat. Serve warm.

NUTRITIONAL INFORMATION PER SERVING

155 calories ▪ 3g protein ▪ 7g carbohydrates ▪ 3g fiber ▪ 0.1g sugar ▪ 14g fat
2g saturated fat ▪ 0.0mg cholesterol ▪ 22mg sodium

Asian Citrus Pear Salad SERVES 4

2 tablespoons olive oil

2 teaspoons sesame oil

2 tablespoons fresh lime juice

1 teaspoon minced shallot

¼ teaspoon dried thyme

1 teaspoon raw, unfiltered honey (optional)

1 cup baby spinach

1 cup radicchio

2 cups Bibb lettuce or other mixed greens

1 pear, thinly sliced

½ red bell pepper, thinly sliced

¼ medium sweet red onion, thinly sliced

2 tablespoons sunflower seeds or slivered almonds

1. In a small bowl, mix olive and sesame oil, lime juice, shallot, thyme, and raw, unfiltered honey, if using. Whisk together thoroughly and set aside.

2. Arrange spinach, radicchio, and lettuce on a platter.

3. Scatter pear, bell pepper, onion, and sunflower seeds or nuts over lettuce.

4. Drizzle dressing over the salad.

NOTE: Raw, unfiltered honey is not appropriate for children under two years of age. Use pasteurized honey in recipes that will be fed to children under two.

NUTRITIONAL INFORMATION PER SERVING

280 calories ▪ 9g protein ▪ 13.6g carbohydrates ▪ 3g fiber ▪ 6.7g sugar ▪ 12g fat 5.5g saturated fat ▪ 73mg cholesterol ▪ 11mg sodium

South of the Border Salad Cups SERVES 6

2 cups fresh green peas
2 cups black beans, presoaked and cooked
2 cups peeled and diced jicama
1 large ripe mango, peeled and diced
½ cup chopped scallions
1 cup diced red bell peppers
1 tablespoon finely chopped fresh cilantro
1 teaspoon ground cumin
½ teaspoon cayenne pepper
¼ cup lemon juice
½ avocado, pitted and thinly sliced
12 large iceberg or butter lettuce leaves

1. Mix peas, beans, jicama, mango, scallions, bell peppers, and cilantro together in a large bowl.

2. Mix cumin, pepper, and lemon juice together in a small bowl so that spices are evenly mixed.

3. Toss salad with lemon juice mixture in the large bowl so that the dressing covers salad evenly.

4. Transfer salad to a serving platter and place avocado slices evenly across the top.

5. Arrange lettuce leaves on plates and scoop salad mix into lettuce cups.

6. Refrigerate until ready to serve.

NUTRITIONAL INFORMATION PER SERVING

208 calories ▪ 10.6g protein ▪ 35g carbohydrates ▪ 11.9g fiber ▪ 12g sugar ▪ 4.4g fat 0.4g saturated fat ▪ 0.0mg cholesterol ▪ 14mg sodium

Cool Kale Salad with Cilantro Dressing SERVES 4

Kale is one of my favorite greens. The greener the better. Eat it every day, and a lot of it!

    ½ cup cilantro
    3 tablespoons fresh orange juice
    1 lime, juiced
    ¼ cup olive oil
    salt and pepper to taste
    4 cups shredded kale
    2 oranges, peeled and sectioned
    ¾ cup peeled and diced jicama
    ½ cup pumpkin seeds

1. In a blender, place cilantro, orange juice, and lime juice. Pulse until cilantro is finely chopped.

2. With the blender running, slowly drizzle olive oil into the blender in a steady stream until blended well. Season with salt and pepper.

3. In a large bowl, mix shredded kale, orange sections, and jicama.

4. Pour the dressing over the kale mixture and toss to coat. Mix in seeds.

5. Refrigerate for 30 minutes before serving.

NUTRITIONAL INFORMATION PER SERVING
251 calories ▪ 5g protein ▪ 27g carbohydrates ▪ 6g fiber ▪ 5.7 sugar ▪ 16g fat 2g saturated fat ▪ 0.0mg cholesterol ▪ 77mg sodium

Warm Spinach Asparagus Salad with Quinoa SERVES 6

This is a great meal option for breakfast or lunch as well. I usually double the portion so I have leftovers for the next morning. Top it with sliced hard-boiled egg and it's a great breakfast on the run.

    2 teaspoons refined coconut oil, or 3 to 4 tablespoons vegetable broth
    ¼ cup finely diced onion
    4 garlic cloves, diced
    1 tablespoon refined coconut oil
    1 cup quinoa, rinsed
    2 cups vegetable broth or water
    1 bunch asparagus tips
    2 handfuls chopped spinach
    1 tablespoon fresh sage, finely chopped

2 tablespoons chives (optional)

¼ cup pine nuts, raw (optional)

Real Salt and pepper to taste

1. Heat coconut oil or vegetable broth in large pot over medium heat. Add onions and sauté for 1 minute.

2. Add garlic and sauté for an additional minute.

3. Add 1 tablespoon of oil to pot. Add quinoa and stir well to coat lightly with oil.

4. Turn heat up to medium-high and stir quinoa constantly for about 10 minutes or until quinoa is lightly toasted.

5. Add broth and turn heat to high. Bring to a boil. Reduce heat to medium-low and simmer for 15 minutes or until liquid is absorbed.

6. Add asparagus tips to quinoa during last 2 minutes of cooking. This will give you crunchy, healthy asparagus tips and ensure that they are not overcooked. It also eliminates the step of having to sauté or steam them separately (but if you prefer softer veggies you may cook them separately and add them).

7. Add the spinach to the quinoa while the quinoa is still warm and mix it in. It will wilt the spinach without overcooking it, thus retaining most of the nutritional value. Add sage and chives, if using.

8. Add pine nuts, if using, and stir well. Add salt and pepper, to taste. Serve warm.

NOTE: You may want to toss salad with 1 tablespoon of refined coconut oil or olive oil to fluff the salad and give it a nice texture. You can also add 1 tablespoon of Bragg's Liquid Aminos.

NUTRITIONAL INFORMATION PER SERVING

210 calories ▪ 8g protein ▪ 24g carbohydrates ▪ 5g fiber ▪ <1g sugar ▪ 11g fat 5g saturated fat ▪ 0.0mg cholesterol ▪ 71mg sodium

Red, White, and Blue Salad SERVES 4

2 tablespoons balsamic vinegar

1 teaspoon honey

¼ cup olive oil

salt, to taste

6 cups mixed greens

1 Persian cucumber, sliced

½ cup chopped cashews

½ cup organic blueberries

½ cup pomegranate seeds

¼ cup sliced jicama

½ bell pepper, diced

1. In a small bowl, mix balsamic vinegar and honey.

2. Slowly whisk in olive oil. Season with salt. Refrigerate until ready to serve.

3. Arrange greens on a large platter.

4. Place cucumber slices around the outer edge of the platter.

5. Put the cashews in a line down the center of the salad. Do the same with the blueberries, placing a line next to the line of cashews. Place another line of pomegranate seeds on the other side of the cashews. Sprinkle the jicama and bell peppers around the outer edges, just inside the cucumber. Serve with dressing on the side.

NUTRITIONAL INFORMATION PER SERVING

244 calories ▪ 1.3g protein ▪ 9g carbohydrates ▪ 1.9g fiber ▪ 18.8g sugar ▪ 19g fat 2.9g saturated fat ▪ 0.0mg cholesterol ▪ 17mg sodium

Roasted Beet Salad SERVES 6

12 baby beets or 4 to 6 large beets (preferably different kinds—red, yellow, and chioggia)

1½ to 2 pink grapefruits

½ cup finely chopped cashews or whole pine nuts

1 shallot, finely minced

2 tablespoons coarsely chopped fresh mint

1 lime, juiced

¼ cup extra-virgin olive oil

1 teaspoon raw, unfiltered honey

2 teaspoons grapefruit zest

pinch of sea salt (optional)

4 cups arugula or mixed greens

1. Preheat oven to 400°F.

2. Individually wrap beets in foil and roast on middle rack in the oven for 30 minutes for baby beets, 40 to 50 minutes for large beets, or until they are soft. Set aside and let cool.

3. Peel and segment the grapefruit. Using a sharp paring knife, remove the ends of each segment, then carefully slice the skin from one end to the other and remove the skin so there is no peel or white pith left.

4. Place grapefruit in a large salad bowl. Combine with nuts, shallot, and mint.

5. Remove beets from foil. Use a paper towel to rub the skin off the beets. (It should rub off easily.) Slice baby beets in rounds. Quarter larger beets. Add to bowl with grapefruit. Set aside in refrigerator.

6. In a small bowl, mix lime juice, olive oil, honey, grapefruit zest, and sea salt, if using.

7. Arrange arugula on individual plates.

8. Gently toss grapefruit-and-beet mixture with half of dressing, or you may serve the dressing on the side.

9. Dish grapefruit-and-beet mixture onto the greens.

10. Refrigerate for 10 minutes or so. This salad should be served cool.

NUTRITIONAL INFORMATION PER SERVING

220 calories ▪ 4.3g protein ▪ 22g carbohydrates ▪ 3.9g fiber ▪ 7.7g sugar ▪ 14.3g fat
2.2g saturated fat ▪ 0.0mg cholesterol ▪ 71mg sodium

Roasted Vegetable Salad SERVES 6

2 tablespoons grape-seed oil
2 red bell peppers, seeded and sliced in thin strips
2 yellow bell peppers, seeded and sliced in thin strips
½ red onion, sliced
2 cups asparagus tips
sea salt and pepper, to taste
Pan-Seared Salmon (page 354)
1 cup diced jicama
1 cup sliced sun-dried tomatoes
1 cup hearts of palm (optional)
1 cup artichoke hearts, diced (optional)
½ cup extra-virgin olive oil
2 tablespoons balsamic vinegar
1 tablespoon red wine vinegar
1 tablespoon gluten-free Dijon mustard
1 garlic clove, minced
1 teaspoon raw, unfiltered honey (optional)
½ avocado, diced
¼ cup shaved, raw almonds

1. Preheat oven to 375°F.

2. Lightly oil a large cookie sheet with a couple teaspoons of the oil. Spread peppers, onions, and asparagus on cookie sheet and brush with remaining oil on both sides. Sprinkle with sea salt and pepper.

3. Bake for 30 to 40 minutes or until vegetables are tender. Turn vegetables halfway through cooking time, after 15 to 20 minutes. Remove from oven and allow to cool for at least 15 minutes.

4. Meanwhile, prepare salmon and cube fillets.

5. In a large salad bowl, mix jicama, tomatoes, and hearts of palm and artichokes, if using. Set aside.

6. In a small bowl, combine olive oil, balsamic vinegar, red wine vinegar, mustard, garlic, and honey, if desired. Whisk until ingredients blend. Refrigerate until ready to use.

7. Combine all vegetables in a salad bowl. Add half of dressing and toss well. Add more dressing and toss. Continue adding dressing and tossing until salad is *lightly* coated with dressing, but not dripping.

8. Serve salad on plates and top with salmon.

9. Sprinkle avocado and almonds over the top.

NOTE: You can also top this salad with chicken or steak.

NUTRITIONAL INFORMATION PER SERVING

415 calories ▪ 53.3g protein ▪ 21.3g carbohydrates ▪ 8.1g fiber ▪ 8.9g sugar ▪ 13g fat
6.9g saturated fat ▪ 122mg cholesterol ▪ 373mg sodium

Pan-Roasted Brussels Sprouts   SERVES 6

I love the flavor of this recipe. Brussels sprouts and other cruciferous vegetables are among the healthiest for you for many reasons, but getting people to eat them has always been a challenge. If you've always avoided Brussels sprouts, give this recipe a try and it may turn you into a fan, too.

2 tablespoons coconut oil
2 leeks, cut in half moons, white parts only
1½ pounds Brussels sprouts, halved
salt and pepper, to taste
1 tablespoon chopped fresh dill

1. Heat the coconut oil in a skillet over medium heat.

2. Add leeks and sauté for 1 minute.

3. Add Brussels sprouts and cook for 5 minutes, or until nicely roasted outside and tender inside, stirring occasionally.

4. Season with salt and pepper, as desired. Sprinkle with fresh dill and serve.

NUTRITIONAL INFORMATION PER SERVING

106 calories ▪ 4g protein ▪ 7g carbohydrates ▪ 5g fiber ▪ 0.0g sugar ▪ 5g fat
4g saturated fat ▪ 0.0mg cholesterol ▪ 34mg sodium

Succulent Roasted Sweet Potatoes **SERVES 6**

3 sweet potatoes, peeled and sliced in rounds
1 tablespoon grape-seed oil or olive oil
½ teaspoon salt
1 teaspoon cinnamon
½ cup raisins or cranberries

1. Preheat oven to 375°F.

2. Place potatoes in a 13x9-inch baking dish. Drizzle with oil. Sprinkle with salt, cinnamon, and raisins. Toss to coat.

3. Arrange potatoes in rows in baking dish and roast for 35 to 40 minutes or until tender and golden brown.

NUTRITIONAL INFORMATION PER SERVING

143 calories ▪ 2g protein ▪ 30g carbohydrates ▪ 4g fiber ▪ 9.6g sugar ▪ 2g fat
0.0g saturated fat ▪ 0.0mg cholesterol ▪ 228mg sodium

Go Green with Sautéed Collard Greens **SERVES 3**

2 tablespoons grape-seed oil (preferably) or olive oil
½ cup diced shallots
3 garlic cloves, minced
8 cups collard greens, rinsed, stems removed, and cut into ribbons
½ cup vegetable broth
1 tablespoon balsamic vinegar
salt and pepper, to taste

1. In a large, deep skillet, heat oil over medium heat. Add shallots and garlic, and sauté for 1 to 2 minutes.

2. Add greens and toss well.

3. Add vegetable broth and balsamic vinegar, and cover. Sauté greens until completely wilted and tender, stirring occasionally, 8 to 10 minutes. Season with salt and pepper, as desired. Serve hot.

NUTRITIONAL INFORMATION PER SERVING

103 calories ▪ 2g protein ▪ 9g carbohydrates ▪ 3g fiber ▪ 0.6g sugar ▪ 7g fat
1g saturated fat ▪ 0.0mg cholesterol ▪ 35mg sodium

Amazing Raw Creamed Spinach SERVES 6

1 avocado, peeled and cut into large chunks

1 garlic clove

1 tablespoon fresh lemon juice

3 tablespoons cilantro

6 tablespoons coconut creamer or full-fat coconut milk

6 ounces baby spinach

¼ sweet red onion, thinly sliced

20 cherry tomatoes, halved

Real Salt, to taste

1. Combine avocado, garlic, lemon juice, cilantro, and creamer in a blender. Blend until smooth and creamy.

2. In a large bowl, toss dressing mixture with spinach and onions.

3. Add tomatoes.

4. Sprinkle with Real Salt.

NUTRITIONAL INFORMATION PER SERVING

66 calories ▪ 2g protein ▪ 6g carbohydrates ▪ 3g fiber ▪ 0.6g sugar ▪ 5g fat
1g saturated fat ▪ 0.0mg cholesterol ▪ 28mg sodium

Rainbow Chard Slaw SERVES 8

- 3 cups shredded or finely chopped Swiss chard
- 1 cup shredded purple cabbage
- ¼ cup shredded carrot
- ½ cup chopped or slivered raw almonds (I like to soak them for 4 to 6 hours, time permitting)
- ¼ cup macadamia-nut oil or olive oil (macadamia-nut oil gives this salad a unique flavor)
- 1 tablespoon apple cider vinegar
- 1 tablespoon Vegenaise (optional)
- ½ teaspoon allspice
- ¼ teaspoon cinnamon
- ¼ teaspoon nutmeg
- 1 tablespoon finely chopped fresh oregano, or ½ teaspoon dried
- 1 tablespoon chopped fresh basil, or ½ teaspoon dried
- ¼ teaspoon black pepper
- ¼ teaspoon sea salt (optional)
- 1 to 2 teaspoons xylitol or 1 packet stevia
- ¼ cup raw hemp seeds
- ½ cup dried, unsweetened blueberries

1. Combine chard, cabbage, carrot, and nuts in a large bowl.

2. In a small mixing bowl, combine oil, vinegar, Vegenaise, allspice, cinnamon, nutmeg, oregano, basil, pepper, salt, and sweetener. Whisk until mixture is blended well.

3. Toss with salad mix.

4. Allow salad to refrigerate for 30 minutes prior to serving, if possible, so flavors can marry. (This salad actually tastes better the following day, after the flavors marry and the chard has a chance to absorb some of the dressing.)

5. Top with hemp seeds and dried blueberries.

NUTRITIONAL INFORMATION PER SERVING

236 calories ▪ 23g protein ▪ 10.2g carbohydrates ▪ 2.9g fiber ▪ 4.4g sugar ▪ 12g fat
1.4g saturated fat ▪ 49mg cholesterol ▪ 153mg sodium

Braised Cauliflower with Basil Sauce SERVES 4

Simple and delicious!

    3 ounces (about 6 tablespoons) fresh basil
    ¼ cup olive oil
    1 tablespoon fresh lemon juice
    salt and pepper, to taste
    2 tablespoons coconut oil or grape-seed oil
    1 large head of cauliflower, cut into 1-inch florets

1. Bring a pot of water to a boil.

2. Blanch basil for 30 seconds. Transfer to a small bowl placed over ice to stop the cooking process. Squeeze out water and place in a blender or small food processor.

3. Add olive oil and lemon juice, and puree. Season with salt and pepper, as desired.

4. In a large skillet, heat oil over medium heat. Sauté cauliflower on both sides until golden brown. Drizzle basil sauce over it and serve.

NUTRITIONAL INFORMATION PER SERVING

207 calories ▪ 5g protein ▪ 12g carbohydrates ▪ 6g fiber ▪ 0.1g sugar ▪ 18g fat 7g saturated fat ▪ 0.0mg cholesterol ▪ 64mg sodium

Cauliflower Garlic Mashed "Potatoes" SERVES 4

  2 cups no-salt-added vegetable broth or purified water
  1 head cauliflower, broken into florets
  ¼ cup unsweetened almond milk
  1 tablespoon Earth Balance butter substitute
  4 cloves garlic, minced
  ½ teaspoon Italian seasoning
  1 tablespoon chopped fresh basil
  2 teaspoons arrowroot mixed with 2 tablespoons purified water
  sea salt and pepper, to taste
  ¼ cup sunflower seeds
  2 tablespoons finely chopped chives
  2 cups baby spinach leaves

1. Pour vegetable broth or water into a medium pot. Put cauliflower florets in pot and bring to a boil over medium-high heat. Cover, reduce heat to low, and simmer for 10 minutes.

2. While cauliflower is cooking, combine almond milk, Earth Balance, garlic, Italian seasoning, and basil in a small saucepan over medium heat. When it reaches a boil, add the arrowroot/water mixture, stirring constantly until the sauce is thickened and smooth. Remove from heat and set aside.

3. Drain as much liquid from cauliflower as possible and place florets in a food processor or blender, blending on high for about a minute. Add sauce and blend until smooth and creamy.

4. Season with sea salt and pepper, to taste.

5. Add sunflower seeds and chives.

6. Serve hot over a bed of spinach.

NUTRITIONAL INFORMATION PER SERVING

105 calories ▪ 3.1g protein ▪ 7.7g carbohydrates ▪ 2g fiber ▪ 1.9g sugar ▪ 7.6g fat
1.3g saturated fat ▪ 0.0mg cholesterol ▪ 62mg sodium

Yellow Beans with Tomatoes SERVES 4

Here is a vegetable dish that is so delicious, even your children will love it!

  1 pound fresh yellow beans
  1 tablespoon coconut oil
  1 small yellow onion, diced
  3 garlic cloves, minced
  2 roma tomatoes, diced

2 tablespoons chopped fresh basil
2 tablespoons chopped walnuts
salt and pepper, to taste

1. Bring water to a boil in a large pot. Drop in beans and cook for 2 minutes.

2. Transfer beans to a large bowl with ice water to stop the cooking process. Drain beans and set aside.

3. In a large skillet, heat oil over medium heat. Stir in onion and garlic, and cook for 3 minutes.

4. Add the tomatoes and cook 1 more minute.

5. Stir in beans and cook until warmed through.

6. Mix in basil and walnuts, and season with salt and pepper, as desired.

NUTRITIONAL INFORMATION PER SERVING

231 calories ▪ 12g protein ▪ 32g carbohydrates ▪ 13g fiber ▪ <1g sugar ▪ 7g fat 4g saturated fat ▪ 0.0mg cholesterol ▪ 276mg sodium

Breaded Zucchini and Squash SERVES 6

1 egg, beaten
¼ cup water
1 cup almond meal or gluten-free bread crumbs
3 zucchini, cut into ¼-inch slices
3 summer squash, cut into ¼-inch slices
1 teaspoon garlic salt, or to taste
1 teaspoon pepper, or to taste
3 tablespoons coconut oil

1. In a medium bowl, mix egg and water.

2. Place almond meal on a flat plate.

3. Season zucchini and squash with garlic salt and pepper, then dip in egg mixture (just enough to coat vegetables).

4. Coat both sides in bread crumbs.

5. In a skillet, heat coconut oil over medium heat. Cook vegetables for 2 to 3 minutes on each side or until golden brown.

NUTRITIONAL INFORMATION PER SERVING

170 calories ▪ 6g protein ▪ 23g carbohydrates ▪ 5g fiber ▪ 0.0g sugar ▪ 7g fat 5g saturated fat ▪ 35mg cholesterol ▪ 198mg sodium

Creamy Asparagus Soup SERVES 6

1 pound asparagus (thickness irrelevant)
1 tablespoon refined coconut oil
½ cup finely chopped white onion
1 leek, chopped, white and light green part only
¼ cup chopped celery
3 cups vegetable broth
2 tablespoons coconut milk (optional)
sea salt and pepper, to taste
1 tablespoon fresh tarragon

1. Cut off asparagus tips and reserve. Discard tough ends. Chop remaining stems.

2. In a medium soup pot heat refined coconut oil. Sauté onions, leek, celery, and asparagus stems over medium heat until onions are translucent, about 5 minutes.

3. Stir until well blended. Stir well while cooking, about 1 minute more.

4. Transfer vegetables to a blender. Add about 1 cup of the vegetable broth (enough to help mixture blend easily). Blend well and transfer back to pot.

5. Add remaining vegetable broth to pot gradually, stirring out any lumps. Bring soup mixture to a boil, then reduce heat and simmer until the soup is smooth and thickened, about 30 to 40 minutes. Stir frequently.

6. Add coconut milk, if desired. Add salt and pepper, to taste.

7. Add asparagus tips to soup and simmer 5 to 10 minutes.

8. Sprinkle with tarragon.

9. Serve warm.

NOTE: Sprinkle with whole-grain croutons or make your own by toasting whole grain bread until hard.

NUTRITIONAL INFORMATION PER SERVING

80 calories ▪ 3g protein ▪ 10g carbohydrates ▪ 2g fiber ▪ 0.0g sugar ▪ 4g fat
1g saturated fat ▪ 0.0mg cholesterol ▪ 520mg sodium

Shirataki Spinach Soup   SERVES 8

This is one of my favorite soups. It's light and healthy. I replace rice or pasta with shirataki noodles. Shirataki noodles are pure fiber and help regulate blood sugar, unlike rice or pasta.

- ¼ cup no-salt-added vegetable broth, or 2 tablespoons coconut oil, for sautéing
- 1 yellow onion, chopped
- 2 garlic cloves, minced
- 8 cups no-salt-added vegetable broth
- 16 ounces shirataki noodles, orzo style (Miracle Noodle, my favorite brand, is available online)
- 3 large tomatoes, peeled, seeded, and diced
- 1 pound baby spinach, cleaned and with stems removed
- 1 cup shiitake mushrooms, sliced
- 2 tablespoons minced fresh basil
- ½ teaspoon black pepper
- 1 teaspoon sea salt (optional)

1. In a large pot, heat ¼ cup broth or oil over medium heat and sauté onions and garlic for about 3 minutes, or until onions look translucent.

2. Add remaining vegetable broth and bring to a boil. Reduce heat to medium-low.

3. Stir in the shirataki noodles, tomatoes, spinach, and mushrooms, and simmer for 10 minutes.

4. Add basil, pepper, and sea salt, if using.

NOTE: To peel and seed tomatoes, carve a shallow X in the bottom of each tomato. Dunk tomatoes in boiling water for a few seconds, then immediately dunk in ice water. This will loosen the skin. Use a paring knife to remove it. Slice tomatoes into quarters. Using your finger or a spoon, scoop out seeds. Then dice tomatoes.

NUTRITIONAL INFORMATION PER SERVING

124 calories ▪ 2.9g protein ▪ 19.4g carbohydrates ▪ 6.1g fiber ▪ 6.9g sugar ▪ 4.5g fat
3.7g saturated fat ▪ 0.0mg cholesterol ▪ 207mg sodium

Tana's Smooth Sweet Potato Soup SERVES 8

6 to 7 cups vegetable broth
½ cup diced onion
⅓ cup diced celery
3 tablespoons diced leeks
2 garlic cloves, minced
1½ pounds sweet potatoes, peeled and diced
1 cinnamon stick
¼ teaspoon nutmeg
½ cup almond milk
1 teaspoon Real Salt
1 teaspoon ground white pepper
¼ cup sunflower seeds (optional)
2 tablespoons finely chopped fresh sage
¼ cup cranberries
cinnamon, sprinkled for garnish

1. Heat ¼ cup of vegetable broth in large soup pot over medium heat. Sauté onions, celery, and leeks for 2 minutes. Then add garlic and sauté for another minute.

2. Add 4 cups of vegetable broth, sweet potatoes, cinnamon stick, and nutmeg. Bring to a boil, then reduce heat to medium-low and simmer until potatoes are tender, about 10 minutes.

3. Remove cinnamon stick.

4. Use immersion blender or pour contents into a blender in batches. Blend until smooth.

5. Pour soup back into pot (if using a blender). Add almond milk. Then slowly add remaining broth according to preferred consistency.

6. Add salt and pepper.

7. Ladle soup into bowls. Sprinkle sunflower seeds, sage, and cranberries in each bowl. Garnish and serve with cinnamon.

NUTRITIONAL INFORMATION PER SERVING

81 calories ▪ 2g protein ▪ 17g carbohydrates ▪ 2g fiber ▪ 4.5g sugar ▪ 0.0g fat 0.0g saturated fat ▪ 0.0mg cholesterol ▪ 234mg sodium

Cream of Broccoli Soup SERVES 8

2 tablespoons no-salt-added vegetable broth or 1 tablespoon grape-seed oil
1 small onion, roughly chopped
1 celery stalk, roughly chopped
8 cups broccoli florets
3 cups no-salt-added vegetable broth
½ teaspoon allspice
¼ teaspoon white pepper
2 tablespoons Earth Balance butter substitute
3 tablespoons almond meal or gluten-free flour
2 cups unsweetened almond milk

1. Heat vegetable broth in medium pot over medium-high heat. Sauté onion and celery until tender and translucent, 3 to 4 minutes.

2. Add broccoli and broth. Bring to a boil. Reduce heat and simmer for 5 minutes.

3. Carefully pour soup into a blender in batches. Do not fill blender bowl more than half full. Start blender on low setting and increase speed to high until soup is creamy and smooth. Return soup to the pot as each batch is finished. You may also use a hand-held blender and blend soup directly in the pot.

4. Keep soup warm on medium-low heat. Add allspice and pepper.

5. In a small saucepan over medium heat, melt Earth Balance butter substitute. Slowly add almond meal or gluten-free flour, stirring so it doesn't clump.

6. Add almond milk slowly. Stir until mixture is thick.

7. Add to soup pot and blend well. Serve hot.

NUTRITIONAL INFORMATION PER SERVING

85 calories ▪ 2.8g protein ▪ 8.5g carbohydrates ▪ 3.3g fiber ▪ 1.3g sugar ▪ 5.1g fat
0.8g saturated fat ▪ 0.0mg cholesterol ▪ 146mg sodium

Harmonizing Vegetable Soup SERVES 6

2 small sweet potatoes, cut into 1-inch cubes

1 small onion, finely chopped

1 tablespoon refined coconut oil

2 cloves garlic, minced

8 cups organic low-sodium vegetable broth

2 celery stalks, cut into 1-inch pieces

½ head cauliflower, cut into small florets

½ head broccoli, cut into small florets

¼ cup finely chopped parsley

1 cup diced carrots

½ red bell pepper, chopped

1 cup fresh green beans, cut into 1-inch pieces

1 tomato, chopped

1 cup baby spinach leaves

½-inch fresh ginger, peeled and sliced

1 tablespoon finely chopped fresh basil

1 teaspoon Real Salt

½ teaspoon pepper

½ teaspoon cayenne pepper

1. Cook potatoes in boiling water for about 20 minutes, or until tender.

2. In separate soup pot, sauté onion in coconut oil over low heat for about 3 minutes.

3. Add garlic and sauté for additional 2 minutes.

4. Add vegetable broth, celery, cauliflower, broccoli, parsley, carrots, red bell pepper, and green beans. Heat until veggies are warm and slightly tender, but still crisp, about 3 to 5 minutes. I prefer vegetables crunchy because they are more nutritious that way. If you prefer your vegetables to be very tender you may need to allow more time for simmering.

5. Add tomatoes, spinach leaves, ginger, basil, salt, pepper, and cayenne.

6. Reduce heat to low and simmer for 10 minutes to allow flavors to "marry."

NOTE: If you are not an onion and garlic lover, skipping the onion and garlic will save you the step of sautéing.

NUTRITIONAL INFORMATION PER SERVING

111 calories ▪ 4g protein ▪ 19g carbohydrates ▪ 5g fiber ▪ 0.96g sugar ▪ 3g fat
2g saturated fat ▪ 0.0mg cholesterol ▪ 527mg sodium

Mindful Minestrone Soup SERVES 6

Minestrone soup is a favorite in the Amen household. Our version is filled with nutrient-rich veggies and high-fiber beans that keep you feeling full longer. If you love pasta in your minestrone soup, try adding 2 cups of shirataki orzo-style noodles.

¼ cup vegetable broth or 2 tablespoons coconut oil (I prefer using broth)
1 onion, coarsely chopped
2 celery stalks, chopped
2 small potatoes, cubed
1 carrot, chopped
1 zucchini, sliced
1 teaspoon fresh thyme
1 bay leaf
one 15-ounce can stewed tomatoes
4 cups low-sodium vegetable broth
2 cups kidney beans, soaked, rinsed, and cooked (only use canned beans in a pinch)
2 cups fresh spinach
2 tablespoons fresh parsley
salt and pepper, to taste

1. Heat ¼ cup vegetable broth for sautéing. Stir in onion, celery, potatoes, and carrot. Stir frequently for about 5 minutes.

2. Add zucchini, thyme, and bay leaf, and cook for another 2 minutes.

3. Stir in tomatoes and vegetable broth. Bring to a boil, reduce heat, and simmer for 10 minutes. Stir in beans, if using, and simmer for 10 minutes.

4. Add spinach and parsley last, just before serving. Stir in and let settle for a minute. Season with salt and pepper, to taste.

NUTRITIONAL INFORMATION PER SERVING

173 calories ▪ 7g protein ▪ 36g carbohydrates ▪ 9g fiber ▪ 3.7g sugar ▪ 1g fat
0.0g saturated fat ▪ 0.0mg cholesterol ▪ 573mg sodium

White Bean Soup for the Wise SERVES 6

1 pound dried white lima beans

2 tablespoons coconut oil

1 onion, chopped

4 celery stalks, sliced

2 leeks, cut in half moons (white parts only)

4 garlic cloves, minced

1 bay leaf

1 teaspoon garlic salt

½ teaspoon curry

⅛ teaspoon nutmeg

⅛ teaspoon cinnamon

2 teaspoons cumin

1 teaspoon chopped fresh rosemary

1 teaspoon chopped fresh thyme

1 teaspoon chopped fresh marjoram

6 cups vegetable broth

3 cups water

1 pound kale, stems discarded and leaves chopped

salt and pepper, to taste

1. In a large bowl, cover beans with cold water and soak overnight.

2. Drain and rinse well.

3. In a large pot, heat oil over medium heat. Add onion, celery, and leeks, and sauté for 5 minutes.

4. Add garlic, bay leaf, garlic salt, curry, nutmeg, cinnamon, and cumin, and cook for 1 more minute.

5. Add beans, rosemary, thyme, marjoram, vegetable broth, and water. Cover, bring to a boil, reduce heat, and simmer for 40 to 50 minutes, stirring occasionally.

6. Stir in kale and simmer for 15 minutes. Season with salt and pepper, as desired. Serve hot.

NUTRITIONAL INFORMATION PER SERVING

207 calories ▪ 7g protein ▪ 33g carbohydrates ▪ 10g fiber ▪ 0.7g sugar ▪ 6g fat
4g saturated fat ▪ 0.0mg cholesterol ▪ 351mg sodium

Shrimp Chowder SERVES 6

This is my daughter Chloe's favorite!

2 teaspoons macadamia-nut oil or coconut oil

4 small sweet potatoes, diced

1 medium yellow onion, diced

8 celery stalks, chopped

3 carrots, chopped

one 14-ounce can coconut milk

2 cups unsweetened almond milk

½ teaspoon Thai green curry paste

½ teaspoon vanilla extract

1 pound fresh shrimp, peeled and deveined (you may choose to remove tails)

1 cup fresh or canned peas

1 cup fresh spinach

½ teaspoon pepper

1 teaspoon sea salt (optional)

1. Heat oil in a large skillet over medium-high heat. Sauté potatoes, onion, celery, and carrots briefly, but do not overcook, about 5 minutes. Add coconut milk, almond milk, green curry paste, and vanilla. Mix well. Turn heat down to a simmer.

2. Add shrimp, peas, spinach, and pepper to the skillet and cook for 3 to 4 minutes or until shrimp are pink and no longer translucent. Do not overcook or shrimp will become tough.

3. Transfer one-third of entire soup mixture to blender to puree. Transfer pureed mixture back to soup pot and mix well. You may skip this step to save time or if you prefer a thinner soup base. However, this step makes the soup more like a chowder.

4. Add sea salt, to taste. Ladle chowder into bowls and serve hot.

NUTRITIONAL INFORMATION PER SERVING

310 calories ▪ 15.3g protein ▪ 24.7g carbohydrates ▪ 6.3g fiber ▪ 8g sugar ▪ 17.6g fat 13.9g saturated fat ▪ 95mg cholesterol ▪ 608mg sodium

Simple Shrimp Scampi SERVES 4

Kids usually love this simple recipe and it tastes great alone or over greens or shirataki noodles. The coconut flavor is a fresh alternative to traditional scampi.

1 tablespoon coconut oil
½ teaspoon crushed red pepper flakes (optional)
1 pound raw large shrimp, peeled and deveined
1 teaspoon minced garlic
1 teaspoon chopped oregano
1 teaspoon chopped basil
½ cup light coconut milk
1 teaspoon fresh lemon juice

1. In a skillet, heat coconut oil over medium heat.

2. Add red pepper flakes, if using. Cook for 1 minute.

3. Add shrimp, and cook for 1 minute on both sides, just until they turn pink. Be careful not to overcook.

4. Add garlic, oregano, and basil.

5. Stir in coconut milk and lemon juice. Cook until slightly thickened, about 1 minute.

NUTRITIONAL INFORMATION PER SERVING

102 calories ▪ 10g protein ▪ 3g carbohydrates ▪ 0.0g fiber ▪ <1g sugar ▪ 6g fat
5g saturated fat ▪ 66mg cholesterol ▪ 76mg sodium

Seared Ahi with Guacamole SERVES 4

two 8-ounce sushi-grade ahi fillets
salt and pepper, to taste
1 to 2 tablespoons refined coconut oil or ghee, for searing

GUACAMOLE INGREDIENTS
1 ripe avocado, pitted and diced
2 tomatillos, finely chopped
2 teaspoons minced shallot
1 tablespoon fresh lime juice
½ teaspoon garlic salt
½ teaspoon pepper

MARINADE INGREDIENTS
2 tablespoons chopped cilantro
2 teaspoons grated fresh ginger
1 shallot clove, minced (about 1 tablespoon)
1 tablespoon fresh lime juice
2 tablespoons low-sodium tamari sauce
½ teaspoon Real Salt
¼ teaspoon black pepper
2 tablespoons refined coconut oil

1. Sprinkle tuna fillets with salt and pepper on both sides and set aside.

2. In a mixing bowl, mash avocado with a fork and mix in diced tomatillos. Stir in shallot, lime juice, salt, and pepper. Set aside until fish is finished.

3. In another mixing bowl, combine cilantro, ginger, shallot, lime juice, tamari sauce, salt, pepper, and coconut oil.

4. Heat a large skillet over moderately high heat. Add 1 to 2 tablespoons of oil or ghee to heated skillet.

5. Place fillets in heated skillet for 1 minute on each side. Turn fillets sideways to ensure that all sides have been seared.

6. Pour cilantro marinade mix into the skillet and coat the fish on both sides. Do not overcook.

7. Remove the fillets from the skillet. Either cut fillets in half or into thin slices and fan out on plates. Drizzle remaining marinade from the skillet onto the fish.

8. Top with guacamole and serve.

NUTRITIONAL INFORMATION PER SERVING
312 calories ▪ 30g protein ▪ 10g carbohydrates ▪ 3g fiber ▪ 0.1g sugar ▪ 18g fat
11g saturated fat ▪ 52mg cholesterol ▪ 880mg sodium

NUTRITIONAL INFORMATION FOR JUST GUACAMOLE PER SERVING
80 calories ▪ 1g protein ▪ 5g carbohydrates ▪ 3g fiber ▪ 0.5g sugar ▪ 7g fat
1g saturated fat ▪ 0.0mg cholesterol ▪ 249mg sodium

Hawaiian Blackened Tuna with Mango Salsa SERVES 2

1 tablespoon grape-seed oil
1 tablespoon fresh lime juice
1 tablespoon chopped fresh marjoram
1 tablespoon chopped fresh cilantro
½ teaspoon ground mustard powder
½ teaspoon chili powder
½ teaspoon garlic powder
½ teaspoon paprika
salt, to taste
2 wild ahi tuna steaks, 4 to 6 ounces each
head of red or green endive

MANGO SALSA INGREDIENTS
1 tablespoon grape-seed oil
1 tablespoon fresh lime juice
1 tablespoon chopped cilantro
1 mango, peeled, pitted, and diced
½ red bell pepper, finely chopped
1 tablespoon finely chopped shallots
1 tablespoon finely chopped chives
½ jalapeño, seeded and minced (optional)
salt and pepper to taste

1. For tuna herb mixture, mix grape-seed oil, lime juice, marjoram, cilantro, mustard powder, chili powder, garlic powder, paprika, and salt in a small bowl.

2. Brush each tuna steak with herb mixture, patting into fish with fingertips. Cover and refrigerate for 1 hour.

3. For mango salsa, mix grape-seed oil, lime juice, and cilantro in a medium bowl.

4. Stir in mango, bell peppers, shallots, chives, and jalapeño, if using. Season with salt and pepper. Set aside.

5. Heat a medium skillet over medium heat. You should not need extra oil for cooking because the fish was marinated in oil. Place tuna steaks in pan and sear, 1 to 2 minutes per side, depending on how cooked you prefer them. Don't overcook; the tuna should be pink on the inside. Transfer tuna to a cutting board and slice against the grain.

6. Arrange the endive leaves on a platter and top with mango salsa. Place sliced tuna on the side of the platter.

421 calories ▪ 39g protein ▪ 34g carbohydrates ▪ 11g fiber ▪ 0.1g sugar ▪ 16g fat
2g saturated fat ▪ 66mg cholesterol ▪ 121mg sodium

NUTRITIONAL INFORMATION FOR ONLY TUNA

233 calories ▪ 35g protein ▪ 3g carbohydrates ▪ 1g fiber ▪ 0.0g sugar ▪ 9g fat
1g saturated fat ▪ 66mg cholesterol ▪ 61mg sodium

Pan-Roasted Salmon with Vegetables SERVES 4

4 salmon fillets (4 to 6 ounces each)

salt and pepper, to taste

2 tablespoons coconut oil

1 onion, chopped

2 garlic cloves, minced

1 fennel bulb, cored and cut into strips

20 plump asparagus spears, woodsy ends removed

2 pinches saffron threads, crushed

2 cups fresh diced tomatoes (or one 14.5-ounce can diced tomatoes in a pinch)

½ cup vegetable stock

2 tablespoons chopped basil

1. Sprinkle salmon with salt and pepper.

2. In a large skillet, heat oil over medium-high heat.

3. Sear salmon for about 1 minute per side (don't cook it through). Transfer to a plate.

4. Add onion and garlic to same skillet, and sauté for 4 minutes.

5. Add fennel, asparagus, and saffron to the skillet. Stir to coat, and cook for 4 minutes.

6. Add tomatoes and vegetable stock. Season with more salt and pepper, cover, and simmer for about 5 minutes.

7. Return fish to pan. Sprinkle with basil, cover, and cook for 3 minutes or until fish is cooked through.

8. Transfer salmon to a plate. Spoon vegetable mixture over fish and serve.

NUTRITIONAL INFORMATION PER SERVING

339 calories ▪ 33g protein ▪ 17g carbohydrates ▪ 6g fiber ▪ 0.0g sugar ▪ 16g fat
7g saturated fat ▪ 80mg cholesterol ▪ 159mg sodium

Pan-Seared Salmon SERVES 4

4 fresh, wild salmon fillets, 4 to 6 ounces each
1 tablespoon grape-seed oil or coconut oil
1 tablespoon chopped fresh basil
sea salt and pepper, to taste

1. Preheat a large nonstick skillet over medium heat for 2 to 3 minutes.

2. Brush the fish with a small amount of oil on each side.

3. Sear the salmon for about 2 minutes. Turn and sear for another 2 to 3 minutes on the other side. You may turn again and cook for another couple of minutes, or remove salmon from the heat, depending on desired doneness and thickness of fillets. Be careful not to overcook or the salmon will taste dry.

4. Garnish with fresh basil. Sprinkle with salt and pepper, to taste.

NUTRITIONAL INFORMATION PER SERVING

272 calories ▪ 33.8g protein ▪ 0.1g carbohydrates ▪ 0.0g fiber ▪ 0.0g sugar ▪ 14.2g fat
2g saturated fat ▪ 94mg cholesterol ▪ 148mg sodium

Ginger-Glazed Salmon SERVES 4

2 tablespoons honey
1 tablespoon fresh lemon juice
1 tablespoon low-sodium tamari sauce
2 tablespoons finely grated ginger root
1 tablespoon gluten-free Dijon mustard
two 8-ounce salmon fillets

1. In a small mixing bowl, combine honey, lemon juice, tamari sauce, ginger root, and mustard. Mix well. Transfer to a shallow baking dish and evenly spread mixture.

2. Place salmon fillets in baking dish and coat one side of fillets with marinade. Turn fillets over and coat the other side. Cover and marinate for 20 to 30 minutes, turning occasionally.

3. Preheat grill to medium heat. Grill fillets for 4 to 5 minutes on each side, depending on thickness. Cut the fillets in half. Serve immediately.

NOTE: Salmon may also be cooked on the stove in a pan over medium heat. It does not fall apart as easily and remains very moist. However, it doesn't have the grilled flavor.

NUTRITIONAL INFORMATION PER SERVING

246 calories ▪ 29g protein ▪ 5g carbohydrates ▪ 0.0g fiber ▪ 8.7g sugar ▪ 9g fat
1g saturated fat ▪ 80mg cholesterol ▪ 245mg sodium

Pan-Roasted Salmon with Vegetables SERVES 4

4 salmon fillets (4 to 6 ounces each)

salt and pepper, to taste

2 tablespoons coconut oil

1 onion, chopped

2 garlic cloves, minced

1 fennel bulb, cored and cut into strips

20 plump asparagus spears, woodsy ends removed

2 pinches saffron threads, crushed

2 cups fresh diced tomatoes (or one 14.5-ounce can diced tomatoes in a pinch)

½ cup vegetable stock

2 tablespoons chopped basil

1. Sprinkle salmon with salt and pepper.

2. In a large skillet, heat oil over medium-high heat.

3. Sear salmon for about 1 minute per side (don't cook it through). Transfer to a plate.

4. Add onion and garlic to same skillet, and sauté for 4 minutes.

5. Add fennel, asparagus, and saffron to the skillet. Stir to coat, and cook for 4 minutes.

6. Add tomatoes and vegetable stock. Season with more salt and pepper, cover, and simmer for about 5 minutes.

7. Return fish to pan. Sprinkle with basil, cover, and cook for 3 minutes or until fish is cooked through.

8. Transfer salmon to a plate. Spoon vegetable mixture over fish and serve.

Pan-Seared Salmon SERVES 4

4 fresh, wild salmon fillets, 4 to 6 ounces each
1 tablespoon grape-seed oil or coconut oil
1 tablespoon chopped fresh basil
sea salt and pepper, to taste

1. Preheat a large nonstick skillet over medium heat for 2 to 3 minutes.

2. Brush the fish with a small amount of oil on each side.

3. Sear the salmon for about 2 minutes. Turn and sear for another 2 to 3 minutes on the other side. You may turn again and cook for another couple of minutes, or remove salmon from the heat, depending on desired doneness and thickness of fillets. Be careful not to overcook or the salmon will taste dry.

4. Garnish with fresh basil. Sprinkle with salt and pepper, to taste.

NUTRITIONAL INFORMATION PER SERVING

272 calories ▪ 33.8g protein ▪ 0.1g carbohydrates ▪ 0.0g fiber ▪ 0.0g sugar ▪ 14.2g fat
2g saturated fat ▪ 94mg cholesterol ▪ 148mg sodium

Ginger-Glazed Salmon SERVES 4

2 tablespoons honey
1 tablespoon fresh lemon juice
1 tablespoon low-sodium tamari sauce
2 tablespoons finely grated ginger root
1 tablespoon gluten-free Dijon mustard
two 8-ounce salmon fillets

1. In a small mixing bowl, combine honey, lemon juice, tamari sauce, ginger root, and mustard. Mix well. Transfer to a shallow baking dish and evenly spread mixture.

2. Place salmon fillets in baking dish and coat one side of fillets with marinade. Turn fillets over and coat the other side. Cover and marinate for 20 to 30 minutes, turning occasionally.

3. Preheat grill to medium heat. Grill fillets for 4 to 5 minutes on each side, depending on thickness. Cut the fillets in half. Serve immediately.

NOTE: Salmon may also be cooked on the stove in a pan over medium heat. It does not fall apart as easily and remains very moist. However, it doesn't have the grilled flavor.

NUTRITIONAL INFORMATION PER SERVING

246 calories ▪ 29g protein ▪ 5g carbohydrates ▪ 0.0g fiber ▪ 8.7g sugar ▪ 9g fat
1g saturated fat ▪ 80mg cholesterol ▪ 245mg sodium

Cedar Plank Salmon SERVES 4

This recipe requires marinating for at least 15 minutes, up to 2 hours. Cedar grilling planks can be found at Whole Foods and many other grocery stores. They can also be purchased online from Target, Lowe's, and many other great sources.

    four (8x5-inch) cedar grilling planks
    1 tablespoon sea salt (optional)
    four 6- to 8-ounce wild salmon fillets with skin on
    2 tablespoons gluten-free Dijon mustard
    1 tablespoon pure maple syrup
    1 teaspoon minced fresh thyme
    2 garlic cloves, minced
    1 teaspoon grated fresh ginger
    ½ teaspoon pepper
    ½ teaspoon sea salt (optional)

1. Soak cedar planks in water for 2 hours if you are grilling, and 30 minutes if you are roasting in the oven. You may add sea salt to the purified water.

2. Rinse and dry the salmon. Set aside.

3. In a small bowl, combine Dijon mustard, maple syrup, thyme, garlic, ginger, pepper, and sea salt, if desired. Whisk until all ingredients are well blended.

4. Put marinade in shallow dish and place fillets with the pink flesh side down in the marinade. Do not cover skin with marinade. Let fillets sit in the marinade for 15 minutes at room temperature, or marinate them for up to a day in the refrigerator.

5. Preheat grill on high. Reduce heat to medium-low after 15 minutes.

6. Remove fillets from marinade. Do not pour marinade over fillets while grilling. Place salmon fillets on cedar planks, skin side down, and place planks on the grill. Cover the grill and cook for 12 to 15 minutes, or until surface fat begins to turn white. Cooking time depends on size of fillets and preferred doneness. For roasting in the oven: Preheat oven to 325°F. Prepare the salmon as described above. Place cedar planks on roasting tray and roast for 12 to 15 minutes. Cooking time depends on size of fillets and preferred doneness.

7. Serve on cedar planks—place cedar planks directly on plates.

NUTRITIONAL INFORMATION PER SERVING
347 calories ▪ 45.2g protein ▪ 5.8g carbohydrates ▪ 0.2g fiber ▪ 3g sugar ▪ 14.4g fat
2.2g saturated fat ▪ 125mg cholesterol ▪ 281mg sodium

Poached Tilapia with Saffron Sauce SERVES 4

1 tablespoon coconut oil or 3 to 4 tablespoons vegetable broth for sautéing
3 garlic cloves, minced
1 tablespoon tomato paste
2¾ cups vegetable broth
2 teaspoons chopped fresh tarragon
1 teaspoon saffron
one 2-inch sliced orange peel
1 bay leaf
1½ cups canned organic tomatoes, stewed or diced
1 leek, sliced, white part only
½ cup chopped fennel
½ cup sliced okra
4 tilapia fillets
Real Salt and pepper, to taste
4 lemon wedges

1. Heat oil in large skillet over medium heat. Add garlic and sauté for 1 minute.

2. Add tomato paste and sauté for 1 minute. Deglaze skillet with 1 cup vegetable broth.

3. Add tarragon, saffron, orange peel, and bay leaf. Simmer for 15 minutes.

4. Remove bay leaf and orange peel. Add tomatoes and remaining vegetable broth. Bring to a boil.

5. Add leek, fennel, and okra. Simmer until vegetables are tender.

6. Season fish with salt and pepper. Add fish to sauce and gently poach for 3 to 4 minutes on each side.

7. Serve immediately in shallow dishes. Garnish each dish with 1 lemon wedge.

NOTE: For those who do not eat animal protein of any kind, this sauce is also excellent served over barley.

NUTRITIONAL INFORMATION PER SERVING

170 calories ▪ 23g protein ▪ 18g carbohydrates ▪ 4g fiber ▪ 0.6g sugar ▪ 0.5g fat
0.0g saturated fat ▪ 55mg cholesterol ▪ 914mg sodium

Simply Delicious Pan-Seared Trout and Cucumber Salad   SERVES 4

SALAD INGREDIENTS
4 Persian cucumbers, thinly sliced
½ avocado, diced
1 tablespoon olive oil
2 teaspoons chopped dill
1 shallot, finely chopped
1 teaspoon fresh lemon juice
salt and pepper, to taste

2 to 3 tablespoons no-salt-added vegetable broth
1 small leek, diced
4 plum tomatoes, seeded and diced
1 tablespoon chopped fresh tarragon
2 tablespoons grape-seed oil
four 6- to 8-ounce wild trout fillets
1 tablespoon chopped fresh basil
3 cups mixed greens

1. Prepare the salad. In a medium bowl, combine cucumber, avocado, olive oil, dill, shallots, and lemon juice, and season with salt and pepper.

2. Cover and refrigerate for 30 minutes.

3. Heat vegetable broth over medium heat in a small pan. Add leek and sauté for 3 to 5 minutes.

4. Add tomatoes and sauté for another 3 minutes. Add tarragon to pan. Remove from heat and set aside.

5. Heat oil in a large nonstick pan over medium-high heat. Add trout fillets, skin side down. Cook for 5 minutes. If trout fillets are large, you may need to cook them two at a time to make sure that they are completely flat in the skillet. The skins should get golden and a little crispy.

6. Turn fillets once for about 30 seconds. Turn back to skin side to be sure trout is cooked.

7. Sprinkle basil evenly over all fillets and remove from heat. Place fillets on plates.

8. Divide greens evenly between 4 plates. Put cucumber mixture over greens.

9. Serve with trout.

NUTRITIONAL INFORMATION PER SERVING
348 calories ▪ 41g protein ▪ 5.8g carbohydrates ▪ 1.2g fiber ▪ 2.6g sugar ▪ 17.2g fat
3.5g saturated fat ▪ 121mg cholesterol ▪ 255mg sodium

Baked Halibut with Creamed Spinach Sauce SERVES 4

2 tablespoons grape-seed oil
2 tablespoons minced shallot
1 garlic clove, minced
¼ cup white wine vinegar
¼ cup dry white wine
2 tablespoons Earth Balance butter substitute
¼ cup light coconut milk
4 halibut fillets, 6 to 8 ounces each
sea salt and black pepper, to taste
¼ cup chopped baby spinach
1 small tomato, diced (about ½ cup)

1. Preheat oven to 400°F.

2. Heat 1 tablespoon of oil in a saucepan over medium heat. Sauté shallot and garlic for 2 minutes.

3. Add vinegar and bring to a boil for about 4 minutes.

4. Add wine and boil for another 3 minutes.

5. Add Earth Balance and coconut milk, and whisk. Take saucepan off heat and set aside for a moment.

6. Lightly oil a baking dish with half of the remaining tablespoon of oil. Place the fish in the baking dish and brush with the remaining oil. Add sea salt and pepper to fish, as desired. Bake until fish is no longer translucent, 10 to 20 minutes, depending on size of fillets.

7. Meanwhile, return sauce to low heat. Mix in spinach and tomato.

8. Serve halibut on plates and spoon a small amount of sauce over each fillet.

NUTRITIONAL INFORMATION PER SERVING

279 calories ▪ 31.1g protein ▪ 2.7g carbohydrates ▪ 0.3g fiber ▪ 0.9g sugar ▪ 16g fat 8.5g saturated fat ▪ 98mg cholesterol ▪ 239mg sodium

Poached Sea Bass in Tomato Broth SERVES 4

2 large sea bass fillets, 8 to 10 ounces each
1 tablespoon refined coconut oil
½ onion, chopped
2 garlic cloves, minced
1 teaspoon ground coriander
½ teaspoon Real Salt
¼ teaspoon cayenne pepper
¼ teaspoon cinnamon
one 14-ounce can whole tomatoes
2 cups vegetable broth
1 cup water
2 fennel bulbs, quartered and sliced lengthwise

1. Prepare sea bass in advance by rinsing with cold water and patting dry with paper towels. Set aside.

2. Heat oil in large pan over medium heat. Sauté onion and garlic for about 3 minutes.

3. Stir in coriander, salt, cayenne pepper, and cinnamon.

4. Add tomatoes, broth, and water.

5. Add fennel when broth comes to a boil.

6. Reduce heat to low and simmer for 5 minutes.

7. Place sea bass in sauce. Increase heat to medium and cook for 5 to 6 minutes. Turn fish over and cover pan. Allow fish to poach for another 5 to 6 minutes.

8. Carefully cut both fillets in half (in the pan). Place in shallow bowls.

9. Spoon sauce over the top of each fillet and serve hot.

NUTRITIONAL INFORMATION PER SERVING

172 calories ▪ 15g protein ▪ 17g carbohydrates ▪ 5g fiber ▪ 3g sugar ▪ 6g fat
4g saturated fat ▪ 27mg cholesterol ▪ 1039mg sodium

Snapper with Tomato Caper Sauce SERVES 2

2 snapper fillets, 4 to 6 ounces each
1 tablespoon grape-seed oil
salt and pepper, to taste
1 shallot, chopped
1 garlic clove, minced
1 anchovy fillet
1 bay leaf
1 tablespoon tomato paste
¼ cup vegetable broth
1 tablespoon capers
1 roma tomato, diced
¼ cup coconut creamer or full-fat coconut milk
1 teaspoon fresh lemon juice

1. Preheat oven to 400°F.

2. Brush snapper with a little oil and sprinkle with salt and pepper.

3. Arrange in baking dish and bake for 20 minutes or until fish flakes easily with a fork.

4. Meanwhile, heat the rest of the grape-seed oil over medium heat. Sauté shallots, garlic, anchovy, and bay leaf for 2 minutes.

5. Stir in tomato paste, and cook for 2 more minutes.

6. Add vegetable broth and deglaze the pan.

7. Stir in capers and tomatoes, and cook for 3 minutes. Remove bay leaf.

8. Add creamer. Season with more salt and pepper, to taste.

9. Simmer until lightly thickened.

10. Add lemon juice. Serve baked snapper with tomato caper sauce.

NUTRITIONAL INFORMATION PER SERVING
297 calories ▪ 33g protein ▪ 15g carbohydrates ▪ 1g fiber ▪ 1.4g sugar ▪ 11g fat
1g saturated fat ▪ 55mg cholesterol ▪ 284mg sodium

Crowd-Pleasing Cioppino SERVES 8

This seafood stew is a favorite among guests!

2 tablespoons coconut oil
1 onion, chopped
1 celery stalk, chopped
3 tablespoons chopped shallots
1 pinch saffron
1 teaspoon paprika
1 bay leaf
5 garlic cloves, minced
2½ cups fresh diced tomatoes (or one 16-ounce can diced tomatoes with
   juice in a pinch)
one 16-ounce can tomato sauce
3 cups vegetable broth
1 pound white firm fish (sea bass, halibut, cod), cubed
1 pound large uncooked shrimp, peeled and deveined
1 pound clams or mussels
½ pound bay scallops
salt and pepper, to taste
3 tablespoons chopped parsley

1. In a heavy-bottomed pot, heat coconut oil over medium heat. Add onion, celery, shallots, saffron, paprika, and bay leaf. Cook for 6 minutes.

2. Add garlic, and cook for 1 more minute.

3. Add tomatoes, tomato sauce, and vegetable broth. Bring to a boil. Reduce heat and simmer for 20 minutes. Remove bay leaf.

4. Add the fish, shrimp, clams or mussels, and scallops.

5. Season with salt and pepper. Simmer for 5 minutes or until fish is cooked through and clams open.

6. Sprinkle with parsley, and serve with a large salad and a vegetable dish.

NOTE: For a rich, savory, San Francisco–style stew, try blending in a blender or food processor about ⅓ of the broth and a few chunks of fish. Place back in the pot and simmer for 5 minutes.

NUTRITIONAL INFORMATION PER SERVING

327 calories ▪ 45g protein ▪ 16g carbohydrates ▪ 3g fiber ▪ 2.6g sugar ▪ 9g fat
4g saturated fat ▪ 157mg cholesterol ▪ 467mg sodium

Macadamia-Crusted Mahimahi SERVES 4

½ cup macadamia nuts
2 tablespoons no-salt-added vegetable broth
2 garlic cloves
½ teaspoon chili powder
1 tablespoon pure maple syrup
1 tablespoon grape-seed oil
4 mahimahi fillets, 6 to 8 ounces each

1. Preheat oven to 450°F.

2. In a food processor, combine nuts, broth, garlic, chili powder, maple syrup, and grape-seed oil. Process until mixture is well blended and fine, but not pasty.

3. Smooth a thin coat of macadamia spread over one side of each mahimahi fillet.

4. Place each fillet in a baking dish with the crusted side up.

5. Place fish on lower rack and bake until crust is golden brown and fish flakes easily, about 12 minutes. Be careful not to overcook crust.

NUTRITIONAL INFORMATION PER SERVING

360 calories ▪ 43.4g protein ▪ 6.4g carbohydrates ▪ 1.6g fiber ▪ 3.8g sugar ▪ 17.7g fat 2.8g saturated fat ▪ 166mg cholesterol ▪ 211mg sodium

Sizzling Chicken Kabobs SERVES 4

2 tablespoons grape-seed oil

1 tablespoon honey

2 tablespoons tamari sauce

1 tablespoon gluten-free Dijon mustard

1 teaspoon rice vinegar

3 garlic cloves, minced

½ teaspoon pepper

2 teaspoons chopped fresh thyme

2 boneless, skinless chicken breasts (4 to 6 ounces each), cut into 1-inch cubes (free-range, hormone-free, antibiotic-free)

1 red bell pepper, cut into 2-inch pieces

1 small red onion, cut into 2-inch pieces

1 zucchini, cut into 1-inch slices

10 small mushrooms

skewers

1. In a large bowl, whisk together oil, honey, tamari sauce, mustard, rice vinegar, garlic, pepper, and thyme.

2. Add chicken, bell peppers, onions, zucchini, and mushrooms. Toss to coat and refrigerate for up to 24 hours.

3. Preheat the grill to high heat.

4. Thread chicken and vegetables alternately onto skewers.

5. Lightly oil the grill. Place skewers on grill and cook, turning frequently, for 15 to 20 minutes, until chicken is cooked through and vegetables are tender. Serve.

NUTRITIONAL INFORMATION PER SERVING

290 calories ▪ 29g protein ▪ 10g carbohydrates ▪ 1g fiber ▪ 4.2g sugar ▪ 15g fat
2g saturated fat ▪ 66mg cholesterol ▪ 669mg sodium

Tomato Curry Chicken with Saffron SERVES 8

Saffron is very expensive, but it gives a wonderful flavor and is considered a brain-healthy spice. If using saffron threads, soak them in a couple of tablespoons of hot water for at least 15 minutes prior to use. Mash the threads with the back of a spoon. If you have time, soak the threads for several hours and do not mash them.

This recipe is best if the chicken is marinated for a minimum of 2 hours, up to 24 hours.

2 to 3 tablespoons no-salt-added vegetable broth for sautéing,
    or 1 tablespoon grape-seed oil
1 large tomato, diced, or one 14.5-ounce jar of low-sodium diced tomatoes
1 small onion, chopped
4 to 5 garlic cloves, minced
½ teaspoon garam masala spice
½ teaspoon mild yellow curry powder
½ teaspoon presoaked saffron threads or ¼ teaspoon dried saffron powder
¼ teaspoon sea salt (optional)
1 cup light coconut milk
8 boneless chicken breast halves (free-range, antibiotic-free, hormone-free)
½ cup raw shaved almonds

PREPARATION FOR MARINADE

1. Heat vegetable broth in a saucepan over medium heat. Sauté tomato and onions for 2 to 3 minutes.

2. Add garlic for 1 minute. Reduce heat and simmer for 5 minutes, stirring occasionally.

3. Add some more vegetable broth if necessary, so mixture doesn't become dry. Add masala seasoning, curry, saffron, and sea salt (if desired). Simmer for 10 minutes more. Remove from heat and cool for several minutes.

4. Pour mixture into a blender bowl and puree on medium until smooth and creamy.

5. Return mixture to the saucepan and add coconut milk. Bring to a mild boil, then reduce heat to a simmer for 5 minutes. Remove from heat.

6. While marinade is cooling, lightly pound chicken breasts with a meat mallet.

7. When marinade cools, place in a bowl and add chicken to sauce. Cover and refrigerate for at least 2 hours, up to 24 hours.

PREPARATION FOR COOKING

1. After marinating chicken, preheat oven to 350°F.

2. Place chicken in baking dish with marinade. Be sure dish is large enough so

chicken isn't crowded together. Cook for 15 minutes on each side, or until cooked through.

3. Place chicken on serving platter and sprinkle with almonds.

NUTRITIONAL INFORMATION PER SERVING

223 calories ▪ 28.4g protein ▪ 4.4g carbohydrates ▪ 1.4g fiber ▪ 1.2g sugar ▪ 9.8g fat
3g saturated fat ▪ 73mg cholesterol ▪ 142mg sodium

Spice of Life Chicken SERVES 8

2 tablespoons sweet paprika
2 teaspoons granulated garlic powder
1 teaspoon sea salt
1 teaspoon ancho chile powder
1 teaspoon ground ginger
1 teaspoon cumin
1 teaspoon onion powder
1 teaspoon black pepper
1 teaspoon fenugreek
1 teaspoon ground allspice
½ teaspoon ground cardamom
½ teaspoon ground cinnamon
¼ teaspoon cloves
4 pounds skinless chicken legs (hormone-free, antibiotic-free, cage-free)
2 tablespoons macadamia-nut oil
1 orange, split into wedges
1 lemon, split into wedges
1 lime, split into wedges
½ cup cilantro leaves (optional)

1. Preheat oven to 400°F.

2. Combine first 13 ingredients together in a small bowl.

3. In a large bowl, toss chicken, oil, and spice mix together. Massage spice mix into chicken.

4. Lay chicken in casserole dish. Bake for 40 to 45 minutes, basting occasionally. Bake until chicken reaches 170°F on a meat thermometer; when pierced, the juice should be clear and not pink.

5. Serve with citrus wedges and chopped cilantro for garnish, if desired.

NUTRITIONAL INFORMATION PER SERVING

201 calories ▪ 28.8g protein ▪ 3g carbohydrates ▪ 1.1g fiber ▪ 0.6g sugar ▪ 11g fat
1.9g saturated fat ▪ 29mg cholesterol ▪ 312mg sodium

Cashew Cream Squash with Turkey and Roasted Peppers SERVES 4

The cashews in the cashew cream need to be soaked overnight, so plan ahead when making this recipe.

    1 cup raw cashews
    1 poblano chile
    1 tablespoon macadamia-nut oil or grape-seed oil
    1 pound ground turkey (free-range, hormone-free, antibiotic-free)
    2 to 4 tablespoons low-sodium vegetable broth for sautéing, or a couple of
        teaspoons grape-seed oil
    1 pound yellow and green summer squash, diced into ½-inch pieces
    1 cup diced red or orange bell peppers
    ½ cup diced sweet onion
    sea salt, to taste

1. To make cashew cream, rinse 1 cup of raw cashews under cold water. Put the cashews in a bowl and cover the cashews with cold water. Cover the bowl and refrigerate overnight. Drain the cashews and rinse under cold water. Place them in a blender with enough fresh cold water to cover them by 1 inch. Using a high- powered blender, blend on high for several minutes until the consistency of a smooth cream.

2. Preheat oven to 450°F.

3. Lightly rub the poblano chile with oil. Roast for about 20 minutes. The skin should blister. Remove the chile from the oven and cool. Rub skin off. Cut pepper open, remove seeds, and dice pepper.

4. Heat the remaining oil in large pan over medium heat. Lightly brown ground turkey, stirring frequently, 7 to 8 minutes. Turn off heat and set aside. Do not overcook.

5. Heat a small amount of broth over medium-high heat. Sauté squash. Add broth as needed to prevent burning.

6. Add the bell peppers, chile, and onion. Stir regularly until the onion is soft or lightly browned, 3 to 5 minutes. Drain off extra broth, if necessary.

7. Add turkey and cashew cream to pan with vegetables. Add salt, if desired. Simmer until the cream is reduced to a thick glaze, about 5 minutes. Serve hot.

NUTRITIONAL INFORMATION PER SERVING

170 calories ▪ 13.7g protein ▪ 11.4g carbohydrates ▪ 4.4g fiber ▪ 1.4g sugar ▪ 9.5g fat 1.3g saturated fat ▪ 32.5mg cholesterol ▪ 336mg sodium

"Spaghetti" with Turkey Meatballs SERVES 4

Another guilt-free meal! Indulge and enjoy!

1 pound ground turkey (free-range, antibiotic-free, hormone-free)

3 scallions, chopped

2 garlic cloves, minced

¼ cup chopped parsley

¾ cup finely chopped celery

½ teaspoon garlic salt

2 tablespoons grape-seed or macadamia-nut oil

one 28-ounce can diced tomatoes, low-sodium (or use 4 to 5 cups fresh diced tomatoes to reduce sodium)

½ to 1 chipotle pepper in adobo sauce (as desired for spicy flavor)

1 onion, chopped

16 ounces shirataki noodles

½ cup coconut creamer or full-fat coconut milk

2 tablespoons chopped fresh basil

1. In a large bowl, mix turkey, scallions, garlic, parsley, celery, and garlic salt. Shape into 1-inch meatballs and place onto a tray.

2. Heat oil in skillet over medium heat. Add meatballs to skillet, browning on all sides, about 5 to 10 minutes.

3. Meanwhile, make the tomato sauce. Place tomatoes, chipotle pepper, and onion in a blender bowl. Blend until smooth.

4. Add the sauce to the browned meatballs, and simmer for 30 minutes.

5. About 5 minutes before meatballs are finished simmering, boil water in a pot. Empty and drain shirataki noodles from package. You may want to cut noodles before boiling. Add to boiling water. Reduce heat and simmer for 3 minutes. Drain the noodles well (they tend to hold water).

6. When meatballs are finished cooking, add creamer and simmer for 2 more minutes. Stir in basil. Serve over shirataki noodles and with favorite greens.

NUTRITIONAL INFORMATION PER SERVING

260 calories ▪ 25g protein ▪ 17g carbohydrates ▪ 3g fiber ▪ 2g sugar ▪ 10g fat 3g saturated fat ▪ 80mg cholesterol ▪ 558mg sodium

Try It, You'll Like It Turkey Bolognese SERVES 6

My husband loves this recipe with the spaghetti squash. But if you are really trying to lose weight, try it with shirataki noodles.

1 large spaghetti squash
1 tablespoon coconut oil
1 onion, chopped
3 garlic cloves, minced
1 pound ground turkey (free-range, antibiotic-free, hormone-free)
3 tablespoons tomato paste
2 cups fresh diced tomatoes, or one 14.5-ounce can chopped tomatoes, in a pinch
2 cups vegetable broth
4 ounces sliced crimini mushrooms
½ cup coconut creamer or full-fat coconut milk
1 tablespoon chopped fresh oregano
1 tablespoon chopped fresh basil
salt and pepper, to taste

1. Preheat oven to 375°F.

2. Cut spaghetti squash in half and clean out seeds. Place squash facedown on a baking dish. Fill baking dish halfway with water. Bake for 40 to 45 minutes or until soft but not overcooked. Squash is finished when fork goes in easily and shreds squash like spaghetti. Place "noodles" in a large serving dish.

3. While squash is baking, heat oil in a skillet over medium heat. Add onions and garlic, and sauté for 3 minutes.

4. Stir in ground turkey. Cook for 7 to 10 minutes, breaking the meat into small pieces with a wooden spoon.

5. When meat is lightly browned, add tomato paste and cook for 3 minutes, stirring frequently.

6. Add chopped tomatoes, vegetable broth, and mushrooms. Lower heat, cover, and simmer for 10 to 15 minutes.

7. Stir in cream, oregano, and basil. Season with salt and pepper and cook for 1 more minute. Serve over spaghetti squash.

NUTRITIONAL INFORMATION PER SERVING

210 calories ▪ 17g protein ▪ 16g carbohydrates ▪ 3g fiber ▪ 2.1g sugar ▪ 9g fat
4g saturated fat ▪ 53mg cholesterol ▪ 299mg sodium

Healthy Turkey Chili SERVES 8

- 1 pound lean ground turkey (free-range, hormone-free, antibiotic-free)
- 1 tablespoon refined coconut oil
- 1 cup chopped onion
- 3 garlic cloves, chopped
- 1 jalapeño pepper (optional: makes chili pretty spicy)
- 1 teaspoon chili powder
- 1 small can Ortega chiles
- 1 tablespoon fresh oregano
- 1 teaspoon cumin seed
- 1 to 2 teaspoons Real Salt
- 3 cups diced tomatoes, fresh or organic canned (no-salt-added variety)
- 2 cups chicken or vegetable broth
- 1 cup chopped bell peppers
- 2 cups chopped celery
- ½ cup chopped zucchini
- 2 cups kidney beans, cooked and drained (you may use canned if you don't have time to cook beans)
- 1 cup black beans or garbanzo beans, cooked

1. In a large saucepan or pot, brown turkey meat in refined coconut oil over medium heat. Crumble turkey and break apart as much as possible. Add onion and stir for about 2 minutes. Meat should be lightly browned.

2. Add garlic, jalapeño (if using), chili powder, Ortega chiles, oregano, cumin seed, salt, and tomatoes. Mix thoroughly until spices are well blended with meat (about 3 minutes).

3. Add broth and bring to a boil, then reduce heat to low, and simmer for 5 minutes.

4. Dish out 2 cups of chili mixture. Put about 1 cup of chili at a time into the blender. Add ½ cup bell pepper, 1 cup celery, and ¼ cup zucchini, and purée. Repeat with other cup of chili and the rest of pepper, celery, and zucchini. Pour each mixture back into the remaining chili pot. Adding the puréed vegetables not only makes the chili tasty, but is a great way to add fiber and vitamins without overcooking.

5. Add the beans. Stir thoroughly and heat through on medium-low, about 5 minutes. Serve hot.

NOTE: It is my preference to cook the vegetables as little as possible. However, if you prefer not to go through the process of blending the vegetables, and prefer cooking the vegetables, you will need to sauté them first. In that case, heat a teaspoon of refined coconut oil in a large skillet over medium heat for about 1 minute. Add bell pepper and celery, and sauté for about 2 minutes. Then add the vegetables in step 2.

NUTRITIONAL INFORMATION PER SERVING
209 calories ▪ 22g protein ▪ 24g carbohydrates ▪ 8g fiber ▪ 0.5g sugar ▪ 4g fat
2g saturated fat ▪ 7mg cholesterol ▪ 687mg sodium

Middle Eastern Steak Salad with Tahini-Dressed Zucchini SERVES 6

I prefer free-range bison London broil. There are several companies that sell it online who certify the bison to be *completely* free-range and naturally raised. This makes them 30 percent lower in fat, so if you use bison London broil, you'll have to reduce the cooking time a bit.

STEAK INGREDIENTS
1 tablespoon grape-seed oil
½ teaspoon cinnamon
¼ teaspoon allspice
½ teaspoon sea salt
¼ teaspoon coarse pepper
16 ounces London broil steak (free-range, hormone-free, antibiotic-free)

SALAD INGREDIENTS
⅓ cup sun-dried tomatoes, no oil
1 teaspoon minced garlic
¼ cup tahini paste
¼ cup fresh lemon juice
2 tablespoons lemon zest
¼ cup orange juice
¼ cup Meyer lemon juice
1 tablespoon grape-seed oil
2 zucchinis, thinly sliced
½ teaspoon ancho chile powder
2 cups green beans, blanched, cut into 1-inch pieces
6 cups mixed baby greens

1. Preheat grill to medium high, or set oven to broil.

2. Combine oil, cinnamon, allspice, sea salt, and pepper.

3. Rub mixture evenly onto the steak. If possible allow the steak to marinate for 10 to 15 minutes in the spices before grilling.

4. Grill or broil for 5 to 7 minutes on each side (internal temperature should reach 145°F), depending on desired doneness.

5. Place on cutting board and cover with foil. Allow to rest for 5 minutes.

6. Meanwhile, prepare salad. Soak sun-dried tomatoes in *hot* water.

7. When they are soft, drain, julienne, and set aside to cool.

8. In a small bowl, combine garlic, tahini, lemon juice, lemon zest, orange juice, and Meyer lemon juice. Stir well.

9. Heat oil over medium heat. Brown zucchini slices for 3 to 5 minutes. Remove zucchini from the stovetop and place in a bowl. Toss with lemon juice mixture and ancho chile powder.

10. Toss green beans with zucchini.

11. Arrange salad greens on plate. Add the zucchini and green beans.

12. Top with the sun-dried tomatoes. Drizzle with any remaining dressing.

13. Slice meat in thin slices. Top the salad with the slices and serve.

NUTRITIONAL INFORMATION PER SERVING

344 calories ▪ 33g protein ▪ 23g carbohydrates ▪ 9g fiber ▪ 7.4g sugar ▪ 12g fat
7g saturated fat ▪ 66mg cholesterol ▪ 207mg sodium

The Best Beef Stroganoff SERVES 6

3 tablespoons coconut oil

1 onion, julienned

2 garlic cloves, minced

8 ounces sliced crimini mushrooms

1½ pounds grass-fed, antibiotic-free beef sirloin, cut into bite-size pieces

1 teaspoon paprika

1 tablespoon fresh rosemary, chopped

2 cups sodium-free vegetable broth

1 bay leaf

1 teaspoon garlic salt

salt and pepper, to taste

¾ cup coconut creamer or full-fat coconut milk

1 tablespoon arrowroot

1 tablespoon chopped fresh parsley

1. In a heavy-bottomed pan, heat 2 tablespoons of the coconut oil over medium heat. Add onions and sauté for 3 minutes.

2. Add garlic and sauté for 1 more minute. Transfer the onion and garlic to a bowl.

3. In the same pan, cook mushrooms for 5 minutes. Set mushrooms aside with onions and garlic.

4. In the same pan, add the rest of coconut oil and beef. Sprinkle with paprika. Cook for 3 to 5 minutes or until the meat is browned on all sides.

5. Add onion, garlic, mushrooms, and rosemary to the beef.

6. Stir in vegetable broth, bay leaf, and garlic salt, season with salt and pepper, and cover. Bring to a boil, reduce heat, and simmer for 50 minutes or until meat is tender. Remove bay leaf.

7. Meanwhile, in a small bowl, mix the creamer and arrowroot. When meat is cooked, add the creamer mixture to the pan. Simmer for 3 minutes. Stir in parsley and serve. Be sure to pair with a large salad or vegetable dish.

NUTRITIONAL INFORMATION PER SERVING

340 calories ▪ 35g protein ▪ 7g carbohydrates ▪ 1g fiber ▪ 0.8g sugar ▪ 18g fat 9g saturated fat ▪ 100mg cholesterol ▪ 303mg sodium

Savory Lubia Rose Stew SERVES 4

I love the versatility of this recipe. Whether you are a protein lover or a vegetarian, you can adapt this recipe to fit your needs. It is simple, tasty, and nutritious.

1 tablespoon refined coconut oil or grape-seed oil

½ small onion, chopped

12 ounces lean lamb, chopped into bite-size pieces (grass-fed, antibiotic-free, hormone-free)

one 28-ounce can diced tomatoes (or 6 fresh, if you have time)

¼ teaspoon salt

¼ teaspoon pepper

½ teaspoon cinnamon

½ teaspoon allspice

2 cups fresh green beans

1 cup cooked brown rice or shirataki noodles

2 tablespoons pine nuts (optional)

1. In a medium-large pan, heat oil over medium heat. Add onions, and sauté for 1 minute.

2. Add lamb and cook until meat is lightly browned on all sides, 5 to 7 minutes. Turn regularly.

3. Add tomatoes, salt, pepper, cinnamon, and allspice. Lower heat, cover, and simmer for 15 minutes.

4. Add green beans and simmer for another 5 minutes.

5. Place rice or shirataki noodles on serving platter and serve lamb-and-tomato mixture over the top. Sprinkle with pine nuts, if desired. Serve with a green salad.

NOTE: Vegetarians may replace the lamb with tempeh or no meat. Try topping it with a few extra pine nuts.

NUTRITIONAL INFORMATION PER SERVING

328 calories ▪ 25g protein ▪ 10g carbohydrates ▪ 6g fiber ▪ <1g sugar ▪ 19g fat 11g saturated fat ▪ 85mg cholesterol ▪ 303mg sodium

Free-Range Bison Meatloaf SERVES 6

Free-range bison (also called buffalo) is one of my favorite meats to eat. I order meat from ranches that allow for a totally natural breeding process, use no antibiotics or hormones, and allow the animals to run free. You can find many such ranches online that are certified by outside third parties. Many of these companies offer discounts if you buy meat in bulk. My suggestion is to get together with friends or family, make a bulk purchase, and freeze it. It brings the cost down substantially, and raises the quality of the meat you are eating significantly!

4 garlic cloves

8 to 10 fresh whole basil leaves

2 tablespoons fresh whole oregano leaves

2 tablespoons fresh whole parsley leaves

1 tablespoon fresh thyme, with thick stems removed

5 to 6 fresh whole sage leaves

4 celery stalks, cut into 2-inch pieces

1 small onion, quartered

¼ cup macadamia nuts

¼ cup cashews

2 pounds ground wild bison (free-range, hormone-free, antibiotic-free)

1 egg (organic, omega-3)

2 tablespoons ground flax seeds (you can grind whole flax seeds in a coffee grinder)

½ teaspoon chili powder

¼ teaspoon black pepper

1 tablespoon low-sodium tamari sauce (you may exclude this if you follow a low-sodium diet)

½ cup no-salt-added organic pasta sauce (optional)

1. Preheat oven to 350°F.

2. In a large food processor, place garlic, basil, oregano, parsley, thyme, sage, celery, and onion. Pulse for 15 to 20 seconds, but do not turn on continuous chop setting or mixture will become soggy. Check mixture for consistency. It should be finely chopped with no large pieces, but not mushy. Remove mixture from food processor and remove any large stray pieces, if necessary.

3. Place nuts in food processor. Pulse for 15 to 20 seconds, but do not turn on continuous chop setting or mixture will become pasty. Check mixture for consistency. It should be finely chopped with no large pieces, but not sticky or pasty. Remove mixture from food processor and remove any large stray pieces, if necessary.

4. Place bison in a large mixing bowl and add the egg. Mix lightly. Bison is lower in fat than beef and gets tough if you overmix it, so do not overwork the meat.

5. Add the herb mixture from step 2 to the bowl. Do not mix.

6. Add chopped nuts, flax seeds, chili powder, pepper, and tamari sauce.

7. Mix all ingredients thoroughly through the meat, blending evenly, but being careful not to overwork the meat.

8. Place meat in a 9x5-inch loaf pan and form. (I prefer not to use Teflon, as it is toxic when heated.)

9. Place pan on the middle rack of the oven and set timer for 1 hour. It usually takes about 1¼ hours to cook.

10. After an hour, check loaf for doneness. You may use a meat thermometer. The internal cooking temperature should be 160°F.

11. You may choose to spread pasta sauce over the top of meatloaf for the last 15 minutes of cooking.

12. Remove from oven and let stand for 5 to 10 minutes before serving.

NUTRITIONAL INFORMATION PER SERVING

277 calories ▪ 36.6g protein ▪ 6.5g carbohydrates ▪ 2g fiber ▪ 1.6g sugar ▪ 11.4g fat
2.5g saturated fat ▪ 125mg cholesterol ▪ 235mg sodium

Bison London Broil SERVES 8

This recipe requires marinating the meat for a minimum of 2 hours, up to 24 hours. You can also substitute the bison with beef. This is great served as a main entrée or over fresh greens as a steak salad for lunch.

4 garlic cloves
2 tablespoons fresh oregano, not chopped
2 tablespoons (about 8 leaves) fresh basil
1 tablespoon fresh rosemary
2 tablespoons grape-seed oil
3 tablespoons red wine vinegar
4 tablespoons fresh lemon juice
2 tablespoons gluten-free Dijon mustard
1 tablespoon low-sodium tamari sauce
½ teaspoon black pepper
¼ teaspoon cayenne pepper, for more kick (optional)
16 ounces bison London broil

1. In a small food processor, place garlic, oregano, basil, rosemary, oil, vinegar, lemon juice, mustard, tamari sauce, black pepper, and cayenne pepper, if using. Chop until herbs and garlic are finely minced and blended with liquid.

2. Put London broil in a large Ziploc bag with marinade. Cover meat completely with marinade. Refrigerate for at least 2 hours, up to 24 hours.

3. Preheat oven to broil.

4. Place London broil on broiler tray with pan to catch juices. Broil for about 7 minutes per side for medium-rare, or until meat reaches an internal temperature of 135°F to 140°F.

5. Remove the broil from the oven, transfer to a cutting board, and let stand for a few minutes before slicing across the grain in thin slices.

NOTE: Bison, elk, and other free-range meats are much lower in fat than beef and farm-raised meats. They tend to overcook quickly and should be cooked for less time.

NUTRITIONAL INFORMATION PER SERVING

245 calories ▪ 29.2g protein ▪ 2.2g carbohydrates ▪ 0.2g fiber ▪ 0.2g sugar ▪ 13.3g fat 4.3g saturated fat ▪ 81mg cholesterol ▪ 261mg sodium

Lentil Lamb Stew SERVES 6

2 tablespoons grape-seed oil

12 ounces ground lamb (grass-fed, hormone-free, antibiotic-free, free-range)

½ onion, chopped

2 garlic cloves, chopped

1 carrot, peeled and diced

1 celery stalk, chopped

½ red bell pepper, diced

3 large tomatoes, peeled, seeded, and diced, or one 14-ounce jar low-sodium, diced tomatoes

4 cups no-salt-added vegetable broth

1 cup red lentils

1 teaspoon chopped fresh rosemary

1 teaspoon chopped fresh thyme

1 teaspoon chopped fresh tarragon

½ teaspoon sea salt (optional)

1. Heat oil in a large stockpot over medium heat. Add lamb, onion, garlic, carrot, celery, and red bell pepper. Cook until lamb is lightly browned, about 3 to 4 minutes, stirring regularly.

2. Add tomatoes, vegetable broth, lentils, the herbs, and sea salt, if using. Bring mixture to a boil. Reduce heat and simmer for 30 minutes or until lentils are soft but not mushy.

3. Ladle the stew into bowls and serve hot.

NUTRITIONAL INFORMATION PER SERVING

333 calories ▪ 19.5g protein ▪ 26.3g carbohydrates ▪ 6.6g fiber ▪ 5g sugar ▪ 16.7g fat 5.4g saturated fat ▪ 43.3mg cholesterol ▪ 529mg sodium

Roasted Rack of Lamb SERVES 4

This recipe requires marinating meat for a minimum of 2 hours, up to 24 hours. The longer you marinate the meat, the more tender and flavorful it will be. Be sure to have the butcher trim off as much excess fat as possible. Grass-fed lamb has up to 30 percent less fat than grain-fed lamb.

- 2 tablespoons grape-seed oil, plus 2 teaspoons
- 1 tablespoon fresh rosemary, not chopped
- 1 tablespoon fresh thyme, not chopped, thick stems discarded
- 2 whole fresh sage leaves
- 2 whole garlic cloves
- 1 teaspoon coarsely ground black pepper
- ½ teaspoon sea salt, or to taste (optional)
- 1½-pound rack of lamb (free-range, hormone-free, antibiotic-free)
- 1 tablespoon gluten-free Dijon or brown mustard

1. Place 2 tablespoons of grape-seed oil and the rosemary, thyme, sage, garlic, pepper, and sea salt, if using, in a small food processor. Chop until herbs and garlic are minced to a fine consistency and there are no large pieces.

2. Rub or brush lamb with the oil mixture.

3. Wrap lamb in plastic wrap, eliminating as much air as possible. Place on a small tray and refrigerate for at least 2 hours, up to 24 hours.

4. When you are ready to cook, preheat oven to 400°F. Remove lamb from plastic wrap.

5. Heat 2 teaspoons of grape-seed oil in a small roasting pan with oven-safe handles over medium-high heat. Make sure pan is hot before introducing lamb.

6. Place the lamb in the pan and brown on both sides, 3 to 4 minutes on each side.

7. When lamb is browned, place meaty side up. Brush a thin layer of the mustard over the lamb at this time, if desired. Place pan in oven, on middle rack. Roast for 20 minutes for medium-rare, 22 to 24 minutes for medium-well, or until meat reaches desired doneness. Remove from oven, place on carving tray, and cover with foil for 5 to 10 minutes before serving.

NUTRITIONAL INFORMATION PER SERVING

240 calories ▪ 21.6g protein ▪ 1.1g carbohydrates ▪ 0.3g fiber ▪ 0.0g sugar ▪ 16.1g fat 3.4g saturated fat ▪ 68mg cholesterol ▪ 351mg sodium

Dr. Amen's Quick and Tasty Pork Chops SERVES 4

Here is how Dr. Amen prepares his favorite pork chops. They are delicious and very simple to prepare. But please note, this is not a low-sodium option. Use the recipe below with fresh ingredients and garlic powder instead of garlic salt if you are on a low-sodium diet or prefer a fresh alternative with the same great taste.

    4 pork chops (free-range, hormone-free, antibiotic-free)
    1 teaspoon garlic salt (use garlic powder for a low-sodium option)
    black pepper, to taste
    2 jars S&W Italian-style stewed tomatoes
    2 cups sliced crimini mushrooms

1. Sprinkle both sides of each pork chop with ¼ teaspoon garlic salt. Pepper both sides. Set aside.

2. In a large skillet, heat tomatoes (with juice) and mushrooms for 3 minutes over medium-high heat.

3. Add pork chops to skillet and reduce heat. Cover and cook for 5 to 7 minutes. Turn pork chops and cook for another 5 minutes.

4. Remove from heat when chops are finished cooking and serve smothered in tomato sauce.

NOTE: Pork overcooks very quickly. The chops are usually finished in about 10 minutes, depending on the heat, number, and size of the chops and the skillet. Check the center of one chop to be sure they are finished cooking.

NUTRITIONAL INFORMATION PER SERVING
282 calories ▪ 24.7g protein ▪ 17.3g carbohydrates ▪ 4.1g fiber ▪ 9.3g sugar ▪ 13.4g fat 5.1g saturated fat ▪ 59mg cholesterol ▪ 785mg sodium

[OMNI DESSERTS]

Dessert Smoothie SERVES 2

2 scoops chocolate protein powder (sweetened with stevia)
1 large scoop ice
1 cup cold water
1 cup chocolate unsweetened almond milk
2 tablespoons walnuts or 1 tablespoon coconut butter
1 tablespoon flax seeds

OPTIONAL
½ cup spinach
1 teaspoon acai powder or pomegranate powder
a few drops of chocolate stevia
½ frozen banana

1. Put all ingredients in a high-powered blender, and mix until ice is crushed and mixture is smooth. I prefer this smoothie to be very thick and icy.

2. Pour into glasses and serve.

NOTE: Use water instead of almond milk if you are still trying to lose weight.

NUTRITIONAL INFORMATION PER SERVING
217 calories ▪ 14g protein ▪ 9g carbohydrates ▪ 2g fiber ▪ 2g sugar ▪ 10g fat
0.5g saturated fat ▪ 0.0mg cholesterol ▪ 140mg sodium

Fresh Berries with Macadamia-Nut Sauce SERVES 8

1 cup fresh blueberries
1 cup sliced fresh strawberries
1 cup fresh raspberries
½ cup macadamia nuts
2 tablespoons coconut flakes
½ cup light coconut milk
10 drops vanilla crème–flavored liquid stevia
1 tablespoon raw honey (optional)
¼ cup unsweetened almond milk, for thinning if necessary

1. In a large bowl, gently toss blueberries, strawberries, and raspberries.

2. In a high-powered blender bowl, add macadamia nuts, coconut flakes, coconut milk, stevia, and honey, if using. Blend until smooth and creamy. If sauce is too

thick, add 2 to 4 more tablespoons unsweetened almond milk until sauce reaches desired consistency.

3. Transfer berries to serving bowls and drizzle with nut sauce.

NUTRITIONAL INFORMATION PER SERVING

273 calories ▪ 3g protein ▪ 21g carbohydrates ▪ 6g fiber ▪ 4g sugar ▪ 23g fat
4g saturated fat ▪ 0.0mg cholesterol ▪ 10mg sodium

Fabulous Fruit Fondue   SERVES 16

2 tablespoons raw cacao butter
1 cup raw cacao powder
½ cup unsweetened almond milk
2 tablespoons pure maple syrup
2 tablespoons erythritol
1 dropperful chocolate-flavored liquid stevia
½ teaspoon pure vanilla extract
½ teaspoon cinnamon
8 large strawberries, stems intact
8 pineapple rings
½ peach, sliced into 8 slices
½ apple, sliced into 8 slices

1. Melt cacao butter over low heat in a small saucepan until completely liquefied.

2. Place cacao powder, almond milk, maple syrup, erythritol, stevia, vanilla, and cinnamon in a high-powered blender bowl. Blend until smooth and creamy.

3. Slowly pour contents from the blender to the saucepan and mix with warm cacao butter.

4. Place a piece of wax paper on a cookie sheet.

5. Dip strawberries three-quarters into chocolate sauce, one piece at a time. Hold for a moment and allow to cool. Place upright on the cookie sheet. Dip pineapple rings halfway into the chocolate sauce. Hold for a moment to allow to cool, then place on the cookie sheet. Dip peach and apple slices halfway into the chocolate sauce. Hold for a moment to allow to cool, then place on cookie sheet.

6. Refrigerate for at least 30 minutes before serving.

NOTE: You may substitute all maple syrup for erythritol, or vice versa. Using erythritol reduces the amount of sugar.

NUTRITIONAL INFORMATION PER SERVING

62 calories ▪ 1.2g protein ▪ 11.9g carbohydrates ▪ 2.5g fiber ▪ 2.5g fiber ▪ 6.4g sugar
2.7g fat ▪ 1.5g saturated fat ▪ 0.0mg cholesterol ▪ 15mg sodium

Frozen Bananas SERVES 4

2 slightly green bananas, peeled
4 popsicle sticks
½ cup chocolate sauce (page 381)
¼ cup cashews, finely chopped, or ¼ cup shredded coconut

1. Cover a small tray with wax paper.

2. Cut bananas in half and insert popsicle sticks in the cut end of each banana.

3. Put chocolate sauce in an open, flat saucer so it's easy to dip and roll the bananas.

4. Put nuts or coconut in a similar type of dish.

5. Holding the stick, dip each banana into the chocolate sauce, rolling and coating the entire banana.

6. Immediately dip the bananas in the nuts or coconut, rolling to coat the chocolate with the topping of your choice.

7. Lay coated bananas on wax paper and place tray in the freezer for at least 20 minutes to allow chocolate to set.

NUTRITIONAL INFORMATION PER SERVING

132 calories ▪ 3.1g protein ▪ 21.3g carbohydrates ▪ 3.4g fiber ▪ 9.5g sugar ▪ 6g fat
2.3g saturated fat ▪ 0.0mg cholesterol ▪ 12mg sodium

Magnificent Cacao "Nut" Macaroons SERVES 16

Besides being beyond delicious, these get my seal of approval because they are a raw, living food. They also contain maca root powder. Touted as the "superfood of the Andes," the maca root contains almost sixty phytonutrients. These macaroons taste great when drizzled with a touch of the macadamia-nut sauce on pages 380–381.

1 cup coconut flakes, unsweetened
1 tablespoon raw cacao powder
⅓ cup finely chopped pecans
⅓ cup dried blueberries or mulberries, unsweetened
2 tablespoons chocolate-flavored pea protein powder (sweetened with stevia)
2 tablespoons honey
2 tablespoons erythritol or xylitol
1 tablespoon hemp seeds
1 teaspoon cinnamon
1 teaspoon vanilla extract
1 tablespoon maca root powder
¼ teaspoon salt
⅓ cup coconut butter
1 tablespoon coconut oil

1. In a medium bowl, mix coconut flakes with cacao powder until all the coconut is dusted with brown powder.

2. Place pecans and blueberries into a food processor and pulse several times until the mixture becomes finely chopped and sticky.

3. Add coconut and cacao powder, protein powder, honey, erythritol, hemp seeds, cinnamon, vanilla, maca root powder, salt, coconut butter, and coconut oil. Blend until mixture holds together when pressed.

4. To shape the macaroons, use your hands to form the batter into round balls, about ½ tablespoon at a time. Leave in round balls or press flat like cookies. Refrigerate for 15 to 20 minutes.

NUTRITIONAL INFORMATION PER SERVING
132.5 calories ▪ 6g protein ▪ 16g carbohydrates ▪ 5g fiber ▪ 7.2g sugar ▪ 13g fat
9g saturated fat ▪ 0.0mg cholesterol ▪ 66mg sodium

Goji Nut Truffles SERVES 16

These simple, raw treats are one of my favorites. Loaded with super-foods and antioxidants, they are intended to be a tasty morsel. A little dollop will do!

¼ cup goji powder
¼ cup vegan vanilla-flavored protein powder (sweetened with stevia)
½ cup raw macadamia nuts
2 tablespoons cacao butter, melted
¼ cup raw honey
5 to 10 drops chocolate-flavored liquid stevia
¼ cup raw cacao nibs
¼ cup whole goji berries
zest from 1 orange (optional)
½ cup shredded coconut

1. Place goji powder, protein powder, and macadamia nuts into a food processor. Pulse several times until blended.

2. While ingredients are blending, slowly add melted cacao butter, honey, and stevia in a steady stream. Be sure not to dump all the liquid at once into the dry mixture. Blend until mixture is smooth and creamy. Transfer mixture to a medium bowl.

3. By hand, blend in cacao nibs, goji berries, and orange zest, if using. Mix thoroughly.

4. Form into teaspoon-size balls and roll in shredded coconut.

5. Place on a cookie sheet. Mixture should yield 16 truffles. Refrigerate for 1 hour.

NUTRITIONAL INFORMATION PER SERVING
64 calories ▪ 7g protein ▪ 10g carbohydrates ▪ 2g fiber ▪ 5.9g sugar ▪ 7g fat
3g saturated fat ▪ 0.0mg cholesterol ▪ 78mg sodium

Mulberry Balls SERVES 24

¼ cup cacao butter

½ cup raw cashews

½ cup dried mulberries

½ cup shelled hemp seeds

½ cup coconut butter

2 tablespoons maca powder

2 tablespoons lucuma powder

1 teaspoon cinnamon

½ teaspoon nutmeg

1 teaspoon pure vanilla extract

2 tablespoons erythritol

2 tablespoons pure maple syrup or raw, unfiltered honey

¼ cup cacao nibs

½ cup raw coconut flakes

1. In a small saucepan, melt cacao butter over low heat.

2. Place next 10 ingredients in a food processor bowl. Pulse ingredients while adding melted cacao butter and maple syrup (or honey) in a steady stream. Do not add liquid all at once, and do not overprocess the mixture or it will become mushy and the natural nut oils will separate.

3. Remove mixture from food processor and place in a large mixing bowl. Add cacao nibs and blend in well.

4. Place shredded coconut in a separate bowl.

5. Form mixture into balls and roll in the shredded coconut until the ball is completely coated with coconut.

6. Place on a tray and refrigerate for 20 minutes before serving.

NOTE: Raw, unfiltered honey is not appropriate for children under two years of age. Use pasteurized honey in recipes that will be fed to children under two.

NUTRITIONAL INFORMATION PER SERVING

124 calories ▪ 2.4g protein ▪ 8.3g carbohydrates ▪ 1.9g fiber ▪ 4.8g sugar ▪ 9.6g fat 5.3g saturated fat ▪ 0.0mg cholesterol ▪ 5mg sodium

Avocado Gelato Squares SERVES 12

Avocado gelato? Yes, it may sound a bit weird, but I haven't met a kid yet who doesn't *love* it. Avocado gelato is a lower-sugar, lighter-calorie adaptation of a recipe from my friend Jenny Ross, who owns the raw-food restaurant 118 Degrees. Raw, live, and luscious!

3 avocados
¼ cup coconut butter
¼ cup honey
3 tablespoons sugar-free chocolate protein powder (vegan)
2 tablespoons raw cacao powder
½ cup almond milk, unsweetened
1 dropperful chocolate-flavored liquid stevia
3 tablespoons coconut flakes, unsweetened

1. In a blender, mix all the ingredients except coconut flakes. Blend until creamy and smooth. Mixture should be very thick.

2. Either smooth entire contents into a cake pan or drop the batter in tablespoon-size round balls (like cookies, but a little thinner) onto a cookie sheet. Note that it is easier to spread the mixture into a cake pan, but it is a little more challenging to cut it after it has been frozen. Dropping batter onto a cookie sheet can be a little messy, but then it is easier to grab and eat after freezing. Try it both ways and see how you like it.

3. Sprinkle coconut over the top.

4. Place cake pan or cookie sheet in freezer for at least 2 hours until frozen.

5. Serve as a frozen treat. They taste like Fudgesicles.

NUTRITIONAL INFORMATION PER SERVING

162 calories ▪ 6g protein ▪ 14g carbohydrates ▪ 4g fiber ▪ 5.7g sugar ▪ 11g fat
4g saturated fat ▪ 0.0mg cholesterol ▪ 23mg sodium

Chocolate Coconut Ice Cream   SERVES 8

2 cups pine nuts
1 cup coconut water
¼ cup coconut butter
2 tablespoons pure maple syrup
2 tablespoons xylitol
¼ cup raw cacao powder
¼ teaspoon pure vanilla extract
½ teaspoon cinnamon
½ cup raw shredded coconut

OPTIONAL
10 drops chocolate-flavored liquid stevia

1. Put all ingredients except shredded coconut in a high-powered blender bowl.

2. Start blender on low and gradually increase speed. Use spatula to mix.

3. Blend until mixture is creamy and smooth. It should be very thick.

4. Scoop mixture into a bowl.

5. Stir shredded coconut into mixture.

6. Cover and freeze for several hours. Serve cold.

NUTRITIONAL INFORMATION PER SERVING

324 calories ▪ 5.9g protein ▪ 14.8g carbohydrates ▪ 4g fiber ▪ 5.3g sugar ▪ 30.1g fat
7.7g saturated fat ▪ 0.0mg cholesterol ▪ 37mg sodium

Omni Apple Cobbler Squares SERVES 16

I like to use red apples for this recipe, or a combination of red and green. Red apples are sweeter.

CRUST INGREDIENTS
¾ cup almond flour
¾ cup all-purpose gluten-free flour
8 dates
4 teaspoons coconut oil

FILLING INGREDIENTS
7 apples
½ cup erythritol
1 teaspoon cinnamon
½ teaspoon nutmeg
¼ teaspoon ginger

CRUMBLE TOPPING INGREDIENTS
¼ cup pecans or walnuts
¼ cup almond flour
2 tablespoons unsweetened almond butter
6 dates

PREPARATION FOR CRUST

1. Preheat oven to 350°F. Coat 9x9-inch glass baking dish with a light coat of coconut oil.

2. In a food processor mix flour, dates, and coconut oil until the mixture is pasty and holds together.

3. Press into pan with fingers, halfway up the sides. Crust should be thin.

4. Bake for 10 to 15 minutes until light golden brown.

PREPARATION FOR FILLING

1. Meanwhile, prepare the filling. Peel and chop apples. Try using the "slicer" attachment on a food processor as a shortcut.

2. Place apples in a medium pan over medium heat. Apples will release fluid and begin to dehydrate. Add erythritol, cinnamon, nutmeg, and ginger. Cook until the apples are hot and soft, about 15 minutes. Don't allow apples to dry out and burn.

3. Remove the apples from heat and pour into the pie crust.

ASSEMBLING COBBLER

1. Mix all topping ingredients in food processor until well blended and chunky.

2. Remove crumble topping from food processor and use hands to sprinkle on top of the apples in the pie crust.

3. Bake the pie for 15 minutes.

NUTRITIONAL INFORMATION PER SERVING

158 calories ▪ 2.8g protein ▪ 15g carbohydrates ▪ 3.8g fiber ▪ 8g sugar ▪ 7g fat
2g saturated fat ▪ 0.0mg cholesterol ▪ 0.0mg sodium

[ACKNOWLEDGMENTS]

IT IS WITH RESPECT AND gratitude that I would like to thank my team for their amazing dedication, hard work, and perseverance in assisting me in completing *The Omni Diet.* I'd like to recognize the following people, who were an integral part of this journey:

My amazing husband, partner, and mentor, Daniel Amen, who offers love and support in all that I do.

Rick Warren, pastor of Saddleback Church, and the participants of the Daniel Plan. Being welcomed as a coach for the Daniel Plan has been an honor and a gift.

Celeste Fine, my agent—and a true rock star!

My assistant and best friend, Jeana Maiocchi, for her loyalty, hard work, and ability to keep up with me.

My professional mentor, Bernie Landes.

Alice Lesch Kelly, for her exceptional writing and organizational skills.

Nichole Argyres, for her dedication in the editing process. Your attention to detail is invaluable.

The team at the Amen Clinics: David Jahr, Ryan Green, Kirsten Iverson, Murray Brennan, Mark Walters, Corey Liebig, Justin Wong, and Brent Ferguson. Your support and effort are a valued part of this process.

Jim Kennedy, my longtime photographer. Your professionalism and skill make you a joy to work with.

My beautiful daughter, Chloe, for inspiring me to leave a legacy of health.

My gorgeous mother, who is a living example that being healthy, beautiful, and sexy into the sixties is possible. You give new meaning to "the golden years."

Robert Sturm, my friend, partner in the Daniel Plan, and chef extraordinaire. Your taste in food is impeccable.

The entire Daniel Plan team: the doctors, Dee Eastman, Jenny Ross, Sally Cameron, and Tony Lattimore. It has been a true honor working with all of you. Through love, dedication, and perseverance you are changing the world!

THE OMNI FAMILY GUIDE: TIPS FOR KIDS

MY HUSBAND AND I GOT USED TO the snickers and smiles we'd get from people when they'd see our daughter, Chloe, eating salmon and avocado at age three. We've long been accustomed to hearing comments from other parents when they see her snacking on red bell peppers and hummus in the airport. Most often, these parents just want to know how we got our strong-willed child to eat anything other than chicken nuggets, pizza, and French fries. But for us, fast food has never been an option. When she was really little, we didn't provide food for her that we didn't want her to have. As a result, she never developed a taste for it or a tendency to reach for it!

Of course, Chloe doesn't live in a bubble—nor do we want her to. She's a normal kid who loves the same things all kids love. If I had cake and ice cream in the house all the time, she'd be eating it regularly in a matter of weeks. But because I don't have unhealthy food in the house and I have fresh fruit and vegetables instead, Chloe has learned to enjoy this way of eating. Psychologists call this the *mere exposure effect:* Human beings just prefer the familiar!

It's easier to make these healthy choices familiar when your children or grandchildren are little and you're still in control of the shopping and the menus at home. If you have older children and you're just beginning to encourage healthy eating, it's a bit more challenging. But here are two steps to put your children—no matter their age—on the path to a life of healthy eating.

STEP 1: STOCK YOUR HOUSE WITH HEALTHY FOODS

IT'S NOT AS HARD AS it sounds. Here are some tips to get you started.

LEAD BY EXAMPLE
IF YOU HAVE FRENCH FRIES, don't expect your kids to crave kale chips. Try some healthy new foods yourself, and share your discoveries—and your enthusiasm—with your children.

DECLARE A "NO JUNK FOOD" ZONE

IF IT'S NOT IN THE house, you—and your kids—can't eat it. Leave the cookies and potato chips at the store. Instead, bring home whole, natural foods like apples, berries, and carrots.

MAKE NEW (FOOD) FRIENDS, BUT KEEP THE OLD

QUICKLY ELIMINATE THE WORST THINGS your kids eat—fast foods and sugary snacks and drinks—then slowly eliminate other less-than-ideal foods. Work toward replacing these foods with more wholesome choices, such as fruit, salads, soups, smoothies, and "raw" homemade desserts.

VEGGIE MAGIC!

USE THESE TIPS TO HELP your kids develop a love for fresh, seasonal vegetables—or sneak them into their meals so they won't even notice they're eating them! Either way, you'll be boosting your children's nutrition and broadening their repertoire of delicious foods.

- Add greens such as spinach to fruit smoothies. They'll never even notice!
- Combine greens with another vegetable that your children like. Most kids like corn, for example—so try adding some sautéed zucchini and some diced tomato.
- Make cauliflower mashed potatoes. Just cook a head of cauliflower until it's soft, then mash, adding a bit of chicken stock or other liquid for creaminess.
- Make "creamed spinach" with almond milk.
- Add small amounts of veggies to some of their favorite foods—they'll never notice the finely diced carrot in meatloaf, for example.
- Cook veggies for longer than you normally would to soften them up.
- Be creative with spices and herbs. Try sprinkling some cinnamon on your kids' oatmeal or waffles, or add some freshly chopped parsley to their scrambled eggs.
- Use raw almond butter on celery sticks and red bell peppers.

STEP 2: HELP YOUR KIDS LIVE A HEALTHY LIFE

REMEMBER, IT'S NOT JUST THE food—it's all the lifestyle choices that make us and our kids fit and healthy (or not). Some habits, like serving meals in front of the TV, can lead to higher cholesterol levels even in preschoolers, potentially putting them at risk for cardiovascular disease as adults, according to a new study. Researchers from the University of Toronto analyzed the eating behaviors and lipid (blood fat) levels of 1,076 kids, ages three to five, and found that the less healthy the youngsters' eating habits were, the higher their levels of bad cholesterol were.[1]

"Our results show that associations between eating behaviors and cardiovascular risk appear early in life and may be a potential target for early intervention," says Dr. Navindra Persaud, a family physician and one of the study's lead researchers.[2]

Parental questionnaires were used to evaluate the preschoolers' eating behaviors, with scores based on the number of meals consumed daily, whether kids were allowed to decide how much to eat, whether or not frequent drinking left them with a poor appetite at mealtimes, and whether they had any trouble with gagging or swallowing food.

Each kid's height, weight, and BMI were checked, and they were given an assessment by a dietician that included their nutritional history and a three-day recall of foods consumed. The study also looked at each parent's level of concern about their kid's eating patterns. After crunching the numbers, the researchers found that preschoolers with the highest cholesterol typically had problematic behaviors that parents can easily modify—reducing their risk for future heart problems. Avoiding these three common mistakes can also help prevent childhood obesity and enhance your child's overall wellness.

MISTAKE #1: EATING IN FRONT OF A SCREEN

DISTRACTED EATING IS UNHEALTHY FOR both kids *and* adults, since it leads to mindless overeating and is a frequent contributor to weight gain. Recent research at the University of Liverpool in the United Kingdom found that distracted eating can cause people to eat up to 50 percent more calories during a meal or snack, compared to attentive eating.[3]

The healthy solution: Avoid eating in "zombie mode." Designate a specific place in your home—such as the dining room or kitchen—where you and your kids eat all meals and snacks *without* any form of screen-based entertainment. Instead, focus on enjoying tasty, wholesome food and family conversation. The simple act of sitting down together for family meals can have many remarkable health benefits—if the TV is turned off.

MISTAKE #2: GIVING KIDS SWEET DRINKS

NOT ONLY DO SUGARY BEVERAGES leave kids too full to eat the nutritious foods they need for optimal growth and health, but many experts also consider these drinks to be the leading culprit in the childhood obesity epidemic. Also known as "liquid candy," sugar-laden beverages are also dangerous, or even lethal, for adults, with a recent study linking sweet drinks to more than 180,000 deaths around the world from heart disease, diabetes, and certain cancers.[4]

The healthy solution: The simplest—and most sure—way to protect kids from the many hazards of sugary drinks is to keep these beverages out of your home. And soda pop isn't the only dietary villain. Also watch out for drinks that have an undeserved "health halo" but which are actually loaded with liquid calories, such as vitamin water, sports drinks, and fruit juice. Encourage your kids to just drink water.

MISTAKE #3: FOOD POLICING

UP TO 66 PERCENT OF parents pressure their kids to clean their plates, even if their kids are overweight or obese, according to a study from the University of Minnesota.[5] And it's even common for parents to try to control how much teenagers eat, while younger kids may be even more likely to be pushed to finish meals after they say they're full.

The healthy solution: Instead of teaching kids to rely on external cues, such as the time of day or how much food is on their plate, encourage them to listen to their bodies and their own appetites. My husband and I are comfortable with our daughter, Chloe, missing an occasional meal if she refuses to eat what's on her plate. We just remind her that there's an abundance of delicious, wholesome food available for her in our home. When she's hungry, she'll eat. Stocking your pantry and fridge with the foods I recommend in the Omni Diet means that every dietary choice you and your kids make will be a healthy one.

[FOOD AND SUPPLEMENT SOURCES]

MANY OF THE FOOD SUGGESTIONS in the book can be found online at the following websites and/or in stores. I often find it more cost-effective to purchase these foods online. Purchasing in bulk, and splitting the investment with a friend, is an economical way to shop for specialty items.

Get familiar with your local health food store, and chain stores such as Whole Foods and Trader Joe's, where many of these items can be found. Traditional grocery stores are good sources for certain foods and staples, but they often don't carry specialty items that are non-GMO and preservative-free. Many of these products can be found online, and Amazon.com carries almost everything.

Some of these suggestions may feel like luxury items, but they are nutritious and delicious alternatives to chemical-filled foods. Make the switch when you can and make the healthiest choice possible when you can't.

BEEF, POULTRY, AND EGGS—FREE-RANGE, HORMONE-FREE, ANTIBIOTIC-FREE

The Buffalo Guys: www.thebuffaloguys.com

Eat Wild: www.eatwild.com

Florida Fresh Meat Company: www.floridafreshbeef.com

Hanover Dexter Cattle Company: www.coloradodexters.com

Homestead Natural Foods: www.homesteadnatural.com

Lazy 69 Ranch: www.lazy69ranch.com

Lindner Bison: www.lindnerbison.com

TX Bar Organics: www.txbarorganics.com

SNACKS

Flax Snax by Go Raw: goraw.com

Green Wala Marketplace for snacks and chocolate

Kale Krunch by Alive & Radiant

Steve's Original for grain-free granola bars and grass-fed beef jerky: www.stevesoriginal.com

Wild Mountain Raw Foods for crackers, chips, and snacks: www.wildmountainrawfoods.com

SPECIALTY PRODUCTS

Acai berries: Whole Foods, local health food stores, some grocery stores

Almond meal: Whole Foods, local health food stores, some grocery stores

Almond milk: most grocery stores

Aloe gel: Whole Foods, local health food stores

Bee pollen: Whole Foods, local health food stores

Bragg's Liquid Aminos: Whole Foods and local health food stores, www. bragg.com

Brain on Joy coconut bars: Amen Clinics Store, www.store.amenclinics.com

Cacao (cocoa), raw: Whole Foods, local health food stores

Cacao nibs: Whole Foods, local health food stores

Camu camu powder, raw: Whole Foods, local health food stores

Chia seeds: Whole Foods, local health food stores

Coconut butter: Whole Foods, local health food stores

Coconut milk: Whole Foods, local health food stores, most grocery stores

Coconut milk creamer: most grocery stores

Coconut oil: Whole Foods, local health food stores, most grocery stores

Coconut powder: Whole Foods, local health food stores

Coconut wraps by Pure Wrap: www.improveat.com

Earth Balance soy-free buttery spread: Whole Foods, local health food stores

Erythritol: Whole Foods, local health food stores, and online

Fenugreek: Whole Foods, health food stores, some grocery stores

Fiber: NOW Foods has a variety of blends and kinds of fiber, and is an easy-to-find brand at Whole Foods and local health food stores

Fish oil: Whole Foods, health food stores

Flaxseed meal: Whole Foods, local health food stores, some grocery stores

Goji powder: Whole Foods, local health food stores

Grape-seed oil: any grocery store

Hemp milk (unsweetened): Whole Foods, local health food stores

Hemp seeds: Whole Foods, local health food stores

Lucuma: Whole Foods, local health food stores

Maca powder: Whole Foods, local health food stores

Macadamia-nut oil: my favorite source is Vital Choice, www.vitalchoice.com; also Whole Foods and local health food stores

Noni juice: health food stores and online

Nut butters, almond and cashew: Whole Foods, local health food stores, some grocery stores

Pea protein powder: Olympian Labs at www.vitacost.com

Powdered greens, also called freeze-dried greens: Green Vibrance is my favorite brand, and you can find it online at www.naturalhealthyconcepts.com or at Whole Foods

Real Salt: Whole Foods, local health food stores, online

Salt Substitute (potassium chloride): any grocery store, Whole Foods, local health food stores

Sea buckthorn oil, raw: Whole Foods, local health food stores, online

Sea buckthorn powder, raw: Whole Foods, local health food stores, online

Shirataki noodles by Miracle Noodle (soy free): www.miraclenoodle.com, specialty grocers, and Amazon.com

Stevia extract: Whole Foods, local health food stores, online

Stevia leaf: Whole Foods, local health food stores, online

Tamari sauce: Whole Foods, local health food stores, online, many grocery stores

Vegenaise: www.followyourheart.com/products, Whole Foods, and local health food stores

Wheat grass: Whole Foods, local health stores

Wheat grass juice: Whole Foods, local health stores

Xylitol: Whole Foods, local health food stores, and Amazon.com

Zevia (soda made with stevia): Whole Foods, local health food stores, and Amazon.com

SPECIALTY STORES

My Natural Market, www.mynaturalmarket.com: super-foods such as cacao, camu camu, goji, pomegranate, maca root, and more

Vital Choice: www.vitalchoice.com for wild fish (steaks and canned), chocolate, macadamia-nut oil, nuts

Erythritol: Whole Foods, local health food stores, and Amazon.com

Stevia: Amazon.com

Xylitol: Whole Foods, local health food stores, and Amazon.com

SUPPLEMENTS

The Amen Clinics Store, www.store.amenclinics.com/: multivitamins, fish oil, vitamin D, Craving Control, Focus and Energy, Brain and Memory Boost, Restful Sleep, Mediclear Plus protein powder

Dr. Ohhira Probiotics, www.drohhiraprobiotics.com: probiotics

Mediclear Plus medical-grade protein powder with super-foods, probiotics, and digestive enzymes, by Thorne, www.store.amenclinics.com/

LaValle Metabolic Institute, www.lmihealthstore.com: herbal remedies, naturopathic alternatives, dried greens

THE AMEN SOLUTION SUPPLEMENTS

When my husband saw that his patients had so much trouble making choices about supplements, he decided to take matters into his own hands and develop a line of Amen Clinics supplements. He spent over a decade developing these top-quality, research-based supplements. We feel good recommending them to patients, friends, and family because we know they are safe, effective, and made with the best possible ingredients. We also have qualified experts available to help people make informed choices and eliminate guesswork.

The Amen Solution: "NeuroVite Plus"

NeuroVite Plus is the multivitamin we make at the Amen Clinics. It contains a complete range of brain-healthy nutrients. Four capsules a day is the full dose and it contains the following:

- Vitamin A and high levels of Bs, plus vitamins C, D (2,000 IUs), E, and K

- Minerals: zinc, copper, magnesium, selenium, chromium, manganese, calcium, and magnesium

- Brain nutrients: alpha lipoic acid, acetyl-L-carnitine, and phosphatidyl-serine

- Equivalent nutrients to a full dose of a stabilized probiotic; one apple (quercitin); one tomato (lycopene); one serving of fresh spinach (lutein); one serving of broccoli (broccoli seed concentrate); two liters of red wine (resveratrol, without the alcohol); a cup of blueberries (pterostilbene)

The Amen Solution: "Omega 3 Power"

Omega 3 Power is our brand to support healthy brain and heart function by providing highly purified omega-3 fatty acids (EPA and DHA) from the most advanced production, detoxification, and purification process in the industry. It is produced under the natural industry's most rigorous standards. Each batch of our oil is independent third-party lab analyzed by Eurofins for 250+ environmental contaminants, including PCBs. And it exceeds all other domestic and international regulatory standards. Two softgels contain 2.8 grams of fish oil, and 860 milligrams of EPA and 580 milligrams of DHA.

The Amen Solution: "Brain and Memory Power Boost"

This is the supplement formulated to help in our brain enhancement work with active and retired NFL players. When used in conjunction with a brain health program, we demonstrated significant improvement in memory, reasoning, attention, processing speed, and accuracy. It was so effective that I take it every day.

Brain and Memory Power Boost includes the super-antioxidant N-acetyl-cysteine, along with phosphatidylserine to maintain the integrity of cell membranes, huperzine A and acetyl-L-carnitine to enhance acetylcholine availability, and vinpocetine and ginkgo biloba to enhance blood flow. This is a novel combination of powerful antioxidants and nutrients essential in enhancing and protecting brain health. It supports overall brain health, circulation, memory, and concentration.

The Amen Solution: "Craving Control"

The key to successful weight management is eating a brain-healthy diet and managing your cravings. In support of this goal, Craving Control was developed. It is a powerful new nutritional supplement formulated to support healthy blood sugar and insulin levels while providing antioxidants and nutrients to the body. Our formulation includes N-acetyl-cysteine and glutamine to reduce cravings, chromium and alpha lipoic acid to support stable blood sugar levels, and a brain-healthy chocolate and DL-phenylalanine designed to boost endorphins.

The Amen Solution: "SAMe Mood and Movement Support"

Research suggests that SAMe helps support comfortable movement and control pain. It has been shown to support healthy joints and decrease pain. And as an added bonus, SAMe supports mood through its involvement in the creation of key neurotransmitters (serotonin, dopamine, and norepinephrine).

The typical dose is anywhere from 400 mg to 800 mg twice a day. It is usually better to take earlier in the day, as it can be energizing. Research suggests you should be cautious with SAMe if you have bipolar disorder.

The Amen Solution: "Serotonin Mood Support"

Serotonin Mood Support promotes normal serotonin levels by providing 5-HTP, a direct precursor to serotonin, along with a proprietary extract of saffron, shown clinically to support a normal mood. Vitamin B6 and inositol are included to provide additional synergistic support. Serotonin Mood Support is especially effective when serotonin levels are suspected to be low, and is helpful for people who tend to get stuck on negative thoughts or negative behaviors. It has also been shown to help support healthy sleep patterns.

The Amen Solution: "Focus and Energy Optimizer"

Formulated without caffeine, Focus and Energy Optimizer supports both focus and healthy energy levels. It is formulated with green tea and choline to help with focus, along with three powerful adaptogens that act synergistically to enhance endurance and stamina. The adaptogens ashwagandha, rhodiola, and panax ginseng have been scientifically shown to improve the body's resistance to stress and support a healthy immune system.

The Amen Solution: "GABA Calming Support"

GABA Calming Support promotes natural relaxation and calm by providing a combination of inhibitory neurotransmitters vital to quieting an overactive mind. It contains clinically tested and natural PharmaGABA shown to promote relaxation by increasing calming, focused brain waves, while also reducing other brain waves associated with worry. Complementing this clinically tested and natural substance are vitamin B6, magnesium, and lemon balm, an herb traditionally known for its calming effects.

[REFERENCES]

Chapter 1

Albert, C. M., et al. "Blood Levels of Long-Chain n-3 Fatty Acids and the Risk of Sudden Death," *New England Journal of Medicine* 346, no. 15 (April 11, 2002): 1113–18.

Amen, D. G., et al. "Reversing Brain Damage in Former NFL Players: Implications for Traumatic Brain Injury and Substance Abuse Rehabilitation," *Journal of Psychoactive Drugs* 43, no. 1 (January–March 2011): 1–5.

Barnes, P. J., and M. Karin. "Nuclear Factor-KappaB: A Pivotal Transcription Factor in Chronic Inflammatory Diseases," *New England Journal of Medicine* 336, no. 15 (April 10, 1997): 1066–71.

Berlett, B. S., and E. R. Stadtman. "Protein Oxidation in Aging, Disease, and Oxidative Stress," *Journal of Biological Chemistry* 272, no. 33 (1997): 20313–16.

Chandra, R. K. "Nutrition and the Immune System: An Introduction," *American Journal of Clinical Nutrition* 66, no. 2 (August 1997): 460S–463S.

Cinti, S. "The Adipose Organ," *Prostaglandins, Leukotrienes and Essential Fatty Acids* 73, no. 1 (July 2005): 9–15.

Collins, A. R., et al. "DNA Damage in Diabetes: Correlation with a Clinical Marker," *Free Radical Biology & Medicine* 25, no. 3 (1998): 373–77.

Freudenheim, J. L. "Study Design and Hypothesis Testing: Issues in the Evaluation of Evidence from Research in Nutritional Epidemiology," *American Journal of Clinical Nutrition* 69, no. 6 (June 1999): 1315S-1321S.

Gao, X., et al. "Immunomodulatory Activity of Resveratrol: Suppression of Lymphocyte Proliferation, Development of Cell-Mediated Cytotoxicity, and Cytokine Production," *Biochemical Pharmacology* 62, no. 9 (November 1, 2001): 1299–1308.

Gohil, K., "Functional Genomics Identifies Novel and Diverse Molecular Targets of Nutrients in Vivo," *Biological Chemistry* 385, no. 8 (August 2004): 691–96.

Goodarzi, M. T., et al. "Oxidative Damage to DNA and Lipids: Correlation with Protein Glycation in Patients with Type 1 Diabetes," *Journal of Clinical Laboratory Analysis* 24, no. 2 (2010): 72–76.

Halliwell, B. "Free Radicals, Antioxidants, and Human Disease: Curiosity, Cause, or Consequence?" *The Lancet* 344, no. 8924 (1994): 721–24.

Hewagama, A., and B. Richardson, "The Genetics and Epigenetics of Autoimmune Diseases," *Journal of Autoimmunology* 33, no. 1 (August 2009): 3–11.

Hruda, J., V. Sramek, and X. Leverve. "High Glucose Increases Susceptibility to Oxidative-Stress-Induced Apoptosis and DNA Damage in K-562 Cells," *Biomedical Papers of the Medical Faculty of the University of Palacky Olomouc Czech Republic* 154, no. 4 (December 2010): 315–20.

Joshipura, K. J., et al. "Fruit and Vegetable Intake in Relation to Risk of Ischemic Stroke," *Journal of the American Medical Association* 282, no. 13 (1999): 1233–39.

Kern, P. A., et al. "Adipose Tissue Tumor Necrosis Factor and Interleukin-6 Expression in Human Obesity and Insulin Resistance," *American Journal of Physiology Endocrinology and Metabolism* 280, no. 5 (May 2001): E745–51.

Kershaw, E. E., and J. S. Flier. "Adipose Tissue as an Endocrine Organ," *Journal of Clinical Endocrinology and Metabolism* 89, no. 6 (June 2004): 2548–56.

Khan, S., and J. Rupp. "The Effect of Exercise Conditioning, Diet, and Drug Therapy on Glycosylated Hemoglobin Levels in Type 2 (NIDDM) Diabetics," *Journal of Sports Medicine and Physical Fitness* 35, no. 4 (December 1995): 281–88.

Liu, S. et al. "Fruit and Vegetable Intake and the Risk of Cardiovascular Disease: The Women's Health Study," *American Journal of Clinical Nutrition* 72 (October 2000): 922–28.

Marette, A. "Molecular Mechanisms of Inflammation in Obesity-Linked Insulin Resistance," *International Journal of Obesity and Related Metabolic Disorders* 27, sup. 3 (December 2003): S46–48.

Pessi, T., et al. "Interleukin-10 Generation in Atopic Children Following Oral *Lactobacillus rhamnosus* GG," *Clinical and Experimental Allergy* 30, no. 12 (December 2000): 1804–8.

Pradhan, A. D., et al. "C-Reactive Protein, Interleukin 6, and Risk of Developing Type 2 Diabetes Mellitus, *Journal of the American Medical Association* 268, no. 3 (July 18, 2001): 327–34.

Shacter, E., and S. A. Weitzman. "Chronic Inflammation and Cancer," *Oncology (Williston Park)* 16, no. 2 (February 2002): 217–26, 229; discussion, 230–32.

Sreelekha, T. T., et al. "Immunomodulatory Effects of a Polysaccharide from *Tamarindus indica*," *Anticancer Drugs* 4, no. 2 (April 1993): 209–12.

Vitetta, L., and B. Anton. "Lifestyle and Nutrition, Caloric Restriction, Mitochondrial Health and Hormones: Scientific Interventions for Anti-Aging," *Clinical Interventions in Aging* 2, no. 4 (December 2007): 537–43.

Yang, F., et al. "The Green Tea Polyphenol (-)-Epigallocatechin-3-Gallate Blocks Nuclear Factor-Kappa B Activation by Inhibiting I Kappa B Kinase Activity in the Intestinal Epithelial Cell Line IEC-6," *Molecular Pharmacology* 60, no. 3 (September 2001): 528–33.

Chapter 2

Adams, P. B., et al. "Arachidonic Acid to Eicosapentaenoic Acid Ratio in Blood Correlates Positively with Clinical Symptoms of Depression," *Lipids* 31, sup. (March 1996): S157–61.

Albert, C. M., et al. "Blood Levels of Long-Chain n-3 Fatty Acids and the Risk of Sudden Death," *New England Journal of Medicine* 346, no. 15 (April 2002): 1113–18.

Amen, D. G., et al. "Reversing Brain Damage in Former NFL Players: Implications for Traumatic Brain Injury and Substance Abuse Rehabilitation," *Journal of Psychoactive Drugs* 43, no. 1 (January–March 2011): 1–5.

Appel, L. J. "The Role of Diet in the Prevention and Treatment of Hypertension," *Current Atherosclerosis Reports* 1, no. 6 (November 2000): 521–28.

Cordain, L., et al. "Plant-Animal Subsistence Ratios and Macronutrient Energy Estimations in Worldwide Hunter-Gatherer Diets," *American Journal of Clinical Nutrition* 71, no. 3 (2000): 682–92.

Couet, C., et al. "Effect of Dietary Fish Oil on Body Fat Mass and Basal Fat Oxidation in Healthy Adults," *International Journal of Obesity* 21 (1997): 637–43.

de Leeuw, J. A., A. W. Jongbloed, and M. W. Verstegen. "Dietary Fiber Stabilizes Blood Glucose and Insulin Levels and Reduces Physical Activity in Sows (Sus scrofa)," *Journal of Nutrition* 134, no. 6 (June 2004): 1481–86.

Ebbeling, C. B., et al. "Effects of a Low-Glycemic Load vs Low-Fat Diet in Obese Young Adults: A Randomized Trial," *Journal of the American Medical Association* 297, no. 19 (May 16, 2007): 2092–2102.

Freed, D. L. J. "Do Dietary Lectins Cause Disease?" *British Medical Journal* 318, no. 7190 (April 17, 1999): 1023–24.

Halton, T. L., et al. "Low-Carbohydrate-Diet Score and the Risk of Coronary Heart Disease in Women," *New England Journal of Medicine* 355, no. 19 (November 9, 2006): 1991–2002.

Hasler, C. M., S. Kundrat, and D. Wool. "Functional Foods and Cardiovascular Disease," *Current Atherosclerosis Reports* 2, no. 6 (November 2000): 467–75.

He, J., and P. K. Whelton. "Effect of Dietary Fiber and Protein Intake on Blood Pressure: A Review of Epidemiologic Evidence," *Clinical and Experimental Hypertension* 21, nos. 5–6 (July–August 1999): 785–96.

Hite, A. H., V. G. Berkowitz, and K. Berkowitz. "Low-Carbohydrate Diet Review: Shifting the Paradigm," *Nutrition in Clinical Practice* 26, no. 3 (June 2011): 300–308.

Horrocks, L. A., and Y. K. Yeo. "Health Benefits of Docosahexanoic Acid (DHA)," *Pharmacological Research* 40, no. 3 (September 1999): 211–25.

Houston, M. C. "The Role of Cellular Micronutrient Analysis, Nutraceuticals, Vitamins, Antioxidants and Minerals in the Prevention and Treatment of Hypertension and Cardiovascular Disease," *Therapeutic Advances in Cardiovascular Disease* 4, no. 3 (June 2010): 165–83.

Houston, M. C., et al. "Nonpharmacologic Treatment of Dyslipidemia," *Progress in Cardiovascular Diseases* 52, no. 2 (September 2009): 61–94.

Howe, G. R., et al. "Dietary Intake of Fiber and Decreased Risk of Cancers of the Colon and Rectum: Evidence from the Combined Analysis of 13 Case-Control Studies," *Journal of the National Cancer Institute* 84, no. 24 (December 16, 1992): 1887–96.

Howes, J., and P. J. Houghton. "Ethnobotanical Treatment Strategies against Alzheimer's Disease," *Current Alzheimer Research* 9, no. 1 (January 2012): 67–85.

Key, T. J., et al. "Insulin-Like Growth Factor 1 (IGF1), IGF Binding Protein 3 (IGFBP3), and Breast Cancer Risk: Pooled Individual Data Analysis of 17 Prospective Studies," *The Lancet Oncology* 11, no. 6 (June 2010): 530–42.

Leaf, A. "On the Reanalysis of the GISSI-Prevenzione," *Circulation* 105 (2002): 1874–75.

Lieb, J. "Antidepressants, Eicosanoids, and the Prevention and Treatment of Cancer: A Review," *Prostaglandins, Leukotrienes and Essential Fatty Acids* 65, nos. 5–6 (November–December 2001): 233–39.

London, B., et al. "Omega-3 Fatty Acids and Cardiac Arrhythmias: Prior Studies and Recommendations for Future Research," *Circulation* 116 (2007): e320–e335.

Moon, D. O., et al. "Sulforaphane Suppresses TNF-Alpha-Mediated Activation of NF-KappaB and Induces Apoptosis through Activation of Reactive Oxygen Species-Dependent Caspase-3," *Cancer Letter* 274, no. 1 (February 8, 2009): 132–42.

Murray, N. R., et al. "Protein Kinase C Beta II and TGF Beta RII in Omega-3 Fatty Acid-Mediated Inhibition of Colon Carcinogenesis," *Journal of Cell Biology* 157, no. 6 (June 10, 2002): 915–20.

Peet, M., et al. "Depletion of Omega-3 Fatty Acid Levels in Red Blood Cell Membranes of Depressive Patients," *Biological Psychiatry* 43, no. 5 (March 1, 1998): 315–19.

Pereira, M. A., and J. J. Pins. "Dietary Fiber and Cardiovascular Disease: Experimental and Epidemiologic Advances," *Current Atherosclerosis Reports* 2, no. 6 (November 2000): 494–502.

Ray, S. D., et al. "Pre-Exposure to a Novel Nutritional Mixture Containing a Series of Phytochemicals Prevents Acetaminophen-Induced Programmed and Unprogrammed Cell Deaths by Enhancing BCL-XL Expression and Minimizing Oxidative Stress in the Liver," *Molecular and Cellular Biochemistry* 293, no. 1–1 (December 2006): 119–36.

Roberts, C. T. Jr. "IGF-1 and Prostate Cancer," *Novartis Foundation Symposium* 262 (2004): 193–99; discussion, 199–204, 265–68.

Salehpour, A., et al. "A 12-Week Double-Blind Randomized Clinical Trial of Vitamin D$_3$ Supplementation on Body Fat Mass in Healthy Overweight and Obese Women," *Nutrition Journal* 11 (September 22, 2012): 78.

Samaha, F. F., et al. "A Low-Carbohydrate as Compared with a Low-Fat Diet in Severe Obesity," *New England Journal of Medicine.* 348, no. 21 (May 22, 2003): 2074–81.

Siri-Tarino, P. W., et al. "Saturated Fat and Heart Disease: Meta-Analysis of Prospective Cohort Studies Evaluating the Association of Saturated Fat with Cardiovascular Disease," *American Journal of Clinical Nutrition* 91, no. 3 (March 2010): 535–46.

Skeaff, C. M., and J. Miller. "Dietary Fat and Coronary Heart Disease: Summary of Evidence from Prospective Cohort and Randomised Controlled Trials," *Annals of Nutrition and Metabolism* 55, no. 1–3 (2009): 173–201.

Škrovánková, S., L. Mišurcová, and L. Machů. "Antioxidant Activity and Protecting Health Effects of Common Medicinal Plants," *Advances in Food and Nutrition Research* 67 (2012): 75–139.

Thomsen, C., et al. "Comparison of the Effects on the Diurnal Blood Pressure, Glucose, and Lipid Levels of a Diet Rich in Monounsaturated Fatty Acids with a Diet Rich in Polyunsaturated Fatty Acids in Type 2 Diabetic Subjects," *Diabetic Medicine* 12, no. 7 (July 1995): 600–606.

Villani, F., et al. "Effect of Dietary Supplementation with Polyunsaturated Fatty Acids on Bronchial Hyperreactivity in Subjects with Seasonal Asthma," *Respiration* 65, no. 4 (1998): 265–69.

Vuksan, V., et al. "Konjac-Mannan (Glucomannan) Improves Glycemia and Other Associated Risk Factors for Coronary Heart Disease in Type 2 Diabetes. A Randomized Controlled Metabolic Trial," *Diabetes Care* 22, no. 6 (June 1999): 913–19.

Wang, H., L. H. Storlien, and X. F. Huang. "Effects of Dietary Fat Types on Body Fatness, Leptin, and ARC Leptin Receptor, NPY, and AgRP mRNA Expression," *American Journal of Physiology, Endocrinology and Metabolism* 282, no. 6 (June 2002): E1352–59.

Chapter 3

Arvill, A., and L. Bodin. "Effect of Short-Term Ingestion of Konjac Glucomannan on Serum Cholesterol in Healthy Men," *American Journal of Clinical Nutrition* 61, no. 3 (March 1995): 585–89.

Chen, H. L., et al. "Konjac Supplement Alleviated Hypercholesterolemia and Hyperglycemia in Type 2 Diabetic Subjects—A Randomized Double-Blind Trial," *Journal of the American College of Nutrition* 22, no. 1 (February 2003): 36–42.

Fanson, B. G., et al. "Nutrients, Not Caloric Restriction, Extend Lifespan in Queensland Fruit Flies (*Bactrocera tryoni*)," *Aging Cell* 8 (2009): 514–23.

Gallaher, D. D., et al. "A Glucomannan and Chitosan Fiber Supplement Decreases Plasma Cholesterol and Increases Cholesterol Excretion in Overweight Normocholesterolemic Humans," *Journal of the American College of Nutrition* 21, no. 5 (October 2002): 428–33.

Mair, W., M. D. W. Piper, and L. Partridge. "Calories Do Not Explain Extension of Life Span by Dietary Restriction in *Drosophila,*" *PLoS Biology* 3, no. 7 (2005): e223.

Martino, F., et al. "Effect of Dietary Supplementation with Glucomannan on Plasma Total Cholesterol and Low Density Lipoprotein Cholesterol in Hypercholesterolemic Children," *Nutrition, Metabolism, and Cardiovascular Diseases* 15, no. 3 (June 2005): 174–80.

Masoro, E. J. "Caloric Restriction and Aging: Controversial Issues," *Journal of Gerontology: Biological Sciences* 61 (2006): 14–19.

Mattison, J. A., et al. "Impact of Caloric Restriction on Health and Survival in Rhesus Monkeys from the NIA Study," *Nature* 489, no. 7415 (September 13, 2012): 318–21.

Smith, D. L., et al. "Telomere Dynamics in Rhesus Monkeys: No Apparent Effect of Caloric Restriction," *The Journals of Gerontology* 66A, no. 11 (2011): 1163–68.

Walsh, D. E., V. Yaghoubian, and A. Behforooz. "Effect of Glucomannan on Obese Patients: A Clinical Study," *International Journal of Obesity* 8, no. 4 (1984): 289–93.

Chapter 4

Aggarwal, B. B., and S. Shishodia. "Suppression of the Nuclear Factor-KappaB Activation Pathway by Spice-Derived Phytochemicals: Reasoning for Seasoning," *Annals of the New York Academy of Sciences* 1030 (December 2004): 434–41.

Agrawal, P., V. Rai, and R. B. Singh. "Randomized Placebo-Controlled, Single Blind Trial of Holy Basil Leaves in Patients with Noninsulin-Dependent Diabetes Mellitus," *International Journal of Clinical Pharmacology and Therapeutics* 34, no. 9 (September 1996): 406–9.

Aherne, S. A., J. P. Kerry, and N. M. O'Brien. "Effects of Plant Extracts on Antioxidant Status and Oxidant-Induced Stress in Caco-2 Cells," *British Journal of Nutrition* 97, no. 2 (February 2007): 321–28.

Atawodi, S. E. "Nigerian Foodstuffs with Prostate Cancer Chemopreventive Polyphenols," *Infectious Agents and Cancer* 6, sup. 2 (September 23, 2011): S9.

Bag, A., et al. "In Vitro Antibacterial Potential of *Eugenia jambolana* Seed Extracts against Multidrug-Resistant Human Bacterial Pathogens," *Microbiological Research* 167, no. 6 (June 20, 2012): 352–57.

Billing, J., and P. W. Sherman. "Antimicrobial Functions of Spices: Why Some Like It Hot," *Quarterly Review of Biology* 73, no. 1 (March 1998): 3–49.

Bravo, E., et al. "*Ocimum basilicum* Ethanolic Extract Decreases Cholesterol Synthesis and Lipid Accumulation in Human Macrophages," *Fitoterapia* 79, no. 7–8 (December 2008): 515–23.

Cheng, D. M., et al. "In Vivo and in Vitro Antidiabetic Effects of Aqueous Cinnamon Extract and Cinnamon Polyphenol-Enhanced Food Matrix," *Food Chemistry* 135, no. 4 (December 15, 2012): 2994–3002.

Chiang, L. C., et al. "Antiviral Activities of Extracts and Selected Pure Constituents of *Ocimum basilicum*," *Clinical and Experimental Pharmacology and Physiology* 32, no. 10 (October 2005): 811–16.

Dailami, K. N., et al. "Prevention of Selenite-Induced Cataractogenesis by *Origanum vulgare* Extract," *Pakistan Journal of Biological Science* 13, no. 15 (August 1, 2010): 743–47.

Deeb, S. J., et al. "Sage Components Enhance Cell Death through Nuclear Factor Kappa-B Signaling," *Frontiers in Bioscience (Elite Ed)* 3 (January 1, 2011): 410–20.

Devi, P. U., and A. Ganasoundari. "Modulation of Glutathione and Antioxidant Enzymes by *Ocimum sanctum* and Its Role in Protection against Radiation Injury," *Indian Journal of Experimental Biology* 37, no. 3 (March 1999): 262–68.

Dhingra, D., and A. Sharma. "Antidepressant-Like Activity of n-Hexane Extract of Nutmeg (*Myristica fragrans*) Seeds in Mice," *Journal of Medicinal Food* 9, no. 1 (Spring 2006): 84–89.

El-Bakly, W. M., et al. "6-Gingerol Ameliorated Doxorubicin-Induced Cardiotoxicity: Role of Nuclear Factor Kappa B and Protein Glycation," *Cancer Chemotherapy and Pharmacology* 70, no. 6 (December 2012): 833–41.

Evans, D. A., J. B. Hirsch, and S. Dushenkov. "Phenolics, Inflammation and Nutrigenomics," *Journal of the Science of Food and Agriculture* 86, no. 15 (2006): 2503–9.

Frydman-Marom, A., et al. "Orally Administrated Cinnamon Extract Reduces Beta-Amyloid Oligomerization and Corrects Cognitive Impairment in Alzheimer's Disease Animal Models," *PLoS ONE* 6, no. 1 (January 28, 2011): e16564, doi:10.1371/journal.pone.0016564.

Ghadrdoost, B., et al. "Protective Effects of Saffron Extract and Its Active Constituent Crocin against Oxidative Stress and Spatial Learning and Memory Deficits Induced by Chronic Stress in Rats," *European Journal of Pharmacology* 667, no. 1–3 (September 30, 2011): 222–29.

Ha, S. K., et al. "6-Shogaol, a Ginger Product, Modulates Neuroinflammation: A New Approach to Neuroprotection," *Neuropharmacology* 63, no. 2 (August 2012): 211–23.

Ito, Y., et al. "Protective Effect of S-allyl-L-cysteine, a Garlic Compound, on Amyloid Beta-Protein-Induced Cell Death in Nerve Growth Factor-Differentiated PC12 Cells," *Neuroscience Research* 46, no. 1 (May 2003): 119–25.

Jayasinghe, C., et al. "Phenolics Composition and Antioxidant Activity of Sweet Basil (*Ocimum basilicum L.*)," *Journal of Agricultural and Food Chemistry* 51, no. 15 (July 16, 2003): 4442–49.

Jeon, S., et al. "A Modified Formulation of Chinese Traditional Medicine Improves Memory Impairment and Reduces Aß Level in the Tg-APPswe/PS1dE9 Mouse Model of Alzheimer's Disease," *Journal of Ethnopharmacology* 137, no. 1 (September 1, 2011): 783–89.

Johnson, J. J. "Carnosol: A Promising Anti-Cancer and Anti-Inflammatory Agent," *Cancer Letters* 305, no. 1 (June 1, 2011): 1–7.

Kim, H. J., et al. "Effect of Methyl Jasmonate on Secondary Metabolites of Sweet Basil (*Ocimum basilicum L.*)," *Journal of Agricultural and Food Chemistry* 54, no. 6 (March 22, 2006): 2327–32.

Kota, N., et al. "Dose-Dependent Effect in the Inhibition of Oxidative Stress and Anticlastogenic Potential of Ginger in STZ Induced Diabetic Rats," *Food Chemistry* 135, no. 4 (December 15, 2012): 2954–59.

Lau, B. H., T. Yamasaki, and D. S. Gridley. "Garlic Compounds Modulate Macrophage and T-Lymphocyte Functions," *Molecular Biotherapeutics* 3, no. 2 (June 1991): 103–7.

Lefort, E. C., and J. Blay. "The Dietary Flavonoid Apigenin Enhances the Activities of the Anti-Metastatic Protein CD26 on Human Colon Carcinoma Cells," *Clinical and Experimental Metastasis* 28, no. 4 (April 2011): 337–49.

Liu, L., and Y. Y. Yeh. "Inhibition of Cholesterol Biosynthesis by Organosulfur Compounds Derived from Garlic," *Lipids* 35, no. 2 (February 2000): 197–203.

Lu, Y., et al. "Cholesterol-Lowering Effect of Allicin on Hypercholesterolemic ICR Mice," *Oxidative Medicine and Cellular Longevity* (2012): 489690.

Ma, L., et al., "Activation of TRPV1 Reduces Vascular Lipid Accumulation and Attenuates Atherosclerosis," *Cardiovascular Research* 92, no. 3 (December 1, 2011): 504–13.

Mahmoud, M. E., et al. "Capsaicin Inhibits IFN-Gamma-Induced MHC Class II Expression by Suppressing Transcription of Class II Transactivator Gene in Murine Peritoneal Macrophages," *International Immunopharmacology* 10, no. 1 (January 2010): 86–90.

Manosroi, J., P. Dhumtanom, and A. Manosroi. "Anti-Proliferative Activity of Essential Oil Extracted from Thai Medicinal Plants on KB and P388 Cell Lines," *Cancer Letters* 235, no. 1 (April 8, 2006): 114–20.

Mechan, A. O., et al. "Monoamine Reuptake Inhibition and Mood-Enhancing Potential of a Specified Oregano Extract," *British Journal of Nutrition* 105, no. 8 (April 2011): 1150–63.

Meyer, H., et al. "Bioavailability of Apigenin from Apiin-Rich Parsley in Humans," *Annals of Nutrition and Metabolism* 50, no. 3 (2006): 167–72.

Munday, J. S., et al. "Daily Supplementation with Aged Garlic Extract, but Not Raw Garlic, Protects Low Density Lipoprotein against in Vitro Oxidation," *Atherosclerosis* 143, no. 2 (April 1999): 399–404.

Nelson, A. J., et al. "Capsaicin-Based Analgesic Balm Decreases Pressor Responses Evoked by Muscle Afferents," *Medicine and Science in Sports and Exercise* 36, no. 2 (March 2004): 444–50.

Nevius, E., P. K. Srivastava, and S. Basu. "Oral Ingestion of Capsaicin, the Pungent Component of Chili Pepper, Enhances a Discreet Population of Macrophages and Confers Protection from Autoimmune Diabetes," *Mucosal Immunology* 5 (January 2012): 76–86.

Ngo, S. N., D. B. Williams, and R. J. Head. "Rosemary and Cancer Prevention: Preclinical Perspectives," *Critical Reviews in Food Science and Nutrition* 51, no. 10 (December 2011): 946–54.

O'Sullivan, L., et al. "Bioaccessibility, Uptake, and Transport of Carotenoids from Peppers (*Capsicum* spp.) Using the Coupled in Vitro Digestion and Human Intestinal Caco-2 Cell Model," *Journal of Agricultural and Food Chemistry* 58, no. 9 (May 12, 2010): 5374–79.

Pande, S., and K. Srinivasan. "Potentiation of Hypolipidemic and Weight-Reducing Influence of Dietary Tender Cluster Bean (*Cyamopsis tetragonoloba*) when Combined with Capsaicin in High-Fat-Fed Rats," *Journal of Agricultural and Food Chemistry* 60, no. 33 (August 2012): 8155–62.

Panickar, K. S., et al. "A Procyanidin Type A Trimer from Cinnamon Extract Attenuates Glial Cell Swelling and the Reduction in Glutamate Uptake Following Ischemia-Like Injury in Vitro," *Neuroscience* 202 (January 27, 2012): 87–98.

Pápay, Z. E., et al. "Pharmaceutical and Formulation Aspects of *Petroselinum crispum* Extract," *Acta Pharmaceutica Hungarica* 82, no. 1 (2012): 3–14.

Park, S. E. et al., "Neuroprotective Effect of *Rosmarinus officinalis* Extract on Human Dopaminergic Cell Line, SH-SY5Y," *Cellular and Molecular Neurobiology* 30, no. 5 (July 2010): 759–67.

Pedraza-Chaverri, J., et al. "Garlic's Ability to Prevent in Vitro Cu2+-Induced Lipoprotein Oxidation in Human Serum Is Preserved in Heated Garlic: Effect Unrelated to Cu2+-Chelation," *Nutrition Journal* 3 (2004): 10.

Prakash, U. N., and K. Srinivasan. "Beneficial Influence of Dietary Spices on the Ultrastructure and Fluidity of the Intestinal Brush Border in Rats," *British Journal of Nutrition* 104, no. 1 (July 2010): 31–39.

———. "Gastrointestinal Protective Effect of Dietary Spices during Ethanol-Induced Oxidant Stress in Experimental Rats," *Applied Physiology, Nutrition, and Metabolism* 35, no. 2 (April 2010): 134–41.

Priestley, C. M., et al. "Thymol, a Constituent of Thyme Essential Oil, Is a Positive Allosteric Modulator of Human GABA(A) Receptors and a Homo-Oligomeric GABA Receptor from Drosophila Melanogaster," *British Journal of Pharmacology* 140, no. 8 (December 2003): 1363–72.

Ramos, A. A., et al. "Protection by *Salvia* Extracts against Oxidative and Alkylation Damage to DNA in Human HCT15 and CO115 Cells," *Journal of Toxicology and Environmental Health (Part A)* 75, no. 13–15 (2012): 765–75.

Saravanan, G., and P. Ponmurugan. "Antidiabetic Effect of S-Allylcysteine: Effect on Thyroid Hormone and Circulatory Antioxidant System in Experimental Diabetic Rats," *Journal of Diabetes Complications* 26, no. 4 (July–August 2012): 280–85.

Seo, H. S., et al. "Apigenin Induces Apoptosis via Extrinsic Pathway, Inducing p53 and Inhibiting STAT3 and NFΊ⁰B Signaling in HER2-Overexpressing Breast Cancer Cells," *Molecular and Cell Biochemistry* 366, no. 1–2 (July 2012): 319–34.

Sharma, M., et al. "Cardioprotective Potential of *Ocimum sanctum* in Isoproterenol Induced Myocardial Infarction in Rats," *Molecular and Cellular Biochemistry* 225, no. 1 (September 2001): 75–83.

Shin, G. C., et al. "Apigenin-Induced Apoptosis Is Mediated by Reactive Oxygen Species and Activation of ERK1/2 in Rheumatoid Fibroblast-Like Synoviocytes," *Chemico Biological Interactions* 182, no. 1 (November 2009): 29–36.

Singletary K., D. MacDonald, and M. Wallig. "Inhibition by Rosemary and Carnosol of 7,12-Dimethylbenz[a]anthracene (DMBA)-Induced Rat Mammary Tumorigenesis and in Vivo DMBA-DNA Adduct Formation," *Cancer Letters* 104, no. 1 (June 24, 1996): 43–48.

Steiner, M., and R. S. Lin. "Changes in Platelet Function and Susceptibility of Lipoproteins to Oxidation Associated with Administration of Aged Garlic Extract," *Journal of Cardiovascular Pharmacology* 31, no. 6 (June 1998): 904–8.

Steiner, M., and W. Li. "Aged Garlic Extract, a Modulator of Cardiovascular Risk Factors: A Dose-Finding Study on the Effects of AGE on Platelet Functions," *Journal of Nutrition* 131, no. 3 (March 1, 2001): 980S–984S.

Steiner, M., et al. "A Double-Blind Crossover Study in Moderately Hypercholesterolemic Men that Compared the Effect of Aged Garlic Extract and Placebo Administration on Blood Lipids," *American Journal of Clinical Nutrition* 64, no. 6 (December 1996): 866–70.

Sun, Q. W., et al., "Apigenin Enhances the Cytotoxic Effects of Tumor Necrosis Factor-Related Apoptosis-Inducing Ligand in Human Rheumatoid Arthritis Fibroblast-Like Synoviocytes," *Molecular Biology Reports* 39, no. 5 (May 2012): 5529–35.

Tohti, I., et al. "Aqueous Extracts of *Ocimum basilicum* L. (Sweet Basil) Decrease Platelet Aggregation Induced by ADP and Thrombin in Vitro and Rats Arterio—Venous Shunt Thrombosis in Vivo," *Thrombosis Research* 118, no. 6 (2006): 733–39.

Vats, V., J. K. Grover, and S. S. Rathi. "Evaluation of Anti-Hyperglycemic and Hypoglycemic Effect of *Trigonella foenum-graecum* Linn, *Ocimum sanctum* Linn and *Pterocarpus marsupium* Linn in Normal and Alloxanized Diabetic Rats," *Journal of Ethnopharmacology* 79, no. 1 (January 2002): 95–100.

Wahba, N. M., A. S. Ahmed, and Z. Z. Ebraheim. "Antimicrobial Effects of Pepper, Parsley, and Dill and Their Roles in the Microbiological Quality Enhancement of Traditional Egyptian Kareish Cheese," *Foodborne Pathogens and Disease* 7, no. 4 (April 2010): 411–18.

Wang, Y., et al. "Antidepressant Properties of Bioactive Fractions from the Extract of *Crocus sativus* L.," *Journal of Natural Medicines* 64, no. 1 (January 2010): 24–30.

Yeh, Y. Y., and L. Liu. "Cholesterol-Lowering Effect of Garlic Extracts and Organosulfur Compounds: Human and Animal Studies," *Journal of Nutrition* 131, no. 3s (March 2001): 989S–93S.

Yeh, Y. Y., and S. M. Yeh. "Garlic Reduces Plasma Lipids by Inhibiting Hepatic Cholesterol and Triacylglycerol Synthesis," *Lipids* 29, no. 3 (March 1994): 189–93.

Yoshikawa, M., et al. "Medicinal Foodstuffs. XVIII. Phytoestrogens from the Aerial Part of *Petroselinum crispum* MIll. (Parsley) and Structures of 6``-Acetylapiin and a New Monoterpene Glycoside, Petroside," *Chemical and Pharmaceutical Bulletin (Tokyo)* 48, no. 7 (July 2000): 1039–44.

Youdim, K. A., and S. G. Deans. "Effect of Thyme Oil and Thymol Dietary Supplementation on the Antioxidant Status and Fatty Acid Composition of the Ageing Rat Brain," *The British Journal of Nutrition* 83, no. 1 (January 2000): 87–93.

Chapter 5

Arruzazabala, M. dL., et al. "Effects of Coconut Oil on Testosterone-Induced Prostatic Hyperplasia in Sprague-Dawley Rats," *Journal of Pharmacy and Pharmacology* 59 (February 2010): 995–99.

Campbell-Falck, D., et al. "The Intravenous Use of Coconut Water," *American Journal of Emergency Medicine* 18, no. 1 (January 2000): 108–11.

Chajès, V., et al. "Association between Serum Trans-Monounsaturated Fatty Acids and Breast Cancer Risk in the E3N-EPIC Study," *American Journal of Epidemiology* 167, no. 11 (June 1, 2008): 1312–20.

Cooper, K. A., et al. "Cocoa and Health: A Decade of Research," *British Journal of Nutriton* 99, no. 1 (January 2008): 1–11.

Dillinger, T. L., et al. "Food of the Gods: Cure for Humanity? A Cultural History of the Medicinal and Ritual Use of Chocolate," *Journal of Nutrition* 130, sup. 8S (August 2000): 2057S–72S.

Franke, A. A., et al. "Tocopherol and Tocotrienol Levels of Foods Consumed in Hawaii," *Journal of Agricultural and Food Chemistry* 55, no. 3 (February 7, 2007): 769–78.

Gonzales, G. F., and L. G. Valerio Jr. "Medicinal Plants from Peru: A Review of Plants as Potential Agents against Cancer," *Anticancer Agents in Medicinal Chemistry* 6, no. 5 (September 2006): 429–44.

Griel, A. E., et al. "A Macadamia Nut-Rich Diet Reduces Total and LDL-Cholesterol in Mildly Hypercholesterolemic Men and Women," *The Journal of Nutrition* 138, no. 4 (April 2008): 761–67.

Hiraoka-Yamamoto, J., et al. "Serum Lipid Effects of a Monounsaturated (Palmitoleic) Fatty Acid–Rich Diet Based on Macadamia Nuts in Healthy, Young Japanese Women," *Clinical and Experimental Pharmacology and Physiology* 31, sup. 2 (December 2004): S37–38.

Jourdain, C., et al. "In-Vitro Effects of Polyphenols from Cocoa and Beta-Sitosterol on the Growth of Human Prostate Cancer and Normal Cells," *European Journal of Cancer Prevention* 15, no. 4 (August 2006): 353–61.

Khonkarn, R., et al. "Investigation of Fruit Peel Extracts as Sources for Compounds with Antioxidant and Antiproliferative Activities against Human Cell Lines," *Food and Chemical Toxicology* 48, no. 8–9 (August–September 2010): 2122–29.

Kurosawa, T., et al. "Suppressive Effects of Cacao Liquor Polyphenols (CLP) on LDL Oxidation and the Development of Atherosclerosis in Kurosawa and Kusanagi-Hypercholesterolemic Rabbits," *Atherosclerosis* 179, no. 2 (April 2005): 237–46.

Lenovich, L. M. "Effect of Caffeine on Aflatoxin Production on Cocoa Beans," *Journal of Food Science* 46 (March 1981): 655.

Matsui, N., et al. "Ingested Cocoa Can Prevent High-Fat Diet-Induced Obesity by Regulating the Expression of Genes for Fatty Acid Metabolism," *Nutrition* 21, no. 5 (May 2005): 594–601.

Matthan, N. R., et al. "Effects of Dietary Palmitoleic Acid on Plasma Lipoprotein Profile and Aortic Cholesterol Accumulation Are Similar to Those of Other Unsaturated Fatty Acids in the F1B Golden Syrian Hamster," *The Journal of Nutrition* 139, no. 2 (February 2009): 215–21.

Radenahmad, N., et al. "Young Coconut Juice Significantly Reduces Histopathological Changes in the Brain that are Induced by Hormonal Imbalance: A Possible Implication to Postmenopausal Women," *Histology and Histopathology* 24, no. 6 (June 2009): 667–74.

Ramiro, E., et al. "Effect of *Theobroma cacao* Flavonoids on Immune Activation of a Lymphoid Cell Line," *British Journal of Nutrition* 93, no. 6 (June 2005): 859–66.

Ramljak, D., et al. "Pentameric Procyanidin from *Theobroma cacao* Selectively Inhibits Growth of Human Breast Cancer Cells," *Molecular Cancer Therapeutics* 4, no. 4 (April 2005): 537–46.

Rinaldi, S., et al. "Characterization of the Antinociceptive and Anti-Inflammatory Activities from *Cocos nucifera L.* (Palmae)," *Journal of Ethnopharmacology* 122, no. 3 (April 21, 2009): 541–46.

Shannon, J., et al. "Erythrocyte Fatty Acids and Risk of Proliferative and Nonproliferative Fibrocystic Disease in Women in Shanghai, China," *American Journal of Clinical Nutrition* 89, no. 1 (January 2009): 265–76.

Shin, B. C., et al. "Maca (*L. meyenii*) for Improving Sexual Function: A Systematic Review," *BMC Complementary and Alternative Medicine* 10 (August 2010): 44.

Sies, H., et al. "Cocoa Polyphenols and Inflammatory Mediators," *American Journal of Clinical Nutrition* 81, no. 1 (January 2005): 304S–12S.

Tarka, S. M. Jr, et al. "Chronic Toxicity/Carcinogenicity Studies of Cocoa Powder in Rats," *Food and Chemical Toxicology* 29, no. 1 (January 1991): 7–19.

Valentová, K., and J. Ulrichová. "*Smallanthus sonchifolius* and *Lepidium meyenii*: Prospective Andean Crops for the Prevention of Chronic Diseases," *Biomedical Papers of the Medical Facility of the University Palacky, Olomouc, Czech Republic* 147, no. 2 (December 2003): 119–30.

Vinson, J. A., et al. "Chocolate Is a Powerful ex Vivo and in Vivo Antioxidant, an Antiatherosclerotic Agent in an Animal Model, and a Significant Contributor to Antioxidants in the European and American Diets," *Journal of Agricultural and Food Chemistry* 54, no. 21 (October 2006): 8071–76.

Weisburger, J. H. "Chemopreventive Effects of Cocoa Polyphenols on Chronic Diseases," *Experimental Biology and Medicine* 226, no. 10 (November 2001): 891–97.

Yamasaki, M., et al. "Alleviation of the Cytotoxic Activity Induced by Trans10, Cis12-Conjugated Linoleic Acid in Rat Hepatoma dRLh-84 Cells by Oleic or Palmitoleic Acid," *Cancer Letters* 196, no. 2 (July 10, 2003): 187–96.

Yong, J. W., et al. "The Chemical Composition and Biological Properties of Coconut (*Cocos nucifera L.*) Water," *Molecules* 14, no. 12 (December 9, 2009): 5144–64.

Zhang, Y., et al. "Effect of Ethanol Extract of *Lepidium meyenii* Walp. on Osteoporosis in Ovariectomized Rat," *Journal of Ethnopharmacology* 105, nos. 1–2 (April 21, 2006): 274–79.

Zomer, E., et al. "The Effectiveness and Cost Effectiveness of Dark Chocolate Consumption as Prevention Therapy in People at High Risk of Cardiovascular Disease: Best Case Scenario Analysis Using a Markov Model," *British Medical Journal* 344 (May 2012): e3657.

Chapter 6

Beulens, J. W., et al. "High Dietary Glycemic Load and Glycemic Index Increase Risk of Cardiovascular Disease among Middle-Aged Women: A Population-Based Follow-Up Study," *Journal of the American College of Cardiology* 50, no. 1 (July 3, 2007): 14–21.

Fortuna, J. L. "The Obesity Epidemic and Food Addiction: Clinical Similarities to Drug Dependence," *Journal of Psychoactive Drugs* 44, no. 1 (January–March 2012): 56–63.

Solfrizzi, V., et al. "Diet and Alzheimer's Disease Risk Factors or Prevention: The Current Evidence," *Expert Review of Neurotherapeutics* 11, no. 5 (May 2011): 677–708.

Villegas, R., et al. "Prospective Study of Dietary Carbohydrates, Glycemic Index, Glycemic Load, and Incidence of Type 2 Diabetes Mellitus in Middle-Aged Chinese Women," *Archives of Internal Medicine* 167, no. 21 (November 26, 2007): 2310–16.

Chapter 7

Christison, G. W., and K. Ivany. "Elimination Diets in Autism Spectrum Disorders: Any Wheat amidst the Chaff?" *Journal of Developmental and Behavioral Pediatrics* 27, sup. 2 (April 2006): S162–71.

Glew, R .H., R. S. Wold, and D. J. VanderJagt. "Comparison of Diets of Urban American Indian and Non-Hispanic Whites: Populations with a Disparity for Biliary Tract Cancer Rates," *Asian Pacific Journal of Cancer Prevention* 13, no. 7 (2012): 3077–82.

Melnik, B. C. "Diet in Acne: Further Evidence for the Role of Nutrient Signaling in Acne Pathogenesis," *Acta Dermato Venereologica* 92, no. 3 (May 2012): 228–31.

———. "Dietary Intervention in Acne: Attenuation of Increased mTORC1 Signaling Promoted by Western Diet," *Dermato-Endocrinology* 4, no. 1 (January 1, 2012): 20–32.

———. "Evidence for Acne-Promoting Effects of Milk and Other Insulinotropic Dairy Products," *67th Nestle Nutrition Workshop Pediatric Program* 67 (2011): 131–45.

Melnik, B. C., et al. "The Impact of Cow's Milk-Mediated mTORC1-Signaling in the Initiation and Progression of Prostate Cancer," *Nutrition and Metabolism* 9, no. 1 (August 2012): 74.

Millward, C., et al. "Gluten- and Casein-Free Diets for Autistic Spectrum Disorder," *Cochrane Database of Systematic Reviews* 2 (April 2008): CD003498.

Silverberg, N. B. "Whey Protein Precipitating Moderate to Severe Acne Flares in 5 Teenaged Athletes," *Cutis* 90, no. 2 (August 2012): 70–72.

Torres-Pinedo, R., and A. Mahmood. "Postnatal Changes in Biosynthesis of Microvillus Membrane Glycans of Rat Small Intestine: I. Evidence of a Developmental Shift from Terminal Sialylation to Fucosylation," *Biochemical and Biophysical Research Communications* 125, no. 2 (December 14, 1984): 546–53.

Chapter 8

Curi, R., et al. "Effect of *Stevia rebaudiana* on Glucose Tolerance in Normal Adult Humans," *Brazilian Journal of Medical and Biological Research* 19, no. 6 (1986): 771–74.

Ferri, L. A., et al. "Investigation of the Antihypertensive Effect of Oral Crude Stevioside in Patients with Mild Essential Hypertension," *Phytotherapy Research* 20, no. 9 (September 2006): 732–36.

Geuns, J. M. "Stevioside," *Phytochemistry* 64, no. 5 (November 2003): 913–92.

Goyal, S. K., Samsher, and R. K. Goyal. "Stevia (*Stevia rebaudiana*) a Bio-Sweetener: A Review," *International Journal of Food Sciences and Nutrition* 61, no. 1 (February 2010): 1–10.

Gregersen, S., et al. "Antihyperglycemic Effects of Stevioside in Type 2 Diabetic Subjects," *Metabolism* 53, no. 1 (January 2004): 73–76.

Hsieh, M. H., et al. "Efficacy and Tolerability of Oral Stevioside in Patients with Mild Essential Hypertension: A Two-Year, Randomized, Placebo-Controlled Study," *Clinical Therapeutics* 25, no. 11 (November 2003): 2797–2808.

Matsui, M., et al. "Evaluation of the Genotoxicity of Stevioside and Steviol Using Six in Vitro and One in Vivo Mutagenicity Assays," *Mutagenesis* 11, no. 6 (November 1996): 573–79.

Nunes, A. P., et al. "Analysis of Genotoxic Potentiality of Stevioside by Comet Assay," *Food and Chemical Toxicology* 45, no. 4 (April 2007): 662–66.

Procinska, E., B. A. Bridges, and J. R. Hanson. "Interpretation of Results with the 8-Azaguanine Resistance System in *Salmonella typhimurium*: No Evidence for Direct Acting Mutagenesis by 15-Oxosteviol, a Possible Metabolite of Steviol," *Mutagenesis* 6, no. 2 (March 1991): 165–67.

Chapter 9

Agerholm-Larsen, L., et al. "The Effect of a Probiotic Milk Product on Plasma Cholesterol: A Meta-Analysis of Short-Term Intervention Studies," *European Journal of Clinical Nutrition* 54, no. 11 (November 2000): 856–60.

Altura, B. M. "Sudden-Death Ischemic Heart Disease and Dietary Magnesium Intake: Is the Target Site Coronary Vascular Smooth Muscle?" *Medical Hypotheses* 5, no. 8 (August 1979): 843–48.

Arterburn, L. M., E. B. Hall, and H. Oken. "Distribution, Interconversion, and Dose Response of n-3 fatty Acids in Humans," *American Journal of Clinical Nutrition* 83, sup. 6 (June 2006): 1467S–76S.

Ayalew-Pervanchon, A., et al. "Long-Term Effect of Dietary {alpha}-Linolenic Acid or Decosahexaenoic Acid on Incorporation of Decosahexaenoic Acid in Membranes and Its Influence on Rat Heart in Vivo," *American Journal of Physiology, Heart and Circulatory Physiology* 293, no. 4 (October 2007): H2296–2304.

Bagchi, D., et al. "Anti-Angiogenic, Antioxidant, and Anti-Carcinogenic Properties of a Novel Anthocyanin-Rich Berry Extract Formula," *Biochemistry (Mosc).* 69, no. 1 (January 2004): 75–80, 1 p preceding 75.

Baur, L. A., et al. "The Fatty Acid Composition of Skeletal Muscle Membrane Phospholipid: Its Relationship with the Type of Feeding and Plasma Glucose Levels in Young Children," *Metabolism* 47, no. 1 (January 1998): 106–12.

Beausoleil, M., et al. "Effect of a Fermented Milk Combining *Lactobacillus acidophilus* Cl1285 and *Lactobacillus casei* in the Prevention of Antibiotic-Associated Diarrhea: A Randomized, Double-Blind, Placebo-Controlled Trial," *Canadian Journal of Gastroenterology* 21, no. 11 (November 2007): 732–36.

Benkovic, V., et al. "Radioprotective Effects of Propolis and Quercetin in Gamma-Irradiated Mice Evaluated by the Alkaline Comet Assay," *Phytomedicine* 15, no. 10 (October 2008): 851–58.

Berggren, A., et al. "Randomised, Double-Blind and Placebo-Controlled Study Using New Probiotic *Lactobacilli* for Strengthening the Body Immune Defence against Viral Infections," *European Journal of Nutrition* 50, no. 3 (April 2011): 203–10.

Besselink, M. G., et al. "Probiotic Prophylaxis in Predicted Severe Acute Pancreatitis: A Randomised, Double-Blind, Placebo-Controlled Trial," *Lancet* 371, no. 9613 (February 23, 2008): 651–59.

Blasiak, J., A. Trzeciak, and J. Kowalik. "Curcumin Damages DNA in Human Gastric Mucosa Cells and Lymphocytes," *Journal of Environmental Pathology, Toxicology and Oncology* 18, no. 4 (1999): 271–76.

Bouhlel, I., et al. "Antimutagenic, Antigenotoxic, and Antioxidant Activities of *Acacia salicina* Extracts (ASE) and Modulation of Cell Gene Expression by H2O2 and ASE Treatment," *Toxicology In Vitro* 22, no. 5 (August 2008): 1264–72.

Braat, H., et al. "*Lactobacillus rhamnosus* Induces Peripheral Hyporesponsiveness in Stimulated CD4+ T Cells via Modulation of Dendritic Cell Function," *American Journal of Clinical Nutrition* 80, no. 6 (December 2004): 1618–25.

Brady, L. J., D. D. Gallaher, and F. F. Busta. "The Role of Probiotic Cultures in the Prevention of Colon Cancer," *The Journal of Nutrition* 130, sup. 2S (February 2000): 410S–414S.

Brash, D. E., and P. A. Havre. "New Careers for Antioxidants," *Proceedings of the National Academy of Science of the United States of America* 99, no. 22 (October 29, 2002): 13969–71.

Bravo, J. A., et al. "Ingestion of Lactobacillus Strain Regulates Emotional Behavior and Central GABA Receptor Expression in a Mouse via the Vagus Nerve," *Proceedings of the National Academy of Sciences of the United States of America* 108, no. 38 (September 20, 2011): 16050–55.

Chakraborty, S., M. Roy, and R. K. Bhattacharya. "Prevention and Repair of DNA Damage by Selected Phytochemicals as Measured by Single Cell Gel Electrophoresis," *Journal of Environmental Pathology, Toxicology and Oncology* 23, no. 3 (2004): 215–26.

Chen, Y., et al. "The Effect of Curcumin on Mismatch Repair (MMR) Proteins hMSH2 and hMLH1 after Ultraviolet (UV) Irradiation on HL-60 Cells," *Journal of Huazhong University of Science and Technology Medical Sciences* 23, no. 2 (2003): 124–26.

Chen, Y. J., et al. "Caffeic Acid Phenethyl Ester Preferentially Sensitizes CT26 Colorectal Adenocarcinoma to Ionizing Radiation without Affecting Bone Marrow Radiore-sponse," *International Journal of Radiation Oncology, Biology and Physics* 63, no. 4 (November 15, 2005): 1252–61.

Dhandapani, K. M., V. B. Mahesh, and D. W. Brann. "Curcumin Suppresses Growth and Chemoresistance of Human Glioblastoma Cells via AP-1 and NFkappaB Transcription Factors," *Journal of Neurochemistry* 102, no. 2 (July 2007): 522–38.

Doron, S. I., P. L. Hibberd, and S. L. Gorbach. "Probiotics for Prevention of Antibiotic-Associated Diarrhea," *Journal of Clinical Gastroenterology* 42, sup. 2 (July 2008): S58–63.

Durlach, J., M. Bara, and A. Guiet-Bara. "Magnesium Level in Drinking Water and Cardio-vascular Risk Factor: A Hypothesis," *Magnesium* 4, no. 1 (1985): 5–15.

Emanuel, P., and N. Scheinfeld. "A Review of DNA Repair and Possible DNA-Repair Adjuvants and Selected Natural Anti-Oxidants," *Dermatology Online Journal* 13, no. 3 (July 13, 2007): 10.

Engelbrektson, A., et al. "Probiotics to Minimize the Disruption of Faecal Microbiota in Healthy Subjects Undergoing Antibiotic Therapy," *Journal of Medical Microbiology* 58, pt. 5 (May 2009): 663–70.

Facchinetti, F., et al. "Magnesium Prophylaxis of Menstrual Migraine: Effects on Intracel-lular Magnesium," *Headache* 31, no. 5 (May 1991): 298–301.

———. "Oral Magnesium Successfully Relieves Premenstrual Mood Changes," *Obstetrics and Gynecology* 78, no. 2 (August 1991): 177–81.

Fischer, J. L., et al. "Chemotherapeutic Selectivity Conferred by Selenium: A Role for p53-Dependent DNA Repair," *Molecular Cancer Therapeutics* 6, no. 1 (January 2007): 355–61.

Francavilla, R., et al. "Inhibition of *Helicobacter pylori* infection in Humans by *Lactobacillus reuteri* ATCC 55730 and Effect on Eradication Therapy: A Pilot Study," *Helicobacter* 13, no. 2 (April 2008): 127–34.

Gallai, V., et al. "Red Blood Cell Magnesium Levels in Migraine Patients," *Cephalalgia* 13, no. 2 (April 1993): 94–81; discussion, 73.

Geetha, T., A. Saini, and I. P. Kaur. "Ginseng Extract Exhibits Antimutagenic Activity against Induced Mutagenesis in Various Strains of *Salmonella typhimurium*," *Indian Journal of Experimen-tal Biology* 44, no. 10 (October 2006): 838–41.

Gohil, K., et al. "mRNA Expression Profile of a Human Cancer Cell Line in Response to *Ginkgo biloba* Extract: Induction of Antioxidant Response and the Golgi System," *Free Radi-cal Research* 33, no. 6 (December 2000): 831–49.

González, S., and M. A. Pathak. "Inhibition of Ultraviolet-Induced Formation of Reactive Oxygen Species, Lipid Peroxidation, Erythema and Skin Photosensitization by *Polypodium leucotomos*," *Photodermatology, Photoimmunology, and Photomedicine* 12, no. 2 (April 1996): 45–56.

Hamilton-Miller, J. M. "The Role of Probiotics in the Treatment and Prevention of *Helicobacter pylori* infection," *International Journal of Antimicrobial Agents* 22, no. 4 (October 2003): 360–66.

Hatakka, K., et al. "Effect of Long Term Consumption of Probiotic Milk on Infections in Children Attending Day Care Centres: Double Blind, Randomised Trial," *British Medical Journal* 322, no. 7298 (June 2, 2001): 1327.

Hickson, M., et al. "Use of Probiotic *Lactobacillus* Preparation to Prevent Diarrhoea Associated with Antibiotics: Randomised Double Blind Placebo Controlled Trial," *British Medical Jour-nal* 335, no. 7610 (July 14, 2007): 80.

Hofseth, L. J., and M. J. Wargovich. "Inflammation, Cancer, and Targets of Ginseng," *Journal of Nutrition* 137, sup. 1 (January 2007): 183S–185S.

Hruby, A., et al. "Higher Magnesium Intake Is Associated with Lower Fasting Glucose and Insulin, with No Evidence of Interaction with Select Genetic Loci, in a Meta-Analysis of 15 CHARGE Consortium Studies," *Journal of Nutrition* 143, no. 3 (March 2013): 345–53.

Jańczyk, A., et al. "A *Polypodium leucotomos* Extract Inhibits Solar-Simulated Radiation-Induced TNF-alpha and iNOS Expression, Transcriptional Activation and Apoptosis," *Experimental Dermatology* 16, no. 10 (October 2007): 823–29.

Jeong, S. J., et al. "Effects of mRg2, a Mixture of Ginsenosides Containing 60% Rg2, on the Ultraviolet B-induced DNA Repair Synthesis and Apoptosis in NIH3T3 Cells," *International Journal of Toxicology* 26, no. 2 (March–April 2007): 151–58.

Ji, F.-D., et al. "Note. Microbial Changes during the Salting Process of Traditional Pickled Chinese Cabbage," *Food Science and Technology International* 13, no. 1 (February 2007): 11–16.

Karppanen, H., et al. "Safety and Effects of Potassium- and Magnesium-Containing Low Sodium Salt Mixtures," *Journal of Cardiovascular Pharmacology* 6, sup. 1 (1984): S236–43.

Kelley, D. S., et al. "Dietary Alpha-Linolenic Acid Alters Tissue Fatty Acid Composition, but Not Blood Lipids, Lipoproteins, or Coagulation Status in Humans," *Lipids* 28, no. 6 (June 1993): 533–37.

Kim, T. H., et al. "Protective Effect of Ginseng on Radiation-Induced DNA Double Strand Breaks and Repair in Murine Lymphocytes," *Cancer Biotherapy and Radiopharmaceuticals* 11, no. 4 (August 1996): 267–72.

Kirjavainen, P. V., S. J. Salminen, and E. Isolauri. "Probiotic Bacteria in the Management of Atopic Disease: Underscoring the Importance of Viability," *Journal of Pediatric Gastroenterology Nutrition* 36, no. 2 (February 2003): 223–27.

Kobrin, S. M., and S. Goldfarb. "Magnesium Deficiency," *Seminars in Nephrology* 10, no. 6 (November 1990): 525–35.

Kovacs, E. "The in Vitro Effect of *Viscum album* (VA) Extract on DNA Repair of Peripheral Blood Mononuclear Cells (PBMC) in Cancer Patients," *Phytotherapy Research* 16, no. 2 (March 2002): 143–47.

Kovacs, E., T. Hajto, and K. Hostanska. "Improvement of DNA Repair in Lymphocytes of Breast Cancer Patients Treated with *Viscum album* Extract (Iscador)," *European Journal of Cancer* 27, no. 12 (1991): 1672–76.

Krasse, P., et al. "Decreased Gum Bleeding and Reduced Gingivitis by the Probiotic *Lactobacillus reuteri*," *Swedish Dental Journal* 30, no. 2 (2006): 55–60.

Krishnaswamy, K. "Traditional Indian Spices and Their Health Significance," *Asia Pacific Journal of Clinical Nutrition* 17, sup. 1 (2008): 265–68.

Kruis, W., et al. "Maintaining Remission of Ulcerative Colitis with the Probiotic *Escherichia coli* Nissle 1917 Is As Effective as with Standard Mesalazine," *Gut* 53, no. 11 (November 2004): 1617–23.

Kubena, K. S., and J. Durlach. "Historical Review of the Effects of Marginal Intake of Magnesium in Chronic Experimental Magnesium Deficiency," *Magnesium Research* 3, no. 3 (September 1990): 219–26.

Letavayová, L., V. Vlcková, and J. Brozmanová. "Selenium: From Cancer Prevention to DNA Damage," *Toxicology* 227, nos. 1–2 (October 3, 2006): 1–14.

Llópiz, N., et al. "Antigenotoxic Effect of Grape Seed Procyanidin Extract in Fao Cells Submitted to Oxidative Stress," *Journal of Agricultural and Food Chemistry* 52, no. 5 (March 10, 2004): 1083–87.

Longtin, R. "Selenium for Prevention: Eating Your Way to Better DNA Repair?" *Journal of the National Cancer Institute* 95, no. 2 (January 15, 2003): 98–100.

Mansour, H. B., et al. "Antigenotoxic Activities of Crude Extracts from *Acacia salicina* Leaves," *Environmental and Molecular Mutagenesis* 48, no. 1 (January 2007): 58–66.

Marcos, A., et al. "The Effect of Milk Fermented by Yogurt Cultures plus *Lactobacillus casei* DN-114001 on the Immune Response of Subjects under Academic Examination Stress," *European Journal of Nutrition* 43, no. 6 (December 2004): 381–89.

Martin, K., et al. "Parthenolide-Depleted Feverfew (*Tanacetum parthenium*) Protects Skin from UV Irradiation and External Aggression," *Archives of Dermatological Research* 300, no. 2 (February 2008): 69–80.

Miranda, D. D., et al. "Protective Effects of Mate Tea (*Ilex paraguariensis*) on H2O2-Induced DNA Damage and DNA Repair in Mice," *Mutagenesis* 23, no. 4 (July 2008): 261–65.

Moiseeva, E. P., et al. "Extended Treatment with Physiologic Concentrations of Dietary Phytochemicals Results in Altered Gene Expression, Reduced Growth, and Apoptosis of Cancer Cells," *Molecular Cancer Therapeutics* 6, no. 11 (November 2007): 3071–79.

Mori, T. A., et al. "Purified Eicosapentaenoic and Docosahexaenoic Acids Have Differential Effects on Serum Lipids and Lipoproteins, LDL Particle Size, Glucose, and Insulin in Mildly Hyperlipidemic Men," *American Journal of Clinical Nutrition* 71, no. 5 (May 2000): 1085–94.

———. "Dietary Fish as a Major Component of a Weight-Loss Diet: Effect on Serum Lipids, Glucose, and Insulin Metabolism in Overweight Hypertensive Subjects," *American Journal of Clinical Nutrition* 70, no. 5 (November 1999): 817–25.

Mukherjee, S., et al. "A Mechanistic Approach for Modulation of Arsenic Toxicity in Human Lymphocytes by Curcumin, an Active Constituent of Medicinal Herb *Curcuma longa* Linn," *Journal of Clinical Biochemical Nutrition* 41, no. 1 (July 2007): 32–42.

Mulero, M., et al. "*Polypodium leucotomos* Extract Inhibits Glutathione Oxidation and Prevents Langerhans Cell Depletion Induced by UVB/UVA Radiation in a Hairless Rat Model," *Experimental Dermatology* 17, no. 8 (August 2008): 653–58.

Näse, L., et al. "Effect of Long-Term Consumption of a Probiotic Bacterium, *Lactobacillus rhamnosus GG*, in Milk on Dental Caries and Caries Risk in Children," *Caries Research* 35, no. 6 (November–December 2001): 412–20.

Nestel, P., et al. "The n-3 Fatty Acids Eicosapentaenoic Acid and Docosahexaenoic Acid Increase Systemic Arterial Compliance in Humans," *American Journal of Clinical Nutrition* 76, no. 2 (August 2002): 326–30.

Niedzielin, K., H. Kordecki, and B. Birkenfeld. "A Controlled, Double-Blind, Randomized Study on the Efficacy of *Lactobacillus plantarum* 299V in Patients with Irritable Bowel Syndrome," *European Journal of Gastroenterology and Hepatology* 13, no. 10 (October 2001): 1143–47.

Niture, S. K., et al. "Increased Expression of the MGMT Repair Protein Mediated by Cysteine Prodrugs and Chemopreventive Natural Products in Human Lymphocytes and Tumor Cell Lines," *Carcinogenesis* 28, no. 2 (February 2007): 378–89.

Olney, J. W. "Glutamate, a Neurotoxic Transmitter," *Journal of Child Neurology* 4, no. 3 (July 1989): 218–26.

Ouwehand, A. C., S. Salminen, and E. Isolauri. "Probiotics: An Overview of Beneficial Effects," *Antonie Van Leeuwenhoek* 82, nos. 1–4 (August 2002): 279–89.

Pacheco-Palencia, L. A., et al. "Protective Effects of Standardized Pomegranate (*Punica granatum L.*) Polyphenolic Extract in Ultraviolet-Irradiated Human Skin Fibroblasts," *Journal of Agricultural Food Chemistry* 56, no. 18 (September 24, 2008): 8434–41.

Parikka, H., et al. "Ventricular Arrhythmia Suppression by Magnesium Treatment after Coronary Artery Bypass Surgery," *International Journal of Angiology* 8, no. 3 (June 1999): 165–70.

Park, J., and M. H. Floch. "Prebiotics, Probiotics, and Dietary Fiber in Gastrointestinal Disease," *Gastroenterology Clinics of North America* 36, no. 1 (March 2007): 47–63, v.

Pedersen, M. H., et al. "The Effect of Dietary Fish Oil in Addition to Lifestyle Counseling on Lipid Oxidation and Body Composition in Slightly Overweight Teenage Boys," *Journal of Nutrition and Metabolism* (2011): 348368.

Price, P. T., C. M. Nelson, and S. D. Clarke. "Omega-3 Polyunsaturated Fatty Acid Regulation of Gene Expression," *Current Opinion in Lipidology* 11, no. 1 (February 2000): 3–7.

Qu, X., et al. "Magnesium and the Risk of Cardiovascular Events: A Meta-Analysis of Prospective Cohort Studies," *PLoS One* 8, no. 3 (2013): e57720.

Rasic-Milutinovic, Z., et al. "Association of Blood Pressure and Metabolic Syndrome Components with Magnesium Levels in Drinking Water in Some Serbian Municipalities," *Journal of Water and Health* 10, no. 1 (March 2012): 161–69.

Rathnasiri Bandara, S. M. "Paranasal Sinus Nitric Oxide and Migraine: A New Hypothesis on the Sino Rhinogenic Theory," *Medical Hypotheses* 80, no. 4 (April 2013): 329–40.

Ravindranath, M. H., et al. "Anticancer Therapeutic Potential of Soy Isoflavone, Genistein," *Advances in Experimental Medicine and Biology* 546 (2004): 121–65.

Ray, S. D., et al. "Differential Effects of IH636 Grape Seed Proanthocyanidin Extract and a DNA Repair Modulator 4-Aminobenzamide on Liver Microsomal Cytochrome 4502E1-Dependent Aniline Hydroxylation," *Molecular and Cellular Biochemistry* 218, nos. 1–2 (February 2001): 27–33.

———. "In Vivo Protection of DNA Damage Associated Apoptotic and Necrotic Cell Deaths during Acetaminophen-Induced Nephrotoxicity, Amiodarone-Induced Lung Toxicity, and Doxorubicin-Induced Cardiotoxicity by a Novel IH636 Grape Seed Proanthocyanidin Extract," *Research Communications in Molecular Pathology and Pharmacology* 101, nos. 1–2 (2000): 137–66.

Reid, G., et al. "Potential Uses of Probiotics in Clinical Practice," *Clinical Microbiology Review* 16, no. 4 (October 2003): 658–72.

Sanders, M. E. "Considerations for Use of Probiotic Bacteria to Modulate Human Health," *The Journal of Nutrition* 130, sup. 2S (February 2000): 384S–390S.

Santos, R. A., and C. S. Takahashi. "Anticlastogenic and Antigenotoxic Effects of Selenomethionine on Doxorubicin-Induced Damage in Vitro in Human Lymphocytes," *Food and Chemical Toxicology* 46, no. 2 (February 2008): 671–77.

Sarker, S. A., et al. "*Lactobacillus paracasei* Strain ST11 Has No Effect on Rotavirus but Ameliorates the Outcome of Nonrotavirus Diarrhea in Children from Bangladesh," *Pediatrics* 116, no. 2 (August 2005): e221–28.

Sazawal, S., et al. "Efficacy of Probiotics in Prevention of Acute Diarrhoea: A Meta-Analysis of Masked, Randomised, Placebo-Controlled Trials," *Lancet Infectious Diseases* 6, no. 6 (June 2006): 374–82.

Schwartz, T. R., and E. B. Kmiec. "Reduction of Gene Repair by Selenomethionine with the Use of Single-Stranded Oligonucleotides," *BMC Molecular Biology* 8 (January 26, 2007): 7.

Seo, Y. R., M. R. Kelley, and M. L. Smith. "Selenomethionine Regulation of p53 by a ref1-Dependent Redox Mechanism," *Proceedings of the National Academy of Science of the United States of America* 99, no. 22 (October 29, 2002): 14548–53.

Seo, Y. R., C. Sweeney, and M. L. Smith. "Selenomethionine Induction of DNA Repair Response in Human Fibroblasts," *Oncogene* 21, no. 23 (May 23, 2002): 3663–69.

Seseña, S., and M. L. Palop. "An Ecological Study of Lactic Acid Bacteria from Almagro Eggplant Fermentation Brines," *Journal of Applied Microbiology* 103, no. 5 (November 2007): 1553–61.

Singh, R. B. "Effect of Dietary Magnesium Supplementation in the Prevention of Coronary Heart Disease and Sudden Cardiac Death," *Magnesium and Trace Elements* 9, no. 3 (1990): 143–51.

Siscovick, J. R., et al. "*Polypodium leucotomos* Inhibits Ultraviolet B Radiation-Induced Immunosuppression," *Photodermatology, Photoimmunology, and Photomedicine* 24, no. 3 (June 2008): 134–41.

Surawicz, C. M. "Role of Probiotics in Antibiotic-Associated Diarrhea, Clostridium Difficile-Associated Diarrhea, and Recurrent Clostridium Difficile-Associated Diarrhea," *Journal of Clinical Gastroenterology* 42, sup. 2 (July 2008): S64–70.

Tubelius, P., V. Stan, and A. Zachrisson. "Increasing Work-Place Healthiness with the Probiotic *Lactobacillus reuteri*: A Randomised, Double-Blind Placebo-Controlled Study," *Environmental Health* 4 (November 7, 2005): 25.

Usha, S., I. M. Johnson, and R. Malathi. "Interaction of Resveratrol and Genistein with Nucleic Acids," *Journal of Biochemistry and Molecular Biology* 38, no. 2 (March 31, 2005): 198–205.

Van Erk, M. J., et al. "Time- and Dose-Dependent Effects of Curcumin on Gene Expression in Human Colon Cancer Cells," *Journal of Carcinogenesis* 3, no. 1 (May 12, 2004): 8.

Weizman, Z., G. Asli, and A. Alsheikh. "Effect of a Probiotic Infant Formula on Infections in Child Care Centers: Comparison of Two Probiotic Agents," *Pediatrics* 115, no. 1 (January 2005): 5–9.

Whorwell, P. J., et al. "Efficacy of an Encapsulated Probiotic *Bifidobacterium infantis* 35624 in Women with Irritable Bowel Syndrome," *American Journal of Gastroenterology* 101, no. 7 (July 2006): 1581–90.

Wollowski, I., G. Rechkemmer, and B. L. Pool-Zobel. "Protective Role of Probiotics and Prebiotics in Colon Cancer," *The American Journal of Clinical Nutrition* 73, sup. 2 (February 2001): 451S–455S.

Xu, J., et al. "Sterol Regulatory Element Binding Protein-1 Expression Is Suppressed by Dietary Polyunsaturated Fatty Acids: A Mechanism for the Coordinate Suppression of Lipogenic Genes by Polyunsaturated Fats," *Journal of Biological Chemistry* 274, no. 33 (August 13, 1999): 23577–83.

Xue, H., et al. "Inhibition of Cellular Transformation by Berry Extracts," *Carcinogenesis* 22, no. 2 (February 2001): 351–56.Erratum in *Carcinogenesis* 22, no. 5 (May 2001): 831–33.

Zulyniak, M. A., et al. "Fish Oil Supplementation Alters Circulating Eicosanoid Concentrations in Young Healthy Men," *Metabolism* 62, no. 8 (August 2013): 1107–13.

Chapter 10

Barres, R., et al. "Acute Exercise Remodels Promoter Methylation in Human Skeletal Muscle," *Cell Metabolism* 15, no. 3 (March 2012): 405–11.

Bouic, P. J., et al. "The Effects of B-Sitosterol (BSS) and B-Sitosterol Glucoside (BSSG) Mixture on Selected Immune Parameters of Marathon Runners: Inhibition of Post Marathon Immune Suppression and Inflammation," *International Journal of Sports Medicine* 20, no. 4 (May 1999): 258–62.

Fujita, S., et al. "Aerobic Exercise Overcomes the Age-Related Insulin Resistance of Muscle Protein Metabolism by Improving Endothelial Function and Akt/dMammalian Target of Rapamycin Signaling," *Diabetes* 56, no. 6 (June 2007): 1615–22.

Gleeson, M. "Immune Function in Sport and Exercise," *Journal of Applied Physiology* 103, no. 2 (August 2007): 693–99.

Holloszy, J. O. "Exercise Increases Average Longevity of Female Rats Despite Increased Food Intake and No Growth Retardation," *Journal of Gerontology* 48, no. 3 (1993): B97–B100.

Kotler, D.P. "Cachexia," *Annals of Internal Medicine* 133 (2000): 622–34.

Manning, J. M., and F. H. Bronson. "Suppression of Puberty in Rats by Exercise: Effects on Hormone Levels and Reversal with GnRH Infusion," *American Journal of Physiology* 260, 4 pt. 2 (April 1991): R717–23.

Mastaloudis, A., S. W. Leonard, and M. G. Traber. "Oxidative Stress in Athletes during Extreme Endurance Exercise," *Free Radical Biology and Medicine* 31, no. 7 (October 1, 2001): 911–22.

Niess, A. M., et al. "DNA Damage after Exhaustive Treadmill Running in Trained and Untrained Men," *International Journal of Sports Medicine* 17, no. 6 (August 1996): 397–403.

Patil, H. R., et al. "Cardiovascular Damage Resulting from Chronic Excessive Endurance Exercise," *Missouri Medicine* 109, no. 4 (July–August 2012): 312–21.

Pereira, C. T., et al. "Age-Dependent Differences in Survival after Severe Burns: A Unicentric Review of 1,674 Patients and 179 Autopsies over 15 Years," *Journal of the American College of Surgeons* 202, no. 3 (March 2006): 536–48.

Rosenberg, I. H., and R. Roubenoff. "Stalking Sarcopenia," *Annals of Internal Medicine* 123, no. 9 (November 1, 1995): 727–28.

Shah, N. R., et al. "Severe Physical Exertion, Oxidative Stress, and Acute Lung Injury," *Clinical Journal of Sports Medicine* 21, no. 6 (November 2011): 537–38.

Tipton, K. D., et al. "Acute Response of Net Muscle Protein Balance Reflects 24-h Balance after Exercise and Amino Acid Ingestion," *American Journal of Physiology, Endocrinology and Metabolism* 284, no. 1 (January 2003): E76–89.

Trushina, E. N., et al. "Dysfunction in Highly Skilled Athletes and Nutritional Rehabilitation," *Voprosy Pitaniia* 81, no. 2 (2012): 73–80.

Williamson, D. L., et al. "Exercise-Induced Alterations in Extracellular Signal-Regulated Kinase 1/2 and Mammalian Target of Rapamycin (mTOR) Signalling to Regulatory Mechanisms of mRNA Translation in Mouse Muscle," *The Journal of Physiology* 573, pt. 2 (June 1, 2006): 497–510.

Wolfe, R. R. "The Underappreciated Role of Muscle in Health and Disease," *American Journal of Clinical Nutrition* 84, no. 3 (September 2006): 475–82.

Zhang, X. J., et al. "The Flow Phase of Wound Metabolism Is Characterized by Stimulated Protein Synthesis Rather than Cell Proliferation," *Journal of Surgical Research* 135, no. 1 (September 2006): 61–67.

[A NOTE ON REFERENCES AND RECOMMENDED READING]

THE INFORMATION AND ADVICE CONTAINED in this book are based on my in-depth analysis of hundreds of scientific studies, articles, and books, as well as discussions and interviews with health experts of every kind and background information from highly reputable sources. To include a bibliography of all of these resources would have extended the length of this book significantly, so I have decided instead to make them available on my website, www.tanaamen.com.

HERE ARE SOME OF THE books that have enlightened and inspired me during my journey to optimal health. I encourage you to take a look at them—they're fantastic sources of information and support as you make changes that will improve your health and your life.

The Blood Sugar Solution: The UltraHealthy Program for Losing Weight, Preventing Disease, and Feeling Great Now!, by Mark Hyman, MD. New York: Little, Brown, 2012.

Change Your Brain, Change Your Body: Use Your Brain to Get and Keep the Body You Have Always Wanted, by Daniel G. Amen, MD. New York: Random House, 2010.

Clinical Natural Medicine Handbook, by Chris D. Melitis, ND, Nieske Zabriskie, ND, and Robert Rountree, MD. New Rochelle, NY: Mary Ann Liebert, Inc., 2008.

Cracking the Metabolic Code, by James B. LaValle, RPh, CCN, ND, with Stacy Lundin Yale, RN, BSN. Laguna Beach, CA: Basic Health Publications, 2003.

Dr. Gundry's Diet Evolution: Turn Off the Genes That Are Killing You and Your Waistline, by Steven R. Gundry, MD, FACS., FACC. New York: Crown, 2008.

The End of Overeating: Taking Control of the Insatiable American Appetite, by David A. Kessler, MD. Emmaus, PA: Rodale, 2009.

Epigenetics in Human Disease, by Trygve Tollesfbok. Academic Press, 2012.

Fat Chance: Beating the Odds Against Sugar, Processed Food, Obesity, and Disease, by Robert H. Lustig, MD. New York: Hudson Street, 2012.

Food, Inc.: Mendel to Monsanto—The Promises and Perils of the Biotech Harvest, by Peter Pringle New York: Simon & Schuster, 2003.

Genetic Roulette: The Documented Health Risks of Genetically Engineered Food, by Jeffrey M. Smith. White River Junction, VT: Chelsea Green, 2007.

Healing ADD: The Breakthrough Program That Allows You to See and Heal the 6 Types of ADD, by Daniel G. Amen, MD. New York: Putnam, 2001.

Loving What Is: Four Questions That Can Change Your Life, by Byron Katie, with Stephen Mitchell. New York: Crown, 2002.

Nutrition for the Focused Brain and the Recovering Brain, by Jeffrey L. Fortuna, PH, MS. Independence, KY: Cengage Learning, 2009.

The Paleo Diet: Lose Weight and Get Healthy by Eating the Foods You Were Designed to Eat, by Loren Cordain, PhD. Jersey City, NJ: Wiley, 2001.

Personal Power 30-Day System by Anthony Robbins (self-published on audio).

Superfoods: The Food and Medicine of the Future, by David Wolfe. Berkeley, CA: North Atlantic Books, 2009.

Toxic Fat: When Good Fat Turns Bad, by Barry Sears, PhD. Nashville, TN: Thomas Nelson, 2008.

What Your Doctor May Not Tell You about Heart Disease, by Mark C. Houston, MD, MS. New York: Grand Central, 2012.

Wheat Belly: Lose the Wheat, Lose the Weight, and Find Your Path Back to Health, by William Davis, MD. Emmaus, PA: Rodale, 2011.

You On a Diet: The Owner's Manual for Waist Management, by Michael F. Roizen, MD, and Mehmet C. Oz, MD. New York: Free Press, 2006.

[OMNI SHOPPING LIST]

MEAT, POULTRY, AND FISH

Choose meats and poultry that are organic, grass-fed, free-range, hormone-free, and antibiotic-free. Fish should be wild, hormone-free, and antibiotic-free.

- Bison
- Herring
- Lamb
- Mackerel
- Shrimp
- Skinless chicken
- Skinless turkey
- Tuna
- Wild salmon

VEGETABLES

Choose fresh, organic vegetables such as:

- Artichokes
- Asparagus
- Avocados
- Bean sprouts
- Bell peppers
- Bok choy
- Broccoli, romaine lettuce
- Brussels sprouts
- Cabbage
- Cauliflower
- Celery
- Chard
- Cucumbers
- Green beans
- Kale
- Mushrooms
- Onions
- Spinach
- Squash
- Sweet potatoes
- Tomatoes
- Watercress
- Zucchini

PANTRY AND REFRIGERATOR BASICS

- Condiments for dipping (hummus, guacamole, salsa)
- Dried beans and lentils in limited amounts
- Eggs. Choose cage-free, organic, DHA-enriched eggs from vegetarian-fed chickens.

- Freeze-dried greens such as Green Vibrance.
- Fresh and dried herbs and spices, which provide rich nutritional benefits and fantastic flavor
- Healthy oils such as coconut oil, almond oil, macadamia-nut oil, grapeseed oil, and olive oil
- Lean meat, fish, and poultry
- Milk alternatives: almond, coconut, hemp, rice milk
- Nut butters and spreads (almond butter and coconut butter)
- Protein powder
- Pure Wrap coconut wraps
- Quinoa
- Raw, unsalted seeds and nuts
- Seeds (chia, flax, hemp)
- Small amounts of fresh and frozen fruit. The best choices are organic strawberries, blueberries, raspberries, and blackberries.
- Super-foods (such as maca root, goji powder, lucuma, and pomegranate) that magnify health-supporting processes
- Sweeteners such as stevia extract and erythritol
- Tamari sauce
- Vegannaise
- Vegetables of all kinds (except white potatoes and nightshades for some of you). Purchase fresh, organic produce when possible.

SPICES

- Basil
- Black pepper
- Cayenne pepper
- Chili powder
- Cilantro
- Cinnamon
- Cloves
- Coriander
- Curry
- Dill
- Garlic
- Ginger
- Marjoram
- Mint
- Nutmeg
- Oregano
- Parsley
- Rosemary
- Saffron
- Sage
- Thyme

[HEALTHY SNACK REPLACEMENTS]

- Green tea latte: steamed almond milk with a bag of green chai tea and a few drops of cinnamon-flavored stevia instead of sugary coffee latte full of milk.

- Light coconut milk in your tea or coffee instead of half-and-half or soy creamer.

- Drink sparkling water sweetened with root beer–flavored stevia instead of diet soda.

- Squeeze lemon or lime or a few drops of lemon-flavored stevia into seltzer, instead of wine.

- Spread almond butter and sliced banana on a coconut wrap in place of peanut butter and jelly.

- Replace candy with Brain on Joy bars.

- Replace ice cream with avocado gelato.

- Eat half an apple with almond butter instead of cookies and candy.

- Eat ¼ cup raw, unsalted nuts and one piece of 70-percent cocoa dark chocolate instead of muffins, candies, and cookies.

- Suck on a handful of frozen grapes instead of sugary ice pops.

- Use flax crackers and veggies for dipping instead of chips.

- Swap butter, cheese, ketchup, and mayonnaise for healthy alternatives: guacamole, salsa, and hummus.

- Use lettuce wraps instead of bread for sandwiches and burgers.

- Use coconut wraps (Pure Wraps) instead of tortillas for burritos.

[FOODS TO DITCH]

- Alcohol (Phase 1)
- Bread, pasta, tortillas, and other foods that contain gluten
- Breakfast cereals (including oatmeal)
- Commercially raised beef and poultry
- Condiments such as ketchup, soy sauce, and barbecue sauce that contain sugar, artificial ingredients, excessive salt, or gluten
- Corn (including popcorn, cornbread, and popped corn chips)
- Dairy foods such as milk, cheese, cream, yogurt, and ice cream
- Farm-raised fish
- Foods that contain genetically modified ingredients
- Foods that contain high-fructose corn syrup or trans (hydrogenated) fats
- Foods that contain sugar, artificial sweeteners, or soy
- Fruit juice (even 100% fresh!)
- Grain-based foods (cereal, rice, instant oatmeal, wheat, barley, rye, and corn)
- Jams, jellies, pancake syrup
- Most cooking oils (corn, safflower, canola, soy)
- Pork and ham
- Processed frozen dinners
- Processed meats such as bacon, sausage, pepperoni, hot dogs, lunch meats
- Salty processed snacks (potato chips, popcorn, pretzels, nacho chips, crackers)
- Soy-based foods such as protein bars, powders, oils, and snack foods
- Sugary processed snacks (cakes, cookies, cupcakes, candy)
- Sweetened drinks such as fruit punch, lemonade, and soda
- White potatoes

[YOUR DAILY SUCCESS PLANNER]

I DESIGNED THIS DAILY JOURNAL to help you stay motivated and on the right track for achieving all of your goals. It allows you to plan your Omni Diet meals for the next day. Remember: "If you fail to plan, you plan to fail." You will also find tips to motivate you and help you stick with your plan.

Each day also includes a checklist of healthy behaviors for you to choose from to help you achieve your goals. Using this journal will keep your goals clearly before you, giving you the motivation to keep going and the strength to make the choices that keep you feeling and looking your best. This journal will be your companion for six weeks. But that's just the beginning. By the end, you'll be seeing the benefits of your healthy new lifestyle and you'll be eager to continue with it.

Before you get started, take stock of your numbers. As my husband, Dr. Daniel Amen, says, "You can't change what you don't measure!" As you start the Omni Diet, make a record of your current physical condition and habits. Then, at the end of the six weeks, compare those numbers with your current stats to see how much progress you've made.

There is space to record that information below. You'll find a two-page journal entry for each of seven days. You can photocopy the pages to give you enough for the next six weeks. Make a commitment to faithfully use this great tool, or simply jot everything down in a notebook or in your smart phone. The important thing is to keep a journal, no matter what format you choose.

	WEEK 1	WEEK 6
Weight		
BMI		
Number of Hours of Sleep per Night		
Blood Pressure		
Blood Work (like cholesterol, thyroid hormone levels, triglycerides)		
Mood		

THE OMNI DIET DAILY JOURNAL

	DAY ONE	Date _____		
Time	**Food & Beverages**		**Calories**	**Healthy?**
	Breakfast			Yes/No
	Snack			Yes/No
	Lunch			Yes/No
	Snack			Yes/No
	Dinner			Yes/No
	Other			Yes/No
	Total Calories Consumed			
	Total Liquid Calories Consumed			
	Total Calories Allowed			

THE OMNI DIET DAILY JOURNAL

Become A Warrior For Your Health!

DAY ONE

What is my desired outcome for the day? (Why MUST I do this?)

_____

_____

Three things I am grateful for today:

1. _____

2. _____

3. _____

Today's Weight	Hours Slept Last Night	Managed stress?

On a scale of 1 to 10 rate the following: (1 = poor, 10 = great)

Mood	Energy	Digestion	Other Symptoms

Write your own mantra. Say it until you believe it.

_____

_____

Choose 5 healthy habits from the list below.

☐ Exercise 1 extra day each week

☐ Lift weights at least 2X each week

☐ Drink 1 extra glass of water daily

☐ Eat 1 extra cup of vegetables daily

☐ Write in a food journal every day

☐ Find an accountability buddy (AB)

☐ Talk to your AB 2X each week

☐ Do "The Work of Byron Katie": www.thework.com

☐ Post a photo of someone you admire who mirrors your goals

☐ Drink fresh green drinks 2X a week

☐ Go in the sauna 2X each week

☐ Write 5 things you're grateful for each morning

☐ Mentor someone who wants improved health

☐ List your daily victories in a victory journal

☐ Review your goals and values

☐ Pray/meditate for 5 minutes daily

MOTIVATIONAL BLAST

The most dangerous thing in the world is to try to leap a chasm in two jumps.
—David Lloyd George

THE OMNI DIET DAILY JOURNAL

Time	Food & Beverages	Calories	Healthy?
DAY TWO		Date _____	
Breakfast			Yes/No
Snack			Yes/No
Lunch			Yes/No
Snack			Yes/No
Dinner			Yes/No
Other			Yes/No
	Total Calories Consumed		
	Total Liquid Calories Consumed		
	Total Calories Allowed		

THE OMNI DIET DAILY JOURNAL

Become A Warrior For Your Health!

What is my desired outcome for the day? (Why MUST I do this?)

_____

_____

Three things I am grateful for today:

1. _____

2. _____

3. _____

Today's Weight	Hours Slept Last Night	Managed stress?

On a scale of 1 to 10 rate the following: (1 = poor, 10 = great)			
Mood	Energy	Digestion	Other Symptoms

Write your own mantra. Say it until you believe it.

_____

_____

Choose 5 healthy habits from the list below.

☐ Exercise 1 extra day each week

☐ Lift weights at least 2X each week

☐ Drink 1 extra glass of water daily

☐ Eat 1 extra cup of vegetables daily

☐ Write in a food journal every day

☐ Find an accountability buddy (AB)

☐ Talk to your AB 2X each week

☐ Do "The Work of Byron Katie": www.thework.com

☐ Post a photo of someone you admire who mirrors your goals

☐ Drink fresh green drinks 2X a week

☐ Go in the sauna 2X each week

☐ Write 5 things you're grateful for each morning

☐ Mentor someone who wants improved health

☐ List your daily victories in a victory journal

☐ Review your goals and values

☐ Pray/meditate for 5 minutes daily

MOTIVATIONAL BLAST

On each side of the river grew a tree of life, bearing twelve crops of fruit, with a fresh crop each month. The leaves were used for medicine to heal the nations. —Holy Bible

THE OMNI DIET DAILY JOURNAL

Time	Food & Beverages	Calories	Healthy?
DAY THREE		Date _____	
	Breakfast		Yes/No
	Snack		Yes/No
	Lunch		Yes/No
	Snack		Yes/No
	Dinner		Yes/No
	Other		Yes/No
	Total Calories Consumed		
	Total Liquid Calories Consumed		
	Total Calories Allowed		

THE OMNI DIET DAILY JOURNAL

Become A Warrior For Your Health!

What is my desired outcome for the day? (Why MUST I do this?)

_____

_____

Three things I am grateful for today:

1. _____

2. _____

3. _____

Today's Weight	Hours Slept Last Night	Managed stress?

On a scale of 1 to 10 rate the following: (1 = poor, 10 = great)			
Mood	Energy	Digestion	Other Symptoms

Write your own mantra. Say it until you believe it.

_____

_____

Choose 5 healthy habits from the list below.

☐ Exercise 1 extra day each week

☐ Lift weights at least 2X each week

☐ Drink 1 extra glass of water daily

☐ Eat 1 extra cup of vegetables daily

☐ Write in a food journal every day

☐ Find an accountability buddy (AB)

☐ Talk to your AB 2X each week

☐ Do "The Work of Byron Katie": www.thework.com

☐ Post a photo of someone you admire who mirrors your goals

☐ Drink fresh green drinks 2X a week

☐ Go in the sauna 2X each week

☐ Write 5 things you're grateful for each morning

☐ Mentor someone who wants improved health

☐ List your daily victories in a victory journal

☐ Review your goals and values

☐ Pray/meditate for 5 minutes daily

MOTIVATIONAL BLAST

The greatest wealth is health. —Virgil

THE OMNI DIET DAILY JOURNAL

If You Fail to Plan, You Plan to Fail. Plan Your Meals for Tomorrow.

Time	DAY FOUR	Date _____	Calories	Healthy?
	Breakfast			Yes/No
	Snack			Yes/No
	Lunch			Yes/No
	Snack			Yes/No
	Dinner			Yes/No
	Other			Yes/No
	Total Calories Consumed			
	Total Liquid Calories Consumed			
	Total Calories Allowed			

THE OMNI DIET DAILY JOURNAL

Become A Warrior For Your Health!

DAY FOUR

What is my desired outcome for the day? (Why MUST I do this?)

_____

_____

Three things I am grateful for today:

1. _____

2. _____

3. _____

Today's Weight	Hours Slept Last Night	Managed stress?

On a scale of 1 to 10 rate the following: (1 = poor, 10 = great)			
Mood	Energy	Digestion	Other Symptoms

Write your own mantra. Say it until you believe it.

_____

_____

Choose 5 healthy habits from the list below.

☐ Exercise 1 extra day each week

☐ Lift weights at least 2X each week

☐ Drink 1 extra glass of water daily

☐ Eat 1 extra cup of vegetables daily

☐ Write in a food journal every day

☐ Find an accountability buddy (AB)

☐ Talk to your AB 2X each week

☐ Do "The Work of Byron Katie": www.thework.com

☐ Post a photo of someone you admire who mirrors your goals

☐ Drink fresh green drinks 2X a week

☐ Go in the sauna 2X each week

☐ Write 5 things you're grateful for each morning

☐ Mentor someone who wants improved health

☐ List your daily victories in a victory journal

☐ Review your goals and values

☐ Pray/meditate for 5 minutes daily

MOTIVATIONAL BLAST

A healthy attitude is contagious but don't wait to catch it from others. Be a carrier.
—*Tom Stoppard*

THE OMNI DIET DAILY JOURNAL

Date _____

Time	Food & Beverages	Calories	Healthy?
Breakfast			Yes/No
Snack			Yes/No
Lunch			Yes/No
Snack			Yes/No
Dinner			Yes/No
Other			Yes/No
	Total Calories Consumed		
	Total Liquid Calories Consumed		
	Total Calories Allowed		

THE OMNI DIET DAILY JOURNAL

Become A Warrior For Your Health!

What is my desired outcome for the day? (Why MUST I do this?)

_____

_____

Three things I am grateful for today:

1. _____

2. _____

3. _____

Today's Weight	Hours Slept Last Night	Managed stress?

On a scale of 1 to 10 rate the following: (1 = poor, 10 = great)			
Mood	Energy	Digestion	Other Symptoms

Write your own mantra. Say it until you believe it.

_____

_____

Choose 5 healthy habits from the list below.

☐ Exercise 1 extra day each week

☐ Lift weights at least 2X each week

☐ Drink 1 extra glass of water daily

☐ Eat 1 extra cup of vegetables daily

☐ Write in a food journal every day

☐ Find an accountability buddy (AB)

☐ Talk to your AB 2X each week

☐ Drink fresh green drinks 2X a week

☐ Go in the sauna 2X each week

☐ Write 5 things you're grateful for each morning

☐ Mentor someone who wants improved health

☐ List your daily victories in a victory journal

☐ Review your goals and values

☐ Pray/meditate for 5 minutes daily

☐ Do "The Work of Byron Katie": www.thework.com

☐ Post a photo of someone you admire who mirrors your goals

MOTIVATIONAL BLAST

He who has health, has hope. And he who has hope, has everything. —*Arabian Proverb*

THE OMNI DIET DAILY JOURNAL

Time	DAY SIX	Food & Beverages	Date _____	Calories	Healthy?
	Breakfast				Yes/No
	Snack				Yes/No
	Lunch				Yes/No
	Snack				Yes/No
	Dinner				Yes/No
	Other				Yes/No
		Total Calories Consumed			
		Total Liquid Calories Consumed			
		Total Calories Allowed			

THE OMNI DIET DAILY JOURNAL

Become A Warrior For Your Health!

What is my desired outcome for the day? (Why MUST I do this?)

_____

_____

Three things I am grateful for today:

1. _____

2. _____

3. _____

Today's Weight	Hours Slept Last Night	Managed stress?

On a scale of 1 to 10 rate the following: (1 = poor, 10 = great)			
Mood	Energy	Digestion	Other Symptoms

Write your own mantra. Say it until you believe it.

_____

_____

Choose 5 healthy habits from the list below.

☐ Exercise 1 extra day each week

☐ Lift weights at least 2X each week

☐ Drink 1 extra glass of water daily

☐ Eat 1 extra cup of vegetables daily

☐ Write in a food journal every day

☐ Find an accountability buddy (AB)

☐ Talk to your AB 2X each week

☐ Do "The Work of Byron Katie": www.thework.com

☐ Post a photo of someone you admire who mirrors your goals

☐ Drink fresh green drinks 2X a week

☐ Go in the sauna 2X each week

☐ Write 5 things you're grateful for each morning

☐ Mentor someone who wants improved health

☐ List your daily victories in a victory journal

☐ Review your goals and values

☐ Pray/meditate for 5 minutes daily

MOTIVATIONAL BLAST

You can set yourself up to be sick, or you can choose to stay well. —_Wayne Dyer_

THE OMNI DIET DAILY JOURNAL

Time	Food & Beverages	Calories	Healthy?
DAY SEVEN Date _____			
Breakfast			Yes/No
Snack			Yes/No
Lunch			Yes/No
Snack			Yes/No
Dinner			Yes/No
Other			Yes/No
	Total Calories Consumed		
	Total Liquid Calories Consumed		
	Total Calories Allowed		

THE OMNI DIET DAILY JOURNAL

Become A Warrior For Your Health!

What is my desired outcome for the day? (Why MUST I do this?)

_____

_____

Three things I am grateful for today:

1. _____

2. _____

3. _____

Today's Weight	Hours Slept Last Night	Managed stress?

On a scale of 1 to 10 rate the following: (1 = poor, 10 = great)			
Mood	Energy	Digestion	Other Symptoms

Write your own mantra. Say it until you believe it.

_____

_____

Choose 5 healthy habits from the list below.

☐ Exercise 1 extra day each week

☐ Lift weights at least 2X each week

☐ Drink 1 extra glass of water daily

☐ Eat 1 extra cup of vegetables daily

☐ Write in a food journal every day

☐ Find an accountability buddy (AB)

☐ Talk to your AB 2X each week

☐ Do "The Work of Byron Katie": www.thework.com

☐ Post a photo of someone you admire who mirrors your goals

☐ Drink fresh green drinks 2X a week

☐ Go in the sauna 2X each week

☐ Write 5 things you're grateful for each morning

☐ Mentor someone who wants improved health

☐ List your daily victories in a victory journal

☐ Review your goals and values

☐ Pray/meditate for 5 minutes daily

MOTIVATIONAL BLAST

It is only the first step that is difficult. —Marie De Vichy-Chamrond

[ENDNOTES]

Chapter 1

1. Diabetes Prevention Program Research Group, "Reduction in the Incidence of Type 2 Diabetes with Lifestyle Intervention or Metformin," *New England Journal of Medicine* 346 (July 7, 2002): 393–403.

2. A. Aljada et al., "Increase in Intranuclear Nuclear Factor kappaB and Decrease in Inhibitor kappaB in Mononuclear Cells after a Mixed Meal: Evidence for a Proinflammatory Effect," *American Journal of Clinical Nutrition* 79, no. 4 (April 2004): 682–90.

3. Takuya Miyahara et al., "D-Series Resolvin Attenuates Vascular Smooth Muscle Cell Activation and Neointimal Hyperplasia Following Vascular Injury," *The FASEB Journal* 27 (June 2013): 2220–32.

4. N. Bhatnagar et al., "3,3'-diindolylmethane Enhances the Efficacy of Butyrate in Colon Cancer Prevention through Down-regulation of Survivin," *Cancer Prevention Research (Philadephia)* 2, no. 6 (2009): 581–89.

5. R. S. Lee, "Chronic Corticosterone Exposure Increases Expression and Decreases Deoxyribonucleic Acid Methylation of Fkbp5 in Mice," *Endocrinology* 151, no. 9 (September 2010): 4332–43.

6. H. H. Hermsdorff et al., "Fruit and Vegetable Consumption and Proinflammatory Gene Expression from Peripheral Blood Mononuclear Cells in Young Adults: A Translational Study," *Nutrition & Metabolism (London)* 7 (May 13, 2010): 42.

7. K. Gross-Steinmeyer et al., "Sulforaphane- and Phenethyl Isothiocyanate-Induced Inhibition of Aflatoxin B1-Mediated Genotoxicity in Human Hepatocytes: Role of GSTM1 Genotype and CYP3A4 Gene Expression," *Toxicological Sciences* 116, no. 2 (August 2010): 422–32.

8. http://www.ars.usda.gov/is/AR/archive/nov96/plant.pdf.

9. Y. Z. Fang, S. Yang, and G. Wu, "Free Radicals, Antioxidants, and Nutrition," *Nutrition* 18 (2002): 872–79.

10. D. Ikeoka, J. K. Mader, and T. R. Pieber, "Adipose Tissue, Inflammation, and Cardiovascular Disease," *Revista da Associação Médica Brasileira* 56, no. 1 (January–February 2010): 116–21.

11. C. Pagnini et al., "Probiotics Promote Gut Health through Stimulation of Epithelial Innate Immunity," *Proceedings of the National Academy of Science USA* 107, no. 1 (January 2010): 454–59.

12. Centers for Disease Control and Prevention: Overweight and Obesity, http://www.cdc.gov/obesity/index.html.

13. S. Sharma and S. Fulton, "Diet-Induced Obesity Promotes Depressive-like Behaviour That Is Associated with Neural Adaptations in Brain Reward Circuitry," *International Journal of Obesity* 37 (March 2013): 382–89.

14. H. Okazawa et al., "Statistical Mapping Analysis of Serotonin Synthesis Images Generated in Healthy Volunteers Using Positron-Emission Tomography and Alpha-[11C]methyl-L-tryptophan," *Journal of Psychiatry & Neuroscience* 25, no. 4 (September 2000): 359–70.

Chapter 2

1. T. Akbaraly et al., "Does Overall Diet in Midlife Predict Future Aging Phenotypes? A Cohort Study," *American Journal of Medicine* 126, no. 5 (May 2013): 411–19.

2. L. Cordain et al., "Plant-Animal Subsistence Ratios and Macronutrient Energy Estimations in Worldwide Hunter-Gatherer Diets," *American Journal of Clinical Nutrition* 71, no. 3 (2000): 682–92.

3. D. S. Weigle et al., "A High-Protein Diet Induces Sustained Reductions in Appetite, ad libitum Caloric Intake, and Body Weight Despite Compensatory Changes in Diurnal Plasma Leptin and Ghrelin Concentrations," *American Journal of Clinical Nutrition* 82, no. 1 (July 2005): 41–48.

4. R. Schmid et al., "Role of Amino Acids in Stimulation of Postprandial Insulin, Glucagon, and Pancreatic Polypeptide in Humans," *Pancreas* 3, no. 4 (1989): 305–14.

5. J. Montonen et al., "Consumption of Red Meat and Whole-Grain Bread in Relation to Biomarkers of Obesity, Inflammation, Glucose Metabolism, and Oxidative Stress," *European Journal of Nutrition* 52, no. 1 (February 2013): 337–45.

6. C. A. Daley et al., "A Review of Fatty Acid Profiles and Antioxidant Content in Grass-Fed and Grain-Fed Beef," *Nutrition Journal* 9 (March 2010): 10.

7. F. Wang and Y. Shan, "Sulforaphane Retards the Growth of UM-UC-3 Xenographs, Induces Apoptosis, and Reduces Survivin in Athymic Mice," *Nutritional Research* 32, no. 5 (May 2012): 374–80.

8. L. Li et al., "Curcumin (Diferuloylmethane) Down-Regulates Expression of Cell Proliferation and Antiapoptotic and Metastatic Gene Products through Suppression of I-kappa-B-alpha Kinase and Akt Activation," *Molecular Pharmacology* 69, no. 1 (January 2006): 195–206.

9. A. Medina-Remón et al., "The Effect of Polyphenol Consumption on Blood Pressure," *Mini-Reviews in Medicinal Chemistry* 13, no. 8 (June 2013): 1137–49.

10. T. L. Zern and M. L. Fernandez, "Cardioprotective Effects of Dietary Polyphenols," *Journal of Nutrition* 135, no. 10 (October 2005): 2291–94.

11. S. Davinelli et al., "Pleiotropicprotective Effects of Phytochemicals in Alzheimer's Disease," *Oxidative Medicine and Cellular Longevity* (2012): 386527.

12. M. J. Brown et al., "Carotenoid Bioavailability Is Higher from Salads Ingested with Full-Fat than with Fat-Reduced Salad Dressings as Measured with Electrochemical Detection," *American Journal of Clinical Nutrition* 80, no. 2 (August 2004): 396–403.

13. "Essential Fatty Acids," Linus Pauling Institute, http://lpi.oregonstate.edu/infocenter/othernuts/omega3fa/.

14. D. A. Khalil et al., "Soy Protein Supplementation Increases Serum Insulin-Like Growth Factor-I in Young and Old Men but Does Not Affect Markers of Bone Metabolism," *Journal of Nutrition* 132, no. 9 (September 2002): 2605–8.

15. K. S. Weber et al., "Dietary Soy-Phytoestrogens Decrease Testosterone Levels and Prostate Weight without Altering LH, Prostate 5alpha-reductase or Testicular Steroidogenic Acute Regulatory Peptide Levels in Adult Male Sprague-Dawley Rats," *Journal of Endocrinology* 170, no. 3 (September 2001): 591–99.

16. E. A. Finkelstein et al., "Obesity and Severe Obesity Forecasts through 2030," *American Journal of Preventive Medicine* 42, no. 6 (June 2012): 563–70.

17. A. P. Simopoulos, "Evolutionary Aspects of Diet, the Omega-6/Omega-3 Ratio, and Genetic Variation: Nutritional Implications for Chronic Diseases," *Biomedicine and Pharmacotherapy* 60, no. 9 (November 2006): 502–7.

18 P. W. Siri-Tarino et al., "Saturated Fat and Heart Disease: Meta-Analysis of Prospective Cohort Studies Evaluating the Association of Saturated Fat with Cardiovascular Disease," *American Journal of Clinical Nutrition* 91, no. 3 (March 2010): 535–46.

19. J. E. Hunter, J. Zhang, and P. M. Kris-Etherton, "Cardiovascular Disease Risk of Dietary Stearic Acid Compared with Trans, Other Saturated, and Unsaturated Fatty Acids: A Systematic Review," *American Journal of Clinical Nutrition* 91, no. 1 (January 2010): 46–63.

Chapter 3

1. L. Fontana et al., "Long-Term Calorie Restriction Is Highly Effective in Reducing the Risk for Atherosclerosis in Humans," *Proceedings of the National Academy of Sciences U S A* 101, no. 17 (April 27, 2004): 6659–63.
2. H. W. Park, "Longevity, Aging, and Caloric Restriction: Clive Maine McCay and the Construction of a Multidisciplinary Research Program," *Historical Studies in the Natural Sciences* 40, no. 1 (Winter 2010): 79–124.
3. L. Fontana et al., "Calorie Restriction or Exercise: Effects on Coronary Heart Disease Risk Factors. A Randomized, Controlled Trial," *American Journal of Physiology, Endocrinology, and Metabolism* 293, no. 1 (July 2007): E197–202.
4. R. Cangemi et al., "Long-Term Effects of Calorie Restriction on Serum Sex-Hormone Concentrations in Men," *Aging Cell* 9, no. 2 (April 2010): 236–42.
5. M. W. Hamrick et al., "Caloric Restriction Decreases Cortical Bone Mass but Spares Trabecular Bone in the Mouse Skeleton: Implications for the Regulation of Bone Mass by Body Weight," *Journal of Bone and Mineral Research* 23, no. 6 (June 2008): 870–78.
6. "Case Western Reserve Student Puts Gorillas on a Diet," Case Western Reserve University, accessed October 30, 2013, http://www.case.edu/magazine/springsummer2011/gorillas.html.

Chapter 4

1. *Guidelines for the Assessment of Herbal Medicines.* Geneva: Programme on Traditional Medicine, World Health Organisation, 1991, www.ncarboretum.org/assets/File/PDFs/Research/WHO_TRM_91.4.pdf.
2. N. Bhala et al., "Vascular and Upper Gastrointestinal Effects of Non-Steroidal Anti-Inflammatory Drugs: Meta-Analyses of Individual Participant Data from Randomised Trials," *The Lancet* 382, no. 9894 (August 31, 2013): 769–79, doi:10.1016/S0140-6736(13)60900-9.
3. P. Rahnama et al., "Effect of *Zingiber officinale* R. rhizomes (Ginger) on Pain Relief in Primary Dysmenorrhea: A Placebo Randomized Trial," *BMC Complementary and Alternative Medicine* 12 (July 10, 2012): 92, doi:10.1186/1472-6882-12-92.
4. V. N. Drozdov et al., "Influence of a Specific Ginger Combination on Gastropathy Conditions in Patients with Osteoarthritis of the Knee or Hip," *Journal of Alternative and Complementary Medicine* 18, no. 6 (June 2012): 583–88, doi:10.1089/acm.2011.0202.
5. J. C. Maroon and J. W. Bost, "Omega-3 Fatty Acids (Fish Oil) as an Anti-Inflammatory: An Alternative to Nonsteroidal Anti-Inflammatory Drugs for Discogenic Pain," *Surgical Neurology* 65, no. 4 (April 2006): 326–31.
6. G. Cappello et al., "Peppermint Oil (Mintoil) in the Treatment of Irritable Bowel Syndrome: A Prospective Double Blind Placebo-Controlled Randomized Trial," *Digestive and Liver Disease* 39, no. 6 (June 2007): 530–36, doi:10.1016/j.dld.2007.02.006.
7. B. Kligler and S. Chaudhary, "Peppermint Oil," *American Family Physician* 75, no. 7 (April 1, 2007): 1027–30.
8. V. Strøm, C. Røe, and S. Knardahl, "Coffee Intake and Development of Pain during Computer Work," *BMC Research Notes* 5 (September 3, 2012): 480, doi:10.1186/1756-0500-5-480.
9. G. K. Beauchamp et al., "Ibuprofen-Like Activity in Extra-Virgin Olive Oil," *Nature* 437 (2005): 45–46.

10. H. Alaa et al., "Olive-Oil-Derived Oleocanthal Enhances ß-Amyloid Clearance as a Potential Neuroprotective Mechanism against Alzheimer's Disease: In Vitro and in Vivo Studies," *ACS Chemical Neuroscience* 4, no. 6 (2013): 973–82, doi:10.1021/cn400024q.

11. K. S. Bora, S. Arora, and R. Shri, "Role of *Ocimum basilicum* L. in Prevention of Ischemia and Reperfusion-Induced Cerebral Damage, and Motor Dysfunctions in Mice Brain," *Journal of Ethnopharmacology* 137, no. 3 (October 11, 2011): 1360–65.

12. T. Dasgupta, A. R. Rao, and P. K. Yadava, "Chemomodulatory Efficacy of Basil Leaf (*Ocimum basilicum*) on Drug Metabolizing and Antioxidant Enzymes, and on Carcinogen-Induced Skin and Forestomach Papillomagenesis," *Phytomedicine* 11, no. 2-3 (February 2004): 139–51.

13. B. Bozin et al., "Characterization of the Volatile Composition of Essential Oils of Some Lamiaceae Spices and the Antimicrobial and Antioxidant Activities of the Entire Oils," *Journal of Agricultural and Food Chemistry* 54, no. 5 (March 8, 2006): 1822–28.

14. G. Shoba et al., "Influence of Piperine on the Pharmacokinetics of Curcumin in Animals and Human Volunteers," *Planta Medica* 64, no. 4 (May 1998): 353–56.

15. J. H. Kang et al., "Dietary Capsaicin Attenuates Metabolic Dysregulation in Genetically Obese Diabetic Mice," *Journal of Medicinal Food* 14, no. 3 (March 2011): 310–15.

16. A. Aissaoui, S. Zizi, and Z. H. Israili, "Hypoglycemic and Hypolipidemic Effects of *Coriandrum sativum* L. in Meriones Shawi Rats," *Journal of Ethnopharmacology* 137, no. 1 (September 1, 2011): 652–61.

17. T. Lu et al., "Cinnamon Extract Improves Fasting Blood Glucose and Glycosylated Hemoglobin Level in Chinese Patients with Type 2 Diabetes," *Nutritional Research* 32, no. 6 (June 2012): 408–12.

18. S. K. Jaganathan and E. Supriyanto, "Antiproliferative and Molecular Mechanism of Eugenol-Induced Apoptosis in Cancer Cells," *Molecules* 17, no. 6 (May 25, 2012): 6290–304.

19. S. Sreelatha and R. Inbavalli, "Antioxidant, Antihyperglycemic, and Antihyperlipidemic Effects of *Coriandrum sativum* Leaf and Stem in Alloxan-Induced Diabetic Rats," *Journal of Food Science* 77, no. 7 (July 2012): T119–23.

20. S. G .Kim et al., "Curcumin Treatment Suppresses IKKß Kinase Activity of Salivary Cells of Patients with Head and Neck Cancer: A Pilot Study," *Clinical Cancer Research* 17, no. 18 (September 15, 2011): 5953–61.

21. G. Q. Zheng, P. M. Kenney, and L. K. Lam, "Anethofuran, Carvone, and Limonene: Potential Cancer Chemopreventive Agents from Dill Weed Oil and Caraway Oil," *Planta Medica* 58, no. 4 (August 1992): 338–41.

22. P. Josling, "Preventing the Common Cold with a Garlic Supplement: A Double-Blind, Placebo-Controlled Survey," *Advances in Therapy* 18, no. 4 (July–August 2001): 189–93.

23. E. Ernst and M. H. Pittler, "Efficacy of Ginger for Nausea and Vomiting: A Systematic Review of Randomized Clinical Trials," *British Journal of Anaesthesia* 84 (2000): 367–71.

24. C. H. Liang et al., "Free Radical Scavenging Activity of 4-(3,4-dihydroxybenzoyloxymethyl) phenyl-O-ß-D-glucopyranoside from *Origanum vulgare* and Its Protection against Oxidative Damage," *Journal of Agricultural and Food Chemistry* 60, no. 31 (August 8, 2012): 7690–96.

25. G. Cappello et al., "Peppermint Oil (Mintoil) in the Treatment of Irritable Bowel Syndrome: A Prospective Double Blind Placebo-Controlled Randomized Trial," *Digestive and Liver Disease* 39, no. 6 (June 2007): 530–36.

26. E. Leiter et al., "Evaluation of the Anxiolytic Properties of Myristicin, a Component of Nutmeg, in the Male Sprague-Dawley Rat," *American Association of Nurse Anesthetists Journal* 79, no. 2 (April 2011): 109–14.

27. A. Ocaña-Fuentes et al., "Supercritical Fluid Extraction of Oregano (*Origanum vulgare*) Essentials Oils: Anti-Inflammatory Properties Based on Cytokine Response on THP-1 Macrophages," *Food and Chemical Toxicology* 48, no. 6 (June 2010): 1568–75.

28. D. Gadi et al., "Flavonoids Purified from Parsley Inhibit Human Blood Platelet Aggregation and Adhesion to Collagen Under Flow," *Journal of Complementary and Integrative Medicine* 9 (August 10, 2012): article 19, doi:10.1515/1553-3840.1579.

29. V. G. Kontogianni et al., "Phytochemical Profile of *Rosmarinus officinalis* and *Salvia officinalis* Extracts and Correlation to Their Antioxidant and Anti-Proliferative Activity," *Food Chemistry* 136, no. 1 (January 1, 2013): 120–29.

30. A. A. Noorbala et al., "Hydro-Alcoholic Extract of *Crocus sativus* L. versus Fluoxetine in the Treatment of Mild to Moderate Depression: A Double-Blind Randomized Pilot Trial," *Journal of Ethnopharmacology* 97 (2005): 281–84.

31. L. Kashani et al., "Saffron for Treatment of Fluoxetine-Induced Sexual Dysfunction in Women: Randomized Double-Blind Placebo-Controlled Study," *Human Psychopharmacology* 28, no. 1 (January 2013): 54–60.

32. M. A. Papandreou et al., "Memory Enhancing Effects of Saffron in Aged Mice Are Correlated with Antioxidant Protection," *Behavioural Brain Research* 19, no. 2 (June 1, 2011): 197–204.

33. D. O. Kennedy et al., "Monoterpenoid Extract of Sage (*Salvia lavandulaefolia*) with Cholinesterase Inhibiting Properties Improves Cognitive Performance and Mood in Healthy Adults," *Journal of Psychopharmacology* 25, no. 8 (August 2011): 1088–1100.

34. L. D. Marín, M. Sánchez-Borzone, and D. A. García, "Comparative Antioxidant Properties of Some GABAergic Phenols and Related Compounds, Determined for Homogeneous and Membrane Systems," *Medicinal Chemistry* 7, no. 4 (July 2011): 317–24.

35. "Oxygen Radical Absorbance Capacity (ORAC) of Selected Foods, Release 2," U.S. Department of Agriculture, Agricultural Research Service, 2010, accessed October 31, 2013, http://www.ars.usda.gov/nutrientdata/orac.

Chapter 5

1. A. A. Papamandjaris, D. E. MacDougall, and P. J. Jones, "Medium Chain Fatty Acid Metabolism and Energy Expenditure: Obesity Treatment Implications," *Life Sciences* 62, no. 14 (1998): 1203–15.

2. K. G. Nevin and T. Rajamohan, "Beneficial Effects of Virgin Coconut Oil on Lipid Parameters and in Vitro LDL Oxidation," *Clinical Biochemistry* 37, no. 9 (September 2004): 830–35.

3. M. G. Shrime et al., "Flavonoid-Rich Cocoa Consumption Affects Multiple Cardiovascular Risk Factors in a Meta-Analysis of Short-Term Studies," *Journal of Nutrition* 141, no. 11 (November 2011): 1982–88.

4. S. Baba et al., "Continuous Intake of Polyphenolic Compounds Containing Cocoa Powder Reduces LDL Oxidative Susceptibility and Has Beneficial Effects on Plasma HDL-Cholesterol Concentrations in Humans," *American Journal of Clinical Nutrition* 85, no. 3 (March 2007): 709–17.

5. D. Grassi et al., "Blood Pressure Is Reduced and Insulin Sensitivity Increased in Glucose-Intolerant, Hypertensive Subjects after 15 Days of Consuming High-Polyphenol Dark Chocolate," *The Journal of Nutrition* 138, no. 9 (September 2008): 1671–76.

6. "Foods Highest in Monounsaturated Fat," accessed October 31, 2013, http://nutritiondata .self.com/foods-000032000000000000000.html.

7. J. D. Curb et al., "Serum Lipid Effects of a High-Monounsaturated Fat Diet Based on Macadamia Nuts," *Archives of Internal Medicine* 160, no. 8 (April 24, 2000): 1154–58.

8. M. L. Garg et al., "Macadamia Nut Consumption Modulates Favourably Risk Factors for Coronary Artery Disease in Hypercholesterolemic Subjects," *Lipids* 42, no. 6 (June 2007): 583–87.

9. W. J. Yoon et al., "Effect of Palmitoleic Acid on Melanogenic Protein Expression in Murine B16 Melanoma," *Journal of Oleo Science* 59, no. 6 (2010): 315–19.

10. R. Vecera et al., "The Influence of Maca (*Lepidium meyenii*) on Antioxidant Status, Lipid and Glucose Metabolism in Rat," *Plant Foods for Human Nutrition* 62, no. 2 (June 2007): 59–63.

11. C. M. Dording et al., "A Double-Blind, Randomized, Pilot Dose-Finding Study of Maca Root (*L. meyenii*) for the Management of SSRI-Induced Sexual Dysfunction," *CNS Neuroscience and Therapeutics* 14, no. 3 (Fall 2008): 182–91.

12. R. A. Alves, "Camu-Camu (*Myrciaria dubia Mc Vaugh*): A Rich Natural Source of Vitamin C," *Proceedings of the Interamerican Society for Tropical Horticulture* 46 (October 2002): 11–13.

13. D. Fracassetti et al., "Ellagic Acid Derivatives, Ellagitannins, Proanthocyanidins, and Other Phenolics, Vitamin C and Antioxidant Capacity of Two Powder Products from Camu-Camu Fruit (*Myrciaria dubia*)," *Food Chemistry* 139, nos. 1–4 (August 15, 2013): 578–88.

14. "Composition," accessed October 31, 2013, http://www.seabuckthornresearch.com/composition.php.

15. I. S. Hwang et al., "UV Radiation-Induced Skin Aging in Hairless Mice is Effectively Prevented by Oral Intake of Sea Buckthorn (*Hippophae rhamnoides L.*) Fruit Blend for 6 Weeks through MMP Suppression and Increase of SOD Activity," *International Journal of Molecular Medicine* 30, no. 2 (August 2012): 392–400.

16. P. Ninfali and M. Bacchiocca, "Polyphenols and Antioxidant Capacity of Vegetables under Fresh and Frozen Conditions," *Journal of Agricultural and Food Chemistry* 51, no. 8 (April 9, 2003): 2222–26.

Chapter 6

1. "Diabetes Statistics 2013," American Diabetes Association, accessed October 31, 2013, http://www.diabetes.org/diabetes-basics/diabetes-statistics/.

2. M. Lenoir et al., "Intense Sweetness Surpasses Cocaine Reward," *PLoS ONE* 2, no. 8 (2007): e698.

3. J. Hu et al., "Glycemic Index, Glycemic Load, and Cancer Risk," *Canadian Cancer Registries Epidemiology Research Group* 24, no. 1 (January 2013): 245–51.

4. S. Sieri et al., "Dietary Glycemic Index, Glycemic Load, and the Risk of Breast Cancer in an Italian Prospective Cohort Study," *American Journal of Clinical Nutrition* 86, no. 4 (October 2007): 1160–66.

5. A. Tavani et al., "Consumption of Sweet Foods and Breast Cancer Risk in Italy," *Annals of Oncology* 17, no. 2 (February 2006): 341–45.

6. C. L. Rock et al., "Plasma Carotenoids and Recurrence-Free Survival in Women with a History of Breast Cancer," *Journal of Clinical Oncology* 23 (2005): 6631–38.

7. K. M. V. Narayan et al., "Lifetime Risk for Diabetes Mellitus in the United States," *Journal of the American Medical Association* 290, no. 14 (October 8, 2003): 1884–90.

Chapter 7

1. M. Leonard, "The Evolution of Lactase Persistence in Europe. A Synthesis of Archaeological and Genetic Evidence," *International Dairy Journal* 22 (2012): 88–97.

2. M. Lorenz et al., "Addition of Milk Prevents Vascular Protective Effects of Tea," *European Heart Journal* 28, no. 2 (January 2007): 219–23.

3. G. H. Docena et al., "Identification of Casein as the Major Allergenic and Antigenic Protein of Cow's Milk," *Allergy* 51, no. 6 (June 1996): 412–16.

4. C. Catassi et al., "Non-Celiac Gluten Sensitivity: The New Frontier of Gluten Related Disorders," *Nutrients* 5, no. 10 (September 26, 2013): 3839–53.

5. J. Visser et al., "Tight Junctions, Intestinal Permeability, and Autoimmunity: Celiac Disease and Type 1 Diabetes Paradigms," *Annals of the New York Academy of Sciences* 1165 (May 2009): 195–205.

6. D. L. J. Freed, "Do Dietary Lectins Cause Disease?" *British Medical Journal* 318, no. 7190 (April 17, 1999): 1023–24.

Chapter 8

1. M. Y. Pepino et al., "Sucralose Affects Glycemic and Hormonal Responses to an Oral Glucose Load," *Diabetes Care* 36, no. 9 (September 2013): 2530–35.

2. Q. Yang, "Gain Weight by 'Going Diet'? Artificial Sweeteners and the Neurobiology of Sugar Cravings," *Yale Journal of Biology and Medicine* 83, no. 2 (June 2010): 101–8.

3. S. E. Swithers and T. L. Davidson, "A Role for Sweet Taste: Calorie Predictive Relations in Energy Regulation by Rats," *Behavioral Neuroscience* 122, no. 1 (February 2008): 161–73.

4. "Opinion of the Scientific Committee on Food on Sucralose," European Commission, Health and Consumer Protection Directorate-General, December 9, 2000, http://ec.europa.eu/food/fs/sc/scf/out68_en.pdf.

5. "Food Additives Permitted for Direct Addition to Food for Human Consumption; Sucralose," 63 Fed. Reg. 64 (April 3, 1998) (to be codified at 21 C. F. R. pt. 172).

6. M. B. Abou-Donia et al., "Splenda Alters Gut Microflora and Increases Intestinal P-Glycoprotein and Cytochrome P-450 in Male Rats," *Journal of Toxicology and Environmental Health* 71, no. 21 (2008): 1415–29.

7. D. J. Brusick, "A Critical Review of the Genetic Toxicity of Steviol and Steviol Glycosides," *Food and Chemistry Toxicology* 46, no. 7 (July 2008): S83–91.

8. N. Lailerd et al., "Effects of Stevioside on Glucose Transport Activity in Insulin-Sensitive and Insulin-Resistant Rat Skeletal Muscle," *Metabolism* 53, no. 1 (January 2004): 101–7; S. Anton et al., "Effects of Stevia, Aspartame, and Sucrose on Food Intake, Satiety, and Postprandial Glucose and Insulin Levels," *Appetite* 55, no. 1 (August 2010): 37–43.

9. X. Chang et al., "Antioxidative, Antibrowning, and Antibacterial Activities of Sixteen Floral Honeys," *Food and Function* 2, no. 9 (September 2011): 541–46.

10. A. B. Ross, "Lifestyle, Genetics, and Disease in Sami," *Croatian Medical Journal* 47, no. 4 (August 2006): 553–65.

Chapter 9

1. "Dietary Supplementation with N-3 Polyunsaturated Fatty Acids and Vitamin E after Myocardial Infarction: Results of the GISSI-Prevenzione Trial," *Lancet* 354 (1999): 447–55.

2. P. C. Calder, "n−3 Polyunsaturated Fatty Acids, Inflammation, and Inflammatory Diseases," *American Journal of Clinical Nutrition* 83, no. 6 (June 2006): S1505-1519S.

3. T. A. Mori et al., "Dietary Fish as a Major Component of a Weight-Loss Diet: Effect on Serum Lipids, Glucose, and Insulin Metabolism in Overweight Hypertensive Subjects," *American Journal of Clinical Nutrition* 70, no. 5 (November 1999): 817–25.

4. C. R. Hooijmans et al., "The Effects of Long-Term Omega-3 Fatty Acid Supplementation on Cognition and Alzheimer's Pathology in Animal Models of Alzheimer's Disease: A Systematic Review and Meta-Analysis," *Journal of Alzheimer's Disease* 28, no. 1 (2012): 191–209.

5. T. A. Mori et al., "Purified Eicosapentaenoic and Docosahexaenoic Acids Have Differential Effects on Serum Lipids and Lipoproteins, LDL Particle Size, Glucose, and Insulin in Mildly Hyperlipidemic Men," *American Journal of Clinical Nutrition* 71, no. 5 (May 2000): 1085–94.

6. A. L Brown et al., "Omega-3 Fatty Acids Ameliorate Atherosclerosis by Favorably Altering Monocyte Subsets and Limiting Monocyte Recruitment to Aortic Lesions," *Arteriosclerosis, Thrombosis, and Vascular Biology* 32, no. 9 (September 2012): 2122–30; Council for Responsible Nutrition (CRN), "Benefits of Long Chain Omega-3 Fatty Acids (EPA, DHA): Help Protect Against Heart Disease," June 2002, http://www.crnusa.org/benefits/chapters.html.

7. W. G. Hodge et al., "Efficacy of Omega-3 Fatty Acids in Preventing Age-Related Macular Degeneration: A Systematic Review," *Ophthalmology* 113, no. 7 (July 2006): 1165–72.

8. R. J. Goldberg and J. Katz, "A Meta-Analysis of the Analgesic Effects of Omega-3 Polyunsaturated Fatty Acid Supplementation for Inflammatory Joint Pain," *Pain* 129, no. 1–2 (May 2007): 210–23.

9. F. Lespérance et al., "The Efficacy of Omega-3 Supplementation for Major Depression: A Randomized Controlled Trial," *Journal of Clinical Psychiatry* 72, no. 8 (August 2011): 1054–62; M. Johnson, "Omega-3/Omega-6 Fatty Acids for Attention Deficit Hyperactivity Disorder: A Randomized Placebo-Controlled Trial in Children and Adolescents," *Journal of Attention Disorders* 12, no. 5 (March 2009): 394–401; T. D. Mickleborough, A. A Ionescu, and K. W. Rundell, "Omega-3 Fatty Acids and Airway Hyperresponsiveness in Asthma," *Journal of Alternative and Complementary Medicine* 10, no. 6 (December 2004): 1067–75; N. Rahbar, N. Asgharzadeh, and R. Ghorbani, "Effect of Omega-3 Fatty Acids on Intensity of Primary Dysmenorrhea," *International Journal of Gynaecology and Obstetrics* 117, no. 1 (April 2012): 45–47.

10. "Omega-3 Fatty Acids," American Cancer Society, accessed November 1, 2013, http://www.cancer.org/treatment/treatmentsandsideeffects/complementaryandalternativemedicine/dietandnutrition/omega-3-fatty-acids.

11. H. A. Bischoff-Ferrari et al., "Fall Prevention with Supplemental and Active Forms of Vitamin D: A Meta-Analysis of Randomised Controlled Trials," *British Medical Journal* 339 (2009): b3692.

12. R. E. et al., "Vitamin D Deficiency and Depression in Adults: Systematic Review and Meta-Analysis," *British Journal of Psychiatry* 202 (February 2013): 100–107; A. J. Whitehouse et al., "Maternal Vitamin D Levels and the Autism Phenotype among Offspring," *Journal of Autism and Developmental Disorders* 43, no. 7 (July 2013): 1495–1504; M. Belvederi Murri, "Vitamin D and Psychosis: Mini Meta-Analysis," *Schizophrenia Research* 150, no. 1 (October 2013): 235–39; S. Lopes da Silva et al., "Plasma Nutrient Status of Patients with Alzheimer's Disease: Systematic Review and Meta-Analysis," *Alzheimer's and Dementia* (October 18, 2013) www.journals.elsevier.com/alzheimers-and-dementia/open-access-articles/; B. Jones, "Multiple Sclerosis: Gene–Vitamin D Interactions Likely to Influence Pathogenesis and Risk of Relapse in Multiple Sclerosis," *Nature Reviews Neurology* 9, no. 9 (September 2013): 486; W. R. Chen et al., "The Effects of Low Vitamin D on Coronary Artery Disease," *Heart, Lung, and Circulation* 2013 Sep 3. pii: S1443-9506(13)01162-1. Published online October 24, 2013. J. Mitri, M. D. Muraru, and A. G. Pittas, "Vitamin D and Type 2 Diabetes: A Systematic Review," *European Journal of Clinical Nutrition* 65, no. 9 (September 2011): 1005–15; W. Qin et al., "Vitamin D Favorably Alters the Cancer Promoting Prostaglandin Cascade," *Anticancer Research* 33, no. 9 (September 2013): 3861–66; E. N. Grineva, T. Karonova, and I. L. Nikitina, "Vitamin D Deficiency Is a Risk Factor for Obesity and Diabetes Type 2 in Women at Late Reproductive Age," *Aging* 5, no. 7 (July 2013): 575–81.

13. F. Wepner et al., "Effects of Vitamin D on Patients with Fibromyalgia Syndrome: A Randomized Placebo-Controlled Trial," *PAIN* 155, no. 2 (2014): 261.

14. Q. Xiao et al., "Dietary and Supplemental Calcium Intake and Cardiovascular Disease Mortality: The National Institutes of Health-AARP Diet and Health Study," *JAMA Internal Medicine* 173, no. 8 (April 22, 2013): 639–46.

15. R. J. Boyle et al., "Probiotics for Treating Eczema," *Cochrane Database of Systematic Reviews* 4 (October 8, 2008): CD006135; G. Reid, J. Dols, and W. Miller, "Targeting the Vaginal Microbiota with Probiotics as a Means to Counteract Infections," *Current Opinion in Clinical Nutrition and Metabolic Care* 12, no. 6 (November 2009): 583–87; T. Matsuzaki et al., "Intestinal Microflora: Probiotics and Autoimmunity," *Journal of Nutrition* 137, no. 3, sup. 2 (March 2007): 798S–802S; L. Ooi, "Cholesterol-Lowering Effects of Probiotics and Prebiotics: A Review of in Vivo and in Vitro Findings," *International Journal of Molecular Sciences* 11, no. 6 (2010): 2499–2522; M. Kumar et al., "Cancer-Preventing Attributes of Probiotics: An Update," *International Journal of Food Sciences and Nutrition* 61, no. 5 (August 2010): 473–96.

16. G. Kiessling, J. Schneider, and G. Jahreis, "Long-Term Consumption of Fermented Dairy Products over 6 Months Increases HDL Cholesterol," *European Journal of Clinical Nutrition* 56, no. 9 (September 2002): 843–49.

Chapter 10

1. "Female Athlete Triad: Problems Caused by Extreme Exercise and Dieting," American Academy of Orthopedic Surgeons, accessed November 6, 2013, http://orthoinfo.aaos .org/topic.cfm?topic=A00342.

2. M. Catoire et al., "Pronounced Effects of Acute Endurance Exercise on Gene Expression in Resting and Exercising Human Skeletal Muscle," *PLoS One* 7, no. 11 (2012): e51066.

3. E. N. Trushina et al., "Immune Dysfunction In Highly Skilled Athletes and Nutritional Rehabilitation," *Voprosy Pitaniia* 81, no. 2 (2012): 73–80.

4. J. B. Kreher and J. B. Schwartz, "Overtraining Syndrome: A Practical Guide," *Sports Health* 4, no. 2 (March 2012): 128–38.

5. J. H. O'Keefe et al., "Potential Adverse Cardiovascular Effects from Excessive Endurance Exercise," *Mayo Clinic Proceedings* 87, no. 6 (June 2012): 587–95.

6. S. C. Moore et al., "Leisure Time Physical Activity of Moderate to Vigorous Intensity and Mortality: A Large Pooled Cohort Analysis," *PLoS Med* 9, no. 11 (2012): e1001335.

7. F. B. Hu et al., "Walking Compared with Vigorous Physical Activity and Risk of Type 2 Diabetes in Women: A Prospective Study," *Journal of the American Medical Association* 282 (1999): 1433–39.

8. G. Wang et al., "Physical Activity, Cardiovascular Disease, and Medical Expenditures in U.S. Adults," *Annals of Behavioral Medicine* 28 (2004): 88–94.

9. "2008 Physical Activity Guidelines for Americans," U.S. Dept. of Health and Human Services, 2008, http://www.health.gov/paguidelines/.

10. C. Kasapis and P. D. Thompson, "The Effects of Physical Activity on Serum C-Reactive Protein and Inflammatory Markers: A Systematic Review," *Journal of the American College of Cardiology* 45, no. 10 (May 2005): 1563–69.

11. "Aging, Chronic Disease, and Telomeres Are Linked in Recent Studies," Jeffrey Norris, University of California, San Francisco, accessed November 6, 2013, http://www.ucsf .edu/news/2011/02/9353/aging-telomeres-linked-chronic-disease-and-health.

12. D. Ornish et al., "Effect of Comprehensive Lifestyle Changes on Telomerase Activity and Telomere Length in Men with Biopsy-Proven Low-Risk Prostate Cancer: 5-Year Follow-Up of a Descriptive Pilot Study," *Lancet Oncology* 14, no. 11 (October 2013): 1112–20.

13. Ibid.

14. M. Du et al., "Physical Activity, Sedentary Behavior, and Leukocyte Telomere Length in Women," *American Journal of Epidemiology* 175, no. 5 (March 1, 2012): 414–22.

15. M. Lee et al., "Inverse Association between Adiposity and Telomere Length: The Fels Longitudinal Study," *American Journal of Human Biology* 23, no. 1 (January–February 2011): 100–106.

16. Ornish et al., "Effect of Comprehensive Lifestyle Changes on Telomerase Activity."

Part Four Phase 1

1. H. R. Wyatt et al., "Long-Term Weight Loss and Breakfast in Subjects in the National Weight Control Registry," *Obesity Research* 10, no. 2 (February 2002): 78–82.

2. E. A. Dennis et al., "Water Consumption Increases Weight Loss during a Hypocaloric Diet Intervention in Middle-Aged and Older Adults," *Obesity (Silver Spring)* 18, no. 2 (February 18, 2010): 300–307.

Part Four Phase 2

1. A. Kong et al., "Self-Monitoring and Eating-Related Behaviors Are Associated with 12-Month Weight Loss in Postmenopausal Overweight-to-Obese Women," *Journal of the Academy of Nutrition and Dietetics* 112, no. 9 (September 2012): 1428–35.

Part Four Phase 3

1. S. R. Patel et al., "Association between Reduced Sleep and Weight Gain in Women," *American Journal of Epidemiology* 164, no. 10 (November 15, 2006): 947–54.

2. E. Dennis, "Water Consumption Increases Weight Loss during a Hypocaloric Diet Intervention in Middle-Aged and Older Adults," *Obesity (Silver Spring)* 18, no. 2. (February 2010); 300–307.

THE OMNI FAMILY GUIDE: TIPS FOR KIDS

1. N. Persaud et al., "Association between Serum Cholesterol and Eating Behaviours during Early Childhood: A Cross-Sectional Study," *Canadian Medical Association Journal* 185, no. 11 (August 6, 2013).

2. Ibid.

3. E. Robinson et al., "Eating Attentively: A Systematic Review and Meta-Analysis of the Effect of Food Intake Memory and Awareness on Eating," *American Journal of Clinical Nutrition* 97 (April 2013): 728–42.

4. G. M. Singh et al., "180,000 Deaths Worldwide May Be Associated with Sugary Soft Drinks" (Study presented at the American Heart Association's Epidemiology and Prevention/Nutrition, Physical Activity and Metabolism 2013 Scientific Sessions, New Orleans, March 19, 2013).

5. K. A. Loth et al., "Food-Related Parenting Practices and Adolescent Weight Status: A Population-Based Study," *Pediatrics*, published online April 22, 2013, doi:10.1542/peds. 2012-3073.

[INDEX]

Boldface page references indicate illustrations. <u>Underscored</u> references indicate tables or boxed text.

Dementia
  Alzheimer's disease, 108
  coconut oil for treating, 88
Deoxyribonucleic acid. *See*
    DNA
Depression
  camu camu for relieving,
    94
  maca powder for relieving,
    93
  as obesity side effect, 108
Dessert
  phase 1, 204, 206
  phase 2, 218–19
DHA. *See* Omega-3 fatty acids
Diabetes, 101–15. *See also* Blood
    sugar; Insulin
  in author's grandmother,
    101–3
  in children, 113, 115
  dangers of, 101, 108
  death and disability due
    to, 104
  diet leading to, 104
  food versus drugs for
    preventing, 9
  health problems due to,
    105
  improved by Daniel Plan, 8
  lifestyle choices affecting,
    105–6
  pre-diabetes, 111
  prevalence of, 8, 101
  process of, 105
  stevia interaction with
    drugs for, 140
  Tami's doughnut habit and,
    106–10
Diabetes Prevention Program,
    9
Dietary fat. *See* Fat, dietary
Diets. *See also* Omni Diet
  author's experience with,
    2, 3–4
  calorie restricting, 61
  high-protein, 4, 29, 32–34, 42
  Plants versus Protein debate,
    28–29
  standard American, 28, 49
  vegetarian, 3–4, 29, 36–39,
    41, 44

Digestion
  of carbohydrates, 104, 111
  herbs and spices aiding, 75,
    79–80, 81
  inability, for dairy foods,
    118–19
  indigestibility of gluten, 124
  probiotics aiding, 158–60
  soluble fiber aiding, 45–46
Dill, 78–79
Dining out, 126, 127
Dinner. *See also* Menus
  in author's typical day, 210
  phase 1, 204
  phase 2, 218
Dirty dozen fruits and
    vegetables, 198
DNA. *See also* Genes
  aging and damage to, 15
  exercise benefits for, 179–81
  genetically modified (GM)
    foods, 40, 132
  plant foods repairing, 35
  protective nutrition for,
    15–16
Docosahexaenoic acid (DHA).
    See Omega-3 fatty acids
Dogs, macadamia nuts toxic
    to, 93
Dopamine, 21, 282
Doughnut dependence,
    107–10
Drugs. *See* Pharmaceutical
    drugs
Dumbbell Single Arm Rows,
    228, **228**
Dutch process cacao, 89

E

Eating out, 126, 127
Egg dishes
  Benedict-Style Poached
    Eggs, 280–81
  Brainy Breakfast Burrito,
    284
  Clear Start Breakfast
    Burrito, 285
  Devil-Less Eggs, 321
  Feel-Good Eggs Ranchero,
    282

Gluten-Free Blueberry
    French Toast, 287
  Herb Garden Frittata, 277
  mood improved by, 282
  Omni-Style Crepes, 278–79
  Pacific Coast Scramble, 274
  Seafood Omelet for Super
    Focus, 275
  sources for healthy eggs, 395
  Southwestern Huevos, 283
  Super Surprise Frittata, 276
Eicosapentaenoic acid (EPA).
    See Omega-3 fatty acids
18-40-60 rule, 249
Emotional health, Omni Diet
    benefits for, 22–23. *See
    also* Mood
Emotions about foods, 119
Energy
  exercise increasing, 173
  Focus and Energy
    Optimizer, 400
  supplements for, 170
Environmental Working
    Group (EWG) dirty
    dozen and clean 15, 198
EPA. *See* Omega-3 fatty acids
Epigenetics, 12–13, 35–36
Equal (aspartame), 137–38.
    See also Artificial
    sweeteners
Erythritol, 139, 398
Essential amino acids, 32–33,
    36–37
Essential fatty acids. *See*
    Omega-3 fatty acids;
    Omega-6 fatty acids
Estrogen, soy foods and, 40
Eugenol, 78, 82
EVOO, 75
EWG dirty dozen and clean
    15, 198
Excitotoxins, 120
Exercise, 172–83
  aging protection from,
    179–81
  amount needed, 183
  burning calories not
    important in, 177–78
  diet interrelated with,
    178–79

doctor's approval for, 224
four-week workout, 233–35
genes and DNA benefited by, 179–81
health benefits of, 172, 173, _174_, 175–77
heart rate for, 226, _226_
interval training workout, 225
Omni Diet Exercise Plan described, 173, 224
overexercising, 172–73, 224
in phase 1, 197
in phase 2, 224–35
sample two-week workout, _233_
strength training myths, 181–83
strength training workout, 225–26, 227–32
stress relieved by, 177, 247–48
sweatiness after, accepting, _174_
warming up and cooling down, _234_
weight loss aided by, 178–79
workout schedule, phase 2, 224
Extra-virgin olive oil (EVOO), _75_

F

Factory farming, 52–53
Failure, 109, _110_, _148_
Farming grains, 121, 122
Fast food, smoothies as, _212_
Fat, body. _See also_ Obesity and overweight
arachidonic acid stored in, _180_
exercise reducing, 177
health dangers of belly fat, 17, _19_
inflammation increased by, 17, _180_
insulin resistance and, 112–13
strength training and, 182
sugar and simple carbohydrates causing, 146–47

Fat, dietary, 46–53. _See also_ Omega-3 fatty acids; Omega-6 fatty acids
conditionally essential fatty acids, 156
demonization of, 43
downside of fat-free foods, 46–47
fat-free foods, 46–47, 145–47
healthy versus unhealthy, 48, 146
hunter-gatherers' consumption of, _144_
low-fat obsession in US, 145–47
monounsaturated, 91
need for, 47
oils, 38, 39, _52_, 86–88, 91–92
in the Omni Diet, 51–52
phase 1 guidelines, 201–2, 203, 204
reduced-fat food products, 133–34
saturated, 49–50, 87–88
in smoothies, _212_, _213_
trans fat, 50–51, 108
unsaturated, 48–49
Fat-free foods
downside of, 46–47, 145–47
trans fat-free, 51
Feelings about foods, _119_
Ferritin level, 193
Fiber
benefits of, 45, 71
insoluble, 46
in the Omni Diet, 46
in shirataki noodles, 343
in smoothies, _212_
soluble, 45–46
Fish and seafood
Ahi Sweet Potato Stew, 304
Baked Halibut with Creamed Spinach Sauce, 358
Cedar Plank Salmon, 355
Crowd-Pleasing Cioppino, 361
Get Smart Mahimahi Burgers with Pineapple Salsa, 309
Ginger-Glazed Salmon, 354

Hawaiian Blackened Tuna with Mango Salsa, 352–53
Macadamia-Crusted Mahimahi, 362
Omni Shopping List, 401
Pacific Coast Scramble, 274
Pan-Roasted Salmon with Vegetables, 353
Pan-Seared Salmon, 354
Peaceful Asian Pear Salad, 289
Poached Sea Bass in Tomato Broth, 359
Poached Tilapia with Saffron Sauce, 356
as protein sources, 32–33, 36–37, 53
Salmon Burgers, 310
Seafood Omelet for Super Focus, 275
Seared Ahi with Cucumber Salad, 291
Seared Ahi with Guacamole, 351
Serrano Chile Shrimp, 308–9
Shrimp Chowder, 349
Shrimp Cocktail, 308
Shrimp over Watermelon Mint Salad, 292–93
Simple Shrimp Scampi, 350
Simply Delicious Pan-Seared Trout and Cucumber Salad, 357
Snapper with Tomato Caper Sauce, 360
Teriyaki Salmon Bowl, 311
Vital Choice canned wild fish, 274
Fish oil. _See also_ Omega-3 fatty acids
as best source of omega-3 fatty acids, 152, 156
neck and back pain relieved by, _74–75_
recommendations for, 155–56
Flax oil, omega-3 in, 38, _52_
Flax seeds, _52_